INVISIBLE ENEMIES

A volume in the series

CULTURE, POLITICS, AND THE COLD WAR

Edited by Christian G. Appy

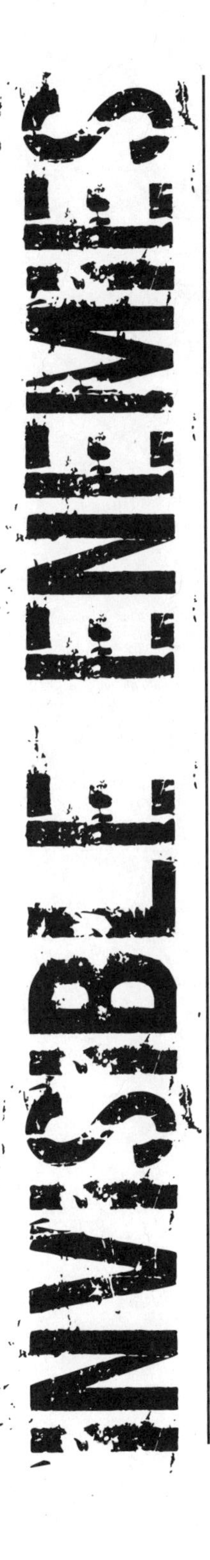

THE AMERICAN WAR ON VIETNAM, 1975–2000

EDWIN A. MARTINI

University of Massachusetts Press
Amherst

Printed in the United States of America

LC 2007007632
ISBN 978-1-55849-609-5 (paper); 608-8 (library cloth)

Designed by Richard Hendel
Set in Scala with ITC Franklin Gothic Demi and Boycott display by dix!
Printed and bound by The Maple-Vail Book Manufacturing Group

Library of Congress Cataloging-in-Publication Data
Martini, Edwin A., 1975–
Invisible enemies : the American war on Vietnam, 1975–2000 / Edwin A. Martini.
p. cm.—(Culture, politics, and the Cold War)
Includes bibliographical references and index.
ISBN 978-1-55849-609-5 (pbk. : alk. paper)—
ISBN 978-1-55849-608-8 (library cloth : alk. paper)
1. United States—Foreign relations—Vietnam.
2. Vietnam—Foreign relations—United States.
3. United States—Foreign relations—1945–1989.
4. United States—Foreign relations—1989–
5. United States—Relations—Vietnam.
6. Vietnam—Relations—United States.
7. Vietnam—Foreign public opinion, American.
8. Public opinion—United States.
9. Vietnam War, 1961–1975—Influence. I. Title.
E183.8.V5M27 2007
327.730597209'045—dc22
2007007632

British Library Cataloguing in Publication data are available.

FOR GENANNE

The President has gone to Vietnam,
A smallish country that we used to bomb
But now would like to send our products to.
And so our corporations take the view
That if the country's ruling class has picked
A form of rule that can be somewhat strict
That's up to them. And Clinton went to say
That there is nothing standing in the way
Of being friends with them forevermore.
Remind me, please: Why *did* we fight that war?
—Calvin Trillin, "The Vietnam Peace" (2000)

CONTENTS

ACKNOWLEDGMENTS

This book would never have been possible without the support of many, many people. I began my work on the project at the University of Maryland, College Park, so it is there my thanks begin. Myron Lounsbury, a trusted and valued adviser during graduate school, taught me a great deal about being an adviser, student, and teacher. David Sicilia, Kandice Chuh, and Mary Sies were all instrumental in helping to develop and refine my work over several years. I owe special thanks to H. Bruce Franklin, who was extremely generous with his time and energy during early stages.

Funding from a variety of sources at Maryland allowed me to focus on research and writing, including a Graduate School Fellowship, a Goldhaber Travel Grant with matching funds from American Studies that allowed me to visit Vietnam in the summer of 2001, and a Graduate School Dissertation Fellowship. I was also lucky enough to work within a stone's throw of the Government Document repository at the University of Maryland. The reference librarians in that section helped me sort through piles of documents and kept me sane while they moved and reorganized the entire section during 2003. A number of staff at the National Archives and the Library of Congress were also extremely helpful on several occasions. Susan Pyzynski of the Farber Archives at Brandeis University gave me first crack at the papers of Stephen Solarz before most of the collection had even been unpacked, let alone catalogued or organized.

I benefited immeasurably from contributions both direct and indirect to this project by Cathy Jones, David Silver, Kelly Quinn, Andrew Johnston, Josh Woodfork, and D Snyder, and I thank them for their friendship and support. Barbara Shaw read nearly every page of this manuscript at one stage or another and provided priceless feedback. Scott Laderman also read the entire manuscript and corrected a number of errors and oversights.

It has been my good fortune to have had the support and guidance of Clark Dougan, senior editor at the University of Massachusetts Press, Carol Betsch, managing editor at the press, and Chris Appy, in his role as series editor, as I revised the manuscript. Likewise the staff at the press were extremely helpful at every stage of turning the manuscript into a book. My new colleagues in the History Department at Western Michigan University have given me time, space, and an environment that is at once supportive and intellectually challenging.

Last, and most important, this work could never have been imagined, let alone completed, without my family. My parents, Shari and Ed, have allowed me to pursue any dream or goal I have ever entertained; my sister Kristen was my first teacher and continues regularly to school me in many things. Anyone is lucky to have one set of amazing parents; I happen to have two. Thanks to Bill and Gennis for their support as well.

Finally, thanks to Genanne Zeller and Gracen Martini-Zeller. Gracen was born in the midst of this project and helped keep it, and all things academic, in much-needed perspective. Genanne has been the most supportive, encouraging, sympathetic, and rock-solid partner I could ever imagine. A wonderful editor and audience—and great cook—G has consistently allowed me to focus on my work, often at great personal sacrifice. Nothing would be possible without her love and support.

ABBREVIATIONS

ADB	Asian Development Bank
ASEAN	Association of Southeast Asian Nations
CGDK	Coalition Government of Democratic Kampuchea
CMEA	Council for Mutual Economic Assistance
DK	Democratic Kampuchea (Khmer Rouge regime)
DRV	Democratic Republic of Vietnam ("North Vietnam")
FEER	*Far Eastern Economic Review*
IMF	International Monetary Fund
NLF	National Liberation Front
NYT	*New York Times*
RVN	Republic of Vietnam ("South Vietnam")
UN	United Nations
VCP	Vietnamese Communist Party
WB	World Bank
WP	*Washington Post*
WSJ	*Wall Street Journal*

INVISIBLE ENEMIES

INTRODUCTION

As the revolutionary forces of Vietnam draped and raised their flags throughout Saigon on April 30, 1975, the sound of gunfire continued. Although the sound was nothing new to the city, the meaning was different. Fired in celebration by troops outside the former Presidential Palace, these were the sounds of victory: the second Indochina war was finally over. Several of the men surrounding Republic of Vietnam General Duong Van Minh were nevertheless understandably startled by the noise. As Colonel Bui Tin of the Revolutionary Forces of Vietnam accepted the formal surrender by the general, he told his former adversaries, "Our men are merely celebrating. You have nothing to fear. Between Vietnamese, there are no victors and no vanquished. Only the Americans have been beaten. If you are patriots, consider this a moment of joy. The war for our country is over."[1] It's unlikely that Minh and his South Vietnamese colleagues were put at ease by Tin's remarks.

What none of the men could possibly have realized was that despite, and in fact because of, the successful campaign against the United States, the war for their country was in fact far from over. Although free from foreign occupation for the first time in over a century, Vietnam remained surrounded by hostile regimes and faced the difficult task of rebuilding a nation devastated and deeply divided after thirty years of sustained warfare. The challenge of national reconstruction would have proven daunting enough under any circumstances; it would have been long and arduous even *with* the billions in American aid that had been promised as part of the 1973 peace accords; it would have been a financially imposing project even *with* the full and unfettered access to sources of international economic and humanitarian aid they were not only in dire need of, but to which they were entitled. But, as the Vietnamese quickly learned in the years immediately following the American withdrawal, one of the few things worse than fighting a war against the United States is *winning* a war against the United States. In contrast to Germany and Japan, which after World War II received billions in American support, Vietnam found itself quickly cut off from American-controlled sources of economic assistance, humanitarian aid, and development loans.

Had the United States simply abandoned the nation altogether, rejecting calls for reparations, aid, and trade, the Socialist revolution in Vietnam might still have failed. The United States, however, instead maintained an aggressively hostile policy under which the nation and people of Vietnam would continue to suffer. Before the guns had even gone silent in Saigon, policymakers in the United States initiated a series of punitive policies that would define the course of relations between the two nations for the next two decades. As the Vietnamese war for national independence reached an end in the spring of 1975, a new phase of the American war against Vietnam began.

Far from ending the war after the defeat of its South Vietnamese client regime, the United States continued to wage economic, political, and cultural war on Vietnam long after 1975. In this book, I examine this post-1975 phase of U.S. relations with Vietnam, which I call the "American war on Vietnam" (1975–2000). In particular, I examine the ways in which cultural representations intersected and interacted with the formation of foreign policy during this period. Both of these activities, I argue, were driven by the same cultural logic of "normalizing" the historical memory of the war, reinserting recuperative American narratives at the center of public discourses about the war while marginalizing and silencing Vietnamese and other alternative and oppositional voices. By rendering Vietnamese subjects silent or invisible in American films, television shows, and comic books about the war, while ignoring the real impact of U.S. policies on Vietnam, the different "fronts" of the American war on Vietnam combined to reconstruct the cultural, political, and economic work of American empire in the wake of a long, devastating, and divisive war. The American war on Vietnam was thus as much a battle for the cultural memory of the war in American society as it was a lengthy and bitter economic, political, and diplomatic war against the nation and people of Vietnam.

I use a range of primary sources to reconstruct the policy history of this period, focusing in particular on many previously overlooked congressional hearings where the principles governing U.S. policy toward all of Southeast Asia after 1975 were discussed, debated, and developed. I focus on congressional hearings for several reasons. First, they are usually less sanitized sources of information than briefings or policy statements from the executive branch; in the back-and-forth of often heated testimony, small windows can be found into the ironies and inconsistencies of the production of foreign policy. Second, the prints of committee proceedings often contain hard-to-find reports from other government agencies, such as the Government Accountability Office, Office of Management and Budget, and Congressional Research Service; they also frequently include contemporary accounts from the news media that have been inserted for the record by participants. Thus not only do these reports save steps in the research process, they also demonstrate which sources informed and influenced policy makers and witnesses at these hearings. Most important, however, congressional hearings are extremely useful in demonstrating not only how policy debates were conducted, but also how they were *constructed*. What interests me are the ways in which discussions of American policy toward Vietnam, whether they took place in Congress, in the news media, or on movie screens, constructed the terms and acceptable limits of debate.[2] Indeed, one of the central characteristics of the American war on Vietnam after 1975 is the way in which it renders certain things completely outside the boundaries of public discourse or cultural representation.

Along with these primary sources, I also bring together a large body of secondary literature from a wide array of fields, including cultural and diplomatic history, cultural studies, political science, and economics. Elements of the story I wish to tell have been produced in each of these fields, but the larger narrative of U.S.-Vietnamese relations has never been linked together in the manner proposed here. Pieced together from these disparate sources, the changes and the continuities in the American war on Vietnam over its twenty-five-year course are traced in the chapters that follow, from the initial imposition of an unprecedented and ill-conceived program of economic sanctions in 1975, to the U.S. backing of anti-Vietnamese forces during the Third Indochina War, to the final ratification of a bilateral trade agreement between the two nations in 2000. The story constructed here relates to a number of interdisciplinary conversations. On one level, it serves to explore the construction of American foreign policy in the final chapter of the cold war, and of the tensions between the legislative and executive branches over the scope and nature of foreign policy in the wake of Watergate and Vietnam; on another, it contributes to recent work on the cultures of U.S. imperialism; it challenges scholars working in a number of fields to reconsider traditional definitions of what constitutes an act of war; and it offers an interdisciplinary approach to the study of American foreign policy that places cultural representations and diplomatic history alongside one another as part of the same historical processes.

By combining approaches from a number of disciplines, I seek to transcend the limits of previous approaches to the problem of U.S.-Vietnamese relations, disrupting and transgressing the intellectual, disciplinary, and chronological boundaries that have contributed to the persistent invisibility of this phase of the American war on Vietnam, and, indeed, of the Vietnamese themselves in American representations of the war. Mine is certainly not the first work to attempt to combine American studies and diplomatic history in such a manner. Indeed, the increasingly productive tension between these fields over the past several years has been central to the formation of the ideas and narrative presented here.

Once a fledgling field attempting to define the true nature of "American civilization" or to demonstrate the uniqueness of "the American mind," American studies has of late become increasingly interested in America's place in the world. In a 1993 essay, Amy Kaplan identified three issues that contribute to the problem of examining empire across several disciplines: "the absence of culture from the history of U.S. imperialism; the absence of empire from the study of American culture; and the absence of the United States from the postcolonial history of imperialism."[3] In 2003, Kaplan echoed these themes in her presidential address to the American Studies Association.[4] Janice Radway had already added another dimension to these conversations in her own 1998 presidential address to the ASA, when she asked members to reconsider the association's name in order to challenge the very definition of "American" studies. This led to a number of calls for the "internationalization" of the field and the further development of research and teaching agendas that would focus equally on the global and the local.[5]

There have been similar appeals in the field of diplomatic history. In his 1990 presidential address, Michael Hunt called upon the Society for Historians of American Foreign Relations (SHAFR) to develop a "practical" agenda for internationalizing the field and thinking about the institutional and professional ramifications of such changes.[6] However, even more common in the pages of *Diplomatic History* have been pleas for greater attention to "culture" as a source of theoretical and methodological innovation for historians of foreign relations—and as a significant factor in the production of American foreign policy. Perhaps the most prominent of these recent calls came from Emily Rosenberg in her 1998 SHAFR presidential address, "Revisiting Dollar Diplomacy."[7] Robert McMahon's 2001 address, "Contested Memory: The Vietnam War and American Society, 1975–2001," noted with great urgency that the issue of national memory of the American war in Vietnam was "far too important a subject for foreign relations specialists to abandon to the cultural historians, the cultural studies specialists, and the political polemicists."[8]

Among recent monographs, too, one could find a number of works that would seem to belie any hard divisions between the fields. To name but a few, Amy Kaplan and Emily Rosenberg, as well as Mark Bradley, Kristin Hoganson, Melani McAllister, and Mary Renda, have all produced landmark scholarship that explores the complex intersections of race, gender, and foreign relations.[9] And yet the relationship between cultural studies and diplomatic history is still in many respects contentious and strained. I could not agree more with Professor McMahon when he argues that the study of popular memory and popular culture is too important to be left to cultural studies scholars alone, and I am equally certain that there are others working in American studies and cultural history who feel a similar sentiment about leaving the study of foreign relations to diplomatic historians. One of the central tasks of this book, then, is to transgress the existing disciplinary boundaries that have limited our understanding of the United States and Vietnam after 1975.

Along with that task, I am also attempting to disrupt some of the narrative frameworks and chronological boundaries of the American war against Vietnam that have resulted from these disciplinary borders, structures which have been central to limiting explanations of what that war was "about." The most basic way in which I am challenging the chronological boundaries of narratives on the war is by placing the entire focus of this project on the post-1975 period. Although bookstore and library shelves continue to be filled every year with new books devoted to some aspect of U.S. involvement in Southeast Asia, none have focused exclusively on this period. As I hope this study makes clear, the time has arrived when the period after 1975 can no longer be ignored or dismissed as an "epilogue" to American involvement in Vietnam. I also challenge existing narratives of the war by focusing on the various narrative structures of texts—not simply the stories and interpretations offered by the text, but how those stories render certain aspects of other narratives outside the realm of discussion. So, for instance, while I will argue that the United States continued to exercise its considerable power over Vietnam after 1975, this power, although it frequently operated through the threat of direct force or military violence, was more often than not exercised by "guiding the possibility of conduct and putting in order the possible outcome" of a given situation.[10] The United States found itself in the rather unique position of emerging in 1975 from the longest—and one of the costliest—wars in its history defeated and divided, yet still armed with the ability to dictate the terms of peace to the enemy at whose hands it had been defeated. The United States was still able, in the late 1970s, to influence, if not control, many of the international institutions to which the Vietnamese sought access and aid; it was still able to govern, more than any other nation, the global flows of capital, technology, and commodities which the Vietnamese were in desperate need of.

In short, the United States was both indirectly and directly responsible for defining the broad terms under which the Vietnamese would reconstruct and rebuild their nation. Michel Foucault's phrase for such manifestations of power is "structuring the possible field of action."[11] In this same sense I will show, for instance, that although the brutal American embargo did not *determine* the fate of a Socialist Vietnam, it did limit the range of possibilities available to the state and its people, by restricting the amount of aid and capital flowing into the country and the amount and type of exports flowing out of it, and by blocking for several years after 1975 Vietnamese applications for membership in the United Nations.

In focusing on narrative structure, I am also drawing on the important and underappreciated work of Jill Lepore. As Lepore shows in her 1999 book, *The Name of War,* acts of war inevitably generate acts of narration. "Waging, writing, and remembering a war" are all parts of the same process of defining the war and the nations and people who fought it: "Both acts [of war and narration] are often joined in a common purpose—defining the geographical, political, cultural, and sometimes national and racial boundaries between people. If you kill me and call my resistance 'treachery,' you have succeeded not only in killing me (and, in doing so, ensuring that I will not be able to call your attack a 'massacre'), but you have also succeeded in calling me and my kind a treacherous people."[12]

Although traditionally such narration is the prerogative of the victors, again the United States found itself in the unique position of losing a devastating war while retaining the ability to define on its own terms the ensuing contest to determine the war's meaning. "If war is, at least in part, a contest for meaning," as Lepore argues, "can it ever be a fair fight when only one side has access to those perfect instruments of empire, pens, paper, and printing presses?"[13] If these statements about the politics of war stories are true for King Phillip's War, on which Lepore focuses, they most certainly hold true as well for the American war in Vietnam, a war that was fought on television and remembered on various "screens." If the pen and the printing press were once the perfect instruments of empire, certainly the American culture industries of the late twentieth century must be considered as key components in narrating the ongoing war on Vietnam after 1975. Indeed, the central role played by the popular media in constructing cultural memory of the war in Vietnam in American society is precisely why it is necessary to consider the intersections of cultural production and policy formation.

The argument I develop here is that the narratives of the American war against Vietnam after 1975, whether constructed in the halls of Congress or on movie screens across the country, operate through the same cultural logic of historical inversion, recasting the history of the war with the United States depicted as the victim of the Vietnamese. Doing so requires that the haunting images and stories of that war—children burned by napalm; rapes, murders, and mass executions by American soldiers and their allies—be erased or, at the very least, marginalized in American cultural memory. Lost in this war for American memory, however, is the consideration of the effects of the war on the nation and people of Vietnam. Any discussion of the massive devastation of Vietnamese life at the hands of the United States is a considerable threat to the historical inversions enacted on the cultural front of the American war on Vietnam. As a result, Vietnam and the Vietnamese are rendered increasingly invisible in narratives of the war after 1975, either rendered outside the discursive construction altogether or dehumanized and marginalized to the point of invisibility and irrelevance. Thus, in debates over the POW/MIA issue, not only are the historical roles of victim and aggressor inverted, but the entire discussion is focused on a small group of American soldiers. Hardly any mention of the estimated 300,000 unaccounted-for Vietnamese soldiers can be found in the historical record. Similarly, in public discussions of the effects of Agent Orange on American soldiers, no consideration is given to the Vietnamese, who were obviously subject to greater exposure to the effects of American chemical warfare. Even in public memorials the Vietnamese and the legacies of the war are carefully and consistently rendered invisible so as not to disrupt the cultural and political work of reconstructing the culture of American imperialism after the ostensible end of the war in Vietnam.

That American forms of memory would focus on Americans, at the expense of any number of possible "Vietnamese Voices," is not at all shocking. Indeed, the patterns of policy making and storytelling that emerge from the American war in Vietnam mirror in many ways those seen after other American wars. That the pattern is not surprising, however, does not mean that it is not significant. It was never a given that representations of the war in Vietnam would seek to recuperate American nationalism or vilify the Vietnamese, any more than it was foreordained that the United States would impose a stringent trade embargo on Vietnam after the war was over. The very idea that such forms of cultural memory are "normal," or taken as common sense, amplifies the need for scholars to show how, and in what contexts, they are constructed and understood, for these representations of war in various forms remain cultural and historical constructions. It is surely not surprising, in this light, that the Vietnam Veterans Memorial in Washington, D.C., does not acknowledge the deaths of millions of Vietnamese; nor are viewers surprised when the Vietnamese characters in *Apocalypse Now* are simply haunting voices in the jungle. But in the wake of a divisive and devastating war that challenged so many Americans' fundamental assumptions about their nation, their government, and their fellow citizens, these silences matter a great deal. How the war was remembered, discussed, and represented, and what role the Vietnamese play (or fail to play) in texts from foreign aid bills to Hollywood films can reveal a great deal about the underlying assumptions Americans held about the war, themselves, and the United States' place in the world from the 1970s into the twenty-first century.

With these and other considerations in mind, I have constructed a narrative here that tells the story of the American war on Vietnam, 1975–2000, examining the intersections and interactions of cultural representations and foreign policy. In the first chapter, I examine the early stages, paying particular attention to the imposition of U.S. economic sanctions on Vietnam during the final hours of the military phase of the war, a policy that constituted a continuation of war by other means, sharing many characteristics with the military phase. In chapter two, I explore the process of "normalizing" the American war in Vietnam through the concept of "mutual destruction" made famous by President Carter in 1977. On both the policy and cultural "fronts" of the ongoing war against Vietnam, the same cultural logic inverting the history and public memory of the war was used to situate the United States as the victim of a savage and cruel enemy. Examining American policy toward Vietnam and Southeast Asia as a whole during the Third Indochina War, I argue in chapter three that in the 1980s the United States entered a new phase of its war on Vietnam, providing various forms of support to the anti-Vietnamese forces in China and Cambodia during this long and bloody conflict. The avowed policy of "bleeding Vietnam," followed by the United States and its allies, was thus an extension of, not a departure from, previous American actions toward Vietnam.

In chapter four, I turn once again to the cultural front. Against the backdrop of the proxy U.S. wars in Cambodia and Central America and the resurgence of American militarism in the 1980s, I argue that a new matrix of representations of the war in Vietnam was established during this period. Texts such as *Rambo, Platoon,* and their progeny only served to further the cultural work of the American war on Vietnam, reconstituting the United States as the primary victim of the war by systematically erasing the Vietnamese from these representations. The final stages of the American war on Vietnam are the focus of chapter five. Tracing the gradual end of hostilities through the first half of the 1990s, I show how U.S. policy continued to erode, both at home and in the international community. The new era of relations between the United States and Vietnam launched in 1994–95, however, continued to reflect the strikingly asymmetrical power relations between the nations, with Vietnam rather than the United States paying what amounted to war reparations as terms of a final settlement. In the last chapter, I explore the larger battle over American cultural memory of the war by examining the Vietnam Veterans Memorial in Washington, D.C. Tracing the evolution of "the Wall," from its design through its digital incarnations, we see that the resulting collection of walls together offer a striking summation of the American war on Vietnam after 1975, reinscribing the war in Vietnam into patriotic and nationalist metanarratives while silencing important questions about the direction, scope, and consequences of American foreign policy.

While the narrative presented in these chapters does seek to include a wide range of events and stories, it is, like all narratives, necessarily incomplete. This story, like all stories, renders certain things outside its narrative boundaries, resulting in a variety of limitations. Some of these I have anticipated; there are likely to be others I have not. For instance, there are several chapters here that could easily be expanded into books in their own right. I have pursued an interdisciplinary approach to the topic, aware that it may satisfy neither diplomatic nor cultural historians and upset both. I gloss over, at times, the type of historical details that one might expect from a more traditional diplomatic history: the myriad memos and conversations that contribute to the formulation of a given policy and other intricacies of policy making. While scholars in a variety of fields could undoubtedly benefit from a tightly drawn history of U.S.-Vietnamese diplomacy from 1975 to 1995, that is not the goal of this project. Similarly, those more interested in the cultural issues discussed here would surely benefit from a reexamination of various "texts," be they policy debates, news articles, or films, through the lenses of race, gender, class, or sexuality. The choice not to place such issues in a more prominent role in these pages is not meant to indicate that they are not part of the story of U.S.-Vietnamese relations after 1975; issues of race, class, gender, ability, and sexuality are, as we will see, inextricably part of every text considered here. While it is impossible to separate issues of race and gender in particular from U.S. representations of the American war in Vietnam, I have attempted to highlight along the way some of the ways in which those analytic categories operate in and against U.S. policy toward Southeast Asia in this period, as well as in American cultural memory of the war, rather than offer sustained discussions on the possible readings of the texts through the lenses of those categories.

Finally, there is the issue of calling this period in U.S.-Vietnamese relations a "war." In doing so, I am not in any way attempting to minimize the devastation of "hot" warfare, particularly the one waged between the United States and Vietnamese forces during the 1960s and 70s. Rather, I am seeking a more expansive definition of warfare in order to identify and name many of the more insidious and invisible aspects of violent relations between nations—economic, cultural, and environmental—that often go unnoticed in military, diplomatic, and even cultural history. For all of the voluminous writings on the philosophy, history, and causes of wars, students of wars still have very few useful definitions of warfare from which to choose in defining their topics. I have no new insights to offer here, only a query: If war, as Karl von Clausewitz claimed, is the continuation of politics by other means, is the inverse not also true? Is politics not the continuation of war by other means, particularly in a case such as that of the United States and Vietnam after 1975, when the policies followed by the United States seem to bear more than a passing resemblance to those enacted during the military phase of the war? As I hope to show, the effects of U.S. policy—a heavy-handed, aggressive policy that had dire consequences for Vietnamese civilians as well as their government—in many ways parallel the consequences of the military phase of the war waged during the previous two decades. From economic embargoes to denials of humanitarian aid, from ignoring the ongoing environmental devastation caused by the United States during the military phase of the war to actively funding and arming the forces fighting Vietnam, many aspects of U.S. policy toward Vietnam after 1975 are difficult to distinguish from similar "wartime" activities. The fact that, after 1975, these activities are supported by a cultural front strengthens this interpretation. Without a simply articulated definition of what does and does not constitute war, then, I leave it to readers to decide for themselves whether or not U.S. policy toward Vietnam both before and after 1975 should be classified as warlike.

Within these and other admitted limits, I have tried to point to the relevant secondary literature in footnotes. Some will have been missed, and I can only hope that I have the chance to expand this study, pursue related projects, and inspire and provoke other works in this area. It is important to note that this study, while presented as a fairly straightforward and largely chronological narrative, is not intended as *the* story, a new narrative to trump all others. It is, I believe, an original contribution to our understanding of the United States and Vietnam after 1975, but it is also an intervention in the contested field of cultural memory. My focus remains set on disrupting the chronological and disciplinary boundaries of the history of the American war in Vietnam. Thus, my story begins where most narratives of the war end: with the toppling of the South Vietnamese regime on April 30, 1975.

A CONTINUATION OF WAR BY OTHER MEANS THE ORIGINS OF THE AMERICAN WAR ON VIETNAM, 1975–1977

As the last helicopters were leaving the roof of the United States embassy in Saigon on April 30, 1975, Henry Kissinger sat helplessly in his West Wing corner office. "Neither Ford nor I could any longer influence the outcome," he wrote in his memoirs. "So we each sat in our offices, freed of other duties yet unable to affect the ongoing tragedy, with a serenity rarely experienced in high office." For the past several years, Kissinger had been the primary architect of the American war on Vietnam. Yet on this day, as he describes it, he was mostly contemplative, his reflections interrupted only by the occasional update from a staff member and, later, a press conference in which he argued that "what we need now in this country, for some weeks at least, and hopefully for some months, is to heal the wounds and to put Vietnam behind us and to concentrate on the problems of the future."[1]

Kissinger was certainly not alone in wanting to put the war in Vietnam behind him. The steady erasure of Vietnam from American attention actually had begun after the signing of the Paris Accords two years earlier. As the United States became engulfed in the Watergate scandal during 1974 and as most American personnel were evacuated from Southeast Asia, interest in the ongoing wars in both Vietnam and Cambodia declined steadily. An essay in *Time* magazine noted that many Americans had for some time "enjoyed a comforting illusion: that Viet Nam and all its horrors had gone away for good" now that the Vietnamese were simply fighting each other.[2] *Newsweek* echoed these sentiments, claiming that after the 1973 Accords "the agony of Vietnam seemed to recede."[3]

In the spring of 1975, however, "the war burst upon the U.S. all over again," making clear to all those in the United States seeking to forget the war that it was the agony of Americans, not the agony of *Vietnam,* that had seemed to recede over the past two years.[4] The Khmer Rouge victory in

Cambodia and the fall of Saigon once again brought the wars in Southeast Asia to the forefront of American consciousness. Images of suffering children, abandoned allies and clients, and fleeing Americans returned to the nightly news, newspaper headlines, and covers of magazines in one final flurry. Since 1950, the cover of *Time* had been devoted to some aspect of American involvement in Southeast Asia sixty-four times. For *Newsweek,* the count was sixty-two times since 1961. From early April until early May 1975, Vietnam was once again *the* story, as the mainstream media pondered the United States' role in the world, the plight of "those we left behind," and, most of all, "where do we go from here?" Just as quickly, though, Vietnam once again disappeared. In the second week in May, the covers of both major newsweeklies featured rising Soviet ballet star Mikhail Baryshnikov, rendering Vietnam increasingly to the back pages, where it would remain indefinitely.

The war thus ended for Americans, but not for America. By the time the Vietnamese were once again out of sight and out of mind in mid-May of 1975, the new war against Vietnam already had begun. As Saigon was being liberated by the revolutionary forces of Vietnam, the Ford White House swiftly imposed harsh economic sanctions on South Vietnam, to match those long in place against the North. In the midst of his meditations on April 30, the secretary of state found time to recommend to the Commerce Department that it freeze an estimated $70 million in South Vietnamese assets held by American-owned banks and their foreign subsidiaries.[5]

Two weeks later the White House was again in crisis mode, after a Khmer Rouge gunboat detained the SS *Mayaguez* in the Gulf of Thailand. Kissinger, returning to Washington on May 13 from a trip to the Midwest, arrived just in time for a meeting of the National Security Council. Soon after, he underwent what he later described as "one of the most bizarre and tense evenings of my experience in government."[6] After another long day of NSC meetings, diplomatic negotiations with the Chinese, and the authorization of military force to rescue the crew of the *Mayaguez,* the White House proceeded with a state dinner for the visiting Dutch prime minister. By the end of the dinner, from which Kissinger and Ford repeatedly took leave to monitor the situation, the ship and its crew of forty had been recovered, although forty-three American military personnel had been killed in the effort. The next morning a 15,000-ton bomb was detonated on the island from which the crew had been released several hours earlier. The White House declared victory, believing it had demonstrated America's resolve to use military force despite the humbling defeat at the hands of the revolutionary forces of Vietnam. "With this," Kissinger wrote, "Indochina disappeared from the American agenda."[7]

Despite all the distractions of the *Mayaguez* incident, however, Kissinger found the time to authorize yet another decision that would keep Vietnam from disappearing from view for at least a little while longer. On May 14, the State Department recommended to the secretary of commerce that South Vietnam and Cambodia be placed in the most restricted category of export controls, under which American citizens were forbidden to send people in those countries any humanitarian aid. Within the year, the United States would enlarge its sanctions program, denying the Vietnamese international aid, access to international capital, and membership in the United Nations. Far from being "unable to affect the ongoing tragedy," as Kissinger put it, the United States began a new campaign against Vietnam before the guns of the old one had even gone silent. Far from receding into isolation, the United States after 1975 remained in a position to shape the direction and contour of events in Vietnam and in Southeast Asia as a whole. The war on Vietnam continued; only the weaponry had changed.

The course of action set in motion on May 14 by Kissinger's authorization of the embargo was not examined at the time for its long-term policy implications and was never intended to be permanent, but it would nevertheless define and limit the range and scope of future interactions between Vietnam and the United States. Decades earlier, the United States had first supported a French war in Indochina and later gone to war there itself, continuing politics "by other means." In the spring of 1975, the United States began a new phase of the battle for Vietnam and Southeast Asia, continuing war by other means.

DEBATING THE EMBARGO: 1975

From the beginning, the economic sanctions placed on Vietnam were problematic. The asset controls invoked under the authority of the Trading With the Enemy Act were put in place as Saigon was being overrun by the revolutionary forces of Vietnam. The Export Administration Act of 1969 provided additional legal cover for the trade embargo, which appeared to be even more hastily conceived than the asset seizures, given that its development took place during the *Mayaguez* crisis in the second week of May 1975. In neither of these decisions was Congress consulted by the administration. As hearings commenced in the early summer of 1975, the White House remained unable to articulate any coherent reason for the implementation of the sanctions program.[8]

As Robert Miller, assistant secretary of state for East Asian and Pacific affairs, told Congress on June 4, the export controls, which had been placed on "the Communist controlled areas of Vietnam" in 1958, were extended to South Vietnam because they "further[ed] significantly the foreign policy of the United States," and that such controls can be authorized by the President "for national security reasons."[9] In 1958, "Communist controlled Vietnam" had originally been placed in Category Z, one normally reserved for nations with which the United States was at war. North Korea and Cuba were the only other nations included in the category at the time. Under this classification, even private shipments of humanitarian aid were subject to licensing by the federal government. Rarely, if ever, were such licenses granted. Category Y, a slightly less hostile category used to identify nations to whom the United States sought to deny "strategically important goods," was at the time applied to the Soviet Union and China, among others. Under that category, military aid and other supplies deemed "strategic" were subject to the same licensing procedures, but humanitarian aid was not. Ironically, this policy placed greater restrictions on aid than had been in place during the war.

Led by subcommittee chair Jonathan Bingham of New York, many committee members took the opportunity to express their concerns over the imposition of the embargo. In his opening remarks, Bingham noted that "It has been my hope, and that of many Members of the Congress, that our peacetime policies toward Indochina would not be mere extensions of our wartime sanctions—that the end of the fighting in Vietnam and the end of U.S. military involvement there would make possible a gradual normalization of relations with the people and governments of Indochina . . . Symbolic gestures with little practical impact when they are invoked, embargoes often become serious hurdles indeed when the time comes for them to be revoked."[10] After listening to Miller's testimony, Bingham offered that he found the administration's reasoning for the trade embargo "totally unconvincing," and a "purely bureaucratic procedure."[11] While Miller continued to focus attention on the asset controls, which most members of the committee found less controversial, it became clear that Bingham's concerns about both the "practical impact" of the embargo and the open-endedness of the measures would become major issues.

The freezing of assets in such situations had indeed become standard operating procedure for the United States government. The Truman administration had frozen close to $200 million in Chinese assets in 1949 ($100 million of which was still held by the United States in 1975), and Kissinger himself had authorized a similar arrangement for holding $9 million in Cambodian assets as Phnom Penh was being overrun by the Khmer Rouge. The blocking of assets was normally justified with the argument that the monies would be used to protect the government against claims from corporations and private individuals who lost foreign investments and property when governments seized or nationalized their assets. Under the Foreign Claims Settlement Act (passed in 1949 in the wake of the Chinese Revolution), American citizens could file claims with the government that eventually could be settled using the foreign assets blocked by the United States. In March of 1977, as the Carter administration was moving closer to normalizing relations with Beijing, the Chinese agreed to pay $80.5 million in cash to help offset the estimated $197 million of American assets frozen since 1949.[12] As the revolutionary forces of Vietnam rolled into Saigon in 1975, the Ford administration acted to ensure that these measures would be in place to protect the millions of dollars abandoned during the American evacuations that year.

Few in Congress took issue with the freezing of assets. The embargo was another matter. Asked to explain how imposing a trade embargo on Vietnam was a matter of national security, Miller answered that the controls would permit the U.S. government "to monitor the evolving attitudes of these new regimes toward the United States and toward its citizens." It would have been "inappropriate," he went on to claim, "to relax the controls on North Vietnam or Vietnam in light of the circumstances that pertained at the time."[13] The policy of the administration, he argued, was to extend the embargo to all of Vietnam and then to evaluate at some later date "the attitude" of the new government. Yet Miller, after further prodding from the committee, also conceded that Vietnam was not at all a threat to the security of the United States, as the legislation demands, but was, rather, *potentially* hostile to "American interests" in Southeast Asia. Having claimed that the North Vietnamese came to power in South Vietnam "in gross violation of the Paris Agreements," Miller was put on the defensive in explaining how an embargo was in the interests of the United States. In a notable exchange with Representative Donald Fraser of Minnesota, Miller revealed the confused and punitive nature of the policy.

FRASER: You agree Vietnam is not threatening the United States?

MILLER: I agree Vietnam is not threatening the United States directly, but that it has taken power in South Vietnam by force of arms against the interests of the United States.

FRASER: This is a form of punishment then. It is for past behavior. It is not a present problem. It is past behavior.

MILLER: Our judgment is that the application of these controls is a prudent and orderly way to establish a basis for judging how the attitudes of these new regimes evolve.

FRASER: Why do we have to put a restraint on trade in order to evaluate the regimes? Does that help our intelligence gatherers?

MILLER: It puts us in a position to monitor the activities of these countries, of these regimes.

FRASER: How does putting an embargo on trade help to monitor their activities?

MILLER: First, as I said, we want to be sure we deny any strategic goods to them. Second, as I have said, the controls already applied to all of Vietnam in effect.[14]

This line of questioning resumed, with Chairman Bingham now chastising Miller:

BINGHAM: Isn't it also true that clearly the purpose of the earlier embargo against North Vietnam was to try to impede North Vietnam's effectiveness in a military struggle to which we were opposed?

MILLER: That is undoubtedly the case; that is correct.

BINGHAM: Then to impose an embargo after the contest is over is to close the barn door after the mare is stolen.

Miller responded that the extension of the embargo was "automatic," but the rest of his testimony made clear that it was hardly that easy. The committee later returned to this question when the underlying policy justifications given by Miller and others remained unclear. Asked if the decisions were made in "routine fashion," as if "they were not very important decisions," Miller replied that, no, "they were given careful consideration," to which Chairman Bingham retorted, again, that the actions "were taken without consultation with Congress and without consultation with any of our friends in Southeast Asia."[15]

Administration officials also testified that President Ford had not been involved in the decision, further demonstrating the surreptitious manner in which the embargo was put in place. When asked why there hadn't been more debate on the matter, Phillip Trimble, a legal adviser at the State Department, stated that "the President has statutory authority, but that has been delegated." The questioning continued:

FRASER: With respect to all of the controls that have now been applied, the Secretaries of the Departments can sign off without involving the President; is that correct?

TRIMBLE: That is correct.

FRASER: No decision is required by the President?

TRIMBLE: The authority is delegated; that is correct. Treasury and Commerce act on the recommendation of the Secretary of State.[16]

In the end, the embargo was pushed through the administration without any trace of a serious policy debate. The ostensible reason given for the embargo was that the United States could "monitor" the new Vietnamese government, and neither Congress nor even the president were apparently consulted or involved in the decision-making process. Authority to impose the trade sanctions rested with the Treasury and Commerce Departments, which acted on the instructions of Secretary of State Kissinger.

Several other things about these hearings are worth noting. First, although it would quickly become the defining policy goal of the embargo, there is not a single mention of the POW/MIA issue in the transcripts of the sessions. For the next twenty years no hearing on any issue related to Vietnam would take place without a significant portion of discussion committed to the topic of missing American personnel, yet in the initial discussion and imposition of the embargo, it is conspicuously absent. Secondly, it is clear that the administration never intended the embargo to be permanent. When asked if the committee was correct in assuming that the sanctions were a "temporary measure," Miller replied, "I don't think anything is permanent, and I think this seriously is our intention, to watch and observe and evaluate the evolving attitudes of these regimes toward us."[17] Yet the administration and Congress failed to prescribe any specific criteria under which the sanctions would be revisited. As Miller told the committee, "I am not aware of any regular or periodic mechanism for reviewing [the policies]."[18] This absence of specifically defined policy goals and procedures allowed for the future malleability of justifications for the program.

Finally, many in Congress were aware that beyond lacking any definitive policy objectives, the sanctions might actually work against U.S. interests in the region in two ways. First, members of the committee assumed the sanctions would push Vietnam further toward the Soviets and/or China. Michael Harrington of Massachusetts was particularly stringent in his criticism on this point, arguing the case of Cuba and numerous "other examples where we have driven the wedge of isolation only then to witness as the isolated nations move closer to the orbit of those with whom they are forced to deal for economic sustenance."[19] In fact, Harrington's fears would be borne out by future events, as the continued isolation of Vietnam by the United States resulted in the formal alliance of Hanoi with the Soviet Union, which in turn led to a triangular proxy standoff in Cambodia between the Soviets, the United States, and China. Second, the White House gave absolutely no economic justification for the embargo. Aside from the direct American military and development aid to South Vietnam, which had already been discontinued and was further restricted by Congress, there was no prior trade relationship with Vietnam that would be missed. In Miller's testimony, he noted that "the trade effect of the export controls was not a major consideration . . . and it is reasonable to assume that even without controls U.S. trade with South Vietnam would be practically nil for the foreseeable future."[20]

As in so many earlier instances, policy makers in Washington were unwilling or unable to realize the Vietnamese desire for better relations between the two nations. Only a few weeks after the fall of Saigon, Prime Minister Pham Van Dong had reached out for American aid. The prime minister was hardly conciliatory, however, demanding the aid by citing "obligations" of the United States stemming from its "criminal war of aggression" against Vietnam.[21] While being less than diplomatic, the Vietnamese did indicate their desire for further discussion on the matter. Rather than seizing the moment as an opportunity for negotiations—or even simply ignoring the gesture—the State Department "issued a stiff denunciation" of the prime minister's comments, reasserting the administration's position that the United States had "no intention of giving aid to any Indochinese communist nation."[22] Senator George McGovern, at a hearing on American MIAs in the spring of 1977, recounted a conversation he had had with Pham not long after the war ended that further demonstrated possibilities for improved U.S.-Vietnamese relations. The senator asked the prime minister what he "thought was a facetious question [about] American oil companies going over there to develop their oil." When the prime minister responded that Vietnam would indeed support American involvement in their offshore oil operations, McGovern was taken aback, having assumed that the last thing the Vietnamese would want was a return of American industry.[23] In fact, according to Nayan Chanda, American oil executives, who had invested hundreds of millions of dollars exploring for oil in the South China Sea during the war, had quietly held several meetings with Vietnamese officials in Paris, and later, in February of 1976, were invited to Hanoi for further discussions. Because the embargo remained in place, however, the contracts never took shape.[24]

In November of 1975, the embargo was given one more public hearing, the last one to be devoted exclusively to the policy until the early 1990s. That fall had seen the issue of normalizing relations with Vietnam briefly resurface in the news, for several reasons. First of all, business groups stepped up pressure on the Ford administration to repeal the embargo and allow them access to the Vietnamese market, while Hanoi's tone softened on the issue of American "financial aid" versus "obligations."[25] But two other developments would set the tenor of the debate in these hearings. First, Hanoi agreed to release the last American "prisoners" of the war: a group of civilians, mostly American missionaries, known originally as the Ban Me Thout Twelve, who had been held by Hanoi since being captured near the village of Ban Me Thout during the final offensive earlier that spring. Second, the American Friends Service Committee (AFSC), a Quaker organization that had been very active in supplying aid to the people of Vietnam during the American war, brought the contradictions of the sanctions program into public view. The AFSC had been quietly subverting the embargo while repeatedly being denied export licenses by the Ford administration. On November 10, several hundred members of the AFSC protested outside the White House, demanding that the State and Commerce Departments approve licenses to the group for humanitarian aid and other supplies.[26] In response to the increasingly visible protest, and to the release of the last nine members of the Ban Me Thout group, the administration made modest revisions to its policy, which seemed only to complicate matters further.

After meeting with Kissinger on November 14, Sonny Montgomery, a Democratic congressman from Mississippi and chair of the House Select Committee on Missing Persons in Southeast Asia, announced that over the weekend the White House had approved the AFSC license and that new requests would be considered on a case-by-case basis. The changes to the policy turned out to be little more than cosmetic, as they attempted to draw a distinction between "humanitarian aid," which would be allowed, and "economic assistance," which would not. The *Los Angeles Times* jumped on the story, calling American policy toward Vietnam "conspicuous silliness" being carried out "as if the war were still being waged." Taking the AFSC licenses as a case in point, the editorial noted that sweaters from the group were approved, but "16 tons of yarn" were not. "Medical supplies, powdered milk, canned pork, school supplies and pediatric drugs are licensed. But not fishing nets, not rotary tiller diesel plows, not the machinery to make prosthetic devices."[27] By the time the Subcommittee opened its hearings on the bill, the State Department did reconsider and approve licenses for the fishing nets and tillers, making clear that they had been granted in response to the release of the American citizens, and did not constitute a new direction in the overall trade policy.

On November 17, the Bingham Subcommittee on International Trade and Finance was again the forum for discussion of the embargo, as members of various church communities were invited to testify about export restrictions to Vietnam. The stated reason for the "Church Views" hearings was consideration of a House resolution, HR 9503, that would amend the Trading With the Enemy Act in order to repeal the embargo on Vietnam. Meanwhile, the release of the Ban Me Thout prisoners had revived the claim that Vietnam continued to hold American prisoners of war. No evidence has ever been found to substantiate the POW/MIA myth, but as the church hearings began in late 1975, it became clear that a marked shift in public debate about U.S. policy toward Vietnam had taken place, with the POW/MIA issue taking center stage.

Inside the committee room, Bingham opened the hearings by stating that the announced change "constitutes no change in policy at all," a point he continued to press with witnesses throughout the proceedings.[28] Edward Doherty of the United States Catholic Conference argued that many American citizens were ready to begin the process of reconciliation with Vietnam, but that the Ford administration was standing in the way of peace. Doherty called upon the United States "to begin a national examination of conscience," asserting that the American government and the American people has [sic] a responsibility to help rebuild Indochina.[29] In questioning from the committee, however, the notion of responsibility was quickly and deftly turned against the Vietnamese, as members asked about Vietnamese assistance regarding "those who are missing in action," as a precondition for bilateral aid, which was completely outside the purview of the committee at the time. Several members also put the question of aid to Vietnam within the context of the larger battle of the period over the distribution of American foreign aid. Congressman Edward Beister of Pennsylvania, for instance, asked why the American people should focus on Vietnam, which would not even be at the "top of the list" of poorest countries.[30]

The next witness, Herman Will of the United Methodist Church, offered similar testimony, noting how active his church had been in providing aid during the American war in Vietnam, and how despite raising hundreds of thousands of dollars in relief aid since the end of the war they were now unable to continue those efforts. Again, however, the talk quickly turned to Vietnamese responsibilities, particularly on the matter of Americans still listed as Missing in Action. Congressman Beister again took the lead, this time arguing that the MIA issue was not a "governmental relationship," but a "human" relationship. Will countered that, given how the United States had "laid waste" to Vietnam, and the vast human tragedies that affected so many Vietnamese lives, the Vietnamese might have difficulty seeing the recovery of American personnel as a priority.[31] Most notably, however, Will made the crucial point that the recent decision of the State Department to consider further opening of the relationship between Washington and Hanoi on a quid pro quo basis actually encouraged the Vietnamese to withhold any information they might obtain about missing American personnel, in order to leverage their overall bargaining position. This claim is important because later debates over normalization of relations and aid to Vietnam would focus on the apparent willingness of Hanoi to trade information, or bodies, for aid. Members of the United Presbyterian Church and of Clergy and Laity Concerned offered similar testimony, and were met with similar reactions by members of the committee. On the other side of the debate, the legislative director of the American Legion submitted a written statement arguing that the United States "should not reward Hanoi's intransigence" on the MIA issue. "Thousands of American families remain in limbo," according to the statement, "because of Hanoi's refusal to assist us in determining the fate of American servicemen who fought for us all in Indochina."[32]

As Bruce Franklin has shown in his close study of the POW/MIA issue, the primary reason that so many American families remained "in limbo" had little, if anything, to do with the Vietnamese. One of the many sad ironies of the POW/MIA myth is that the Vietnam War produced the lowest percentage of unaccounted-for American service personnel in major wars waged by the United States. As the government's own study of the topic indicates, of over 360,000 American soldiers killed in action during World War Two, 22 percent were never recovered, even with unfettered access to all sites of battle.[33] In the Korean War, according to Franklin, over 15 percent of the 33,000 American casualties were not accounted for. The number for Vietnam was significantly lower: of close to 60,000 Americans killed in Vietnam, around 2,500, or 4 percent, were initially unaccounted for.[34]

Beginning with the Paris peace negotiations of 1969, the Vietnamese delegation was consistently met with unparalleled demands by the United States. In late 1969, the U.S. delegation presented to the Vietnamese a list of personnel it considered "missing or captured." Attached to the list, notes Franklin, was a "bizarre" and "unprecedented" statement: "We are holding the Communist authorities in Southeast Asia responsible for every individual on this list whether or not he is internally classified by the services as captured or missing." Franklin's description of the impact of this attachment is worth quoting at length:

> This demand is probably unprecedented in the annals of warfare. It has no basis in international law, which hardly requires belligerent powers to furnish each other with information on the identities of those they have killed. It could never even conceivably be met, for it holds all the opposing forces individually and collectively "responsible for every individual" missing, including those in planes lost at sea or exploding above mountains and jungle. It thoroughly and effectively confuses the question of the missing with that of prisoners. It has been the official policy of the United States since it was issued in 1969. It is the foundation upon which the entire POW/MIA myth has been built.[35]

Even the congressional Select Committee on Missing Persons agreed with this assessment:

> There are no convenient historical examples to serve our interest. What is now being demanded of the Indochinese governments is unusual. After the 1946–54 war, the French did not receive information on their missing. The United States has never asked for such a volume of information on its missing, especially from a former enemy that was not defeated, and in a war as complex as the Vietnam war proved to be. There are no examples in world history to compare with the accounting now being requested.[36]

This demand further demonstrates that the continuing construction of Vietnam as an "enemy" state—in the later stages of the war and, especially, after the fall of Saigon—was hardly the result of "business as usual" in Washington. As always, Vietnam proved to be an exception to the rule.

What is perhaps even more remarkable than this request, however, is that the Vietnamese repeatedly went above and beyond the call of what could have been reasonably expected from a former adversary that was still fighting off a war of aggression and, later, rebuilding a devastated and deeply divided country. Constantly bombarded with conflicting numbers from the Pentagon, the Vietnamese and Laotian governments initially produced an accounting "for fifteen *more* prisoners than the Defense and State departments had listed as likely prisoners," even though those numbers were themselves inflated. In fact, as Franklin goes on to argue, "what was truly remarkable about the accounting of American POWs was how closely each side's list correlated with that of the other."[37] The Vietnamese, it turned out, were keeping better track of missing Americans than the United States.

Had it been left to the military, the issue might well have disappeared, despite the initial embarrassment of having the "Communist authorities in Southeast Asia" demonstrate superior recordkeeping of American forces. But the POW/MIA issue became what Franklin accurately terms a "Frankenstein's monster": the myth succeeded in shoring up support for Nixon's escalations of the war from 1969 to 1972, but it became an uncontrollable creature that would create policy dilemmas for all future administrations, turning bereaved and misled citizens against their own government.[38] The Vietnamese, of course, remained the primary object of this ire, caught in the twisted logic of the POW/MIA matrix. Instructed by the American government and public that they would not receive any aid until they released these phantom captives, and later accused, as Franklin points out, "of withholding prisoners *because* the United States had not carried out its promise to help rebuild Vietnam," the Vietnamese people became the true prisoners of this myth.[39]

In the period of just a few short months, the focus of the congressional debate over the American embargo on Vietnam had gone from discussion of the statutory authority under which such measures could be imposed to Vietnamese responsibility for assisting the recovery of missing American military personnel.[40] Lost in this shift were the fact that the United States seemed to be continuing the war by other means, and questions over whether the trade embargo was actually a practical, effective, or humane means to an ill-defined end.

THE UNITED NATIONS

The embargo was but one piece of the initial phase of the American war on Vietnam. The United States further demonstrated its ongoing obstinacy with regard to Vietnam at the United Nations. On August 6, 1975, the United Nations Security Council denied a hearing to South Korea's application for membership. Although the South Koreans had been repeatedly denied admission since their first application in 1949, the decision not even to hold a hearing on the matter was somewhat unusual. The standard UN position had been that divided nations, such as Korea, Germany, and Vietnam between 1954 and 1975, would not be admitted unless both parties agreed on entrance. East and West Germany were not admitted until 1973, when they signed a mutual recognition treaty.[41] North Korea's continued intransigence on joining the United Nations effectively rendered void its southern counterpart's request. As it turned out, however, the refusal of the Security Council to consider the Korean question provided the Ford administration the pretext it desired to take the unprecedented step of vetoing the two Vietnams' applications.

The Vietnamese applications provided an unusual case in their own right. At the time of the applications, North Vietnam remained clearly in control of South Vietnam, and there was little doubt in Southeast Asia, the United States, or the rest of the world that the two would soon be reunified. As the *Economist* opined at the time, "there are now about one and a half Vietnams," united politically and militarily and separate primarily in economic planning. Regardless of the politics involved, given that the Democratic Republic of Vietnam had taken over the Republic of Vietnam by force, the dual applications from "two governments, one of which has just helped overthrow the other's predecessor in a war fought to decide, among other things, whether their countries should be two or one," certainly constituted a unique situation.[42] The United States, though, was not interested in a debate on the subtleties of UN procedure, as the White House quickly made up its mind to reassert its power over the process.

The members of the American delegation were unanimous in their opinion on how to respond to the applications, according to Daniel Patrick Moynihan, then the American ambassador to the UN. Although the admission of "the Vietnams" would "symbolize and confirm" the humiliation of the United States and serve as yet another marker of "the end of the period in which the United States was *the* principal actor in world affairs," the mission agreed that an American veto would provoke the General Assembly into some form of retaliation, perhaps even the expulsion of Israel, an idea being circulated at the time.[43] In a lengthy cable to the White House, Moynihan informed Kissinger that a veto would be a calamity. "We would be seen to act out of bitterness, blindness, weakness, and fear. We would be seen not only to have lost the habit of victory, but in the process to have acquired the most pitiable stigma of defeat. But there would be little pity. The overwhelming response would be contempt."[44] Kissinger and President Ford were unwavering. They instructed Moynihan to veto the Vietnamese applications. The August 11 votes were only the eighth and ninth vetoes ever cast by the United States in the Security Council, and the first against the admission of another nation.[45]

When the General Assembly convened in September, it responded to the American action with a vote of 123–0, instructing the Security Council to "reconsider" the applications "immediately and favorably." The United States and a few allies abstained from this vote. In an address to the assembly on September 22, Kissinger denied any great animosity toward the Vietnamese: "So we say to all peoples and governments: Let us fashion together a new world order. Let its arrangements be just. Let the new nations help shape it and feel it is theirs. Let the old nations use their strengths and skill for the benefit of all mankind. Let us all work together to enrich the spirit and to ennoble mankind."[46] One week later, however, the United States again cast the lone veto against the admission of Vietnam into the United Nations. In December of 1975, when members of the Select Committee were meeting with Vietnamese leaders in Hanoi, Foreign Minister Phan Hien was told by members of the American delegation that the U.S. veto "was nothing directed at the Vietnamese," at which Hien and his colleagues could only laugh.[47]

Even taking into consideration the unusual nature of the Vietnamese applications, the clear international consensus was to allow the admission of both states under the assumption that reunification was little more than a formality. Although it has become increasingly common since the end of the war in Vietnam for the United States to be on the short end of near-unanimous UN votes, at the time it was a major departure.[48] While Moynihan's comments in the Security Council justified the vetoes on the grounds that the simultaneous denial of the South Korean application constituted a procedural misstep, it seems clear that the administration's motives were far less idealistic. Kissinger and Ford could easily have instructed Moynihan to abstain from the votes, voicing displeasure at the process without making such a radical shift in policy. By noisily, publicly, and solitarily denying Vietnamese membership in the UN, the Ford White House echoed its actions after the fall of Saigon, enacting unnecessary measures that only made the nation appear more like a "petty and frustrated tyrant."[49]

This view was borne out a year later, when the recently reunified and renamed Socialist Republic of Vietnam applied for United Nations membership and was promptly greeted with an announcement by the Ford administration that it would once again veto the application in the Security Council. Although understandably frustrated, the Vietnamese were persuaded by the French to wait to apply until after the upcoming American elections. Working behind the scenes, Kissinger had secured this arrangement the previous week in Paris.[50] Public statements by Hanoi, echoed by many in the international press, suggested that the continued obstinacy of the United States was based more on the personal pettiness of Kissinger than anything else. These feelings were seemingly confirmed yet again when, after the 1976 presidential elections, the United States cast the lone vote against Vietnam's application. Yet again the General Assembly responded with an adamant message to the Security Council to reconsider, and yet again the United States used its veto power to deny the application.

The real story in the latest round of vetoes was the shift in justifications for the votes. From the muddled "procedural concerns" of 1975, the United States was in the fall of 1976 asserting its rejection of the application solely on the basis of the POW/MIA issue. Ambassador William Scranton, who replaced Moynihan as head of the U.S. delegation, claimed that Vietnam was not fit for membership in the United Nations because the unwillingness of Hanoi to provide a "full accounting" of missing American servicemen violated the precepts of "humanitarianism" and "peaceful intent" set forth in the UN charter. As *Far Eastern Economic Review* columnist Louis Halasz pointed out at the time, however, the relevant section of the document says nothing about humanitarianism.[51] In the meantime, Hanoi had made a number of gestures, both to its neighbors and toward the United States, indicating its desire for improved bilateral and international relations, and was continually met only with increasing demands by the United States.

By the time the final veto was cast against Vietnam in December of 1976, Jimmy Carter had defeated Ford for the presidency. Although the Carter administration would reverse the veto policy by 1977, during the course of the campaign the POW/MIA issue had been firmly established as the central facet of American policy toward Vietnam. As Christopher Jespersen has accurately described it, Vietnam had little to do with Ford's defeat, but the domestic electoral process had a "substantial impact on decisions relating to Vietnam."[52] Ford had been forced to move further to his political right on the POW/MIA issue, to ward off a conservative challenge from Ronald Reagan and to deflect Carter's criticisms of his policies during the campaign. Ironically, the POW/MIA issue would play a far greater role in the normalization process of the 1990s than it did in the 1970s. But even without the POW/MIA issue on center stage, the Vietnamese faced a stalwart opponent in the United States Congress. During the early years of the Carter administration, the House and Senate would seemingly pave the way for the White House to pursue full normalization, only to later throw up new roadblocks.

THE CARTER ADMINISTRATION AND CONGRESS

According to the February 28, 1977, edition of *Time,* the Carter administration began making "top secret" overtures to the Vietnamese shortly after the inauguration.[53] In late January, Carter met with several members of Congress, including members of the Select Committee on Missing Persons, reiterating his intention to move toward normalized relations. The article went on to note that the Vietnamese had softened their stance on American reparations over the past two years, indicating that they were equally interested in opening ties to American business interests. So certain of developing these ties were the Vietnamese, that a group of oil executives visiting from Japan had been told in late 1976 that future development of Vietnam's substantial petroleum interests "was reserved 'for the American sector.'" "Washington, in turn," concluded the piece, "seems almost ready to accept the fact that the fate of most of the MIAs will never be known."[54]

Although the Select Committee had all but declared the MIA issue a red herring, Carter clearly thought he needed one final show of his attention to the matter before beginning to negotiate with the Vietnamese. On February 25, the White House announced that a delegation led by Leonard Woodcock, president of the United Auto Workers (which had helped deliver the White House to Carter), would visit Hanoi to pave the way for negotiations. Woodcock would be accompanied by four others, including former Senate Majority Leader Mike Mansfield and Sonny Montgomery. In the announcement, the administration indicated a new phase in Vietnamese-American relations by noting that it would be "more flexible" in its policies, including easing the current embargo.[55] Presumably, this also meant an end to the official stance of requiring the impossible "full accounting" of missing Americans by the Vietnamese.

The mission was marked from the beginning by a tension between the dictates of domestic politics and foreign relations. In his close study of the Carter administration's policy toward Vietnam, Stephen Hurst shows that although the public purpose of the commission was to "discuss matters affecting mutual relations as part of a long-term goal of establishing normal relations,"[56] the real reason for the mission was more complex. Frederick Brown, a State Department spokesperson at the time of the commission, claimed the administration needed to "neutralize" the MIA question as a domestic political issue. According to an internal White House memo unearthed by Hurst, however, National Security Advisor Zbigniew Brzezinski further wanted to "defuse the MIA issue" for the Vietnamese, taking away what most policymakers viewed as the only card held by Hanoi in negotiations.[57] Defusing either side in this confrontation, though, would prove more difficult than anyone in the White House had expected.

In Hurst's account, when the delegation landed in Hanoi, it was met with immediate assertions by the Vietnamese foreign minister, Nguyen Duy Trinh, that the United States was still under a legal obligation, arising from both the Paris Accords and the infamous Nixon letter, to provide aid. The 1973 letter from Nixon to Pham Van Dong, which had not yet been made public, promised a commitment of several billion dollars. The money would never materialize, but at the time of the commission's visit the Vietnamese clearly still felt entitled to the aid.[58] Without it, Trinh allegedly told Woodcock, "there would be no accounting for the MIAs."[59] If this was indeed the note on which the negotiations began, both parties kept the tension hidden from the press accompanying the mission. All major accounts of the meetings reported in the American press took special note of the friendly manner in which the delegation was greeted. "From the moment the Americans arrived in Hanoi," noted *Time*, "they were made to feel welcome by the Vietnamese, who avoided any macabre linkage between the remains of U.S. servicemen and money for reconstruction."[60] The article went on to quote Foreign Minister Phan Hien's remark that "[t]his is not a question of what amount of money. It is a question of responsibility, honor, and conscience, and it does not relate to Nixon—it relates to the U.S. . . . If the U.S. does not make any contribution toward the healing of the wounds of war, then we will do it all ourselves. We've already begun doing that."[61] The *Economist* also took note of the conspicuously outgoing nature of the Vietnamese leaders, noting in particular that Prime Minister Pham Van Dong "had given the mission a friendly welcome" and was the prime mover in proposing formal negotiations later in the spring.[62]

There is no question that the Vietnamese felt entitled to war reparations from the United States. The issue here has to do with how the Vietnamese are portrayed in terms of the MIA issue—whether as a friendly, peace-loving people interested in putting the wounds of the American war behind them, or as a cruel and heartless Asian menace, holding knowledge of missing Americans, if not the missing Americans themselves, ransom for several billion dollars. Although the encounters were all described in glowing terms at the time, the Vietnamese had initially suggested that the biggest obstacle to normalization lay not with them, as the Americans had long suggested, but with the continuation of "erroneous policies of the past," including the trade embargo and the veto of Vietnam's United Nations application.[63] In the final analysis, the Vietnamese were looking for an indication that the United States would stop its hostile economic and diplomatic policies and make some commitment, however nebulous, to provide some form of economic assistance to Vietnam. As a result of discussions with Woodcock, the Vietnamese dropped the terminology of reparations and obligations as well as their demand for the $3.25 billion promised by Nixon in 1973. As Woodcock put it, "They put the emphasis on bilateral, multilateral, on the many ways it could be done."[64]

The Woodcock Mission appeared at the time to be a success for Vietnam as well as the United States. Aside from this demonstration that it was willing to continue to assist in the recovery of MIAs, the spring of 1977 saw a number of developments that boded well for Vietnam's own economic recovery. "It was not a coincidence that the Woodcock delegation's trip was preceded by an unpublicized three-week trip by the World Bank and two separate missions by United Nations Development Program [UNDP]," Nayan Chanda wrote in *Far Eastern Economic Review.* Although neither program committed to specific aid projections at the time, the understanding among those agencies and the Vietnamese was that a normalization of relations with the United States would result in greater development aid for Vietnam. As Chanda described it, the UNDP informed the Vietnamese that the current allocations for two projects were insufficient and "that they would have to look for additional donors. As one diplomat noted: 'The Vietnamese know who the donors could be.'"[65]

Unfortunately for the Vietnamese, the refusal of the United States Congress to follow though with a pledge of some form of aid would remain the primary obstacle to normalization. While some legislative committees consulted members of church communities, and the White House continued to exercise its veto power at the UN, other members of Congress had already initiated proceedings to significantly revise the Trading With the Enemy Act (TWEA), under which the initial embargo had been imposed. The corrective legislation called for in 1975 would not be passed for two years. The changes to the law made in 1977, however, further demonstrate the extent to which many policymakers at the time considered the sanctions program against Vietnam to be a mistaken course of action put in place under questionable authority. The revisions to the TWEA also limited the application of the law "to the case of a declared war," although the bill's authors were careful to allow for sufficient gray area in the language of the legislation so that it might be applied in instances of undeclared wars such as the war on Vietnam.[66]

The discussion and testimony in the hearing make it clear that members of both the legislative and executive branches found the previous policy regime haphazard, yet no one involved in the hearings was willing to extend the discussion to consider terminating the various sanctions programs in place at the time under the auspices of the TWEA. Instead, the existing sanctions against Vietnam, Cuba, North Korea, and a few Eastern Bloc countries were grandfathered into the new law. Congressman Bingham, who chaired the initial embargo hearings described above, and who was one of the authors of the TWEA revisions, explained the decision to continue those measures by the need for an "uncontroversial" bill: "What we are focusing on is a procedural arrangement, and we are avoiding substantive issues of controversy. I think for us to attempt to deal with those controversial issues would be a mistake even though I personally favor lifting the embargo against Cuba and Vietnam . . . I think in time those embargoes will be lifted, but I think that will probably not occur until the President has made up his mind that that should be done and then persuades the Congress to concur in that judgment."[67]

The new law did alter the terms of the embargoes, such that if the president did decide to continue the sanctions, he would need to make an annual declaration to Congress, stating why it was in the national interest to do so. Certainly Bingham was right in noting that a congressional cancellation of the existing embargoes, particularly against Cuba and Vietnam, would have greatly complicated the passage of the bill, but the multiple ironies are difficult to ignore. The entire congressional backlash against executive misuse of power during the war in Vietnam and Watergate—

including the election of the Watergate class of 1974, the War Powers Act, and the National Emergencies Act—was ostensibly intended to curb those abuses by reasserting the role of the legislative branch in constructing foreign policy. Yet the only ongoing material policies stemming from those abuses, embodied in the sanctions program, were basically delegated back to the White House. Furthermore, in the 1975 embargo hearings, several members of the committee had chastised representatives from the State and Commerce Departments for putting the sanctions in place as a matter of "bureaucratic procedure," but by the time of these 1977 hearings they had adopted the same procedural approach, eschewing any debate about the merits, purpose, or impact of the policy. Congress would not remain passive for long, however.

On May 3, 1977, Phan Hien met Assistant Secretary of State Richard Holbrooke in Paris to begin negotiating the terms for diplomatic normalization between the United States and the Socialist Republic of Vietnam. Both of the men had been aides during the 1968 peace negotiations.[68] Holbrooke's intention was to inform the Vietnamese delegation that the United States would end its practice of vetoing UN membership for Vietnam, and, more importantly, that the United States was prepared to accept unconditional normalized relations between the two nations.[69] According to Elizabeth Becker, who later interviewed both men, Holbrooke began the meeting with this request: "May we go out this afternoon and announce normalization? The United States has no preconditions. After our embassies are established, we'll lift the trade embargo." To which Hien replied, "just as simply: 'No, without aid it is impossible.' "[70]

The talks broke off immediately, but events continued to spiral when Hien addressed the press (which had been expecting the announcement of normalization as well), quoting directly from the Nixon letter and declaring, "Vietnam would not agree to normalization without an American promise of aid." Nixon's letter was still classified at the time, and Hien's statement to the press revealed it to the world. The letter would be declassified a few weeks later, and become the subject of new hearings in Congress, but the fallout from the revelation was immediate. The day of Hien's statement, the House voted 266–131 to further obstruct American aid to Vietnam. Such aid, of course, was already prohibited, but the new measure barred the administration from even discussing the matter with Hanoi. The resolution, part of a State Department appropriations measure in the foreign aid bill, specifically prohibited "negotiating reparations, aid or any other form of payment to Vietnam." On May 5, the State Department issued a statement affirming that the United States indeed would not provide aid to Vietnam.[71]

Although they clearly misread both the intentions of the United States government and the loyalties of the American public, one can certainly make an argument that the Vietnamese were rightly insistent that the United States should provide a promise of aid up front. Had Hien agreed to announce normalized relations that afternoon in Paris, there was absolutely no guarantee that the United States would be willing or able to provide aid. As the numerous congressional hearings and legislative maneuvers in the spring and summer of 1977 would demonstrate, many policymakers, despite the intentions of the White House, were not interested in the symbolic healing that normalization would represent, much less the actual healing to which the United States could contribute by providing trade and aid to Vietnam. Even assuming that the embargo would have in fact been lifted after diplomatic recognition (which was far from certain), there was little chance that any aid would be headed to Hanoi.

Even the possibility of *trade* with the United States was beginning to recede. While business interests were nowhere near as visible in their lobbying efforts, they were beginning to take their place alongside the POW/MIA lobby as one of the most active forces in constructing U.S. policy toward Vietnam. American firms had collectively lost over $100 million in Vietnam, and several began pushing proposals that tied the resumption of normal trade relations to the settlement of these claims. While many companies, especially in the oil and telecommunications industries, were anxious to reenter the Indochinese market so as not to lose out to European companies, others were more firm in their resolve to recoup the cost of their abandoned assets. Frank Zingaro, CEO of oil giant Caltex, was a particularly vocal opponent of normalization, let alone aid. "We are not ready to forgive and forget," he told *Far Eastern Economic Review* before the administration's resumption of negotiations with the Vietnamese. "We are deeply interested in getting paid."[72] With several other major American corporations lined up against Vietnam as well, the possibility of normalization was fast eroding.

THE BATTLE OVER IFI'S

Clearly, given the tone of U.S.-Vietnamese negotiations taking place in Paris and the domestic sentiment in the United States, direct bilateral aid was out of the question. Any attempt would already be doomed by layer upon layer of prohibitive legislation—but that still did little to ease the most vehement opposition to economic assistance. Many in Congress, identifying what they considered to be a possible loophole, moved to prohibit American funds from reaching Vietnam through international aid agencies or international financial institutions (IFIs). As numerous congressional investigations had made plain, even without direct assistance from the United States, Vietnam could still become the indirect recipient of American dollars. Although Congress had thus far failed—or refused—to seize many opportunities to reclaim control over the economic tools of foreign policy, many in the capitol remained determined to exercise control over the direction of foreign aid, particularly to IFIs.

In September 1976, the Socialist Republic of Vietnam assumed the place of the former South Vietnamese regime in relation to the Asian Development Bank, World Bank, and International Monetary Fund. This was a very significant development for a number of reasons. Symbolically, it further legitimized the newly reunified nation and demonstrated Vietnam's desire for independence and sovereignty. At the time, neither the Soviet Union nor China had agreed to participate in these institutions because they were unwilling to divulge all the economic data required of member nations. Vietnam's willingness to participate in the process confirmed both its independence from those nations and its need for international aid. The Vietnamese would soon come to realize that the Bretton Woods institutions were not democratic, nor did they offer a particularly healthy path for developing nations. Despite their charters, these institutions were subject to the will of the United States, the largest contributor to the IFIs. The 1976 *Final Report of the Select Committee on Missing Persons in Southeast Asia* noted that through these agencies and the United Nations, the Vietnamese would be receiving around $34 million in indirect United States aid in 1977, $24 million in low interest loans, and $10 million in grants. The Select Committee recommended that the administration not "lose sight of these indirect contributions to Vietnamese humanitarian projects."[73]

In June of 1977 it became clear that Congress would not allow the Carter White House or the Vietnamese to lose sight of the contributions. On June 2, Hien and Holbrooke met in Paris for another round of negotiations. The Vietnamese delegation delivered information on twenty Americans listed as Missing in Action, and were again hopeful that some agreement on aid could be reached. Holbrooke's response remained the same, however, as he informed them that any question of aid would have to be deferred until after normalization. He did inform Hien that the United

States could "help you through different international organizations," but he could not pledge a given amount nor guarantee that Congress would agree to the general increase in funding to IFIs the administration was already promoting. Hien remained particularly frustrated by Holbrooke's insistence that congressional measures could continue to determine the fate of Vietnamese aid. "What would you do if I said the Vietnamese National Assembly had passed a law prohibiting searches for the MIAs?" he asked Holbrooke. "How can I go back to Hanoi empty-handed?"[74] Again, no progress was made, and Hien indeed left empty-handed.

Back in Washington, however, the resumption of negotiations had again raised the specter of aid to Vietnam, and the fact that Holbrooke had discussed even the *possibility* of channeling aid through IFIs set off yet another firestorm of legislation. Just as after the May meetings, Congress took only a day to respond to the actions of the administration. On June 4, the House voted 359–33 to approve another amendment to the foreign aid bill. The measure, sponsored by Lester Wolff of New York, chairperson of the subcommittee, was supposedly designed for Congress to put to rest the idea of reparations as promised in the Nixon letter, adding "reparations" to the categories of aid which the United States could not provide to Vietnam—as if somehow the government would approve reparations but not humanitarian aid. Although basically redundant, the amendment served to further demonstrate the degree of congressional hostility toward Vietnam.[75]

Congress was just getting warmed up. In the Senate on June 14, Robert Dole introduced an amendment that would force the United States to oppose funding to Vietnam provided through the World Bank and other IFIs, and, if outvoted, to hold back the amount of funds used toward the projects from the next American contribution. Describing the amendment, political scientists Joseph Zasloff and McAllister Brown took note of the "emotion aroused by the Vietnam aid issue." After John Glenn of Ohio spoke against the measure, citing the stance of the Select Committee and the State Department, "that to get tough may be counterproductive," his office received a barrage of angry calls from the POW/MIA lobby arguing that getting tough was exactly what was required. The next day, claiming that his remarks had been misinterpreted, he introduced his own amendment, "barring any commitment by U.S. negotiators 'to assist or pay reparations' to the Indochina states. It passed 90–2."[76]

Ironically, it was in part the rhetoric coming from the Carter White House that provided the fodder for consolidating the anti-Vietnam sentiment in Congress. Throughout his administration, Carter had pursued a foreign policy defined, in word if not in deed, by its focus on "human rights" issues, and it was precisely this idea that many congressional opponents used to derail many of the administration's foreign aid requests in 1977. To Carter's opponents, Vietnam and other "Communist-controlled states" were guilty of numerous violations of basic human rights, including, they claimed, withholding information about unaccounted-for American servicemen. It was an effective foil to Carter's policy. As Susumu Awanohara wrote in the *Far Eastern Economic Review,* "the human rights issue boomeranged on Carter" when "pro–human rights liberals" and "anti-aid conservatives" aligned in support of the various amendments restricting aid to a number of countries.[77] Although the battle over human rights never coalesced into a coherent policy, it did further hamstring Carter's efforts at increasing foreign aid and provided yet another angle from which the Vietnamese became dehumanized in cultural and political discourses. The general hypocrisy of a foreign policy based on a muddily defined concept of "human rights" would become even more pronounced as Carter began to move toward normalized relations with China while further alienating Vietnam.

To be sure, the many amendments to foreign aid legislation were part of the larger battle over foreign policy taking place in the late 1970s. Throughout the Carter administration the White House and Congress locked horns on the substance, direction, and means of American foreign policy, particularly on the question of foreign aid. But it took a persistent hostility toward Vietnam to help solidify the general distaste for aid among many in Congress into a coherent, if troubling, expression of policy. Previous targets of state-specific aid restrictions, such as South Korea, Chile, and Angola, had never provoked such ire on the part of Congress. The most vociferous advocates of the anti-Vietnam policy, though, claimed that they were simply voicing the concerns of their constituents. Dole responded to questions about his amendment by claiming that "Vietnam is still such a controversial issue, from an emotional standpoint. My folks tell me that they want no part of this so-called normalization of relations with Vietnam."[78] Although it is difficult to assess public support for aid to Vietnam in the late 1970s, A *New York Times*/CBS News poll in July of 1977 indicated that "66 percent of Americans favored food or medical assistance to Vietnam and 49 percent favored assistance in industrial and farm equipment." As Hurst points out, however, that same poll dropped to around twenty percent on the question of providing "actual money and grants."[79]

Even if Dole and the *Times* poll were correct in assessing Americans' feelings about normalization and aid, there is no evidence whatsoever that the public favored the draconian measures taken by Congress to deny the nations of Indochina access to humanitarian and international aid. That, in the end, is one of the most unfortunate aspects of the debates over aid to Vietnam. Lost in the debate over providing aid to or allowing trade with Vietnam was any meaningful attention to the radical nature of the sanctions themselves.

Also very troubling was the battle over funding for the World Bank and IMF, or what Hurst refers to as "the politicization of the IFIs." Given Carter's pledge to increase foreign aid and help increase the capital reserves of the World Bank and IMF, many legislators were prepared for a battle over the role of the United States in the Bretton Woods institutions. Just as, earlier, Vietnam had become the convenient test case for a new, preemptive sanctions policy, in the battle over foreign aid in the summer of 1977 Vietnam became the testing ground for a reassertion of American hegemony over the international financial order.

Throughout the summer, Congress and the administration battled over American contributions and veto powers at the IFIs. An appropriations bill containing $5.2 billion in funds for the World Bank and the Asian Development Bank, which had already been subject to amendments restricting loans to Vietnam and other countries, also became a battleground for protectionists in Congress, including Tom Harkin of Iowa and W. Henson Moore of Louisiana. The protectionist bloc, like the "anti-Vietnam" bloc, took advantage of the White House's human rights platform in proposing their restrictions. The Harkin amendment, for instance, prohibited American aid from reaching "any government guilty of a consistent pattern of gross violations of internationally recognized human rights."[80] Such measures, of course, were in direct violation of the World Bank charter, which specifically prohibits basing lending decisions on political matters.[81]

The amendments also prompted a sharp response from the World Bank itself, leading to one of the supreme ironies of the ongoing American War against Vietnam. Robert McNamara, who had taken over as president of the World Bank in 1967 after leaving the Johnson administration, came, in effect, to Vietnam's defense a decade later, admonishing Congress not to place any restrictions on American contributions to the World Bank.[82] McNamara's letter was instrumental in eventually getting the restrictions dropped, but the foreign aid battle still ended badly for the people of Southeast Asia. Taking heat from numerous factions in the legislature, and having already committed an enormous amount of political capital on other international issues, Carter was ultimately forced to give in to the politicization of the IFIs. In September, Congress and the White House reached an agreement on the foreign aid bill, which placed no restrictions on American contributions to the IFIs, but only after the White House agreed that it would instruct its representatives at those institutions to vote against any aid to Vietnam and the other countries. As Hurst notes, "the administration thus closed off the last avenue by which it could reach an accommodation with Hanoi involving the provision of aid. All it could do now was wait and hope that the Vietnamese would drop their demand."[83]

The Vietnamese, however, desperate for aid and still suffocating under the embargo, were in no position to drop their demand. On December 19, the two delegations again met in Paris, and Holbrooke informed Hien that he had no instructions to offer any aid, even as a private, off-the-record statement. Holbrooke later told Nayan Chanda that during a break in the sessions Hien said, "You just whisper in my ear the amount you'll offer, and that is enough." "I said, 'I am sorry. I have no authority to do that.'" Holbrooke also informed Hien that the United States was not willing to drop the embargo, and the talks once again ended with no substantive progress.[84]

The prospects for normalization, so strong only a few months earlier, had been greatly diminished. As Hurst describes it, the failure to advance toward normalization in 1977 should be chalked up to both Hanoi and Washington. Without question, the Vietnamese underestimated the level of aversion to Hanoi felt by many in Congress, and could have played their hand much better when confronted with such congressional animosity. Nevertheless, the ultimate responsibility for failure must be placed with the United States. The Vietnamese, despite their initial obstinacy on the matter of reparations, continually demonstrated their flexibility in seeking some form of aid that would be acceptable to the United States. In the spring of 1977, the same type of amendments restricting aid through IFIs had been defeated in Congress, and the Vietnamese had indicated their willingness to receive aid through those institutions. But, as Hurst argues, an "opportunity was missed" because of the Carter administration's "overconfidence and unwillingness to provide Vietnam with aid."[85]

By way of contrast, consider the actions of France and Japan in their relations with Vietnam. In 1973, France began to provide aid through both loans and grants, with an initial $20 million (in U.S. dollars) as a "contribution to the reconstruction and development of the country." Over the next five years France would make another $350 million available.[86] After Japan and Vietnam normalized relations in 1975, Japan made an immediate contribution of $40 million in direct foreign aid to Vietnam, acknowledged by both sides as reparations for the brutal Japanese occupation during World War II.[87] Yet France and Japan, although central to Vietnam's economy as investors and trading partners, did not hold the keys to the global economy; they could not single-handedly proscribe international aid or IFI funds from reaching Vietnam. The Vietnamese and the rest of the world were well aware that, in their search for international aid, no nation was more important than the United States.

Despite winning their decades-long war for independence, the Vietnamese were learning that the world had changed a great deal since their declaration of independence from the French thirty years earlier. Although Vietnam was now a sovereign nation, with a new constitution and a seat in the United Nations, the leaders in Hanoi were learning that "independence" in the late 1970s had more to do with their position in the regional and global economy than with their political hegemony in Indochina. Vietnam had cast off the yoke of several colonizing powers, at an unimaginable cost. They were much less prepared, and would be much less successful, in their battle against the neocolonial global economic order.

CONSTRUCTING MUTUAL DESTRUCTION THE CULTURAL LOGIC OF NORMALIZATION, 1977–1979

15.35 million tons of bombs.
2.5 million occupying troops.
2 million hectares of forests defoliated or destroyed.
80 million liters of chemical agents deployed.
300,000 missing in action.
14 million wounded.
More than 3,000,000 dead.[1]

For many of the statistics of the American war in Vietnam listed above, a comparison or equivalency with the United States is not even possible. The Vietnamese did not, of course, occupy, bomb, defoliate, or wage chemical warfare on the United States at any time. Yet even for those for which a comparison is possible, the numbers clearly suggest who the victims in the war were. For example, the United States at the end of the war had only a few thousand servicemen unaccounted for, compared with three hundred thousand Vietnamese. The United States lost close to sixty thousand personnel in the war, which, while tragic, stands in stark contrast to several *million* Vietnamese. Before 1975, with numbers like these, few in the United States—regardless of their feelings about the war or the Vietnamese—would ever have suggested that the destruction was "mutual."

Indeed, it is difficult to fathom what "mutual destruction" would have looked like. The Environmental Conference on Cambodia, Laos and Vietnam, in a 2003 report titled *Long-Term Consequences of the Vietnam War*, attempted such a comparison, and the numbers are nearly impossible to comprehend. If the United States had experienced similar consequences to those of Vietnam, the reports shows, the figures would be as follows:

Bombs Dropped: 430 million tons
Occupying Troops: 12.5 million
Hectares Defoliated or Destroyed: 56 million
Chemical Agents Deployed: 2.24 trillion liters
Wounded: 70 million
Dead: 17,500,000[2]

Even these numbers, however, do not do justice to the scale of destruction to which they refer. They do not, for instance, fully acknowledge the effects of the war on Cambodia or Laos, which are difficult to separate from those felt by Vietnam.

More importantly, however, the numbers do not indicate some of the most devastating aspects of the United States' war on Vietnam: the terrible legacies of the war that continued to harm the Vietnamese after the departure of the United States. For instance, 3.5 million land mines remained in the ground in Vietnam after 1975. Twenty-three million bomb craters littered the country's landscape. Since 1975, land mines and unexploded ordnance have killed at least thirty-eight thousand people throughout the Vietnamese countryside. Another seventy thousand have been injured.[3] Most significantly, however, and most horribly, the deadly chemicals dumped on the region remain in the ground, poisoning the water and food supply and contaminating future generations of Vietnamese children. Decades later, extraordinarily high levels of dioxin, the carcinogen found in Agent Orange, are still present in "hot spots" throughout Vietnam. The chemical can still be found in animals and groundwater, has been detected in the milk of nursing women, and has actually been found in the genetic code of some Vietnamese. Recent studies have also shown that the levels of dioxin present in the chemical agents are at least twice as high as previously thought.[4] While these and other horrible environmental legacies of the American war in Vietnam could not have been known to Americans in the immediate "postwar" era, the figures from the military war itself certainly were.

Less than a year after the fall of Saigon, a United Nations mission visited Vietnam and detailed firsthand the ruins in which much of Vietnam found itself, the results of what the report called "a savage war of *destruction*."[5] It detailed the utter devastation of Vietnam's industrial infrastructure, agricultural base, and transportation system, and it spoke of the large loss of life experienced by the Vietnamese and how that loss would affect the nation's ability to rebuild. When this report was included in a Staff Report for Senator Ted Kennedy's Senate Judiciary Committee in 1976, the senator noted in the introduction how stark the situation was in Southeast Asia and how the United States was finally positioned to help, rather than harm, the people of that region. "Having contributed so heavily to the years of war, our country must not fail now to pursue policies and programs that will contribute to the peace."[6]

But far from pursuing peace and reconciliation in the years immediately following the end of the American war in Vietnam, the American government began to pursue "war by other means," reclassifying the newly reunited nation of Vietnam as an "enemy" and pursuing openly hostile and unprecedented economic and diplomatic policies against the Vietnamese. Although the election of Jimmy Carter initially held out the promise of peace and progress between the two nations, the period was ultimately shaped by a different type of "normalization."

Usually understood as a political, economic, and diplomatic term used to denote a state of open, peaceful, and, theoretically, mutually beneficial relations between nations, "normalization" can also be understood as a cultural and political process which revised the history of the then-recent war by dehumanizing the Vietnamese and casting Americans as the principal victims of the conflict. Beginning in late 1977, however, this process, already underway in the halls of Congress, was supplemented by major contributions from the American culture industries. On the big screen, Vietnam "came home" in the first wave of Hollywood films to deal directly with the war. The familiar images, already fading in the relative absence of cultural representations of the war in 1975–76, began to be contested by another set of images: wounded and deranged American servicemen, fractured American communities, and savage Vietnamese characters, often depicted as torturers. Just as Ford and Kissinger's policies toward Vietnam were shaped by what Christopher Jespersen has called the "national mood of denial and punishment," the same sense of mutual destruction that helped the Carter administration navigate its foreign policy priorities in the late 1970s shaped cultural representations of the war in American society as well.[7]

The notion of mutual destruction did not originate in 1977, however. To understand the evolution of this idea in the late 1970s, we must begin at the root of revisionism concerning the war: the POW/MIA myth.

THE POW/MIA MYTH AND THE ROOTS OF MUTUAL DESTRUCTION

In his landmark work *M.I.A., or Mythmaking in America,* H. Bruce Franklin offers a definitive history of the rise of the POW/MIA myth as both a "national religion" of sorts and as "a basis—or at least an ostensible basis—for foreign policy."[8] From 1954 to 1968, he demonstrates, there was no POW/MIA issue, largely because no such classification existed. In other wars, missing service personnel and prisoners were categorized separately.[9] But in the spring of 1969, conservative forces in American society conspired with the incoming Nixon administration to conjure up an issue that would provide justification for Nixon's escalation of the war, serve as an obstacle to negotiations, and remain the primary impediment to normalizing relations between the United States and Vietnam for the next quarter of a century. In the 1980s, the POW/MIA myth took on a life of its own, but from 1969 to 1979 the issue drew the boundaries within which Vietnamese-American relations would be established. By dehumanizing the Vietnamese, portraying them as ruthless and cold-blooded figures, and helping to recast the United States as the primary victim of the American war in Vietnam, this issue came to define the matrix of the American war on Vietnam in the production of both foreign policy and cultural representations.

Immediately after Nixon's inauguration, members of his administration raised the issue of American prisoners of war at the Paris Peace Talks in terms of a "prisoner exchange." The Vietnamese, they claimed, were using the prisoners as political bargaining chips.[10] As Ambassador William Sullivan later described this view to Congress, the Vietnamese "are attempting coldly, ruthlessly to use prisoners that they hold, our prisoners, as leverage for the achievement of political objectives which they have not been able to accomplish by military or psychological means . . . We think, however, that in making and in formulating proposals we have to treat that sort of mentality as one would treat any other blackmailer attempting to extract ransom and extortion from a law-abiding citizen."[11]

While it is certainly true that the North Vietnamese used cruel and inhumane methods in dealing with American POWs during the war—just as it is true the United States and South Vietnamese forces tortured captured prisoners—the use of "cruel and inhumane" to describe the Vietnamese negotiating position reflects the broader attempt to dehumanize the Vietnamese in the eyes of Americans. The equation of the United States with a "law-abiding" citizen alongside a portrayal of a "cold" and "ruthless" enemy is indicative of the cultural logic of inversion that would define the period of "normalization" in the late 1970s.

As became clear over the next several years, it was the United States, not Vietnam, that would use the POW/MIA issue for political gain, at home and abroad. On March 1, 1969, the White House launched its "Go Public" campaign, which garnered immediate support in the mainstream media and gained resonance with the public throughout the summer as it became closely aligned with organizations of POW families and billionaire H. Ross Perot. Particularly effective was the campaign's use of language describing the Vietnamese as "inhuman." The *New York Times,* Franklin notes, was among the major newspapers to take hold of the issue, denouncing North Vietnam in an editorial titled "Inhumane Stance on Prisoners." In December, using similar language, the House of Representatives unanimously passed a resolution condemning the "the ruthlessness and cruelty of the North Vietnamese."[12] As the coverage of the POW issue intensified, Franklin notes, not only the history of the war but cultural representations of the war began to be inverted: "America's vision of the war was being transformed. The actual photographs and TV footage of massacred villagers, napalmed children, Vietnamese prisoners being tortured and murdered, wounded GIs screaming in agony, and body bags being loaded by the dozen for shipment back home were being replaced by the simulated images of American POWs in the savage hands of Asian Communists."[13]

In the late 1960s these images were still being contested in daily newspapers and televised news reports from Vietnam. Now, in relation to a war so often defined by mediated images, the very fact that the inverted logic of the POW/MIA myth became part of the battle over the *cultural memory* of the war is itself significant. The more crucial point, however, in the context of post-1975 American relations with Vietnam, is that the inverted constructions begun with the POW issue would continue to resonate in the production of both cultural representations and foreign policy. No longer constrained by competing images of American violence and atrocities, by the mid-1970s the dehumanization of the Vietnamese and the representation of the United States as victim could proceed relatively unfettered.

Ironically, given the initial promise of diplomatic normalization in 1977, it would be the Carter administration that fully articulated the dogma of "mutual destruction." On March 24, Carter held a press conference to highlight the work of the Woodcock Mission. Addressing the question of normalization, Carter noted that he would favor normalizing relations with Vietnam when "convinced that the Vietnamese had done their best to account for the service personnel who are missing in action." The president then reiterated some of the successes of the trip: "They not only gave us the bodies of 11 American servicemen, but they also set up a Vietnamese bureaucracy" to assist in further efforts. In short, Carter was already convinced that "I think this is about all they can do. I don't have any way to prove that they have accounted for all those about whom they have information. But I think, so far as I can discern, they have acted in good faith . . . In the past, the Vietnamese have said that they would not negotiate with us nor give us additional information about the MIA's until we had agreed to pay reparations. They did not bring this up, which I thought was an act of reticence on their part." [14]

Later, Ed Bradley of CBS began a line of questioning that would produce an accurate indication of the administration's stance on Vietnam.

> BRADLEY: Mr. President, on the subject of Vietnam, if you feel the United States is not obligated to uphold the terms of the Paris Peace Accords because of the North Vietnamese offensive that overthrew the South Vietnamese Government, do you feel, on the other hand, any moral obligation to help rebuild the country?
>
> CARTER: I can't say what my position would be on some future economic relationship with Vietnam. I think that could only be concluded after we continue with negotiations to see what their attitude might be toward us.

After further elaboration, the questioning continued.

> BRADLEY: Beyond that, do you still feel that if information on those American servicemen who are missing in action is forthcoming from the Vietnamese, that then this country has a moral obligation to help rebuild that country, if that information is forthcoming?
>
> CARTER: *Well, the destruction was mutual.* You know we went to Vietnam without any desire to capture territory or to impose American will on other people. We went there to defend the freedom of the South Vietnamese. And I do not feel that we ought to apologize or to castigate ourselves or to assume the status of culpability. *Now, I am willing to face the future without reference to the past.* And that is what the Vietnamese leaders have proposed. And if, in normalization

> of relationships, there evolves trade, normal aid processes, then I would respond well. But I don't feel that we owe a debt, nor that we should be forced to pay reparations at all.[15]

This has to be considered one of the most remarkable utterances ever made by an American official about the war in Vietnam. Leaving aside Carter's statements about why the United States "went" to Vietnam, and even his belief that the United States did not owe Vietnam anything—sentiments likely shared by many Americans in 1977—an assertion that there was "mutual destruction" can only be understood in terms of the ongoing cultural and political reconstruction of the war taking place in the mid-1970s. During and immediately after the war, few in the United States would have accepted that Americans endured hardships on a par with those suffered by the Vietnamese. But in the "normalizing" process, such statements became not only possible, but accepted logic. Carter's willingness "to face the future without reference to the past" should thus be read not simply as an attempt to "put the war behind us," but as part of a larger will-to-forget, a critical assertion in the contest over cultural memory that defined this period in American life.

Thus, as 1977 came to a close, there was little to be optimistic about in Hanoi. Failure either to normalize relations with the United States or to secure other significant international aid—both of which were central to the Vietnamese Politburo's economic plans for postwar reconstruction—and increasing border tensions with Cambodia all loomed large. In less than a year, Vietnam would once again be at war, and normalization with the United States would be shelved indefinitely. While all this was going on, another front in the American war on Vietnam opened, this time in the United States: the cultural front.

"VIETNAM COMES HOME": NORMALIZING THE WAR ON THE BIG SCREEN

The policies of the period immediately following the fall of Saigon were established in a relative absence of cultural representations of the war. After the flood of discourse and images to which Americans had grown accustomed during the period of direct American military involvement, Vietnam disappeared from the nightly news, from the pages of daily and weekly newsmagazines, and was all but banned as a subject for films. The same cannot be said to be true after 1977. "Vietnam" was never completely erased in the cultural sphere, of course. As Julian Smith pointed out in

Looking Away: Hollywood and Vietnam, the first major work to deal with the relative absence of the war from American film, for a number of years the war was simply marginal to the plot, even of films which ostensibly treated Vietnam as a direct issue.[16] Films ranging from *Shampoo* (1975), in which the war becomes literally background noise from the television, to such early veteran exploitation movies as *Welcome Home, Soldier Boys* (1972), *The Visitors* (1972), *Heroes* (1977), and *Rolling Thunder* (1977) presented the war in Vietnam as literally on the margins of American consciousness, something not yet completely forgotten but certainly of minor importance. As Rick Berg describes it, this marginalization is in fact deeply rooted in American films of the period connected even secondarily to Vietnam: "For Hollywood, Vietnam—both the country and the war—seemed to be just off screen, at the edge and on the frontier, always about to be found." Indeed, from the middle through the end of the twentieth century, Vietnam, in film and foreign policy, would always be viewed through the colonial "gaze."[17]

But from late 1977 to 1979 Vietnam "came home" to the United States, as the floodgates of cultural production opened to produce a series of landmark movies, novels, memoirs, and television shows about the war. Commentators of all stripes, recognizing the significance of the moment, wrote extensively about the reappearance of Vietnam in American culture. The focus of the commentary, as well as of public debate, was and has been motion pictures. Few critics at the time, however, and fewer scholars of the subject since, have connected the cultural representations of the war in films of the late 1970s to the formation and consolidation of American policy toward Vietnam in the same period.

In her book *Epic Encounters,* Melani McAllister argues for the fundamental interconnectedness of cultural and political "fields," and demonstrates convincingly that "cultural productions help make meanings by their historical association with other types of meaning-making activity": "This suggests that we might ask less about "what texts mean"—with the implication that there is a hidden or allegorical code to their secret meaning—and more about how the texts participate in a field, and then in a set of fields, and thus in a social and political world."[18]

While what the films discussed here have to say about the war in Vietnam—and even about its effects on the United States—is certainly important, I am less concerned here with how cultural texts function as representations of the war itself than with how they intersect and interact with both public discourses about Vietnam and the production of foreign policy toward Vietnam. In *Epic Encounters,* McAllister uses a similar model to demonstrate how a variety of cultural representations related to the Middle East in the post–World War Two era coincided with the dictates of American foreign policy. A similar phenomenon was at work in the "normalization" of the American war in Vietnam in the late 1970s. Just as American policy toward Southeast Asia actively denied American responsibility for the war, refused to contribute to healing the wounds of war in Vietnam, and dehumanized the Vietnamese as violators of humanitarian accords, the films of this period work according to the same cultural logic and within the same matrices of representation. Along with the economic and political assaults on Vietnam, this cultural front helped to pave the way for the reconstruction of the American imperial project in the wake of the war. The first step in this process was the concept of mutual destruction, which turned the focus onto the effects of the war on the United States, rather than the devastation of Vietnam itself.

The most notable examples of this first wave of films accomplished this in different ways. Most of the smaller movies of 1977 and 1978, such as *Rolling Thunder, Who'll Stop the Rain, Go Tell the Spartans,* and *The Boys in Company C,* were overshadowed by three films that quickly came to constitute the early canon of American films about the war: *Coming Home, The Deer Hunter,* and *Apocalypse Now.* As Peter Marin wrote in *Harper's* in 1980, the "big three" of the late 1970s "were not necessarily the best or most intelligent films; they were *events*. Despite the fact that they failed to confront the moral issues of the war, they were treated with the same seriousness and granted the same attentiveness that we ordinarily reserve for important books; many regarded them as summary statements about the war, which tells us something about ourselves, if not about Vietnam."[19]

It is undoubtedly true, as Marin and others have argued, that these films tell us more about Hollywood than they do about the American war in Vietnam. Similarly, it is not at all unusual that American films about this or any other war would focus attention on American characters. Yet if the fields of cultural production are relevant to the production of meaning in other fields, including the production and reception of foreign policy, then certainly the images of the Vietnamese offered by these popular, widely seen and discussed films matter. The fact that they work within established conventions of narrative and presentation is not surprising; indeed, working within those conventions helps make the representations in the films more "normalized." But the ways in which the appropriations of those conventions interacted with the larger project of normalizing the Vietnam War in American culture is worthy of exploration. By rendering the Vietnamese completely invisible (as in *Coming Home*), or as savage, inhumane villains (as in *The Deer Hunter*), or by taking an ambivalent stance about American responsibility for the war (as in *Apocalypse Now*), these films worked within the same grid of representations that defined and shaped American policy toward Southeast Asia in the period.

To truly understand the context in which these films were being received, the story of the "big three" must begin in the summer of 1977. Major newspapers and magazines began running articles anticipating the fact that, as one piece from the *New York Times* put it, Hollywood finally appeared ready "to come to grips with the Vietnam War."[20] Stories emerged that several stars and directors, from Jane Fonda to Robert DeNiro to Francis Coppola, were developing projects that would attempt to deal with the war. Given Coppola's recent fame and fortune, derived from the success of the first two *Godfather* films, the shadow of his project was cast over all other comers.

Even by the summer of 1977, before any of these films had been seen by the public, Coppola's Vietnam film was becoming legendary for its troubles. The *Times* piece on August 2 noted that *Apocalypse Now* was already "so far over budget that Mr. Coppola had to mortgage his home and many of his assets to United Artists, the distributor that is financing the project in part." At that point, *Apocalypse Now* was still scheduled to be released the following spring. Although it would not actually premiere until the spring of 1979, the fact that United Artists had greenlighted the project to begin with, and the fact that a filmmaker of Coppola's stature and reputation was tackling the war in Vietnam, allowed several other projects to proceed as well.[21]

As Coppola trudged on, in the Philippines and in the editing room, the other films that his initiative had helped make possible began to open around the country. The fall of 1977 witnessed the arrival of *Rolling Thunder*, based on a script written by Paul Schrader, who had previously penned the screenplay for *Taxi Driver*. The film, which focuses on the violent escapades of a former POW, was roundly panned by critics upon its release. The *Washington Post* noted that it would appeal to fans of violent action films, but did little to "attempt to graft the nation's most recent scar tissue onto the scene."[22] Early in 1978, *The Boys in Company C* met a similar fate. The marketing slogan for the film was telling: "You may want to forget the war, but you'll never forget the Boys in Company C." The "boys," a diverse platoon of soldiers taken out of any stock combat-film screenplay, battle the Viet Cong and corrupt South Vietnamese officials before the action culminates in a dramatic *soccer game* with their Vietnamese counterparts. Many critics accused director Sidney Furie of the same sin ascribed to John Wayne in his 1968 film *The Green Berets:* attempting to translate the war in Vietnam into narratives and imagery taken from World War II.[23]

Despite the growing anticipation throughout 1977, Hollywood's attempts to deal with the war were disappointing filmgoers and critics alike. It would take one of the more talked-about projects, Jane Fonda's *Coming Home,* to change the conversation about Hollywood and Vietnam in 1978.

COMING HOME

In the *New York Times* on February 19, 1978, the weekend entertainment pages were nearly entirely devoted to this conversation. In a lengthy review piece on recent Vietnam war films, Vincent Canby asked whether it was "inevitable that commercial movies must trivialize intense feelings and complex ideas because of the nature of a system that must appeal to as many people as possible?"[24] After surveying the cultural landscape of films about the war, Canby's answer was an unqualified yes. From *Tracks* to *Rolling Thunder* and *Heroes* to *The Boys in Company C,* Canby found nothing more in these films than the common theme of using the war as an "excuse" for irrational or erratic behavior, usually by combat veterans. Canby had held some hope that the recently released *Coming Home* would be different. He called it "the most ambitious, pious attempt to date to deal with the Vietnam War in a commercial American fiction film," but ultimately labeled it a "fine mess," more about Fonda and Freud than the war itself.

The other major piece in that weekend's section focused on the "five-year struggle to make *Coming Home,*" from changes to the screenplay to dealings with the Veterans Administration to challenges in casting.[25] As that piece and others at the time revealed, the genesis of *Coming Home* lay as much in the vision of Jane Fonda as that of director Hal Ashby, although the final product owes less to the political convictions of the artists involved than to the genre conventions and financial realities of Hollywood. In *The Land of Nam: The Vietnam War in American Film,* Eben Muse describes how Fonda, who worked with wounded American veterans during the war, originally wanted to make "an anti-war polemic" focusing on the return of American soldiers, but was persuaded by Ashby to tone down the politics of the film to reach a wider audience. "The film thus became a love story with a Vietnam era backdrop," he writes. "It makes the war palatable to a general audience by sentimentalizing the issues surrounding the conflict while evading the war itself."[26]

As the film begins, however, viewers could be forgiven for thinking that they were watching a documentary rather than the melodrama that ensues. The opening scene shows a group of American veterans around a pool table, discussing the various rationalization mechanisms they and their peers have used to justify their roles in the war and the injuries that resulted from their participation. "They don't want to see what they did as a waste," says one. One of the vets, Luke (Jon Voight), lays flat, face down, and motionless on a gurney. The scene then shifts from Luke to a pair of legs, running during the opening credit sequence. The legs are revealed to belong to Bob (Bruce Dern), in the first of what becomes a seemingly endless series of juxtapositions of the two men. Ironically, Voight, who would go on to win the Academy Award for Best Actor for his performance, was initially slated to play the part of Bob.

Voight had been active in the antiwar movement. He had also grown close with several antiwar veterans, and reportedly coveted the role of the antiwar paraplegic. But United Artists, which was financing the film along with two other Vietnam-themed films, *Who'll Stop the Rain* and *Apocalypse Now,* both still in production, felt it needed a bigger star for the role. Only after Sylvester Stallone and Jack Nicholson both turned down the role was Voight able to convince the producers that he fit the part.[27]

Coming Home revolves around the transformation of the two men, and of Bob's wife, Sally (Fonda). As Bob heads, headstrong, off to war, determined to bring home a Russian-made rifle as a keepsake, Sally begins her transformation by moving out of officers' housing and volunteering at the local VA hospital. There she meets Luke, a former high school classmate, who became a paraplegic in Vietnam. As Luke sheds his anger and hostility for sensitivity and intimacy, Sally's transformation is highlighted, although hers is more physical and material than emotional: she remains passive and submissive in relationships while letting her hair down and buying a new sports car. "In short," as Gilbert Adair has written of Sally's metamorphosis, *"she turns into Jane Fonda."*[28] Sally and Luke eventually strike up a romance, which culminates in a long love scene.

Bob has undergone his own change, although *Coming Home* is much less concerned with exploring his experience. Upon returning from the war he walks with a limp, which we later learn is a result of a self-inflicted mishap. The mood of the scenes suggests something is different, but other than his reluctance to talk about the war, we learn little of Bob's story. The implication is that the transformations of all the characters are a result of the war—but, as the film moves on, the love triangle becomes the plot's catalyst. As one reviewer suggested at the time, "as the romance develops, Vietnam recedes and Hollywood takes over."[29] Indeed, Bob is pushed "over the edge" only when he learns of Sally's infidelities during his tour of duty.

During Sally and Luke's romance, Luke becomes the object of FBI surveillance as a result of protesting the war by locking himself to the gate of the local army base. The surveillance tapes include sexual encounters between he and Sally. The FBI makes Bob aware of the affair while questioning him about Luke, leading Bob to confront Luke. Instead of focusing on the affair, however, Bob simply warns Luke about the surveillance. Upon his return home, Bob takes his rifle from the garage and enters the house silently. After Sally confronts him and they argue, Luke shows up, and Bob threatens them both with the bayonet end of the rifle. As Sally passively watches, Luke tells Bob, "I am not the enemy. The enemy is the fucking war. And you don't want to kill anyone here." Bob drops the rifle and both men exit, leaving Sally alone in the house.

The original ending of *Coming Home* was to have been a rehash of other "vetsploitation" films of the era such as *Rolling Thunder:* after confronting Sally and Luke, Bob goes crazy and ends up in a wild shootout with police. That ending was scrapped, however, after Ashby received feedback from veterans who were tired of "always being depicted as totally crazy."[30] Instead, the film ends with a montage of the characters, leaving it unclear what really becomes of any of them. Luke gives a moving speech to a group of high school students, instructing them about the realities of war: "I have killed for my country. And I don't feel good about it . . . I don't see any reason for it. And there's a lot of shit I did over there that I find fucking hard to live with." Interspersed with the speech are shots of Bob walking along the beach, stripping from his uniform, removing his wedding ring, and swimming out into the ocean. Many reviewers read this as a suicide, but the film leaves Bob's fate open and unresolved. Sally, in the final shot of the movie, enters a market to buy steaks for a barbecue. The door of the market swings open to display the word "out."

The responses to *Coming Home* ranged widely. Conservative groups predictably reacted to "Hanoi Jane" with the same venom they had years earlier when Fonda visited North Vietnam. In his more balanced account, Peter Marin noted "the smugness and self-satisfaction at work" in the film, which he saw as sidestepping an honest attempt to deal with the problems of veterans in favor of "a ritualized love story and a vehicle for Ms. Fonda's perpetual moral posturing." Frank Rich of *Time* found many faults with the film, but they were artistic, not political or moral in nature.[31] In certainly one of the most evenhanded reviews of *Coming Home,* Morris Dickstein, in *Partisan Review,* praised the film, despite its many faults, simply for being made: "Modest, flawed, even a little compromised by box office conventions, the film is nevertheless a serious act of witness, made by obsessed people with long memories and a determined conscience, a refusal to forget. This is what Coming Home finally means: bringing the war home. For once the Hollywood left has done itself proud."[32] For Dickstein, the film's attempt to break "the silence itself, the graveyard calm, the mood of national forgetfulness that is one of the hallmarks of the seventies," was reason enough to celebrate.

But to what, exactly, does *Coming Home* bear witness? What is it that Ashby and Fonda are seeking not to forget? The film has been credited with raising awareness of the treatment of veterans, which Dickstein sees as part of a larger struggle for public memory: "Our callous treatment of the unwelcome veteran is part of the avoidance of the memory of the war itself, and we may be condemned to repeat it unless we're willing finally to face it."[33] Perhaps Dickstein was simply being overly optimistic in his hope that, as the opening act in the veritable Vietnam War film festival that was 1978, *Coming Home* would be followed by films that would help Americans to "face" Vietnam. In fact, a dialogue about the war is proposed but not engaged in by the film; to the extent that *Coming Home* presents views of or on the war at all, they remain inward-looking and myopic.

For all its drama and its place in the pantheon of Vietnam War films, *Coming Home* has almost nothing to say about the war. Muse argues that "[a]ll we know of the war we learn from Bob—we never see any of it apart from a flash of news coverage—and his description is tantalizingly obscure: "I don't know what it's like; I only know what it is. TV shows what it's like.' "[34] We do learn that war is hell, from the shots of wounded men at the hospital, from Luke's final speech, and from Bob's brief recounting of troops under his command cutting the heads off of dead Vietnamese soldiers, the only moment in which he speaks about the war. One could argue that one of the messages of the film is the need for veterans, and indeed for all Americans, to *talk* about the war. Luke, the figure of redemption, does his duty by passing on his knowledge to the students, while Bob, who again and again refuses to talk about the war, ends the film in silence and, perhaps, suicide. The implication of this dichotomy, for many, is that the film is thus "antiwar" because redemption came to the supposed antiwar figures.[35] Yet the film itself does not provide any space for commentary about the war in Vietnam; the war itself is completely and conspicuously absent, and the enemy invisible. Instead, through the images of the mentally, emotionally, and physically traumatized American veterans, the film explores only what Vietnam did to "us."

As such, the film should be seen as part of the larger myopia of American society in the late 1970s. Even if successful in drawing attention to the plight of American veterans, *Coming Home* and the other 1978 representations of the American war in Vietnam follow the logic of "mutual destruction" proposed by President Carter. They deliberately silence the past and situate Americans as the primary victims of the war. In short, Ashby's film, like most of the other films of 1977 and 1978, face the war by not facing it at all. By keeping "Vietnam"—and the Vietnamese, especially—silent and invisible, *Coming Home* asks viewers to remember certain things at the expense of others. It focuses attention on what Vietnam did to us, at the expense of what we did, and what we were continuing to do, to the people of Vietnam. As Hans Koning pointed out in the *New York Times,* in *Coming Home,* as in the other films of this wave, the Vietnamese remained "as invisible as they have been during all the war years," and the war itself provided little more than "a convenient place" to have American characters explore "questions of life, courage, and death." In Hollywood treatments of the war, it appeared by 1978 that, in order to appeal to a wider audience, films had not only to "trivialize intense feelings and complex ideas," but to render the Vietnamese invisible as well.[36]

THE DEER HUNTER

The Deer Hunter has never been accused of rendering the Vietnamese invisible; quite the opposite. Michael Cimino's film, which had garnered far less pre-release attention than was lavished on *Coming Home* and *Apocalypse Now,* quickly gained notoriety for its portrayal of Viet Cong soldiers as dehumanized savages who torture their American captors. In many respects, *The Deer Hunter* changed the way in which commentators wrote about the Vietnam War film. For example, *Coming Home* only began to be widely discussed as overtly political when juxtaposed with *The Deer Hunter.* With the exception of *Rambo* (1985), no American film dealing with the war in Vietnam has aroused such vehement responses. However, although *The Deer Hunter* has been critiqued on a number of levels, it has yet to be connected to the formation and consolidation of American foreign policy toward Vietnam in the late 1970s.

The American public first became aware of the film in late 1978, when it was put into limited release in order to qualify for that year's Academy Awards. Cimino's film would go on to win several Oscars, including the awards for Best Director and Best Picture. Like *Coming Home, The Deer Hunter* had been, at least in anticipation, consistently overshadowed by and judged against *Apocalypse Now,* which in late 1978 was still in its post-production phase. On a Saturday night in early December, Cimino and Coppola met at Cimino's hotel room in Manhattan. "You beat me, baby," Coppola reportedly remarked to Cimino, who responded that he had actually been hoping for the opposite result. He had been counting on *Apocalypse Now* to "break the ice." [37] Instead, that task fell to *The Deer Hunter* (which reveals the extent to which *Coming Home* was quickly forgotten in American culture, only to be resurrected in the race for the Academy Awards the next spring).

When the film appeared in New York theaters in December of 1978 it immediately generated a major buzz among filmgoers and critics alike. So much attention was given to the film upon its re-release for nationwide distribution in February of 1979 that tickets in many American cities had to be preordered. Reports abounded in the press that many in the audience, including veterans of the war in Vietnam, had been so troubled by what they saw on the screen that they had walked out of the theater, some in tears and others physically ill. The *Washington Post* review noted that some would find it an "exploitative, simplistic, perhaps reactionary" interpretation of the war, while others "will consider it a justifiably brutal and realistic rendering." For most, however, the review concluded, "it will be a shock to the psyche and the senses." [38]

The film comprises three acts. In the first, the audience is introduced to the community of Clairton, a Pennsylvania steel town. In the opening scene we see the steel mill where Michael (Robert DeNiro), Nick (Christopher Walken), and Steve (John Savage) are ending their final shift before leaving for a tour of duty in Vietnam. On their way through the locker room, their co-workers wish them well. One encourages Michael to "kill a few for me." As the friends make their way to their local bar we meet the rest of the gang, who are all preparing for Steve's wedding. The wedding and reception, long and elaborate scenes set in the VFW hall, portray a tightly knit community grounded in tradition and nationalism. The head table and reception floor, where the guests perform Russian folk dances, are adorned with red, white, and blue banners proclaiming "Serving God and Country Proudly." At the reception, after Michael has made an awkward, halfhearted, and unsuccessful pass at Nick's girlfriend, Linda (Meryl

Streep), the three soldiers-to-be notice a Green Beret at the other end of the bar and buy the man a drink. "We're going over there. We're going airborne," Michael tells him. "I hope they send us where the bullets are flying," Nick adds. The soldier, with a blank stare, simply responds, "Fuck it," as he drinks the shot. "What's it like over there?" they ask. Again, the same response: "Fuck it."

The next day, the men go hunting. On the way to the cabin Michael has a blowout with their friend Stanley and the others over his "fanatical" ways about hunting (Michael will not allow Stanley to use an extra pair of boots because Stanley is never properly prepared). Michael, whom Cimino constructs as an outsider, not entirely comfortable in the community, tracks a deer by himself, shunning the group dynamic. He shoots the deer with "one shot," the only acceptable way to hunt, for Michael, as he explains to Nick in an earlier scene. Immediately, the film cuts to the boys driving back through town. They pull up to the bar with the ubiquitous steel mill in the background. Upstairs in the bar, a raucous celebration turns somber as John, the bartender, sits at the piano and plays a quiet ballad. The men exchange glances as the song gradually ends.

The next shot is a jarring cut to a village being bombed, with bamboo huts engulfed by flames while the sound of a helicopter rages in the background. Over an hour into the film, we finally reach act two, set in Vietnam. We see Michael lying injured as a Viet Cong soldier comes into the village and throws a hand grenade into a bunker filled with villagers. A lone Vietnamese soldier shoots down a defenseless woman carrying a baby, and Michael attacks him with a flamethrower, later killing him with his rifle after reinforcements, including Nick and Steve, appear. Soon other Vietnamese forces arrive, though, and the men are taken captive, setting up the scene for which the film became famous. In just a few short minutes, Cimino establishes that the Viet Cong are cold and ruthless killers, executioners of women and children. The Americans are there to protect the Vietnamese people from such figures, but are themselves captured and taken prisoner.

In the Viet Cong's POW camp, based on the "tiger cages" regularly employed by the South Vietnamese forces allied with the United States, the prisoners are forced by their savage, caricatured Vietnamese captors to play Russian roulette. The Viet Cong figures speak in sharp tones (in Chinese, by the way, not Vietnamese) and they cackle and exchange money when one of the prisoners "loses" the game. In later scenes that continue the roulette theme, all Vietnamese act in this same manner, an implication of national depravity for which Cimino was heavily criticized.

When Michael and Steve are forced to play the game against one another, a bullet glances off Steve's head, leaving him wounded but alive. He is then relegated to "the pit," an underwater holding cage littered with rats and corpses. In another cage, Michael hatches a plan to convince their captors to allow him to play the game with more bullets in the chamber. This allows them to kill their captors and escape. The enemy is on screen for less than fifteen minutes, but the sequence, described by one reviewer as "one of the most frighteningly, unbearably tense sequences ever filmed, and the most violent excoriation of violence in screen history,"[39] leaves a horrific and lasting impression. While *Coming Home* argues for an acceptance of all Americans as victims of "the war," *The Deer Hunter* puts a face on both the enemy (cruel and inhuman Vietnamese) and the victim (well-intentioned Americans). As Bruce Franklin argues in *Vietnam and Other American Fantasies*, this scene was central to the revisionism of the war that seized American culture well beyond the 1970s: "*The Deer Hunter* succeeded not only in reversing key images of the war but also in helping to canonize U.S. prisoners of war as the most significant symbols of American manhood for the 1980s, 1990s, and beyond."[40]

After their escape, Nick is rescued by a helicopter, but Michael stays behind with Steve, who is too weak to hang on to the chopper. In Saigon, Nick recovers, but upon his release from the hospital wanders back into the Saigon underworld, where he discovers a Russian roulette "club" where people play the game for money. Michael finds him there by chance, but Nick flees after the encounter in the club, and Michael returns home without him.

A shot of the familiar steel mill indicates that the final act, back in Clairton, has begun. Michael avoids his welcome home party and only later sneaks into his own house, where Linda has been staying. With Nick's status unknown, the romantic tension between Michael and Linda gives way to an affair. Another hunting trip ensues, during which Michael has yet another blowout with Stanley, this time over the gun that Stanley carries. But now Michael is unable, or unwilling, to shoot a deer when he comes face-to-face with it. Instead, he fires a shot into the air and repeatedly yells "O.K!"—which the forest echoes back to him.

Unable to fully enter the community, even after he brings Steve home from the VA hospital, Michael returns to Vietnam to fulfill his promise to bring Nick home. It is now 1975 and the war is all but over, which further confuses the admittedly skewed chronology employed by Cimino in de-historicizing the war. Refugees clamor at the gate of the American embassy while Michael wades back into Saigon to find the Russian roulette club. Michael arranges to play against Nick, who still does not recognize him. Michael puts the gun to his head, looks at Nick, says "I love you," closes his eyes, and fires a blank. Nick takes the gun, while Michael pleads with him, "Come on, Nicky, come home. Just come home." Nick smiles as Michael reminds him of the trees in the mountains back home. "One shot?" he asks Michael, finally making a connection. "One shot," Michael tells him. Nick smiles, places the gun to his head, fires, and falls dead. The scene cuts to news footage of the war's closing days, viewed on a television screen that could be anywhere. "This seems to be the last chapter in the history of American involvement in Vietnam," says an ABC news reporter.

In the final scene, second in infamy only to the POW camp Russian roulette sequence for those who indicted the film as jingoistic, the group reassembles after Nick's burial for breakfast at the bar. John, cooking eggs in the kitchen, begins to hum "God Bless America." As he walks to the main room, the others, including Michael, join in, as Cimino demonstrates through close shots of the individual figures. On the second verse we see the whole table, and Linda leading the singers. The singing gets louder on the bridge and the chorus, although it never reaches a triumphant pitch. As the song ends, Linda smiles at Michael, who toasts, "Here's to Nick." The frame freezes and cuts to credits.

The controversial ending, along with the rest of the film, became an immediate lightning rod for debate among critics about representing the war on screen. In *American Myth and The Legacy of Vietnam,* John Hellmann argues that "smaller films," including *Coming Home,* "more consistently pleased film critics" because the politics of such films were clearer. *The Deer Hunter* and *Apocalypse Now* "were widely attacked in reviews and articles for being implausible and incoherent."[41] While that account may hold for *Apocalypse Now, The Deer Hunter* brought forth a more diverse set of responses than Hellmann acknowledges.

When the film was first released in late 1978 in time to be considered for the Academy Awards, several critics seized on it as a fascist, racist, gross oversimplification of the war. Peter Marin lambasted Cimino for his "intentional misrepresentations of the war, his implicit absolution of Americans for any illegitimate violence or brutality, and a xenophobia and racism as extravagant as anything to be found on the screen."[42] Peter Arnett, who covered the war as a reporter, labeled the film "fascist trash."[43] Jane Fonda joined Arnett in calling the film "fascist," adding that it was "a racist, Pentagon version of the war."[44] In international circles, reaction against the film was just as strong. At the 1979 Berlin International Film Festival, where *The Deer Hunter* represented the United States, the delegations from the U.S.S.R. and several Soviet-aligned countries withdrew over what they termed "an affront to the struggles of the Vietnamese people."[45]

Yet, although the charges of racism and de-historicizing the war are justified, the film is not without its contradictions. For all the violence *The Deer Hunter* does to the Vietnamese people, and to the memory of the war itself, it is, as Rick Berg points out, the only film of its time, and perhaps since, that "bothered to look at the community that fought the war." While he acknowledges that Cimino's representation of working-class life in Clairton is as essentialized as that of the Vietnamese, Berg praises the director for focusing on how the war in Vietnam destroyed many working-class communities. Even in the controversial final scene, one "that many read as just another attempt to recuperate the patriotic myths that led us into the war," Berg finds an intimate portrayal of the impact of the war on those Americans who fought it: "What we see," he concludes, "is a community shattered by Vietnam, trying to express a deeply rooted nationalism, with all its ironies and contradictions."[46]

Leonard Quart, however, offers a counterview of this final scene, which he describes as "politically disturbing." "There is no directorial irony in the sequence," he notes. "The *mise-en-scène* and camera setups move us toward total empathy with their feelings. As a result, *The Deer Hunter* leaves us with the indelible image of Vietnam as an abattoir but then implicitly absolves the U.S. of the responsibility for helping bring it about by creating a working class who are viewed as both the war's heroes and its victims. The portrait is so sympathetic that it allows the late 1970s audience to feel somewhat relieved of its uneasiness and distress about America's role in Vietnam, and with some hope that the American Dream can be renewed by men like Michael Vronsky."[47] Implicit in both of these accounts, though, regardless of whether the sequence seeks to exonerate the United States, is the focus on what the war "did" to Americans. My intent is not to criticize the films for their myopic and often narcissistic focus on American culture; indeed, as with *Coming Home*'s focus on the plight of veterans, *The Deer Hunter* should be credited for bringing attention to previously marginalized or ignored effects of the war on Americans.

However, to ignore the parallels of the logic of mutual destruction at work in the texts is to miss a great deal of their significance. These films effectively functioned as the cultural front of the ongoing war on Vietnam in the late 1970s. Reinforcing the structure and content of American policy toward Southeast Asia, the texts either render the Vietnamese invisible or represent them as cruel and inhuman subjects, thus solidifying the distorted cultural memory that the United States was the primary victim of the war. And, just as with the films themselves, the discourses of contemporary critics and commentators did the cultural work of "normalization" during 1978, framing the public discussion of events in such a way as to render the United States as victim of both the war and the Vietnamese.

Certainly, the quotes above demonstrate that many critics on the left took issue with the film, but many others praised *The Deer Hunter* for its "courage" and for its politics, or, rather, the perceived lack thereof. In *Time*, Frank Rich held up Cimino's film as "the first movie about Vietnam to free itself from all political cant," pointing out that *The Deer Hunter* has no antiwar characters at all and that "its pro-war characters are apolitical foot soldiers, not fire-breathing gook-killers" (failing, apparently, to remember the only combat scene in the film, in which Michael sprays a "gook" with his flamethrower). "Cimino," Rich concludes, "has attempted to embrace all the tragic contradictions of the U.S. intervention in Southeast Asia."[48] In *Newsweek*, Jack Kroll likewise extolled what he viewed as the apolitical nature of the film, calling it "the first film to look at Vietnam not politically, but as the manifestation of an endemic murderousness." "Many people will react angrily to the film as politically reactionary," he predicted. "But *The Deer Hunter* is a film of great courage and overwhelming emotional power." Kroll took special pains to defend the Russian roulette scenes, calling them "dramatic and moral," not "political," a symbol of a society committing moral suicide.[49] Leonard Quart later describes the view of the war in *The Deer Hunter* as "a politically indifferent one," but then finds himself "politically troubled" by the final scene.[50] One might wonder, from these interpretations, how such a supposedly apolitical film could ever be charged with being "politically reactionary."

Indeed, what is perhaps most troubling is that *The Deer Hunter* is described even by many of its strongest critics as apolitical. It is hard to imagine *any* representation of the American war in Vietnam as being apolitical, but particularly one appearing only a few years after the end of the war and offering such troubling representations of the Vietnamese. Cimino himself consistently stated both that the film was not "about" the war in Vietnam and that it was not meant to be "political." The director acknowledged referencing events such as the My Lai massacre and the fall of Saigon, but told one reporter, "The film is not realistic, it's surrealistic . . . If you're attacking this film on its facts, then you're fighting a phantom, because literal accuracy was never intended." Cimino hoped that filmgoers would identify with the characters in the film, not his interpretation of the war. "This is not a film of the intellect," he argued. "It's a film of the heart."[51] Even in August of 1977, more than a year before its release, Cimino was claiming that the role of the war in his film was merely "incidental" to the development of his characters. "I have no interest in making a 'Vietnam' film, no interest in making a direct political statement." All the same, his assertion appeared in an article titled "A Vietnam Movie That Does Not Knock America."[52] As Cimino was finding out, the war in Vietnam could no more be divorced from politics than its meaning could be strictly controlled within his narrative. The war always was, and continues to be, an overtly political matter on a number of levels.

Ultimately, the contemporary and ongoing debate over the politics of these first major American films about the war rests on a very narrow and myopic view of the meaning of "politics." In these discussions, the term refers almost exclusively to "pro-war" or "antiwar" stances, as though the films were released in 1968, not 1978. Thus, *Coming Home,* because it has a recognizable real-world antiwar figure in Jane Fonda, and because it seems to tilt toward a traditional antiwar bias in its redemption of Luke and condemnation of Bob, can be described as antiwar. Because *The Deer Hunter,* as Kroll and Rich argued, is conspicuously *not* antiwar, especially when read alongside *Coming Home,* it can be described as apolitical. Such simplistic characterizations, aside from doing a gross injustice by reducing complex texts with multiple contradictions to a binary construction, also fail to consider the many ways in which texts are always already political. Just as there were many reasons for one to be antiwar or pro-war during the American war in Vietnam, there are multiple ways in which a film could "be" pro-war or antiwar. Certainly, to de-historicize the war, as Cimino does, is a political act, as is the rendering of the war itself invisible in *Coming Home.* The decision not to address the historical and political implications of the war in Vietnam, while understandable within the genre conventions and Hollywood mode of production, is a political act.

But the larger problem inherent in such constructions of the political is that by focusing the debate over the films in terms of domestic political attitudes, it ignores the implications of the films for foreign policy. As

Melani McAllister's work has demonstrated, the point is not whether or not a particular representation is accurate, realistic, or racist. Our focus is more usefully placed on how the texts participate, intersect, and interact with other constructions—including the construction of foreign policy.

The dehumanized portrait of the Vietnamese offered by *The Deer Hunter* has a wider significance when considered alongside the similar portraits offered in congressional debates about the POW/MIA issue (or myth). The POW/MIA films of the early 1980s make explicit such connections to ongoing political and diplomatic battles, but *The Deer Hunter* has never been implicated in the failures of normalization in the late 1970s. At the very least, the film argues for an acceptance of Carter's notion of "mutual destruction," according to which the working-class communities of, say, Appalachia were as devastated by the war, if not more so, as the villages of the Mekong Delta. It is also important to situate the representations offered by *The Deer Hunter* in the context of the dearth of any other images of the Vietnamese in American culture at this moment. If Bruce Franklin's assertion that the cultural inversion of the war began with the POW myth of the late 1960s is correct, then certainly the Russian roulette scenes and the dehumanized portrayal of the Vietnamese in Cimino's film would seem to deal a fatal blow to any hopes of reversing the process.

APOCALYPSE NOW

In one of the many articles to declare that Vietnam had "come home" in 1978, a piece in *Time* took note of the rather remarkable spectacle presented by the Oscar ceremony in April of 1979. Already that night, Jane Fonda and Jon Voight had won awards for best performances for their roles in *Coming Home,* but the highlight came when John Wayne, of all people, gave the final award of the night, Best Picture, to Cimino for *The Deer Hunter.* The piece also mentioned headlines around the country that cleverly appropriated the awards to comment on the irony of the situation, such as when the *Los Angeles Examiner* proclaimed, "The War Finally Wins."[53] A month later, a *Times* overview of recent representations of the war in film, television, and the theater noted that "no writer or director has yet dealt with 'the other side,'" with the result that "the bottom-line question: 'Are we a moral nation?,' has not yet been asked, let alone answered. Francis Coppola's Vietnam film 'Apocalypse Now' will be released August 15 in New York and may change this; many who have seen an early print of the film report it does."[54]

The film that had already cast its shadow over Hollywood representations of the war had finally arrived. Though Cimino had once hoped that Coppola's film would "break the ice" with American audiences, the producers of *Apocalypse Now* were by 1979 more optimistic about breaking even financially because of the success of *The Deer Hunter.* "All these years, the industry has thought that audiences did not want to deal with the Vietnam war," said Fred Roos, co-producer of *Apocalypse Now.* " 'The Deer Hunter' is the first tangible proof that this may not be true."[55]

By the time it was screened at the Cannes festival in May, *Apocalypse Now* needed no more hype from the industry. The film had become a legend even before it hit the big screen. Rumors had long circulated in Hollywood about Coppola's Vietnam film: that he had mortgaged his house and his rights to royalties from *The Godfather;* that it was based on Joseph Conrad's *Heart of Darkness;* that he and his crew had been stranded in the Philippines for almost a year. In the summer of 1978, about halfway between the releases of *Coming Home* and *The Deer Hunter, Newsweek* ran a special piece by Maureen Orth titled "Waiting for the Apocalypse." In it, she chronicled the various disasters that had put the film years behind schedule and tens of millions of dollars over budget. Harvey Keitel, originally slated to play the lead role of Captain Willard, had been fired. Martin Sheen, his replacement, had a heart attack. Marlon Brando, cast in the role of Colonel Kurtz, wouldn't work unless he was given one million dollars per week and finally arrived seventy-five pounds overweight, forcing Coppola to rewrite and reconceptualize many of Kurtz's scenes. The Philippine army helicopters that were lent to Coppola by the Marcos administration were diverted for several days to put down a political insurrection.[56]

Among all these difficulties, however, "the longest running battle on the set was over what the film was really about." In the article, everyone from Coppola on down weighs in with his or her view on the message of the film, and not one of them sounds remotely like the other. As later reviews and essays would further demonstrate, the film was pieced together on the fly, not simply in the face of production challenges, but thanks to a continually reworked narrative expressing an uncertain message. Although it was originally based on *The Odyssey* and Conrad's *Heart of Darkness,* the film draws on such a variety of influences, from The Doors to T. S. Eliot, as to make it all but incoherent at times. Peter Marin accurately described it as "a sampler, a variety show of Coppola's talents: bits and pieces of successive scripts, fragments of John Milius's originally hawkish screenplay, Michael Herr's antiwar narrative added late in the day, set pieces of surreal exaggeration derivative of *Catch-22* or *MASH,* mawkish images of the

Vietnamese, and, finally, the entire last convulsive third of the film, a pastiche of borrowed meanings and second-hand myths, in which Coppola, striving to locate the significance of his work, loses his way completely."[57]

Screenwriter John Milius would later tell *Film Comment* that the character of Willard was a combination of "Adam, Faust, Dante, Aeneas, Huckleberry Finn, Jesus Christ, the Ancient Mariner, Capt. Ahab, Odysseus, and Oedipus."[58] The politics of Coppola and Milius also collided on the project. Milius, who believed that the war in Vietnam was lost "on the campuses" in the United States, originally viewed his script as hawkish. Coppola, however, wanted it to make a more "liberal" statement about the war. In the end, they agreed to disagree and attempted, like Cimino, to make an "apolitical" film.[59]

To a certain degree they were more successful than Cimino in this regard, as the moral and political message of *Apocalypse Now* was seen by most at the time as, at best, muddled. Nevertheless, if any of the "big three" films was a spectacle, *Apocalypse Now* was it. "My movie isn't about Vietnam," Coppola told an audience at the 1979 Cannes Film Festival, where the film shared the Grand Prize. "It *is* Vietnam." Although he was referring in part to the disastrous quagmire of production experienced while working on the film, Coppola's statement becomes all the more loaded when considered within the matrix of normalization I am proposing here. In the context of the rewriting of the war in late 1970s American culture, his claim constitutes the ultimate act of cultural appropriation: allowing a fictional representation to displace and silence the historical reality of the war.

Coppola's mythic journey upriver follows Willard on his mission to "terminate the command" of Colonel Walter Kurtz. Willard has been informed that Kurtz, once a rising star in the military bureaucracy, has gone insane, and is now using "unsound methods" to wage his own war, without borders or boundaries of any kind. As he is escorted up the river, Willard pores through Kurtz's file. Struggling to balance his concern over Kurtz's descent into madness with his own personal identification with the man, Willard recognizes at least the insanity of his own mission and, perhaps, the war itself: "Charging a man with murder in this place," Willard comments in a voiceover, "is like handing out speeding tickets at the Indy 500." This statement also defined what critics would come to call the film's moral ambiguity. In Coppola's Vietnam, there is no useful distinction to be made between the killing of enemy combatants and the slaughter of innocent civilians.

The journey becomes increasingly surreal as the crew moves toward Kurtz. In one of the most legendary sequences in any American combat film, they meet up with Colonel Kilgore (Robert Duvall), a character originally intended to play the Cyclops figure to Willard's Odysseus.[60] After mopping up the wreckage from his air cavalry unit's latest assault on the Vietnamese, Kilgore agrees to drop Willard and his crew at the mouth of a river in a "hairy" Viet Cong–controlled area—but only after Kilgore learns that Lance, one of the men escorting Willard, is a legendary California surfer and is advised that Willard's destination offers particularly good waves. Kilgore, who is apparently more than passionate about surfing, decides that the point can be taken and held long enough for his own purposes. When one of his troops shows reluctance, saying, "It's Charlie's [the Viet Cong's] point, sir," Kilgore shouts back, "Charlie don't surf!"

The next morning, Kilgore's unit attacks the village, blaring "The Ride of the Valkyries" from speakers specially mounted on its helicopters. "I use Wagner," Kilgore tells Lance. "It scares the hell out of the slopes." The village, including a seemingly innocuous schoolyard, turns out to be a Viet Cong stronghold replete with antiaircraft weaponry. Kilgore rewards one crew with "a case of beer for that one" as they take out one of the guns. "Don't these people ever give up?" Kilgore asks as he takes out a vehicle on the bridge and then sips his coffee. The men land on the beach and begin to take the village. An American soldier is shown close up (in far greater detail than we ever see Vietnamese subjects), suffering from a severe leg wound. As a helicopter sets down in the schoolyard to evacuate the wounded, a young girl throws a grenade into it, blowing it up. "Fucking savages," Kilgore responds. "I'm going to get that dink bitch," we hear from another pilot over the radio. The girl and her mother run, and are gunned down from above. After landing on the beach, the colonel further secures his position by ordering in a napalm strike along the tree line. The odor of the strike puts Kilgore into a kind of reverie: "I love the smell of napalm in the morning. The smell, that gasoline smell . . . smells like . . . *victory*." Looking directly at Willard, Kilgore concludes, "Someday this war's gonna end."

The scene sums up the ultimate ambivalence of *Apocalypse Now*. On the one hand, it seems determined to demonstrate the absurdity of the entire American involvement in Vietnam: wiping out an entire village in order to surf. Coppola also makes a point of alluding to the racism and hypocrisy of Kilgore and his men, who refer to the Vietnamese as "slopes" and "savages." That the Americans are clearly the initiators of the violence is itself somewhat remarkable. It is very rare, in fact, for the American forces in a Vietnam War film to initiate the action that results in a large battle or in the deaths of Vietnamese subjects. Normally, American troops are ambushed or caught off guard. Even in atrocity scenes, such as the one in *Platoon,* the American violence is set up by the gruesome killing of an American soldier. Yet the film at another level justifies the attack by showing this to be a Viet Cong–controlled village. This is not the slaughter of innocents; they are the enemies of the Americans, who shoot back at the aircraft and throw grenades into helicopters. The ends of the particular mission are unquestionably absurd, but the battle itself and the killing of Vietnamese women and children are not.[61]

Later, upriver, the film offers another instance of American-initiated violence, just as ambiguous in its moral implications. On a "routine" stop of a Vietnamese family's boat, the young and frazzled crew members accompanying Willard are ordered to inspect the cargo. Willard pleads with his boat's commander to ignore the Vietnamese boat so they can continue toward his destination. "Chief" (Albert Hall) insists, and "Chef" (Frederick Forrest) reluctantly boards the other boat. Frustrated and scared, he pushes a young girl down. "Shut up, slope," yells "Mr. Clean" (Laurence Fishburne), who keeps the American boat's mounted gun fixed on the family. As Chef moves to inspect another basket, the girl gets up and rushes toward him, and Mr. Clean opens fire, killing the girl. Lance joins in, and in a frantic scene they slaughter the entire family. Chef finds that the girl was only trying to protect her puppy, hidden in the basket. Then Chief points out that the girl is moving, still alive. He insists that they take her to an ARVN hospital, according to regulations. Willard informs Chief that they will not, and executes the girl on the spot. "I told you not to stop. So let's go." In the voiceover that follows, Willard observes, "It was a way we had over here. We'd cut 'em in half with machine guns and give them a Band-Aid. It was a lie. And the more I saw of them, the more I hated lies." Through the device of the voiceover, Willard justifies his murder, chalking it up to the "lie" of American policy in Vietnam.

Perhaps the most remarkable scene in *Apocalypse Now,* however, is one that was not included in the original 1979 release. After reaching the apex of surrealistic adventure at the Do Long Bridge, where haunting and hallucinatory music accompanies the taunting voices of the Vietnamese in the wilderness ("Hey, GI, fuck you, GI! I kill you, GI!"), the crew comes upon a surviving French rubber plantation. The owners, who have been on the land since the early years of French colonization, treat the crew to dinner and offer Willard a historical lesson on the First and Second Indochina Wars. The patriarch of the family explains to Willard that the Americans have never understood the primacy of Vietnamese nationalism. "If the Vietnamese are Communist tomorrow," he says, "they will be *Vietnamese* Communists." A younger man, recounting the domino theory, appears more supportive of what he perceives as the American position: "They are fighting for freedom," he tells the patriarch. The conversation turns, at considerable length, to the Vietnamese victory at Dien Bien Phu. "Why don't you Americans learn from us, learn from our mistakes. You are stronger, you could win," the younger man pleads with Willard. In a twisted defense of colonialism, the patriarch states that the family stays because they "worked very hard bringing the rubber from Brazil. We worked very hard with Vietnamese to build something out of nothing. That is why we stay. Because it belongs to us. It keeps our family together. But you Americans are fighting for the biggest nothing!"

The scene offers no definitive historical account of either the French or American historical involvement; it actually reads as more of a strange hybrid of several explanations for Franco-American failures than anything else. In the redux version of the film, released in 2001, the inserted scene stands out as a halfhearted attempt to historicize the otherwise largely surreal, mythic narrative. Nevertheless, it is worth questioning why the scene was not included in the original version. Like *The Deer Hunter, Apocalypse Now* is unconcerned with the historical realities of the American war in Vietnam, attempting instead, according to Coppola, to get at larger questions of human nature.[62] In the end, it is simply one more contradiction in the film, which comes across as unsure whether the already historical American involvement matters, or whether, as President Carter claimed in his press conference on Vietnamese aid, the United States should move forward "without reference to the past."

The final scenes at Kurtz's compound are similarly noteworthy, as much for what they are as for what they are not. As Coppola explains in the documentary *Hearts of Darkness,* shot during the filming by his wife, Eleanor, and released in 1991, the improvisational nature of the story began to catch up with the filmmaker in the final scenes. On top of the various crises and adaptations detailed in the 1978 *Newsweek* piece, Coppola was unable to come up with a suitable ending for the film. As Eben Muse explains in *The Land of Nam,* three separate endings were shot: one in which Willard joins Kurtz, one in which Willard dies alongside Kurtz after calling in an American air strike on the compound, and one in which Willard kills

Kurtz. The last was eventually used, but only after several audience focus groups found it the most satisfying of the three.[63] In fact, even after its debut at Cannes in May 1979, Coppola referred to the film as "a work in progress," hinting that several scenes, including the ending, could still be changed.[64]

[Coppola told many reporters and reviewers that his film was about "moral choice." Yet if he was unable to articulate that intent coherently, or to comment through the film as to what the appropriate choices would have been or still were for the United States in Vietnam, he did succeed in sparking a debate about the representation of morality in the film itself.[65] For many reviewers and scholars, Coppola's inability to articulate or symbolize any coherent message in the film's climax was indicative of its larger moral and political failures. Even among sympathetic reviewers, Coppola was often criticized for falling prey to his own delusions of grandeur. In *Newsweek,* Jack Kroll called *Apocalypse Now* "the ultimate war movie," a "searching and deeply committed probing of the moral problem of the Vietnam War," while admitting that *in the film* he could not locate what that "moral problem" was. Should the United States have been in Vietnam? Should it have waged the war differently, as Colonel Kurtz argued?[66] A perhaps more unlikely source of praise came from the Soviet Union. The Associated Press reported on August 22 that the Soviet press, which had bitterly lambasted *The Deer Hunter,* was giving a "thumbs up" verdict to *Apocalypse Now,* which it saw as containing a "strong message against the American war."[67]]

The judgment of the film by Vincent Canby of the *New York Times* as "a failed masterpiece" was more indicative of the evaluations offered by most reviews in the United States. Canby praised the artistry and cinematography while noting that, at its heart, the film was "confused" and the ending an "intellectual muddle."[68] Others were not as generous. Peter Marin derided the film as "morally stupid": "an essentially unintelligent investigation of themes too complex for Coppola to handle . . . crippled by a morally incoherent attitude toward the war and its attendant issues."[69] Author and Vietnam veteran James Webb, writing in the *Washington Post,* called the film an "illogical absurdity," "a remarkably bad and thoroughly offensive emotional amalgam, an insult to both the experience and those who fought there."[70] Gary Arnold, also of the *Washington Post,* called it "lamentable," "mangled," and "ruinously pretentious."[71] Another reviewer in the *Post* was more kind, but ultimately came to the same common conclusion, that the film essentially avoids taking a moral stand on anything, attempting to show instead that "moral ambiguity" is itself rather "complex."[72]

Frank Tomasulo, also, later took the film to task for its moral and political ambivalence. Coppola, in Tomasulo's account, wanted to have it both ways—to have both an antiwar and pro-war film, as well as a film that aestheticizes the violence of war while still attempting to comment critically on the events depicted.[73] One of Tomasulo's concerns has to do with what he terms "the politics of film reception." Working against the grain of theories that promote an "open," multivalent text, Tomasulo argues that "what is really needed—at least in terms of Vietnam War movies—is a *closed* text, a film that takes an *un*ambiguous stance on the imperialist involvement and illegal conduct of the Vietnam Conflict."[74]

Tomasulo misses, however, the very point of reception theories that focus on the polyvalence of textual meaning. It is not that artists actively *create* "open" texts, and could therefore simplify the articulation of a particular message by creating a less ambiguous text. Ambiguity, after all, is not synonymous with polyvalence. Reception theory holds that texts, by dint of the manner in which they are produced, received, and consumed, are open to a variety of readings dependent on the subject positions of their audience. Thus, both Cimino and, to a lesser degree, Coppola considered their films "apolitical," but audiences and reviewers generally disagreed. Furthermore, as seen in the reaction to *The Deer Hunter,* to attempt to locate films about the Vietnam War within the narrow confines of pro-war or antiwar debate only results in reductive simplification. Nevertheless, Tomasulo's larger point is well taken: films such as *The Deer Hunter* and *Apocalypse Now,* which seek to displace and abstract "political realities onto the universal and ambiguous realm of myth," contribute to the "social amnesia" of American culture.

Coppola's avowed attempt to explore the larger moral implications of the American war in Vietnam, then, as opposed to its ongoing political significance, were seen by most critics at the time as a failure. Yet *Apocalypse Now* has held up as well as any Vietnam film of its period. In part, this is likely due to its artistic triumphs, particularly the cinematography and sound quality for which it was recognized at the 1979 Oscar ceremony. But, further, as an ultimately ambivalent tale riddled by ambivalence in its execution, it may best reflect the way most Americans felt about Vietnam in the late 1970s. Aside from the most vocal and visible of the hawks and doves, were not most Americans confused about the purpose and direction of the war both throughout its duration and after? Did not many who opposed the war by the early 1970s do so because they simply disagreed with the way in which it was being carried out? Many Americans were both prowar and antiwar at the same time, just as Coppola was accused of being. Even in 1979, Americans were confused and ambivalent about the war and its legacies, which may help to explain why such a long, troubling film was so immensely popular, though blasted by contemporary critics.

Apocalypse Now made nearly $79 million domestically in 1979, well exceeding expectations and ensuring that Coppola could keep both his estate in Napa and his *Godfather* royalties. Only five films that year made more money: *Alien, Star Trek, Rocky II, The Amityville Horror,* and *Kramer v. Kramer,* with only the last taking in over $100 million.[75] Of course, *The Deer Hunter* and *Coming Home* also did well at the box office. *Coming Home,* while initially a disappointment, was put back into wide release in early 1979 when it was nominated for several awards. *The Deer Hunter* had fared much better, even given its limited release in a more competitive year in film, with blockbusters like *Grease, Animal House, Superman,* and *Jaws 2* all taking in over $100 million. *The Deer Hunter*'s $49 million take placed it sixth for 1978 in terms of box office receipts, albeit well behind these other films. Despite and partially because of their controversial subject matter, the big three had shown the film industry and the American public that films about the Vietnam War could be both popular and profitable.

Clearly, the success of all three films was to a certain degree related to their position in Hollywood's hierarchies. *Coming Home* had significant star power and built-in publicity with Jane Fonda's prominent role. *The Deer Hunter*'s star power was even greater: Streep, DeNiro, and Walken all helped allay concerns about thirty-six-year-old director Cimino and a controversial topic. Excitement over *Apocalypse Now* was enhanced not only by the public personae of Coppola, Brando, and Duvall, but, as we have seen, by the mythic stories that emerged regarding the production itself. For all of these reasons, as much as thanks to the stories they told—and the stories they avoided—these films became cultural events, seen and discussed around the country.

Whether or not the films sacrificed complexity for the sake of popularity was, and is, debatable. A more pertinent question might be, Why did the films have to sacrifice the *history* of the war? Were audiences, and film studios, so reluctant to visit a more realistic representation of the war that they sought out, instead, the mythic landscapes of Coppola and Cimino?

Was there no way in the late 1970s to make a film about Vietnam that did not sacrifice the entire history of the war?

GO TELL THE SPARTANS

The answer to this question may lie in one of the most overlooked films of this wave—the rare film about the Vietnam War of this period that was praised by critics and completely ignored by the public: *Go Tell the Spartans.* Released in the summer of 1978, scheduled between the first runs of *Coming Home* and *The Deer Hunter, Spartans* was based on Daniel Ford's novel, *Incident at Muc Wa.* Unlike *The Deer Hunter* and *Apocalypse Now,* the film is not only precise and consistent in place and time but is set in 1964, before the war became a full-scale military conflict. As one reviewer put it, "the film limits itself to a narrow strip of geographical and narrative terrain, and doesn't try to sum up the war or everything it may have meant in two glib hours."[76] It was shot in California, not the Thailand or Philippines settings of *The Deer Hunter, Boys in Company C,* or *Apocalypse Now,* so the landscape does look less like Vietnam than those films, but the film retains a certain authenticity in its nonvisual elements that those films do not. Director Ted Post and principal lead Burt Lancaster had neither the budget, the supporting cast, nor perhaps the talent of the crews assigned to these other films, so *Spartans* has the look and feel of a B movie, which is exactly how it was marketed and likely one of the reasons why even many critics ignored it.

From the outset, the film makes clear that it will be more grounded in history than the other Vietnam war films of the period. The first title sequence provides "historical background" to the story:

> In 1954, the French lost their war to keep their Indochina colonies and those colonies became North and South Vietnam.
>
> Then the North aided a rebellion in the South and the United States sent in "Military Advisors" to help South Vietnam fight the Communists.
>
> In 1964, the war in Vietnam was still a little one—confused and far away.

While historians may quibble with elements of causality here, the opening titles alone offer more fidelity to the development of the war than any other Vietnam-themed film from the era. They also help establish the feel of authenticity and historical accuracy that continue throughout most the film. In *Go Tell the Spartans,* South Vietnamese officials are corrupt and protective of their supplies, but they are not the caricatured evil figures from *Boys in Company C;* American forces are hamstrung by the political realities of South Vietnam, but never in an oversimplified way. American troops make just as many mistakes in combat as the ARVN forces, and the competition between idealism and cynicism embodied in various characters is normally well balanced.

The film centers on the decision by American military commanders to build up a garrison near the village of Muc Wa, an outpost that has been abandoned since the end of the French war in 1954. No enemy patrols have been noticed within fifty miles of Muc Wa, but the orders are nevertheless passed down to the command of Major Asa Barker (Lancaster), a grizzled and somewhat cynical veteran of the Korean War, who chews on cigars constantly and has been denied promotion to colonel over the years because of his fondness for both drink and women, including the wife of a former commanding officer. The soldiers under Barker's command include a typical Hollywood war-film assortment of Americans, from fellow Korean war veteran Oleo (short for Oleonowski) to a green draftee named Courcey, and of Vietnamese fighters as well, including local villagers and uniformed ARVN troops. The most significant figure in the troop is a South Vietnamese soldier nicknamed "Cowboy," who works as a translator for Barker's unit. Cowboy speaks several languages and dialects and is the most intuitive soldier under Barker, but he regularly beats suspected Viet Cong prisoners, and, in one instance, beheads one who was not cooperating with his interrogation.

Barker is skeptical about the order to build a defense force at Muc Wa, and his concerns are only heightened when he receives into his unit a new expert in psychological warfare who bases his intelligence assessments on computer models and displays threat levels for local areas in a color-coded chart. Barker thinks so little of Muc Wa that he sends his least experienced officer, Hamilton, to command the outpost, despite the warnings from a more trusted soldier that "Charlie shows up wherever we go." When the team reaches Muc Wa they find an old French graveyard. There is an inscription over the entrance gate, which Courcey translates as, "Stranger, when you find us lying here, go tell the Spartans we obeyed their orders." This is a reference to the Battle of Thermopylae, in 480 B.C., where a Spartan-led army of approximately seven thousand soldiers for two days held a mountain pass against a Persian army estimated to have been between a quarter of a million and half a million strong. They were eventually defeated—and around fifteen hundred of them died—but the delay was crucial to preparations for the successful defense of the Greek city-states, and to the subsequent rise of the Athenian empire. The contrast with the French plantation scene in *Apocalypse Now* is striking. Coppola's sequence offers the lone discussion of history and context in an otherwise ahistorical, surreal landscape; in *Spartans,* the theme of a failure to learn lessons from the past is consistently developed throughout the film. Juxtaposed to this history lesson, written, as it is, literally on the wall for the Americans to read, are several statements made throughout the film by overly confident troops and commanders that the United States would not fall prey to the same fate as the French—or the Spartans.

But, of course, the Americans do fall prey to that same fate. In building up the outpost at Muc Wa, the noisy American and South Vietnamese forces attract the attention of the Viet Cong, and Muc Wa slowly moves up the color-coded chain of threat levels back at Barker's office. During the buildup, the forces at Muc Wa encounter and take into their care a band of local villagers. Cowboy insists they are "Cong," but Courcey is not convinced. "Besides, who cares? They're hungry," he tells Cowboy. The villagers are brought back to the base, where Cowboy repeats his claims to Hamilton. Hamilton informs his troops that part of their mission is "to win the hearts and minds of the peasants." When Oleo protests, affirming that "Cowboy thinks they're a Cong family," Hamilton responds, "They don't look like communists to me." Oleo tells him, "Sir, I've been in this fucking war for three years, and I still don't know what a communist looks like," but Hamilton remains firm, and the refugees join the encampment at Muc Wa. In the film's final sequences, U.S. forces, under increasing siege from the Viet Cong, are ordered to evacuate and abandon the outpost they have just spent weeks creating. The command post informs Barker that Muc Wa "no longer has sufficient strategic value" over which to risk an engagement with the enemy. The United States had been forced to fight a seemingly senseless battle over a location that was strategically unimportant—a tightly but not overly drawn parallel to the war as a whole.

The choice, then—a clearly drawn moral choice the likes of which never appears in *Apocalypse Now*—is what to do about our Vietnamese allies and the refugees. As the American forces withdraw, they are ordered to leave the refugees and the South Vietnamese forces behind. Courcey refuses to obey this order, and Barker reluctantly joins him to help all the Vietnamese escape under cover of darkness before the Viet Cong arrive. Shortly before their escape, Barker and Courcey hear gunfire, and go out to find that

Cowboy has killed most of the refugees because they were, in fact, a "Cong family" which had stolen weapons and ammunition from the outpost. As they are making their escape, they run through the French graveyard to the road back to the base. On the road, however, they are ambushed by an enemy even Cowboy did not see—a young Vietnamese woman from the refugee family, who escaped Cowboy's attack and is now waiting in the bunker with the Viet Cong. The forces are tied down in battle and everyone except Courcey is killed. The next morning, Courcey catches a final glimpse of a one-eyed Viet Cong soldier he has seen before on ambush. The Vietnamese soldier raises his rifle to kill Courcey, but instead collapses, weeping, and Courcey mumbles, "I'm going home, Charlie—if you'll let me." As Courcey stumbles out of the graveyard, on the screen flashes "1964," a reminder that ten more years of a much heavier war lay ahead—regardless of the lessons of history.

What is perhaps most remarkable about *Go Tell the Spartans,* particularly when considered alongside the other films surveyed here, is how visible the Vietnamese are throughout the film. Adding to the "authenticity" of the film is the fact that several Vietnamese soldiers and members of the refugee family *were* played by South Vietnamese refugees, living in the Los Angeles area after fleeing Saigon in 1975, as opposed to the Chinese, Thai, and Filipino stand-ins of Cimino and Coppola's films.[77] The Vietnamese in this film, whether ARVN forces, villagers, refugees, or guerilla forces from the National Liberation Front, are visible throughout the entire film; and yet, at the same time, the forces are still elusive. The guerillas move without detection, and only Cowboy can distinguish innocent refugees from "Cong." We see Vietnamese faces, friendly and unfriendly; we hear their voices and sense their emotions. Director Ted Post shows us that in order to represent the invisible enemy as experienced by American soldiers, filmmakers need not render all Vietnamese invisible or silent.

At the time of its release in the summer of 1978, *Spartans* certainly did not receive the media treatment of the Big Three. Yet reviewers paid some attention to the film, which was generally hailed as an understated masterpiece, one that, unbeknownst to reviewers at the time, seemed to accomplish all that Coppola, still at work on *Apocalypse,* was attempting to do—and more. Critics roundly hailed its economy and lack of pretension, noting that it dealt with complexity and ambiguity without eschewing authenticity. Writing in the Style section of the *Washington Post,* Tom Shales praised the "surprisingly powerful" film for reaching beyond the oversimplifications of films like *Coming Home* and *The Boys in Company C.* Shales acknowledged the film's "liberal" tilt, but noted that Post still "tussled with devastating moral ambiguity" and managed to move beyond a simple "rhapsody of American guilt." *Post* film reviewer Judith Martin likewise commended the film for its "authenticity" and its "intellectual refusal to simplify," even as she labeled it an overall failure.[78] In *Newsweek,* Jack Kroll called it "the best movie yet made about the Vietnam war," and wrote that it "embodies the military and moral confusion that would shortly escalate to apocalypse." It is telling, however, that Kroll's review came out in October, only after the film had been praised by other critics but largely ignored by audiences. Kroll acknowledged, in closing his review, that this "tough, compassionate, unpretentious film will have to fight for the audience it deserves."[79]

The question, then, is why *Go Tell the Spartans,* but not *Coming Home* or *The Deer Hunter,* like them a small-budget film and released in the same year, would have to fight for an audience, for media attention, and for recognition, even when it was clearly a bigger critical success than either of those films or *Apocalypse Now,* not to mention the likes of *Boys of Company C* or *Rolling Thunder.* A major component of the explanation lies surely in the economics of the Hollywood system. Despite his recognizable face and mannerisms in this, his sixtieth feature film role, Burt Lancaster had none of the rising-star qualities of Robert DeNiro; and Ted Post, best known at the time for his work on *Beneath the Planet of the Apes,* was no Hal Ashby, let alone Francis Coppola. The studio and distributors marketed the film as an underwhelming B movie, more along the lines of *Company C* than *Coming Home,* and thus failed to devote the resources that might have helped it find a larger audience.

Yet, some part of the explanation for the failure of *Spartans* at the box office must lie in the public's desires as well. At the time of the film's run, millions of Americans were demonstrating their willingness to sit through three-hour epics, replete with heavy doses of graphic violence, that explored the war in Vietnam through different lenses. Because its lukewarm reception led to scant media coverage or discussion, historians have little explanation for why those who did see *Go Tell the Spartans* did or did not appreciate the film. It is plausible, however, and would fit with the larger myopia and lack of historically driven introspection taking place in American culture at the time, that filmgoers were more willing to see films that *interpreted* the war than films that sought to *explain* the war—that is, films that treated the war as part of America's mythic narratives, rather than those depicting a failed military intervention. It is not unreasonable to assume that many Americans in 1979 had less interest in debating the *lessons* of Vietnam—including those from the French—than in exploring the *legacies* of Vietnam.

"Vietnam" had indeed been brought home in 1978 and 1979. The films explored in this chapter, as well as the critical discourses they engendered, contested American cultural memory of the war by "normalizing" it, translating it into terms acceptable to American cultural production and foreign policy. Through the act of cultural appropriation constituted by making the war "about us," as the Big Three do, the texts reinforce the myopic and narcissistic tendencies of American policy toward Vietnam in the 1970s. All three of the main texts examined here are part of the larger "normalization" of the United States' war on Vietnam, doing for the cultural sphere what the legislative and policy discussions had accomplished in the political field. These films helped to lift the moral burden of the war off Americans, countering any collective sense of guilt with self-indulgent appeals to victimization. By the time of the 1979 Oscars and the release of *Apocalypse Now,* the familiar images of the American war in Vietnam—of children being burned by napalm, of American allies executing their enemies on the streets of Saigon, of a mass of bodies, executed by young American soldiers, lying in a ditch at My Lai—were being edged out, if not entirely displaced, by images of traumatized American veterans, fractured communities, and, importantly, sinister and cruel Vietnamese figures torturing Americans. "Vietnam" had successfully been brought into American cultural memory: it was no longer a war, and had long since ceased being a country. It was now an "experience," something that happened *to* America and Americans.

Peter Marin still wondered in 1980 if American representations of the war would ever consider it "from the Vietnamese point of view—in terms of their suffering rather than ours."[80] The political and cultural work of normalization, however, sought not simply to ignore the Vietnamese, but to silence them. By rendering what the war did to the nations and people of Southeast Asia outside the realm of discussion, the cultural logic of mutual destruction constructed and disseminated in the late 1970s laid the groundwork for the escalation of the United States' ongoing war on Vietnam—and for another major shift in the matrix of representations of the war during the 1980s. The inverted (a)historical representations of the war implicit in the constructions we have seen here would provide the lens through which many Americans were later to view the Third Indochina

War, this time between Cambodia, China, and Vietnam. The government and mainstream media, both agents of normalization in the late 1970s, had already chosen sides in that conflict by early 1979, letting China and their Khmer Rouge clients off rather easily while condemning the Vietnamese as the aggressors and transgressors.

Equally important, though, is the way in which this next military conflict allowed the process of rewriting the American war in Vietnam to continue.

BLEEDING VIETNAM
THE UNITED STATES AND THE THIRD INDOCHINA WAR

In his 1976 national address marking Tet, Le Duan, the longtime secretary general of the Vietnamese Communist Party (VCP), promised that every family in Vietnam would have a radio, a television, and a refrigerator in their home within ten years.[1] While these specific goals may not have been exactly what one might have expected from one of the central figures of the Vietnamese socialist revolution, Le Duan's comments reflected the sanguinity of Hanoi after the end of the Second Indochina War. Having defeated the Americans and their South Vietnamese clients, the Party leadership was now seemingly free to confront the task of socialist economic transformation.

In 1976, optimism reigned supreme in Hanoi. That July, Vietnam would be officially reunited as the Socialist Republic of Vietnam. In the fall, representatives from the United States would visit and recommend the normalization of relations between the two nations. Later that year, the Party announced its incredibly ambitious Second Five Year Plan (FYP), the first such plan since the Democratic Republic of Vietnam's First FYP of 1961–65. In the new plan, the VCP announced that, as part of its three ongoing revolutionary tracks (science and technology, relations of production, and cultural-ideological), the Vietnamese economy would exceed all expectations.[2] The projected increases in agricultural production (8–10 percent), industrial output (16–18 percent), and national income (13–14 percent) would have been ambitious for any economy, let alone one still emerging from three decades of sustained warfare.[3] Moreover, the Fourth Party Congress at which the FYP was announced also produced a statement of economic independence. Anticipating a massive influx of foreign aid, especially from the United States, the Party angered the Soviets by declaring their agenda for genuine economic independence. Although committed to international socialism, the Vietnamese leadership prized nothing more than national sovereignty, which they knew would come only from a position of economic strength and international multilateralism. It certainly appeared to many at the time that the Vietnamese would soon, as Ho Chi Minh had predicted years earlier, rebuild their land "ten times more beautiful."[4]

Ten years later, in early 1986, the dreams of Ho, Le Duan, and the Vietnamese people lay in tatters. Le Duan had died the previous summer at the age of 79; many of his former comrades, including Vo Nguyen Giap, had been forced out of power, and others, including Le Duc Tho and Pham Van Dong, would soon share a similar fate. The vanguard figures of the revolution were being replaced, and another transformation was underway. The Vietnamese economy, which continued to struggle throughout the late 1970s, became increasingly market-oriented in the mid-1980s. As early as 1978 it became clear that the goals for the Second FYP would not be met: agricultural production showed only two percent growth, industrial growth was only six-tenths of a percent, and growth in national income, far from the double-digit gains projected, remained at less than one half of one percent.[5] Although the economy would perform better during the Third FYP of 1981–85, the gains in that period also fell considerably short of both the expectations of the government and the needs of the people. Far from achieving economic independence, Vietnam had been forced into accepting membership in the Council for Mutual Economic Assistance, the Soviet-bloc common economy. Most importantly, the Vietnamese in 1986 found themselves mired in another long, bloody, and costly war, this time with their neighbors and occasional allies, Cambodia and China.

Far from becoming "a land ten times more beautiful," Vietnam by the mid-1980s was surrounded by unfriendly regimes, beset with serious economic woes, and remained the target of an alternatively hostile and indifferent United States. Without question, the Vietnamese leadership must shoulder a good portion of the blame for this situation. The VCP managed its economy poorly and at times remained needlessly obstinate in the face of world opinion during its occupation of Cambodia. What has often been obscured in the rush to judgment concerning the failures of the Vietnamese, however, is the role played by the United States in the multiple tragedies of Southeast Asia during the 1980s. The United States (in concert with China and the ASEAN nations[6]) followed a policy of "bleeding Vietnam white" during this period, needlessly prolonging the devastating war in Cambodia while using the war as a justification for its continued hostility toward Vietnam. Far from a response to the Vietnamese invasion and occupation of Cambodia, U.S. strategy toward Southeast Asia during the late 1970s and 1980s was merely a continuation and extension of its previous policy of continuing the war by other means.

COMING TO TERMS WITH CAMBODIA

The suppression of long-standing national disputes and coalescing of Asian Communist and nationalist factions that had been engendered by the American war in Vietnam were quickly erased when the Americans left. The revolutionary forces of Vietnam and the Khmer Rouge of Cambodia, both of which had been supported by the Chinese during their wars to liberate their countries from American-backed regimes, exchanged messages of congratulations on their victories in April of 1975. Less than a month later, the two nations were battling over disputed territories in the Gulf of Thailand. By the end of 1976, the Khmer Rouge had become *the* major threat to the stability of Southeast Asia, having aggravated tensions with Thailand and Vietnam and, unbeknownst to much of the world, slaughtered millions of its own people.[7]

As conditions in Southeast Asia deteriorated in the late 1970s, the United States was forced to rethink its approach to the region. In doing so, it would be forced to revisit its role in the creation of those conditions. Normalization with Vietnam was no longer the only issue under consideration. The security of close allies such as Thailand, relations with China (which the Carter administration had been quietly working to normalize), and the question of military and/or humanitarian intervention in Cambodia were all on the table in Washington, D.C.

When the stories of Khmer Rouge atrocities began to make their way into the outside world, however, the initial response in American policymaking circles revolved around the role of the United States in helping create the conditions that allowed the regime to seize power in 1975. In the summer of 1977, the House Subcommittee on International Organizations held the first major government hearings on the situation in Cambodia. As William Shawcross would later write, the most remarkable thing about these hearings was that they *were* the first to be held on the matter, a full two years after the Khmer Rouge assumed power and had begun their program of auto-genocide.[8]

In the first of two sessions devoted to the situation, the committee heard testimony from several academics, who sparred with various House members about the tension between the moral responsibility of the United

States for the existing situation in Cambodia and the moral obligation to help in righting that situation. Two of the witnesses in particular, David Chandler of Harvard and Gareth Porter, an independent scholar working in Washington, D.C., took their opportunity before the committee to castigate the United States' policy toward the region during the previous war. Chandler, while admitting that it was difficult to tell exactly what was happening in Cambodia at the current moment, argued that the roots of the crisis lay in the American attacks on Cambodia during the Nixon administration. "To a large extent, I think the American actions are to blame" for the rise of the Khmer Rouge, he told the committee. "It is ironic, to use a colorless word, for us to accuse the Cambodians of being indifferent to life when, for so many years, Cambodian lives made so little difference to us." Chandler had no concrete recommendations for what course the United States should follow with regard to Cambodia, but he was adamant in his insistence that the United States face the complicated reality of the situation in that nation: "We should accept the fact, even if it might be a sad one, that Democratic Kampuchea is a sovereign independent state, and we should formulate our policies toward it, in part, by remembering rather than forgetting, what we have done."[9]

Porter's testimony was far more contentious. Along with some other intellectuals on the left, most notably Noam Chomsky (whose name arose in the course of Porter's testimony), Porter erred on the unfortunate side of caution, downplaying the possibility of a Cambodian holocaust. Pointing to previous exaggerations by Western powers of communist atrocities, such as the land reform program in North Vietnam in the mid-1950s and the Hue Massacre of 1968, on which he was an expert, Porter argued that the postwar policies of the Khmer Rouge, such as mass evacuations and a return to collectivized agriculture, were "rational" given the devastated state of the country's infrastructure. In a lengthy and meticulously documented written statement, he argued that reports of genocide were completely overblown. Whatever "mistakes" the Khmer Rouge committed, Porter claimed, were "dwarfed" by the destruction previously caused by the United States. "It is the worst kind of historical myopia and hypocrisy," he concluded, "to express more moral outrage at the revolutionary government for its weaknesses than at the cause of overwhelmingly greater suffering: the U.S. policy in Cambodia from 1970 to 1975."[10]

The rest of the afternoon featured a series of vitriolic exchanges between Porter, Chandler, and several members of the subcommittee. Before Porter arrived, Chandler was grilled about his stance on the moral quandary facing the United States. Chairman Donald Fraser of Minnesota asked if Chandler thought the United States should refrain from action "for perpetuity" because of "our own conduct in Cambodia." Chandler rejected this simplification, drawing attention once again to the "complicated" position facing the United States. He reiterated his hope that, at the very least, attitudes and policy toward Cambodia would be formulated "in a context of memory," rather than "in a vacuum, as if we had nothing to do with the situation there."[11] The representative from Illinois, Edward Derwinski, claimed that one of the statements before the subcommittee should not be titled "Human Rights in Cambodia," but, rather, "Justification for Slaughter."[12] William Goodling of Pennsylvania also refused to accept Chandler's point about the complexity of the situation, calling his testimony "very annoying." Yet, in his own muddled statement, Goodling revealed the brutal nature of the American war on Cambodia. Comparing the United States' bombing of Cambodia to the murderous Khmer Rouge seemed specious to Goodling: "Our bombs didn't single out certain segments or certain peoples in Cambodia. Our bombs hit them all. And whether you thought it was right or I thought it was right, the military at that time thought it was right."[13] That such a statement could be presented as a defense of American policy reveals the tangled and twisted nature of American relations with Southeast Asia.

A much more nuanced position on the Cambodian situation came from Stephen Solarz, the Democratic congressman from Long Island who came to Washington as part of the Watergate class of 1974. Jewish and thus acutely concerned with issues of genocide and diaspora, Solarz took an early and passionate interest in both the Cambodian holocaust and the refugee crisis facing Southeast Asia. At the May 3 hearing, Solarz battled with Porter about the conditions in Cambodia, demonstrating a concern and knowledge of the subject that were unrivaled in the United States Congress during his tenure. He ridiculed witnesses who seemed to defend the Khmer Rouge, compared Porter to those who continued to deny the Jewish holocaust, and pressed them about their assumptions, their evidence, and their politics. Most impressively, he alone among the congressional representatives acknowledged both the complexity of the situation in Southeast Asia and the moral ambiguity inherent in the formulation of American foreign policy toward the region. "I hold no brief for what we did in Cambodia," he told the witnesses and the committee. "I fully agree that we bear a measure of the responsibility for setting in motion a course of events which ultimately led to this most monstrous evil. But how anybody can suggest, by virtue of that fact, that we are morally absolved of any obligation to attempt to deal with this crime seems to me an act of moral insensitivity."[14] Over the course of this and numerous subsequent hearings, over which he would come to preside as chair, Solarz continued to demonstrate his unique grasp of the issues surrounding the region.

Despite the palpable animosity in the room, the one item on which everyone at the hearings appeared to agree was that humanitarian aid should be sent to Cambodia.[15] Ironically, of course, such aid was prohibited by the sanctions placed on Cambodia under the terms of the Trading With the Enemy Act and the Export Administration Act. The hearings did reveal that U.S.-made DDT had been sold to Cambodia to combat malaria. Any such transaction was prohibited under the sanctions program, yet no one in the hearings was disturbed by this development. In his statement to the subcommittee at related hearings later in the summer of 1977, Assistant Secretary of State Richard Holbrooke noted, almost as an aside, that "the United States has made exceptions to the Export Administration controls on Cambodia to permit sales of DDT as a means of easing the outbreak of malaria there."[16] It was clear to all those involved that malaria infections had been at epidemic levels in Cambodia since at least the height of the American bombing campaign. Even the government experts who testified at these later hearings conceded that the number of deaths from malaria under the Khmer Rouge was "even greater than those executed."[17]

That the need for assistance in some form was a point of agreement in these hearings reveals as much about the state of lingering animosity and indifference toward Vietnam as it does about the state of concern about Cambodia. During this same period—the spring and summer of 1977—Congress was developing new and unprecedented regulations designed to prevent U.S. direct aid to Vietnam, aid through international organizations, and the possibility of even *discussing* aid to Vietnam during normalization negotiations. While the famines plaguing Vietnam in 1977 and 1978 do not constitute horrors parallel to the suffering of the Cambodian people, it is nevertheless remarkable that such proposals for Cambodian aid were made and received so casually during the hearings. Aid to Cambodia, which would certainly have to have been provided via the Khmer Rouge, was discussed as though it was a given that the needs of the Cambodian people trumped the possibility of further propping up a murderous and possibly genocidal regime. In and of itself, this is not a radical sentiment; it is precisely the point of humanitarian aid to provide aid to populations without regard to politics or diplomacy. The question is, What is the reason for the double standard on aid to Vietnam and Cambodia?

During their rise to power, the Khmer Rouge had played upon the role of the "U.S. imperialists" in destroying their country and propping up the Lon Nol regime. Long after the war, they continued to blame the United States for committing genocide against the Cambodian people, while denying their own auto-genocidal practices. Even well into 1978, Pol Pot and Ieng Sary accused "the U.S. imperialists and their lackeys" of killing over a million Cambodians. The number itself is not a matter of great dispute. American officials at the July 1977 hearings testified that the number of Cambodians killed during the American involvement in that country was "probably close" to one million.[18] Yet the number of Vietnamese who were killed during the American war there is likely at least twice as high; even conservative estimates place Vietnamese casualties somewhere near two million. (While significant divisions remain among scholars about how many Vietnamese died, the most commonly agreed-upon figure is around 2.5 million.)

Even so, the Vietnamese entered the postwar era with an attitude of openness, speaking of healing the wounds of war and developing a mutually beneficial relationship with the United States. They went to unprecedented lengths in the face of unprecedented demands by the United States on the POW/MIA question, only to be met with greater skepticism and more demands. The Khmer Rouge, on the other hand, refused all American attempts at diplomatic contact. The House Select Committee on Missing Persons in Southeast Asia took particular note of the complete lack of assistance from the Khmer Rouge, and when the Woodcock Commission attempted to schedule a visit to Phnom Penh during their tour of the region in early 1977, they received no response from the Cambodian regime.[19]

In fact, the question of aid to Cambodia at the time was largely moot. The regime was still largely closed to the outside world, had rejected previous offers of aid from various countries, and certainly was not interested in any assistance from the United States. On the other hand, the Vietnamese had made clear that they both needed and desired aid from the United States and the world community. Although they initially *demanded* such aid, which turned out to be a gross political and diplomatic miscalculation, the Vietnamese grew increasingly flexible regarding the scope, form, and substance of aid. Yet Congress refused even to consider such a possibility.

As Bruce Franklin writes of the double standard for the Vietnamese and Cambodians with regard to the POW/MIA question: "Nowhere else does the hypocrisy and cynicism of U.S. government policy on the MIA question stand so nakedly exposed."[20] The same could be said of the more general policy of the United States on aid to the nations of Southeast Asia. The question of aid to Cambodia would continue to be raised during the next several years without ever reaching an adequate answer. The double standard to which the United States government was holding the Khmer Rouge and Vietnamese would also remain, and would grow increasingly hypocritical as the years, and the war for Cambodia, dragged on.[21]

CONSTRUCTING A "POST-VIETNAM" POLICY: CHOOSING CHINA

In June of 1978, Assistant Secretary of State Richard Holbrooke addressed the Western Governors' Association in Honolulu, describing to the group what he labeled the "changing perspectives" of American foreign policy in Southeast Asia. Holbrooke at the time was still leading the charge within the White House for normalizing relations with Vietnam, but on this day he revealed the extent to which that goal had fallen in the administration's priorities. He spoke of maintaining a strong military presence in the region, keeping up good relations with Japan, increasing trade and investment with the ASEAN nations, and "our commitment to normalizing relations with China." Holbrooke labeled the overall shift in perspective "our post-Vietnam Asia policy." Certainly this nomenclature reflects chronology, but in the context of the summer of 1978 it also foreshadows the erasure of Vietnam from at least the visible part of the American policy agenda. Holbrooke told the governors that time would not permit a discussion of Vietnamese-American relations, but did note in closing that the United States had "made a reasonable offer to establish diplomatic relations and to lift the trade embargo," implying that the ball was in Hanoi's court.[22]

Hanoi, however, was already making its own overtures to the United States in the summer of 1978. As Stephen Hurst has shown, throughout May, June, and July, Vietnamese officials made several public pronouncements revealing their willingness to drop outright the demand for American economic aid as a precondition for normalization. In July, the Vietnamese deputy foreign minister told journalists, "even if the U.S. Congress rejects the reconstruction aid, we look forward to establishing full diplomatic ties."[23] Another Vietnamese official noted, later that summer, "it is clear that in matters of normalization, the ball is on the American side."[24]

The United States, however, insisted that it had not received any "official" proposal from the Vietnamese, and thus had no official basis of its own upon which to respond. At a Senate hearing in August, Deputy Assistant Secretary of State Robert Oakley told the Subcommittee on East Asian and Pacific Affairs "we are waiting for a clarification of precisely what the Vietnamese have in mind. We have not yet had a direct, official explanation of their present position on establishing normal diplomatic relations with the United States."[25] It is curious, given the amount of attention the administration had already devoted to the issue of normalization, that it was now "waiting" for further Vietnamese clarification. As Hurst puts it, "[t]he significant question is not 'why did the Vietnamese not officially drop the aid precondition.'" Instead, one should ask "'why did the United States not immediately kick the ball back?'" The answer, Hurst argues, has primarily to do with external developments of the period, including several Soviet-related issues that had nothing to do with Southeast Asia but helped to reinforce the Soviet-centric Brzezinski worldview within the administration.[26] When Vietnam became a full member of the Council for Mutual Economic Assistance (CMEA) in June, the administration's view of Hanoi as a Soviet proxy power was only further solidified. Even when a CIA study demonstrated that the Soviets were not actively involved in Vietnam at the time, this view continued to dominate White House policy making.[27] The United States maintained its hostile stance toward Vietnam in international organizations, casting the lone veto at the 1978 meeting of the Asian Development Bank, thus blocking new loans and grants to Vietnam.[28] In fact, policies such as these were greatly responsible for pushing the Vietnamese back into the Soviet orbit.

In August, Sonny Montgomery led a congressional delegation to Hanoi and met with several members of the VCP, including Pham Van Dong. The POW/MIA issue, which had momentarily ceased to be a central one in the normalization process, was still the ostensible reason for the visit, but the Vietnamese used the occasion to claim "officially" that they were willing to move forward without concrete aid commitments.[29] "We are friends with you now, and we want to be even better friends," Dong told Montgomery. "We had the wind against us in the past. Now let it be at our backs." Montgomery told reporters not only that he was still "completely convinced that there are no more Americans alive in Southeast Asia," but also that he had become much more sympathetic to the difficult position in which Vietnam found itself. Although Montgomery made a noticeable gaffe by referring to his hosts as "the North Vietnamese," he pointed out that if the United States wished to combat the Soviet presence in Southeast Asia, "it would be useful if we had some presence in this part of the world to see what the Russians are trying to do."[30]

The Vietnamese had for many years made clear their desire for bilateral trade and aid agreements with many nations, as well as for participation in multilateral agreements. The openness of the Vietnamese Communist Party to international financial institutions in the years immediately following the Second Indochina War demonstrated their desire for genuine economic independence. Its decision to join the World Bank, IMF, and Asian Development Bank had distanced Hanoi from both Moscow and Beijing, which at the time refused to open their books to the organizations. The VCP continued to strive for economic autonomy in the face of the American embargo, gradually increasing trade with regional partners and rebuffing Soviet pressure to join the CMEA on several occasions. In December of 1976, for instance, the VCP rejected a Russian proposal for further economic integration, "confining themselves," as Derek Davies later noted in *Far Eastern Economic Review,* "to a conventional expression of thanks for Soviet aid—but asking the French to build an integrated steel mill which Moscow had turned down."[31] In August 1978, shortly before Montgomery's visit, Pham Van Dong restated the VCP's position: "Whenever in our four-thousand-year history Vietnam has been dependent on one large friend, it has been a disaster for us."[32] Only as a final resort, facing severe economic crises, potential famine, and the threat of a war with China, did the Vietnamese move toward full membership in the CMEA.

In fact, even the State Department acknowledged that Vietnam's primary motive was one of moving toward political and economic independence, rather than toward a close relationship with other communist nations. Responding in August to questions put to it by a Senate committee, the State Department set forth its official position on Soviet-Viet relations as follows:

> We doubt that Vietnam will seek too close ties to the Soviet Union if relations with China continue to deteriorate unless actual military conflict appears certain. Hanoi has traditionally cherished its independence and sovereignty and has sought to avoid too close identification with any one nation. Vietnam continues to receive international support and advisers from the U.S.S.R. However, we do not anticipate that the

Vietnamese will be willing to give the Soviets bases in Vietnam, and allegations to date that this has occurred have been found to be inaccurate. Vietnam compensated for joining the Soviet Union's economic zone—COMECOM—by active wooing of western nations, Japan, Australia, and ASEAN.[33]

There was still clearly a split between the State Department position and that of Brzezinski throughout the summer and fall of 1978. Nevertheless, while it is clear that it may not have been the intent of the Carter administration to push the Vietnamese into the Russian camp—or to set the stage for its own complicity in the ensuing war in Southeast Asia—that is precisely the result of its foreign policy decisions of late 1978. By essentially "choosing" China, the United States entered into what historian Michael Haas has termed a "Faustian pact" in which China and the United States would support the Khmer Rouge, one of the most murderous regimes in history.[34]

The lines were thus drawn early in what would, within months, become the Third Indochina War. Throughout the fall, the Chinese had been moving tanks, artillery, and aircraft toward the northern border of Vietnam. Vietnamese forces had also been active, securing the area north of Hanoi against a possible Chinese attack while concentrating troops along the Cambodian border in anticipation of an invasion designed to oust the Pol Pot regime.[35] U.S. intelligence agencies had been aware of all these troop movements for some time, and were apparently less concerned about the Chinese buildup than that of the Vietnamese. Even so, all available evidence indicates that, although Washington was concerned about the ongoing border conflict and the possibility of a Vietnamese invasion, few in the United States thought that events would result in a prolonged occupation of Cambodia.

In August of 1978, the Senate Committee on Foreign Relations held its "first review of Indochina developments" since April of 1975.[36] Robert Oakley from the State Department and Douglas Pike, then a scholar in residence at the Congressional Research Service, testified that a full-scale Vietnamese invasion and occupation was unlikely. When several members of the committee, particularly former presidential candidate George McGovern, inquired about the possibility of overthrowing the Khmer Rouge and stopping the genocide, Oakley replied that there had been reports from the region about "resistance movements" supported by Vietnam, but he was skeptical about their chances for success.[37] Pike concurred:

> For the Vietnamese, or anybody, to change the governmental structure would involve putting teams or military units into virtually every village in the country in a kind of military occupation that would be an extraordinarily dangerous, bleeding kind of operation which I cannot really believe the Vietnamese would entertain. So the Vietnamese, I think, would like to do the Socialist world a favor by getting rid of Pol Pot and his associates, but there are intractable problems, technical problems, involved in doing it, which are unique. You would not find them in any other country in the world.[38]

McGovern pressed the witnesses, suggesting that if the Vietnamese were not up to the task, perhaps the United States could do the job of ridding the world of Pol Pot. Oakley responded, "I don't believe that this is an option that is being studied anywhere."[39] Toward the close of the hearing, a seemingly exasperated Senator John Glenn, then chairman of the subcommittee, wondered if anyone in the government was "really coordinating this whole picture . . . I don't want to form another committee or another study group. But who is in charge of our policy here that is laying out the short term and the long term?"[40] Pike later offered an apparently unsatisfactory but nevertheless honest reply: "You know, to plan ahead requires that you anticipate and that you predict. Those of us who have worked in Asia were burned early, and have long learned, that it is extremely dangerous to try to predict anything."[41]

As the in-house expert on Southeast Asia, however, Pike was asked several times over the next several months to do precisely what he had advised against: predict. In early October of 1978 he delivered a report to the House Subcommittee on Asian and Pacific Affairs on the "Vietnam-Cambodia conflict." Pike indicated that although a protracted occupation was a possibility, given the limited options available to Vietnam, it was unlikely. Echoing what he had told the Senate committee two months earlier, Pike concluded that "the most likely future of the war appears, as of this moment, to be indeterminate." While a Vietnamese client state would be "an attractive prospect" for Vietnam, that was only a slightly more likely outcome than a negotiated settlement.[42]

Yet despite the ongoing American hostility and intransigence toward the Vietnamese, and despite the concerns of the United States about recent developments in Southeast Asia, when Holbrooke arranged for secret meetings in New York with Nguyen Co Thach in late September of 1978, normalization was still a possibility. At those meetings Thach made a last-ditch effort to secure a promise of American aid, but none was forthcoming. According to Nayan Chanda, after yet another stalled session Thach told Holbrooke, "Okay, I'll tell you what you want to hear. We will defer other problems until later. Let's normalize our relations without preconditions." He then pressed Holbrooke to sign a memorandum of understanding immediately. Although Holbrooke refused to do so, he felt assured on leaving the meetings that normalization could be accomplished in the near future.[43] He passed word of the breakthrough to Carter through Cyrus Vance. Thach told Holbrooke he would be in New York for another month and would await notification of Carter's approval.

Once thought to be a dead end, the long road to normalization seemed finally to have led to an agreement. The United States would have a relationship with Vietnam, a symbolic and a strategic victory for the Carter administration. Vietnam would not have the aid it had long needed, but it would have a new relationship with Washington, the possibility of future aid, and, presumably sooner rather than later, an end to the American embargo. Unfortunately, 1978 was an election year in the United States. When Carter agreed in principle to normalize with Vietnam, he did so with the caveat that it would have to wait until after the midterm elections.[44] Once again, the future of Vietnam would be subject to the considerations of American domestic politics.

With the elections approaching in late October, Pike delivered yet another report, this time to the Senate, titled *Vietnam's Future Foreign Policy.* This report was noticeably different in tone, if not substance; if anything, much of the material was outdated given the developments in normalization talks earlier that fall. Pike described the Vietnamese as being paranoid and anti-American in their policy views. Hanoi perceived the United States "as a relentlessly aggressive and eternally hostile force stalking the world," he argued.[45] Furthermore, Vietnamese leaders continued to act "as if the war were still being fought." Those who claimed that Vietnam has adopted a conciliatory approach to the United States were wrong, Pike claimed. The internal message being circulated by the Party was "the U.S. is our enemy, the world's enemy; and we will bury the U.S., or at least hope to do so."[46] The evidence offered for these sentiments was scant, with Pike referring to a few scattered editorials in *Nhan Dan,* the official Party newspaper. More troubling were Pike's claims that Hanoi was still solely focused on economic aid ("privately labeled war reparations"). That Vietnam had dropped its precondition of aid since the previous spring was completely ignored in the report. At the same time, Pike grossly minimized the ongoing American hostility toward Vietnam; the only mention of the U.S. sanctions program was when he noted that "certain legal prohibitions exist on U.S. money or goods going to Vietnam." [47]

This rather sudden shift in Pike's thinking could be explained, it would seem, by his politics, and his concern that the United States was perhaps moving close to normalization with Hanoi. Pike had long been strongly anti-Communist, and made no secret of his feelings in his published work. In the preface to his 1966 book, *Viet Cong,* Pike wrote that "Victory by the Communists would mean consigning thousands of Vietnamese, many of them of course my friends, to death, prison, or permanent exile," and that "If America betrays the Vietnamese people by abandoning them, she betrays her own heritage." [48] Pike had also been a vocal opponent of the Vietnamese Communist Party, and in this case, at least, his politics may have bested his scholarship. Despite the anti-Vietnamese tone of the report, however, Pike's overall assessment of the Cambodia situation remained unchanged: the most likely outcome of the border conflict was "indeterminate," a stalemate.[49]

In late 1978, this was the accepted wisdom and sentiment about Vietnam in Congress: the Vietnamese, for a number of reasons, were still undeserving of American aid or trade, and, although the border conflict with Cambodia was a source of concern, it was unlikely that Vietnam would invade and begin a protracted occupation. Furthermore, Pike and the various congressional committees recognized that the development most likely to change the situation in Cambodia was a change of Cambodian leadership. As we have seen, few if any in Washington considered that a likely possibility. The world would find out soon enough how wrong these assumptions were.

When the United States made its choice, moving toward normalization with China, Hanoi made its own final decision. On October 30, Holbrooke's assistant, Robert Oakley, informed the Vietnamese delegation in New York that the United States could not proceed on normalization because of the situation in Cambodia, the refugee crisis, and Vietnamese-Soviet ties.[50] On November 1, Thach met Le Duan, Pham Van Dong, and other Vietnamese leaders in Moscow. The next day, the two nations signed a twenty-five-year "Treaty of Friendship and Co-Operation," which included provisions for military assistance to Vietnam in the event of an attack or "the threat of an attack."[51] That same day, Carter's proposal for normalization with China, still unknown to the American public, reached Deng Xiaoping, who had recently solidified control of the Chinese Communist Party. The terms offered, as Nayan Chanda has observed, were almost identical to those rejected by China a year earlier, including those on the delicate question of American military support for Taiwan. Faced with the prospect of a potential Soviet military threat in the region, however, and poised for a confrontation with Vietnam, Deng realized that normalization with the United States should happen quickly. China and the United States would normalize relations before the end of the year.[52]

Between December 1978 and February 1979, the entire landscape of Southeast Asia was rapidly transformed. On December 2, Hanoi announced the formation of the Kampuchea National United Front for National Salvation, working to remove the Pol Pot regime from power. On December 15, the United States and China announced their normalization of relations. By then, two Vietnamese divisions were already encamped well into Cambodian territory. On December 25, another eleven divisions poured across the border and began to cut swiftly through the countryside; Khmer Rouge forces hastily retreated. As the Vietnamese forces closed in on the capital, they discovered a wealth of unused Chinese-supplied military equipment, including a fleet of MiG aircraft; two more Chinese ships loaded with weapons and ammunition, it was later revealed, were en route to Cambodia at the time of the invasion. The Khmer Rouge's peasant army, Nayan Chanda later wrote, "knew how to kill with machetes but had not had time to learn to fly fighter planes or man antiaircraft guns."[53] On January 7, Vietnamese forces consolidated control of an again abandoned Phnom Penh; the Khmer Rouge leaders and their Chinese advisers had fled to the Thai border. On January 14, Thai, Chinese, and Khmer Rouge leaders agreed upon a plan to wage a guerilla war against the Vietnamese.[54] The invasion no one had predicted, yet which many feared, had come. Another invasion was on the horizon, but it would not take the United States so nearly by surprise.

As President Deng Xiaoping flew to Washington in January of 1979 to celebrate the normalization of relations with the United States, American intelligence was monitoring massive movements of Chinese troops to their southern border. By the end of the month well over two hundred thousand troops were poised along the border with Vietnam. Various members of the Carter administration reiterated several times in late 1978 that the United States would "not take sides" in the burgeoning war between Cambodia and Vietnam, anticipating the moral dilemma that would confront the administration if forced to choose between accepting an aggressive Vietnamese incursion and backing the return to power of the genocidal Khmer Rouge. That already difficult position was only worsened with what appeared to be a likely Chinese invasion of Vietnam. Rather than put normalization at risk, the Carter administration chose to "wink" at China's invasion plans. Meanwhile, the Chinese had been publicly denouncing the Vietnamese invasion of Cambodia, informing the world that they planned on "teaching Vietnam a lesson." Deng repeated these statements during his visit, both in the Oval Office with Carter and at a press conference later that day. Officially, Carter urged Deng to exercise restraint with regard to Vietnam, but the recommendation was hollow at best.[55]

On February 17, 1979, the Chinese army swept across the Vietnamese border and began its brief punitive action, a two-week invasion of Vietnam that was later described by Chanda as a "pedagogical war" designed to teach a stern "lesson" to an insolent nation. The United States called for an emergency meeting of the United Nations Security Council and the removal of both Vietnamese troops from Cambodia and Chinese troops from Vietnam.[56] It is clear from its statements describing the Chinese response as a logical outcome of Vietnam's invasion of Cambodia, however, that the administration continued to view Vietnam as the primary aggressor in the region.[57] Like China and the Soviets, the United States expressed little interest in the actual situation in Cambodia, continuing to use the nation, in Michael Haas's analogy, as a superpower "chessboard," with the Vietnamese and Cambodian people as their pawns.

THE VIETNAMESE OCCUPATION

The Chinese forces withdrew from northern Vietnam in March of 1979, leaving tens of thousands dead on both sides. The destruction in Vietnam went beyond casualties, however. Government officials and sources on the ground in the north estimated that close to a million people had been displaced as a result of the attack, and 85,000 hectares of badly needed rice fields destroyed, along with several hundred thousand cattle and water buffalo. Bridges, factories, farms, and mineral mines were obliterated or crippled by the invasion. Although the destruction wrought by the Chinese dealt a severe blow to an already weak Vietnamese infrastructure, it stopped short of being fatal. Maintaining the threat of another invasion, Beijing announced upon its withdrawal that it "reserved the right" to "teach Vietnam another lesson."[58]

If there was, indeed, a lesson taught to the Vietnamese by the Chinese invasion, it remains unclear what that lesson was. Although it caused further injury to an already unstable Vietnamese economy and devastated a large portion of its northern infrastructure, the invasion had no measurable effect on the situation in Cambodia. If anything, it confirmed for the Vietnamese leadership what many already believed to be true: that Vietnam was surrounded by hostile regimes and that China in particular was bent on undermining Vietnamese independence. Nayan Chanda has wondered whether it was not China that had learned a lesson. "Far from diverting troops from Cambodia, a cocky Vietnamese leadership did not even send regular troops to the border, leaving the job instead to the militia and regional forces." Yet China was unable to secure a victory over such opposition, suffering comparable losses and coming to the realization that its own armed forces were "not able to conduct a modern war."[59] The Vietnamese, however, remained convinced for several years that another round of military engagement with China was inevitable. The question in Hanoi was no longer if, but "how and when" China would attack again.[60]

In Cambodia the occupation continued, unhindered by the events on Vietnam's northern border. A 1979 United Nations report acknowledged that, although the Cambodian people continued to suffer, given the horrors that preceded the occupation, "the Vietnamese army was and is still welcomed as the liberator of a nightmare."[61] In fact, while it was clearly not their primary goal in invading Cambodia, the Vietnamese had been successful in what no other nations were willing to take on: halting the Cambodian genocide. Unfortunately, this positive outcome would be tempered in perception by international concern over possible Vietnamese designs on other neighboring countries, particularly Thailand, and in reality by the ongoing suffering of the Cambodian people. While there is little question that the majority of Cambodian citizens were better off under Vietnamese rule than they had been under the Khmer Rouge, a host of new problems quickly emerged. When the Vietnamese removed Pol Pot from power, the Cambodian people, who had suffered under the Khmer Rouge for nearly four years, were suddenly freed from the forced agricultural collectives, allowed to return to their homes and search for their families. This newfound freedom, however, went along with the harsh reality of occupation. With the almost instant, large-scale abandonment of collective agricultural production, the famine only worsened. Most of the 1979 crop was lost.[62] Mass starvation accompanied by death on an unfathomable scale was, sadly, nothing new to Cambodians. Ironically enough, it was the Vietnamese invasion that brought the suffering of the Cambodian people to the attention of the West, including the United States government.

In the fall of 1979, a delegation from the U.S. Senate visited the vast refugee camps along the Thai-Cambodian border to witness the devastation firsthand. They informed the governing authorities that their interests were purely humanitarian, stressing that they "were not interested in political considerations."[63] The politics of food were inextricably tied to the politics of regime recognition during the occupation, which meant that the Cambodian people would once again be held hostage by geopolitical considerations. To provide food through Phnom Penh was seen by some as a boon to the Vietnamese-backed regime; to run the food through Thailand into the refugee camps would provide aid to the Khmer Rouge forces that had made the camps their own.[64] The leaders in Hanoi and Phnom Penh were deeply suspicious of aid, and were unwilling to have it funneled through the Thai border area. They suspected—rightly, as it turned out—that food-based aid would easily turn into financial and military aid to the Khmer Rouge resistance. In Cambodia in the late 1970s and 1980s, food was power, and it was, as one U.S. senator put it, "being used as a weapon by all factions."[65]

Although rationally suspicious of some Western aid overtures, the Vietnamese leadership did play a shameful role in actually obstructing humanitarian aid during the occupation. Aside from other abominable practices, such as the development of permanent Vietnamese settlements inside Cambodian territory, the Vietnamese and their Soviet allies regularly denied even the possibility of widespread starvation and famine in the initial years of occupation.[66] Meanwhile, refugees, reporters, and aid workers accused the Vietnamese-led forces of using starvation as a political and military tactic to consolidate their hold on the countryside.[67] There is little question that, while the Cambodian people starved, they were forced to send both rice and fish to feed Vietnamese citizens.[68]

Such policies only invited and sharpened criticism of Vietnam's presence in Cambodia. The Vietnamese had once again failed to accurately gauge the tide of opinion in the international arena. As Elizabeth Becker wrote, "While it is clear Cambodia started the border war with Vietnam, it is less obvious why Vietnam interpreted that challenge as an invitation to invade and occupy Cambodia." Her account, and others, make it clear that a complex mixture of sociohistorical and political reasons can at least in part explain the invasion and occupation—but, the longer the Vietnamese occupation went on, the more obscured those reasons became. Increasingly, the Vietnamese occupation of Cambodia (or Kampuchea) was causing the history of both the Second and Third Indochina Wars to be revised.

Once the victim of a devastating and famously undeclared war at the hands of the United States, Vietnam was now derided as the aggressor, confirming, to many longtime critics, that Hanoi was bent on dominating all of Southeast Asia. Whereas a year earlier even Douglas Pike had testified to Congress that the Vietnamese were in a particularly difficult position, with few good options available, he was now blaming the Vietnamese for the entire Third Indochina War. "Vietnam's war with Cambodia and takeover of Laos," he wrote in a June 1979 report to the House Committee on Foreign Affairs, "triggered hostile Chinese behavior, which caused Vietnam and the U.S.S.R. to move closer together, which in turn caused concern in Japan, Southeast Asia, and the United States."[69] It is worth recalling that a year earlier, several members of Congress had largely agreed with Pike that ridding the world of Pol Pot and the Khmer Rouge would, at least, be a beneficial outcome of a Vietnamese-sponsored revolution in Cambodia. A year into the Vietnamese occupation, though, Congress debated the situation as if the Khmer Rouge was no longer an issue, and as if the paramount goal of policy should be to remove the Vietnamese from Cambodia, regardless of the consequences.

The invasion and occupation succeeded, then, in obscuring the horrors of the Khmer Rouge rule of Cambodia. In Southeast Asia, Vietnam was now viewed by its neighbors "with revulsion," as "a country which has installed its own puppet regime, an action which completely overshadows the fact that the Pol Pot regime was one of the most despicable ever to reign in Asia."[70] This only benefited the Khmer Rouge. Shortly after the Vietnamese invasion, the same Thai government against which the Khmer Rouge had spent several years launching unprovoked attacks offered Foreign Minister Ieng Sary an armed escort to secure his passage to a United Nations meeting. William Shawcross offered a particularly vivid description of the event: "In a first-class cabin, being plied with champagne, went the man who, until a few days earlier had been reviled as a leader of one of the most vicious regimes in the world—a regime, moreover, that prided itself on abjuring most of the world. Until now the Khmer Rouge leadership had been mass murderers. Now they were also a government that had been overthrown by a regime seen as a surrogate of the Soviet Union."[71] Amnesia regarding the Khmer Rouge's program of auto-genocide spread across the globe as the Vietnamese occupation lengthened. "Much of the world—not just the Western World and ASEAN," Shawcross wrote, "has chosen to see the Khmer Rouge first as the defenders of national sovereignty rather than as the perpetrators of massive crimes against man."[72]

The Vietnamese occupation of Cambodia and the Chinese invasion of Vietnam had the effect of internationalizing what many nations, including the United States, had wished to relegate to being a regional conflict. The United Nations became, in the 1980s, a battleground for deciding the future of Cambodia, and, by extension, of Vietnam as well. For most of the world's nations—nearly all of which had established relations with Vietnam, yet with many recognizing the Khmer Rouge as well—the situation required a new approach appropriate to the complexity of the situation. For the United States, the Cambodian question was framed by several years of relations and negotiations with Vietnam: the question was whether it would be better for the United States to recognize Vietnam, and thus have a political and economic presence in Hanoi to exert leverage on Vietnamese policy, or to isolate the country on all fronts while using steps to normalization as reward for actions and policies that pleased Washington. As it turned out, although the situation in Southeast Asia had radically changed since the American withdrawal from Vietnam, U.S. policy would remain the same: an aggressive, hostile program that sought to isolate Vietnam politically, economically, and diplomatically.

BLEEDING VIETNAM

The primary diplomatic battle over the Third Indochina War revolved around an issue that was at one level largely symbolic, and, at another, of the utmost political significance: which regime would be seated as the Cambodian delegation to the United Nations. The UN had already spent considerable time debating the situation in Cambodia after the Vietnamese and Chinese invasions. In the Security Council and the General Assembly, the Vietnamese and their allies in the Soviet bloc initially argued for the UN to leave the situation alone while the Chinese drafted a Security Council resolution calling for United Nations intervention. After the Chinese invasion of Vietnam, however, the Soviets drafted a new resolution calling for the withdrawal of Chinese troops and the payment of reparations to Vietnam. Deadlocked by mutual vetoes and a divided Security Council, no progress was made in either direction.[73]

The issue of seating the Cambodian delegation was far more complicated, for it forced nations either to take sides in the war or remain staunchly neutral. The Vietnamese had been attempting to promote international acceptance of the People's Republic of Kampuchea (PRK) since the fall of Phnom Penh, but only the Soviet bloc and a few members of the nonaligned movement had formally recognized the Heng Samrin–led regime. In September of 1979, the United Nations for the first time took up the issue of seating the PRK in place of the Khmer Rouge delegation. The Credentials Committee, on which a United States representative sat, was the first to weigh in on the matter, voting on its recommendation to the General Assembly, which would in turn be voting later in the month.

Thus the United States, still smarting a bit from the embarrassment of the Chinese invasion following so closely upon the heels of normalization between the two nations, was placed in yet another awkward situation. It was forced to choose between Vietnam, the nation it had spurned, ignored, and punished over the past several years, and the Khmer Rouge, the group that only a year earlier President Carter labeled "the worst violator of human rights in the world today."[74] The United States had four options: it could vote in favor of the Vietnamese-sponsored PRK, which would certainly anger the Chinese and the ASEAN nations, all of which had been vocal in their opposition to the Vietnamese occupation; it could vote to seat the Khmer Rouge, which would demonstrate support for the China/ASEAN position, but also signify support for the murderous regime; it could vote to leave the seat empty until such time as the situation in Cambodia was resolved, a stance seen by many as lending legitimacy to the Vietnamese occupation and leaving the Cambodian people without representation; and, finally, the United States could abstain from the vote, which would likely displease both ASEAN and China, but lend credence to the Carter administration's supposed stance of neutrality on the issue.

Secretary of State Vance was reportedly "agonized" by the decision, but ultimately joined Brzezinski in recommending that the United States vote to seat the Pol Pot delegation as the representative of the Cambodian people in the United Nations.[75] The Credentials Committee agreed, voting 6–3 to recommend to the General Assembly that it accept the Democratic Kampuchea regime as the legitimate government of Cambodia, which the assembly did on September 21 by a vote of 71–35 with 34 abstentions. The United States again cast its vote in favor of the Khmer Rouge—a vote that, in Chanda's words, "linked U.S. support to a murderous group with whom U.S. officials were forbidden to shake hands," and a position for which many in Congress now sought an explanation.[76]

A week after the UN vote, Assistant Secretary of State Holbrooke appeared at a Senate hearing about the situation in Southeast Asia. Although the hearings were ostensibly about the refugee crisis, the subcommittee members inquired about other matters, including the administration's vote to support the Khmer Rouge delegation. Chairman John Glenn asked why the United States did not abstain from the vote, inferring that "we indicated by our vote that we supported Pol Pot at the United Nations, and that sort of flies in the face of our human rights emphasis around the rest of the world."[77] Holbrooke responded that an abstention would have meant

> a public break with the policies that we, the ASEAN countries, Japan, Australia, New Zealand, and the People's Republic, have all followed in regard to the representation question. The costs of that would have been very great for our foreign policy. At the same time, we felt that any vote should not be misunderstood as implying any sort of support for Pol Pot. Therefore, our delegates in New York were instructed to deliver what some people described as a clothespin vote—you hold your nose and vote. We were voting only for the claim of this delegation to sit for Kampuchea at this time. We made it clear again and again that this regime is not acceptable to us or to the [Khmer] people, and that we will not recognize it or have anything to do with it.[78]

A vote for abstention, Holbrooke concluded, "would have put us on the side of Moscow and Vietnam."[79]

The position of the Carter administration regarding the issue of UN representation for Cambodia was thus not a departure in policy at all. Having for the past four years refused to "recognize" Vietnam in its own right, the administration was certainly not about to recognize what was clearly viewed as a Vietnamese puppet regime in Cambodia. Moreover, as they had for the past several years, the White House and Congress refused to move toward policies that would, even at a secondary level, indicate even the most minute acceptance of the Vietnamese government. Holbrooke's statement that the Khmer Rouge regime "is not acceptable to us," and that "we will not recognize it or have anything to do with it," could easily be confused with the government's stance toward Vietnam.

The following year, Holbrooke once again appeared before a congressional committee to update them on the status of the Cambodian situation. The discussion largely focused on the refugee issue, but the hearings also dealt with military and political developments. Senator Glenn's statement in opening the hearings indicated the U.S. government's overriding perception of the situation: that Vietnam's occupation was one of three "separate but interrelated dangers" threatening the region. The second was "the turmoil and upheavals" the invasion had caused to the agricultural system, which were leading to widespread famine. The third danger was "Vietnam's harsh policies and conflict with China," which had led to the refugee crisis.[80] Conspicuous in its absence from this list of dangers was the danger posed by the return to power of the Khmer Rouge, who continued to use the refugee camps along the Thai border as a base camp for much of their activity.

This view was essentially echoed by Holbrooke, who informed the committee that the administration "would not oppose" a coalition government that included the Khmer Rouge. The problem, he pointed out, was that neither the Khmer Rouge nor the Heng Samrin government were interested in a coalition government at the time. The administration's belief, Holbrooke went on to explain, was that the Democratic Party of Kampuchea regime would not survive without the maintenance of large numbers of occupying Vietnamese troops. The Vietnamese-backed regime was only able to muster what popular support it had, he argued, because of the lingering fear of the return of the Khmer Rouge; the "unifying symbol" of Pol Pot had been exploited by the Heng Samrin regime "to coalesce opposition to a commonly hated foe."[81] The administration was essentially arguing that the Vietnamese *needed* the Khmer Rouge as an enemy to help consolidate their hold on Cambodia, the same way that the Khmer Rouge had needed Vietnam as an external threat to help secure their revolutionary program years earlier. The rest of the hearings focused on the logistical difficulties of relief efforts in the region, which was fairly appropriate given that such efforts would remain the only United States engagement with the Third Indochina War for the duration of the Carter administration. In fact, not much movement of any kind would take place in Cambodia, as China and the Soviet Union continued to funnel millions of dollars into the region to prolong the stalemated proxy war.

For the first several months of the Reagan administration there was little or no mention of the war at all. On the campaign trail, Reagan had offered sharp criticisms of the Carter administration's hypocrisy in decrying the Khmer Rouge regime as the "worst violator of human rights" in the contemporary world, while voting to seat its delegation at the United Nations. In July 1981, at the first International Conference on Kampuchea (ICK), the new administration was given an opportunity to offer its own solution. Instead, the conference demonstrated that Reagan would simply continue the ineffective policies of the previous administration, attempting to have it both ways by publicly offering empty denunciations of the same murderous regime that it continued to support through its diplomacy.

The Khmer Rouge leadership had made for strange bedfellows with nearly any government's representatives, aside, perhaps, from the Chinese. Certainly the spectacle of even a strained alliance between Democratic Kampuchea representatives and Carter administration officials, whose foreign policy rhetoric had been so consumed with issues of human rights, was strange enough. Perhaps the only thing stranger, as William Shawcross pointed out, would be support from Reagan's first secretary of state, Alexander Haig, who a decade earlier had helped orchestrate the American war on Cambodia from inside the Nixon White House. Nevertheless, when the ICK came to New York that summer, Haig quietly helped to organize the administration's policy on Cambodia, with the ultimate result of at least indirect United States support for the Khmer Rouge. Using the language of international law and cloaking their support under the banner of the United Nations charter, the United States and China succeeded at the conference in getting the ASEAN representatives to withdraw provisions both for disarming the Khmer Rouge and establishing an interim government following the Vietnamese withdrawal. The resulting declaration from the conference was a muddled, unclear call for "appropriate measures for the maintenance of law and order."[82]

While the United States let China take the lead in supporting the Khmer Rouge, the American role in the conference was clear: in both word and deed, it had broken from its stated position of supporting the ASEAN policy toward Cambodia and Vietnam in order to placate the Chinese and isolate the Vietnamese. In public, however, the United States continued to express contempt for the Khmer Rouge, such as when Haig led a walkout of the delegation when Ieng Sary addressed the conference. "That bit of theatrics made the front page of the *New York Times,*" an ASEAN delegate to the conference later told Chanda, "but behind the scenes, they pressured us to accept the Chinese position."[83] After the formal negotiations of the ICK wrapped up, the United States delegation, including Haig, spent a good portion of that evening's reception dodging the advances of the Khmer Rouge delegates, who wished to thank the Americans for supporting their cause.[84] The United States' support for the Khmer Rouge, first in the decision to support its claim to the Cambodian seat at the United Nations, and then in helping persuade ASEAN representatives to the ICK that the regime should not be disarmed, was placed at the center of several congressional inquiries over the coming years. Stephen Solarz, a member of the U.S. delegation to the ICK, used his recent rise to chairmanship of the House Subcommittee on Asian and Pacific Affairs as an opportunity to probe and alter American policy toward Cambodia. His first hearing on the matter came only days after the ICK had concluded.

In his opening statement, Solarz expressed his "disappointment" with the American delegation's role at the conference, particularly its "acquiescence" to the final declaration. "What is at stake," he argued at the hearing, "is much more than simply getting Vietnam out of Cambodia. What is at stake is making it possible for the people of Cambodia to determine their own future without fear that Pol Pot and his people will reimpose their authority over them by force of arms . . . There can be little doubt that if the Khmer Rouge were not disarmed, they would promptly march into Phnom Penh and undoubtedly proceed to reimplement their policies of auto genocide. That is something which I think the United States cannot acquiesce in or permit."[85] Over the course of this hearing and those that followed, Solarz continued his passionate attempts to provide for a Cambodia free from both Vietnam and the Khmer Rouge, a goal toward which the Reagan administration, and most other members of Congress, had little interest in actively working. Yet, beginning with this hearing, the positions of Solarz and the White House would begin to converge in the search for an elusive "non-Communist resistance" force to battle the Vietnamese and prevent the return of the Khmer Rouge.

Over the next several months, Solarz continued to explore the possibility of U.S. support for a viable non-Communist Cambodian resistance force (NCR). In October of 1981 he held an extensive, three-day set of hearings on "U.S. Policy toward Indochina since Vietnam's Occupation of Kampuchea." The first round of hearings focused on the existence or potential for the emergence of NCR forces in Vietnam or Cambodia. Testifying were two Vietnamese expatriates—Truong Nhu Tang, a founding member of the National Liberation Front for South Vietnam but now an anti-Hanoi dissident, and Doan Van Thai, author of a book on the "Vietnamese Gulag"—along with David Elliot, a Southeast Asia specialist formerly of the RAND Corporation, and Douglas Pike. Tang and Thai attempted unsuccessfully to convince the committee that the vast majority of the Vietnamese people were ready and willing to take up arms against their own government and "its master—the Soviet Union." Tang, who went on to write a successful book, *A Viet Cong Memoir,* informed representatives that as a former leader of "the present regime of Vietnam," he was certain "that over 90 percent of the Vietnamese people desire to fight against the present regime and Soviet intervention."[86] Thai echoed both the sentiment and the statistic—ninety percent of the Vietnamese people allied against their government—in his remarks.

There was, of course, no such level of support for another revolution in Vietnam, which became clear as the hearing went on. When Solarz queried Elliot and Pike on the "prospects for a viable, non-Communist, indigenous resistance movement" in either Vietnam or Cambodia, both responded that the prospects were "bleak."[87] Returning to Tang, Solarz once again asked for his assessment of the possibility for such forces to develop. Backing off from his earlier statements, Tang acknowledged that although there was actually no current movement, he was "convinced that in time the people will rise to overthrow the regime." "This passive resistance," he argued, "is now turning into armed political violence," but offered no evidence of such a transformation.[88] If Solarz was hoping to uncover a viable Third Force in Southeast Asia, clearly he was going to be disappointed. As these hearings went on the following week, similar testimony emerged from other witnesses who reinforced much of what the committee already knew: that Vietnam would not invade Thailand, that the Soviet presence in Vietnam and Laos was growing, and that there was no viable NCR in the region. Aside from the occasional callous remark, such as Representative Henry Hyde's statement on October 21 that the United States should be "pleased that the Soviets and the Chinese are glaring at each other" in a proxy war in Southeast Asia, rather than funneling those resources into "Western Europe," the hearings went off without much excitement or revelation—until the final day, when Solarz sparred with Assistant Secretary of State John Holdridge.

Solarz began by pressing Holdridge on why the United States should not offer the possibility of normalizing relations with Vietnam in exchange for Hanoi's removing its troops from Cambodia. "[I]f the policy is ultimately going to work," Solarz offered, "it has to include carrots as well as sticks."[89] As Holdridge went on to explain, the position of the White House was that "the Vietnamese have taken whatever carrots have been offered them and then proceeded right along the same lines without any basic adjustments." This problem, he argued, dated at least back to the failure of Hanoi to abide by the terms of the 1973 Paris Accords.[90] Ignoring the numerous gestures toward normalization by the Vietnamese over the years and the far more notable intransigence of the United States, Holdridge pointed out that the removal of Vietnamese troops from Cambodia was not the only obstacle to normalization. Along with the POW/MIA issue, which saw a dramatic resurgence in popular and official attention in the Reagan years, the administration had adopted a policy of withholding normalization as long as Vietnam "generally remains a menace to other countries of the region."[91] Although he insisted that this was not a new policy at all, it was clearly new language, and it serves as useful evidence against later statements that the fate of normalization was not specifically dependent upon the situation in Cambodia.

The more immediate question concerned United States assistance to indigenous Cambodian resistance movements. Although the White House had denied any knowledge of funding of the NCR forces in the region, the increasing discussion of what would come to be called the Reagan Doctrine—funding anti-Communist "freedom fighters" throughout the developing world—lent credence to the idea of arming various factions in the Third Indochina War. Solarz, who was clearly interested in such a proposal, was nevertheless concerned that the Reagan administration had already begun planning covert operations to support anti-Vietnamese forces in Southeast Asia.

SOLARZ: Mr. Secretary, are we considering providing military assistance, directly or indirectly, to any of the resistance movements in Indochina?

HOLDRIDGE: No.

SOLARZ: Not in Cambodia?

HOLDRIDGE: Not in Cambodia.

SOLARZ: In Laos?

HOLDRIDGE: No.

SOLARZ: Vietnam?

HOLDRIDGE: No.

SOLARZ: Then what did you mean in your statement on the trip with Secretary Haig, that we had to put diplomatic, economic, and I think yes, even military pressure on the Vietnamese?

HOLDRIDGE: That was a collective "we," Mr. Chairman. I wasn't talking about the United States . . . If there is military pressure being exerted, that is for others to do.[92]

The issue of military aid to any nation of Southeast Asia had remained a loaded one since the American withdrawal from Vietnam, as had the balance between the executive and legislative branches of government in formulating and implementing foreign policy. Although many in Congress,

Solarz included, were pressing for some type of aid program for some type of Cambodian resistance, they were also apprehensive about the White House acting on such issues without congressional approval.

A year later, in the fall of 1982, the situation in Cambodia had changed, slightly but noticeably. The Vietnamese remained in occupation and the war was still at a stalemate, but a loose coalition, which China and ASEAN had been increasingly pushing for, had finally been established. The Coalition Government of Democratic Kampuchea (CGDK), announced in the spring of 1982, included Son Sann's Khmer People's National Liberation Front (KPNLF), and featured Prince Norodom Sihanouk as a cabinet leader and public face, but there was little question as to who was in charge. The Khmer Rouge, by far the largest and best equipped of the three primary member movements, was the force behind the CGDK.[93] Even with this understood, the formation of the CGDK made an impact on Hanoi, which ceased challenging the Cambodian delegation at the United Nations after 1982. It seems to have had a similar impact within U.S. leadership circles, because by the time Solarz held his last hearing on the question of the UN seat, the focus of debate on American policy had clearly shifted to the question of supporting, and possibly arming, the non-Communist Cambodian resistance.

In the October 1982 hearings Solarz and Holdridge again sparred over the question of Cambodian representation at the United Nations, but saved most of their discussion for gauging the relative viability of the NCR in Cambodia and determining to what extent the United States was supporting that coalition. Holdridge testified that the United States was not providing any military assistance to the KPNLF at that point, but was less clear in response to Solarz's question about more general economic assistance: "We are providing humanitarian assistance to the refugee camps along the border. We are helping feed the Kampucheans who are in the camps whether astride the border or on the Thai side. We are also providing medical assistance, food, clothing, and so on. As I say, we are carefully watching ASEAN, we are considering how we will be of further help. This will not in any event be military assistance. We will not provide assistance of any kind to the Khmer Rouge."[94] As Solarz well knew, however, the Khmer Rouge controlled many of the refugee camps, so a significant amount of international aid flowing through the camps was, in effect, helping to replenish those forces. Solarz pushed Holdridge on this question, accusing him of being unresponsive and avoiding difficult questions.

HOLDRIDGE: I am trying to answer the question as best I can. We do not have a program of assisting the Khmer Rouge. We make refugee supplies available to the international organizations. They in turn distribute them to women and children, some of whom are in camps which are controlled by the Khmer Rouge. Would you prefer the international organizations not to give any aid to women and children?

SOLARZ: If they are in camps controlled by the Khmer Rouge, my answer would be yes.[95]

Solarz suggested that the United States encourage and, where possible, direct the international relief organizations working in the camps to focus on providing aid to camps controlled by the KPNLF, a recommendation that Holdridge rejected as "playing life and death" with the refugees.[96] As the hearings went on, opinions on these matters were solicited from others, including a representative of the KPNLF and a member of an American-based Christian relief organization working in Cambodia, but few offered any evidence that would change Solarz's mind about the current situation in Cambodia.

Solarz's comments throughout the series of hearings he chaired in the early years of the Reagan administration reveal not only his concern for the people of Southeast Asia, but his growing concerns about the direction of the Reagan administration's foreign policy. As it turns out, Solarz was right to be suspicious of the activities of the White House. Although he was clearly not aware of it at the time, the Reagan administration had already begun covert funding of the KPNLF to wage a war of resistance against the Vietnamese occupation. Quietly, invisible to the American public, the American war on Vietnam had entered a more active phase. Moving beyond the political and economic warfare of the late 1970s, during the 1980s the United States began to wage a proxy military battle against Vietnam.

THE REAGAN DOCTRINE AND THE KHMER ROUGE

Unlike the Carter administration, which maintained a stance—in word if not in deed—of neutrality toward the situation in Southeast Asia, the Reagan administration had fewer qualms about providing aid to the Khmer Rouge–led "coalition" in Cambodia. As Christopher Brady argues in his study, *United States Foreign Policy toward Cambodia, 1977–92,* the administration's vision of the Third Indochina War fit perfectly into the world view promoted by the Reagan White House: an expansionist Soviet empire was actively promoting revolution around the globe and had to be turned back.

In spite of this world view, for the first several years of his administration Reagan failed to articulate a clear vision of his foreign policy, particularly with regard to Southeast Asia. While the White House continued to support the seating of the Khmer Rouge delegation at the United Nations, it publicly refused to offer any commitment to aid—military or otherwise—to the KPNLF. Behind the scenes, however, the United States had already begun covert funding of the Khmer Rouge–dominated group. In 1985, as Congress was debating a substantial increase in foreign aid to anti-Communist insurgencies around the world, the *Washington Post* revealed that the KPLNF had been receiving American funds since at least 1982. The story by Charles Babcock and Bob Woodward revealed that "millions of dollars" over several years had been funneled to the group through Thailand.[97] On the day the story ran, Stephen Solarz's office released a statement to the press saying that he would not comment on intelligence matters, but that he remained "fully committed to [his] initiative to provide assistance for the non-Communist Cambodian resistance groups . . . As is the case in Afghanistan, I am convinced that such assistance . . . is in the American interests."[98]

CIA sources for the *Post* article insisted that the aid had not been reaching the Khmer Rouge, but other anonymous sources acknowledged the hollowness of this claim, as well as the larger dilemmas posed by the policy. To begin with, they noted, any aid from the United States freed up the recipient's other resources for military expenditure, rendering the distinction between "lethal" and "nonlethal" aid irrelevant. Furthermore, several of those involved in the program recognized that their attempt to strengthen the "non-Communist" elements of the coalition was unlikely to succeed. One "informed source" told the authors, "if the coalition wins, the Khmer Rouge will eat the others alive."[99] The goal of the United States, however, was never victory for the KPNLF. Rather, as became clear during the mid-1980s, the goal of the United States was to "bleed Vietnam white" on the fields of Cambodia, much as it had been bleeding Vietnam economically and diplomatically during the decade since it withdrew its forces.

Supporters of this policy, from congressmen like Solarz to various administration officials, reiterated this goal often. Paul Wolfowitz, then a deputy secretary of state for Asian and Pacific affairs, told the House Appropriations Committee in 1985 that the United States' goal for the KPNLF was "definitely not a military victory and no one is deluded enough to think the Vietnamese are going to be beaten militarily."[100] Solarz echoed these statements months later in a response to a *New York Times* op-ed criticizing his support of the Cambodian resistance. The purpose in providing overt aid to the KPNLF, Solarz wrote, was not "to win a war," as the previous piece had argued. "Not even the non-Communist resistance groups believe it is possible to achieve military victory . . . But there is unlikely to be progress at the negotiating table unless Vietnam faces greater difficulty on the battlefield."[101] With a working majority in Congress supporting the goal of aiding the KPNLF, the bleeding of Vietnam thus became policy. With the full backing of the White House, it became part of a doctrine.

First declared in the 1985 State of the Union address and further articulated in several speeches and statements by various administration officials that year, the Reagan Doctrine was an updated policy of supporting proxy wars around the world. As Mark Lagon explains in his study of the doctrine, "the Reagan administration declared that it reserved the right to aid insurgent 'freedom fighters' against pro-Soviet regimes recently established in the Third World."[102] The point of the Reagan Doctrine was to aid and abet such insurgencies around the globe without the direct involvement of U.S. forces; to bleed the target regimes slowly and painfully rather than seek a swift military victory. As *Newsweek* put it in late 1985, " the Reagan doctrine is a policy of harassing the Soviets on peripheral battlefields—and of doing it on the cheap, without any commitment of U.S. forces."[103] Because of the lack of direct U.S. involvement, the policy was widely acceptable at home and solicited little sustained attention, positive or negative, among the American public. The wars waged under the mantra of the Reagan Doctrine were not meant to be covert; they were publicly defended and justified by the White House and its congressional allies. But neither were they meant to garner much public attention. Painless, cost-effective, and nearly invisible to the American public, the wars of the Reagan era were designed to be everything the American war in Vietnam was not.

The biggest problem with the government's policy, however, was that it was still embedded within the binary logic of the cold war, imposing a Manichean framework on a variety of nations, regions, and regimes that often did not fit the world view of the Reagan administration. Under such a framework, it was possible for many policymakers to turn a blind eye to the seedy coalitions within which the Reagan Doctrine placed the United States. In dealings with the formative elements of what would become the Taliban in Afghanistan, the murderous Khmer Rouge, or similar client forces around the globe, the true character of the "allies" of the United States during the 1980s was always of secondary interest in the struggle against opposing Soviet proxy forces. Cambodia, in particular, was a place where simplistic distinctions were exploited and the lines always blurred. Whether they were framed as a choice between humanitarian aid and development aid, between the "non-Communist resistance" and the Khmer Rouge, or between lethal and nonlethal aid, binary constructions of the issues and actors involved could not explain away the exceedingly complex and muddled alliances formed on the killing fields of Cambodia.[104] Although it clearly remained on the periphery of American foreign policy and public discourse, the situation in Cambodia would continue to be marked by the broad footprint of the United States.

In the summer of 1985, the revelation that covert aid had long been funneled from the United States to the Khmer Rouge caused little more than a brief distraction, as foreign aid negotiations went on in Washington. That covert funding was being directed to the Contra forces in Nicaragua would create a major scandal for the administration in the following year, but the Cambodian aid situation was barely a blip on the radar in 1985. Although there are several reasons for the difference in reaction to the two situations, the most significant was that congressional leaders and the White House had forged a certain consensus on the issue of aid to Cambodia, even as most Democrats, at least, in Congress, including Solarz, continued to oppose funding of anti-Sandinista forces in Central America.[105] Having long pushed for more funding to Cambodian resistance movements, Solarz won enough allies in the summer of 1985 to secure funding to KPNLF-identified entities during the appropriations process for FY 1986. Earlier that spring, Solarz had begun a major lobbying effort for his amendment to any foreign aid bill, one that would provide significant overt aid to the KPNLF. In a letter to Dante Fascell, chair of the House Committee on Foreign Affairs, Assistant Secretary of State for Legislative Affairs William Ball informed the committee that the administration would support the amendment "as an important signal to Hanoi regarding Congressional and public attitudes toward Vietnam's illegal occupation of Cambodia and the threat it poses to its neighbors."[106] Congress eventually passed the measure, including Solarz's proposal. Although the White House threatened to veto the final version of the bill because it did not include enough military aid to other regions and countries, the funding was eventually approved—and the United States began *overt* funding of the Khmer Rouge–led KPNLF. The Cambodian forces received $5 million, a third of the sum appropriated for the anti-Soviet factions in Afghanistan.[107] Now with triangulated support from all three major powers, the war in Cambodia would remain mired in stalemate for several more years.

STALEMATE BY PROXY

Even by the standards of official Cambodian-American relations, the extent to which the Third Indochina War remained a sideshow in American society during the 1980s is remarkable. Rendered invisible by the administration's other wars, and by the Iran-Contra scandal in particular, the Third Indochina War dragged on and on in a proxy stalemate. By the end of the Reagan administration, the United States had been funding the anti-Vietnamese forces, including the Khmer Rouge, for the better part of a decade. The overt support for these forces, including the possibility that American aid was being funneled to the Khmer Rouge, had been public knowledge since 1985, as was the fact that covert aid had been sent since 1982. Neither the publicity surrounding 1984's *The Killing Fields,* a film depicting the Cambodian genocide, nor the enormity of the Iran-Contra scandal succeeded in arousing the American public's ire over their government's support of the Khmer Rouge. Oddly, however, in the latter part of the decade, as the Vietnamese were finally withdrawing their military forces from Cambodia, another round of hearings in Congress and a series of news pieces focused on the problems encountered by the United States' aid programs in Cambodia. In fact, the issue of U.S. aid in the region received more attention from 1988 through 1990 than it had at any point since 1975.

In June and July of 1988, Solarz convened another round of hearings devoted to the situation in Cambodia. These hearings, more than any others discussed in this chapter, demonstrate the deep contradictions of U.S. policy toward Southeast Asia during the 1980s. The hearings were designed ostensibly to debate a joint resolution pending in the House, authored by Chester Atkins of Massachusetts, calling for the United States, "in cooperation with the international community," to "use all means available to prevent a return to power of Pol Pot, the top echelon of the Khmer Rouge, and their armed forces so that the Cambodian people might genuinely be free to pursue self-determination without the specter of the coercion, intimidation, and torture that are known elements of the Khmer Rouge ideology."[108] As the hearings made clear, however, the United States had no intention of backing up this sentiment. Despite numerous statements to the contrary by representatives of the White House as well as several congressional allies, it became evident during these sessions that a lingering hostility toward the Vietnamese, rather than any concern for the nation or people of Cambodia, was driving United States policy toward the region.

After testimony was heard from Dith Pran and Haing Ngor of *Killing Fields* fame, as well as from Kitty Dukakis, human rights activist and then wife of the Democratic nominee for president, Michael Dukakis, various administration officials appeared to discuss the administration's aims for Cambodia. Deputy Assistant Secretary of State David Lambertson expressed "uncertainty" about the extent of the Vietnamese withdrawal. He went on to argue that the White House was simply following the ASEAN-led policy of "isolating Vietnam economically and diplomatically." This was hardly ASEAN's policy, however. Most ASEAN nations had resumed trade with Vietnam by the late 1980s, as had France and Japan. Each ASEAN member also had some degree of diplomatic presence in Hanoi at the time. Lambertson pressed his case, however, claiming that the administration was determined to follow a policy of "'no trade, no aid, and no normal relations' except in the context of a political settlement and an end of Vietnam's occupation of Cambodia."[109] This policy, he continued, did not "reflect any lingering animus toward Vietnam resulting from the war. They are not a function of *what Vietnam did* in 1975, but of what it is doing right now—occupying militarily a once sovereign neighbor. The United States indeed looks forward to the time when we will be able to *resume* normal relations with Vietnam. We have made it clear that we in fact will be prepared to do so in the context of an acceptable Cambodian settlement which provides for the withdrawal of all Vietnamese forces."[110] Given the relations between the United States and Vietnam since 1975, it is difficult to accept Lambertson's premise that the policy of bleeding Vietnam was not based on "lingering animus." The economic and diplomatic war against Vietnam had begun long before the invasion and occupation of Cambodia. The invasion was simply the latest in a long series of justifications used by various administrations to continue a hostile policy. Furthermore, the United States had never had "normal relations" with Vietnam, so "resume" was at the very least a poor choice of verb in that context.

What is most remarkable about Lambertson's testimony, however, is that it all but ignores the issue on which the hearings were supposed to focus: preventing the return to power by the Khmer Rouge. When Lambertson and other administration officials spoke of an "acceptable settlement" in Cambodia, they focused their attention almost solely on the issue of the Vietnamese withdrawal. In his testimony, Deputy Assistant Secretary of Defense Karl Jackson argued even more strongly in favor of keeping the status quo policy toward Vietnam. Jackson claimed, without any evidence, that "the concerted Western diplomatic and trade embargo" had been successful, and that the United States "should resist all moves to normalize relations or to ease the trade embargo unless and until a satisfactory solution has been found to the Cambodian problem."[111] Like Lambertson's, Jackson's definition of a "satisfactory" solution did not concern itself with the status of the Khmer Rouge forces.

By the summer of 1988, however, the Vietnamese were clearly in the process of ending their occupation. Even if some in Washington remained "uncertain" about the scope and speed of the withdrawal, they admitted that the process was well under way. Yet, despite the fact that the line from Hanoi had remained the same for several years—Vietnam would end its occupation of Cambodia when the remnants of the Khmer Rouge had been eradicated and there was no possibility of their return to power—this goal was far from accomplished. Largely because of aid from China and the United States, Pol Pot's regime remained a major force inside Cambodia. As the Vietnamese continued to demand throughout the period of withdrawal that the Khmer Rouge be excluded from any political settlement, China continued to press strongly for their inclusion.

This was a moment for the other players, particularly the superpowers that had been prolonging the bloody conflict for a decade, to make a concerted effort to keep the Khmer Rouge from returning. In such a situation, with Vietnam already pulling out of Cambodia, it could not have been seen in any way as mollifying the Vietnamese for the United States to push the international community (especially China and U.S. allies in Southeast Asia) to help bar the Khmer Rouge from returning to power or disrupting national elections. The representatives from the Reagan administration, however, told Congress that it was "very hard" to "describe certain scenarios" leading to the exclusion of the Khmer Rouge from any negotiated settlement, even though a variety of proposals had been made at the United Nations and by the Vietnamese.

Despite the administration's reluctance to take a strong stance against the Khmer Rouge, a resolution calling for the United States to oppose their return to power was eventually passed by Congress—and signed into law by President Reagan in October of 1988.[112] Unsurprisingly, this represented more of a symbolic gesture than a significant policy shift. The administration continued to ignore calls to pressure China and Thailand to end their aid programs, and it continued to ignore and isolate Vietnam. Dating from its decision to back the Chinese invasion of Vietnam, through the 1981 International Conference on Kampuchea, through a decade of warfare that remained largely invisible to the American public and most of the Western world, the United States had displayed an absence of substantive policy rather than any coherent approach to Southeast Asia. Now, in the fall of 1988, as yet another administration stood poised to take the reigns in Washington, Vietnam and Cambodia continued to bleed.

The 1988 hearings about the situation in Cambodia did help to bring some attention to U.S. involvement in the Third Indochina War. In October, the *New York Times* and the *Washington Post* each ran a series of articles devoted to the role of the United States vis-à-vis the Cambodian coalition. At the center of this story was the enigmatic Prince Norodom Sihanouk, whose complicated relationship with the United States stretched back to the 1950s. In Washington at the time to visit the Reagan administration, Sihanouk told a group at the Carnegie Endowment that China's recently reported decreases in aid to the prince's forces and allies had not hurt the coalition, because they were still "getting some weapons and ammunitions and equipment" from "some countries." Although he initially stopped short of stating that the United States was offering military assistance, Sihanouk later said that administration officials had promised political, diplomatic, and "material" aid to the non-Communist forces in Cambodia—all of which forms of assistance, he insinuated, had long been provided already "via Thailand."[113]

Two weeks later the *Post* highlighted a serious scandal in the Cambodian aid program, revealing that over $3.5 million in covert funding to the anti-Vietnamese forces had been embezzled by Thai military officers. According to the report, the 1988 budget for the covert aid program—which it called "the least controversial and least known of the Reagan administration's secret operations"—was around $12 million. The Thai scandal resulted in a decrease in congressional funding to the Cambodian program the following year, from $12 to $8 million.[114] The *Times* ran a similar story a few days later, reiterating many of the points made in the *Post*. "Because the program is the least contentious of the Reagan administration's covert aid programs," it noted, "and complements overt assistance of $3.5 million a year approved by Congress in 1985, it has received little publicity over the years."[115]

These articles are instructive for at least two reasons. First, both stories maintain the arbitrary distinction between "lethal" and "nonlethal" aid, relying on administration assurances that it was only providing "nonlethal" aid to the coalition. This distinction, a hallmark of policy debates about the

Cambodian situation dating back to the earliest congressional hearings on the Khmer Rouge, remained as hollow in 1988 as it had in 1978. When coalition members received nonlethal aid from the United States, that freed up resources or allowed other allies and donors to provide the "lethal aid" the forces required. Second, the articles both mention in passing that the covert aid program run by CIA operatives working on the Thailand-Cambodia border was uncontroversial. The *Post's* claim that the Cambodian aid program was both the least controversial and the least known of the Reagan Doctrine's proxy wars begs the question as to whether there is not some relationship between the media's complicity in silence about the situation in Cambodia and the government's role in prolonging that war. The *Times* went a step further, and in a sense rendered the question irrelevant, by claiming that the program had received such scant attention over the years *because* it was "the least contentious" of the many proxy fights waged by the Reagan White House. These statements defy logic as well as the historical record. We know, for instance, that even in the midst of the relative consensus that emerged around U.S. policy toward Cambodia in the 1980s, there were significant differences over the scope, scale, and target of aid to the anti-Vietnamese forces. The circular logic of these pieces not only seeks to justify the American role in prolonging the Third Indochina War, it also implicitly exonerates the American press for its own role in helping to maintain the war's invisibility and the American role in it.

THE SIDESHOW GOES ON

Contention over U.S. policy toward Cambodia continued to be evident in future hearings on the scope and nature of American aid, particularly as the first Bush administration wavered on supporting a coalition that included the Khmer Rouge. In a series of congressional hearings debating appropriations for overt and covert aid to the NCR, the same battles over indirect aid to the Khmer Rouge and their involvement in a coalition government continued to be waged.[116] In early 1990 these tensions came to a head when ABC News aired a special program, "From the Killing Fields." Hosted by Peter Jennings, the report argued that the United States was aiding the return to power of the Khmer Rouge by funneling aid to Sihanouk and his allies. The special was followed by a two-hour "town meeting" on Cambodia, titled "Beyond Vietnam." This portion of the program included a live studio audience and a wide array of guests, from important policymakers such as Richard Holbrooke and Stephen Solarz to figures such as Senator John McCain, General William Westmoreland, and Dith Pran.

The first segment of the program, the special report on U.S. aid to Cambodia, featured interviews with Sihanouk, deputy secretary of state for the Bush administration Richard Solomon, former CIA Director William Colby, and Representative Chester Atkins. Sihanouk, as he had for several years, claimed that the United States was supplying both lethal and nonlethal aid to his forces, an argument backed up by interviews with aid workers on the ground in Cambodia. When he confronted Solomon with Sihanouk's claims, Jennings asked the secretary what the Bush administration would do if they "found out" that the non-Communist resistance and the Khmer Rouge were, as Sihanouk claimed, fighting "side by side" using American military aid. In a telling slip, Solomon responded that if the administration discovered "a violation of the law, we would cut off arms," although he had previously denied that the United States was supplying lethal aid to any forces in Cambodia. Solomon quickly "corrected" himself, saying, "I'm sorry. I made a mistake there. We do not supply any lethal assistance to the non-Communists." Jennings was clearly not convinced by the administration's line, implying throughout the program that the United States was simply turning a blind eye, in what was at the very least de facto acceptance that aid was being received by the Khmer Rouge.[117]

Among the various public figures appearing in the town meeting segment were several diplomats and politicians who had been implicated by the ABC News report. Charles Pickering, the United States representative to the UN, said he was "appalled" by it. Solarz, equally offended, dismissed the charges, noting that he "wrote the law" forbidding aid to the Khmer Rouge.[118] Solarz, Pickering, and others claimed that Sihanouk was simply "mistaken" or that he "misspoke" in his statement about American military support. The program gradually descended into chaos, with various figures from the government brushing aside charges of complicity in the Khmer Rouge's designs on power, and others accusing the United States of everything from direct military aid to Pol Pot to lending the Khmer Rouge "moral legitimacy." Tellingly, despite Jennings's efforts to focus the debate on the issues framed in his report, the discussion shifted to issues concerning the United States' relationship with *Vietnam:* whether or not to normalize relations and end the trade embargo, and the status of American soldiers still listed as Missing in Action. As the credits began to roll, a cacophony of shouting could still be heard from the soundstage. Once again, the suffering of the Cambodian people had been relegated to the background of the ongoing American war on Vietnam.

"I AM REALITY"
REDRAWING THE TERMS OF BATTLE, 1985–1989

Amid the ongoing tragedy in Cambodia and the United States' continuing policy of "bleeding" Vietnam, the spring of 1985 brought with it the ten-year anniversary of the end of the Second Indochina War. The occasion was marked in the United States by official state department addresses, several academic symposia, editorials and special sections in most major American papers, cover story retrospectives in leading weekly news magazines, and numerous television reports. In Vietnam, the anniversary received less sustained attention. Aside from a few official pronouncements from the Party and the occasional flag-waving ceremony, the liberation of the South was quietly commemorated in the North. In the South itself, however, where the "ideological and cultural" component of the Vietnamese revolution continued to lag, a major festival was planned.

Although more than a thousand Western journalists had applied for visas to cover the events, the Vietnamese government was wary of allowing too much media coverage. The official reason for reticence was that the press corps might constitute a "security risk." Hanoi, after all, was not on particularly good terms with the United States and most of its allies at the time. The Vietnamese government was also taken aback at the interest in covering the events, particularly among the Americans whose defeat they were celebrating. "I'm not quite sure," a media relations representative for the government told Jonathan Alter of *Newsweek,* "why there is this great desire by you Americans to relive this terrible defeat." Alter explained in his article that the reason, "of course," was "to learn from it."[1] Even the American media itself, Alter included, seemed surprised at the scope of the coverage. All three major U.S. television networks devoted substantial airtime to the anniversary, with ABC and NBC sending, at considerable cost, extensive crews to provide live satellite feeds from Ho Chi Minh City.[2]

The coverage proved both difficult and disappointing. ABC's *Nightline* featured a "debate" between Le Duc Tho and Henry Kissinger, the two men who once shared the Nobel Peace Prize for negotiating the shaky agreement to end U.S. involvement in Vietnam (Le Duc Tho declined the prize, arguing that the agreement had not achieved peace). The broadcast was a disaster, beset with logistical and technical difficulties. Mixed audio signals caused a cacophony of overlapping voices, with host Ted Koppel, Tho, and his translator constantly speaking over one another. A frustrated Kissinger, who felt unable to break through the noise, complained to the network, with which he had a consulting contract at the time, and succeeded in extending the show ten minutes to allow him a proper "response."[3] NBC's *Today* show had other problems. Throughout the week, the morning show aired live segments from Ho Chi Minh City, where it was late in the evening. During several pieces, Vietnam's legendary insects took aim at host Bryant Gumbel and his guests. As media critic Tom Shales put it in the *Washington Post,* "the huge TV lights attracted great hordes of winged creatures that encircled and bombarded the anchorman."[4]

Shales also reported that most network executives considered the coverage a complete technical and financial failure. Many had hoped for a "big story," particularly "a break in the MIA story," but they had decided by midweek that no news was being made. For Shales, though, the fact that the Vietnamese commemorations turned out not to be newsworthy paled in significance, in light of the construction he chose to put on the anniversary. After taking the networks to task for their shoddy reports, he pointed out that the main problem with the entire effort was that the media missed the "real" story: "One crucial thing that none of the network newsbobs seems willing to consider is that by going to Vietnam, and with such a flurry, they missed the real Vietnam story, which can be covered without leaving the United States. This is where the American soldiers who fought and survived are, this is where the government officials who engineered the war are, and this is where the real scars are, as far as American involvement is concerned."[5]

Of course, "the real Vietnam story," as we will see shortly, was more than adequately covered by the American press, which had no difficulty focusing its attention on the United States. In fact, Shales's remarks demonstrate the extent to which the boundaries of narratives about the war and its legacies in American culture had by 1985 already been drawn so as to exclude any consideration of Vietnam and the Vietnamese. Meanwhile, the "scars" of "American involvement" are everywhere in Southeast Asia. For every American veteran afflicted with cancer or other conditions related to U.S. use of chemical agents during the war, there are thousands of Vietnamese. For every amputee veteran there are thousands of Vietnamese left with deformities from the war itself, not to mention the ongoing problem of unexploded ordinance remaining throughout the Vietnamese countryside. And certainly, in the spring of 1985, one need have looked no further than Cambodia to see the most horrific legacies of American involvement in the region.

Beginning with the ten-year anniversary, the second half of the 1980s brought a new phase in the battle over the cultural memory of the American war in Vietnam, one that played out largely in the field of American popular culture.. In the debates over these representations, what the United States did and was continuing to do to Vietnam (and to all of Southeast Asia) remained essentially outside discussion of the contested reality of the war. Moreover, the texts of this period helped move American society from the sense of "mutual destruction"—which at least acknowledged the *existence* of the Vietnamese—to a "reality" in which the Vietnamese ceased to matter, or even, in some cases, to exist. After this restructuring of the debate, including by the texts examined below, it was not an uncommon sentiment in the United States that, "in the end," as the lead character in *Platoon* put it, Americans "did not fight the enemy. We fought ourselves." With the significant aid of *Rambo, Platoon,* and the comic book *The 'Nam,* which I will also examine, efforts on the cultural front to effectively erase the Vietnamese themselves from American popular consciousness achieved extraordinary success—thereby masking the ongoing effects of the war on the nations and people of Southeast Asia.

THE TEN-YEAR ANNIVERSARY

In the United States, the anniversary of the "fall" of Saigon was an opportunity to reflect on "the legacy of Vietnam," as *Newsweek* put it, or, in the words of *Time,* "The War That Went Wrong, [and] The Lessons It Taught."[6] Like other commentary and events marking the period, these special issues, which appeared two weeks prior to the actual anniversary, demonstrate that the battle over the cultural memory of the war, begun over a decade earlier, was ongoing. From the perspective of these news magazines, the main focus for retrospection was what the war did, and was continuing to do, to Americans. When the Vietnamese were mentioned at all, they were portrayed as corrupt ideologues and villains—in the case of Party leaders—or as the helpless victims of a repressive "Stalinist" regime.

Newsweek was largely obsessed with what the war did to the United States, but its presentation began with an attack on the legacy of the Vietnamese victory. "The events of the past decade—the occupation of Cambodia, the plight of the boat people, the dreary neo-Stalinist isolation of Vietnam today—have deflated the hopeful expectations of those who saw Ho Chi Minh as the liberator of his country."[7] This strategy, of using the failures and shortcomings of the Vietnamese regime to support a revisionist history of the war (an increasingly common tactic in American culture by 1985), was normally coupled with statements to the effect that, unlike the Vietnamese, who were clearly imperialists in disguise, the United States had fought in a noble cause with the best intentions. *Newsweek* was no exception, as seen elsewhere in the same issue: "A war fought with the best of intentions and the worst of results—a war in which, unless one counts the hollow triumph of national liberation celebrated 10 years ago this month in Saigon, there were no winners at all."[8]

While it is undoubtedly fair to criticize the leadership of Vietnam on a number of levels, only the most narrow-mindedly American view would see such deserved criticism as justifying such a spurious argument. Leaving aside the notion of the United States' "good intentions," the belief that the expulsion of the United States from Southeast Asia in 1975 constituted "the worst of results" can only be sustained in the context of an invisibility and silence of the Vietnamese themselves.

To be fair, when in the same issue two *Newsweek* reporters bothered to record the views of Vietnamese citizens, the otherwise solid editorial line was at least disrupted, if not entirely abandoned. Tony Clifton and Ron Moreau, who traveled throughout the country during their visit, took careful note of the roads paved with America's good intentions. Praising the "benefits" brought by previous imperialists, they wrote that "The French left their language, their graceful colonial architecture, even their excellent crusty bread. The Chinese left their philosophy, their tombs, their arts and their dragon temples. But the Americans have left only rust."[9] More immediately, the Vietnamese quoted by Clifton and Moreau made it far too clear that the legacy of the U.S. occupation consisted of more than the "rusty metal" left by the military, and now appropriated by the people of Vietnam to roof their homes. As a professor at Can Tho University told them, "You gave us some very good roads, of course, and you trained some of our best scientists and technicians. But you also gave us Agent Orange, social diseases, and more bombs than have been dropped on any other country."[10]

This piece, titled "A Wounded Land," was a rare exception in the flood of coverage of the anniversary in the American media. Although it did mistakenly state that the economic blockade of Vietnam began only in 1979, at the time of the full-scale invasion of Cambodia, the piece stands out for its presentation of an actual Vietnamese reality. By making the effort to speak with Vietnamese citizens, from around the country, the authors drew praise from even as harsh a critic of mainstream U.S. media as Noam Chomsky. Yet, as Chomsky noted, the account constituted only four of the magazine's thirty-three pages devoted to the topic. For the most part, he observed, the coverage of the anniversary by *Newsweek,* among others, avoided discussion of the conduct of the war by the United States, or of the effects of the war on Southeast Asia. "It is a classic example of Hamlet without the Prince of Denmark."[11]

Time's coverage was particularly myopic. "The war destroyed many lives, American and Vietnamese. But it did other damage: to American faith in government and authority, for one thing." This lead article in *Time's* special issue did not stop with equating the deaths of millions of Vietnamese to that of 58,000 Americans (not that such tragedy can be adequately measured in numbers), or the physical destruction of an entire nation to the symbolic trauma done to many Americans' "faith in government." Going further, the piece placed the blame for the destruction visited on the United States squarely upon Vietnam—not only as a nation, but as a country: "Charles de Gaulle called Vietnam 'a rotten country,' and he was right in a psychic as well as a physical sense. Rotten, certainly for Americans. Vietnam took America's energy and comparative innocence—a dangerous innocence, perhaps—and bent it around so that the muzzle fired back in the nation's face. The war became America vs. America."[12]

In this confused construction, the tragic irony of the war was not that American "energy" and "comparative innocence" had forged a weapon, pointed at Vietnam, but rather that the Vietnamese caused the gun to backfire. This view is reinforced by the title of the special issue itself: "The War That *Went* Wrong." In this and other retrospectives, there was little to no attention paid to the *origins* of American involvement in Southeast Asia—thus leaving outside the realm of acceptable debate the question of whether or not the war was "wrong" in the first place.

In the meantime, by blaming the Vietnamese, *Time* denied the historical actors who expelled the American invaders from their country the agency of their victory: "the war became America vs. America." In the end, as *Time* would have it, "Vietnam was a crisis of the American identity," and even, "Vietnam may have been a hallucination."[13] The erasure of the Vietnamese from the narrative of the war was thus fully accomplished. By the end of the essay, the war was seamlessly constructed as a completely American event.

Yet even as *Newsweek* labored to dismiss Vietnam as a "rotten country," and the war as a virtual figment of the collective American psyche, its constructions of each would pale in comparison to that of a film timed to coincide with 1985's ten-year anniversary. *Apocalypse Now* had already offered a vision of the war as a dark, hallucinatory nightmare. *Rambo* would provide a new fantasy, in which the view of Vietnam as a rotten country only fed the cultivated and growing desire to see the United States as the primary victim—and ongoing hostage—of that war.

REWRITING REALITY: *RAMBO*'S REVISIONISM

The second wave of American films about the war came in the early 1980s. Most notably, *First Blood* (1982), *Uncommon Valor* (1983), and *Missing in Action* (1984) looked and sounded completely different from the films of the first wave. In terms of content, these new treatments, focusing entirely upon the plight of American veterans in the United States and those supposedly still being held by Hanoi, were unapologetic in their revisionism. For one thing, they took the POW/MIA myth as fact, with American viewers even returning to Southeast Asia to rescue POWs, in the case of *Uncommon Valor* and *Missing in Action* (each spawning sequels). By such means, America learned that its Vietnam veterans not only hated the evil Asians who were still holding their buddies hostage, but abhorred their own government, which continued to deny—and even cover up—the very fact that those buddies were prisoner.[14]

One irony of the principal POW films is that they made a part of the argument that I am making: specifically, that the war with Vietnam was still going on . . . after 1975, through the 1980s, and well into the 1990s at least. Unfortunately they, along with the entire POW/MIA industry, inverted the roles of victim and aggressor, choosing to represent Americans as being held hostage by the Vietnamese, never mind acknowledging the ongoing war against Vietnam. Meanwhile, release of the films coincided with several paramilitary operations in Southeast Asia undertaken by the Reagan administration. Segments of Hollywood joined the cause. As Bruce

Franklin revealed in *Mythmaking in America,* in a strange alliance Colonel James "Bo" Gritz (an Army Special Forces veteran and fervent believer in the POW cause), William Shatner, and Clint Eastwood put together a 1982 covert rescue mission into Laos—with the full knowledge of the president, who reportedly told Eastwood that, if the team found one POW, he would "start World War Three" to get the rest out.[15]

This mission, as well as other efforts supposedly directed by Gritz, turned up no evidence of surviving American POWs. The task of suggesting that there was such evidence was left to, and picked up by, Hollywood. In *Uncommon Valor* (1983) and *Missing in Action* (1984), teams led by Gene Hackman and Chuck Norris, respectively, turn up dozens of POWs still being held in Southeast Asia. Although *Uncommon Valor* was more commercially successful, *Missing in Action* was more influential in the genre, helping to pave the way for its own sequels and other related films. Central to the plot of *Missing in Action* and the films that would follow it was the complete inversion of victimization. American war crimes are unmentioned or exonerated while the Vietnamese are depicted as barbarous criminals. Franklin sums up this strategy of historical inversion in *M.I.A.*: "Just as the POW issue was consciously created in 1969 amid shocking revelations about U.S. conduct . . . *Missing in Action* uses the POW issue to indoctrinate the audiences of the 1980s with the notion that Americans were not the victimizers but the victims. Those who have forgotten, or are too young to remember, learn that all accusations of U.S. war crimes are merely insidious Asian Communist propaganda designed to hide the crimes the Vietnamese are still perpetrating against innocent Americans."[16]

It may seem to be granting such mere action films too much influence to suggest their power as a force for historical revisionism, but the inverted discourse of victimization constructed in and through these films had implications far beyond the movie screen. The American cultural front was still a battlefield, and films such as *Uncommon Valor* and *Missing in Action* would help to set the premises for and terms of debate regarding the stories that would come to be told about the American war in Vietnam to "post-Vietnam" generations of Americans.

None of these earlier films, though, had anything like the impact of 1985's *Rambo: First Blood Part II.*

Timed to coincide with the ten-year anniversary of the end of the war, the pre-release press kit for the film contained a video treating the POW/MIA issue and hyping *Rambo*'s connection to the myth of surviving prisoners being held by Hanoi. A sequel to 1982's *First Blood,* a surprising box office success, *Rambo* revolves around the character of John Rambo, a misunderstood and tortured American veteran of the war in Vietnam. The script for *First Blood* had circulated for years in Hollywood, undergoing numerous plot changes and tentative casting. In the body of rising superstar Sylvester Stallone, however, the character became a veritable superhero in the 1980s, a cultural phenomenon that would reshape the ways in which Americans told and discussed stories about the war in Vietnam.[17]

The opening shot of *Rambo* reveals the prison labor camp in which Rambo (Stallone) has spent the last several years since single-handedly destroying the town of Hope, Oregon, in *First Blood.* Rambo's former commander, Colonel Trautman, arrives at the prison, requesting that Rambo accompany him on a new mission: "Recon for POWs in 'Nam." After hearing the details of the mission and agreeing to join Trautman, Rambo asks the question for which the film became infamous. "Sir, do we get to win this time?" "This time it's up to you," Trautman replies. Unfortunately for Rambo, Trautman is not in charge of this mission. Marshall Murdoch, a Washington bureaucrat working for a congressional committee, is leading the team, along with a group of mercenaries. The committee, Murdoch explains to Rambo, is simply attempting to find evidence that will disprove any beliefs that POWs are still being held by the Vietnamese. Rambo is only supposed to take photographs of the empty camp, the very one in which he was held during the war. "Under no circumstances," he is informed by Murdoch, "are you to engage the enemy."

After being dropped in Vietnam from the base in Thailand, Rambo meets up with Co Bao (played by Hawaiian actress Julia Nickson), his Vietnamese guide, who speaks in short, choppy English. As they move down the river toward the camp, escorted by pirates, Rambo tells Bao his story—how, when he returned from Vietnam, he found another war going on in the United States, a "quiet war" against veterans. Bao relates that she is working against her own government because her father, an "intelligence officer," had been killed. When the mission is over, she tells Rambo, she would very much like to go to America. When they arrive at the camp, Rambo defies his orders and, with Bao's help, infiltrates the camp, which is of course populated with a dozen American POWs. He easily kills and outmaneuvers several Vietnamese guards, all of whom appear even less Vietnamese than Bao. Rambo rescues one POW and brings him along to the extraction point where he is to be picked up by Murdoch's men. Along the way, as they elude the inept Vietnamese soldiers, the POW tells Rambo how timely his rescue was. "They move us around a lot—to harvest crops." Thus the film's first explanation for why the Vietnamese would still be holding American soldiers: during a devastating famine and an ongoing war with Cambodia, the Vietnamese need some help with their agricultural production. The plot thickens, however, when they reach the extraction point. Rambo informs Murdoch that he has an American POW with him, which leads Murdoch to abort the mission, leaving Rambo and the man to be captured by the Vietnamese and returned to the camp. At the camp, the Vietnamese soldiers and their Russian "advisors" torture Rambo. The representation of the relationship between the Soviets and the Vietnamese offers an accurate reflection of the Reaganite, cold warrior world view, in which the incompetent and diminutive Asian subjects are merely the lackeys of the powerful and forceful Russians. The Soviets in *Rambo* seem to respect the Americans more than they do their Vietnamese allies, whom they dismiss as "vulgar" and "lacking compassion." The film also refuses even to bother with such inconveniences as subtitles when languages other than English are being spoken. The leader of the Russian troops even gives his orders to the Vietnamese in English.[18] Clearly, though, whatever the Vietnamese are saying is irrelevant, as they are merely the Asian puppets of the Kremlin.

Rambo, however, is much less concerned with the Vietnamese, or even the Soviets, as an enemy than it is with the United States government. Rambo's mission was never intended to prove the existence of POWs. The government, which the film ultimately shows to be more evil and corrupt than either the Russians or the Vietnamese, had no intention of rescuing any POWs found by Rambo. This is consistent with both the tone and content of the POW/MIA myth, whose adherents strongly believed in a government-led cover-up of evidence confirming the existence of remaining POWs. It is also consistent with domestic Reaganism in general, which blamed government for the troubles of the country. Trautman, angry at Murdoch for abandoning his man, tells him that he knows what the cover-up is really about: "Money. In '72, we were supposed to pay the Cong four and a half billion dollars in war reparations. We reneged. They kept the POWs." Murdoch doesn't dispute this story; he in fact admits that the POWs are being held as ransom. But the alternatives to a cover-up are either "paying blackmail money" that would end up "financing the war effort against our [Cambodian] allies," or, worse, "starting the war up all over again" to save "a few forgotten ghosts."

Back at the POW camp, Rambo escapes with the help of Co Bao, who returns disguised as a prostitute servicing the Vietnamese guards. After their escape, Bao and Rambo share a romantic encounter, during which he agrees to take her with him back to the United States. After the kiss, however, Bao is gunned down by a Vietnamese soldier, which sets off Rambo on a killing rampage, leading him back to the camp to rescue the remaining POWs rather than escape alone. During this sequence, Rambo becomes a one-man death squad, destroying helicopters and entire villages, and sending all the Vietnamese into a frenzied panic and, eventually, to their deaths. After a final face-off with the Russians, Rambo takes a helicopter and returns to the base in Thailand, ready to confront his betrayers. Removing the large mounted gun from the helicopter, Rambo completely destroys the huge supercomputers lauded by Murdoch at the beginning of the film. He then goes after Murdoch, stabbing his knife into a desk right next to Murdoch's head, but allowing him to live. "You know there's more men out there," he tells Murdoch. "Find them. Or I'll find you." As Rambo is on his way out of the camp, Trautman implores him to stay rather than wandering off. "The war, everything that happened here, may be wrong. But, dammit, don't hate your country for it," he tells him. "Hate?" Rambo responds. "I'd die for it." Rambo also goes on to offer a final statement on behalf of his men: "I want what they want, what every guy who came over here and spilled his guts and gave everything they had wants: for our country to love us as much as we love it."

The initial critical response to *Rambo* suggested that critics did not love the film as much as Stallone loved it, although many acknowledged, as one put it, that "*Rambo* works."[19] Jack Kroll of *Newsweek* was completely unconcerned by *Rambo*'s acceptance of the POW/MIA myth, the representation of the Vietnamese, or the anti-government message of the film. For Kroll, it was all about Stallone's masochism and narcissism.[20] Richard Shickel of *Time* admitted feeling "shame" at being somewhat amused by the action sequences and Rambo's "superhero ploys," because the film was preying upon the "live moral issues" of the POW/MIA myth. "Whether such victims are real or fiction," he noted, "the films exploit and travesty emotions that a decent movie would try to help us share more deeply."[21] The *Washington Post* and *New York Times* were unique not for their criticisms of *Rambo,* but rather for their brief attention to the dehumanized portrayal of the Vietnamese. The *Post* assailed the film for its revisionist approach to the war, comparing it to the Nazi-led revisionism regarding the First World War, and noted that the Vietnamese in the film "are caricatures out of 1960s anticommunist propaganda. They are flunkies of the

Russians, and their cause is neither anti-colonialism, nationalism nor even imperialism, but raw evil."[22] Vincent Canby of the *Times* sounded a similar note, focusing on the film's "plausibility" problem: "Among other things, *Rambo* seems to believe the Vietnamese, apparently out of sheer Asiatic crudeness, would waste the manpower represented by 50 to 60 of their soldiers to guard a heavily armed jungle prison, which contains no more than a dozen or so P.O.W.'s used as farm laborers. If the Vietnamese are so hard up for labor, why not just use the soldiers and get rid of the prisoners? Are these captors not only mean but also stupid? Well you might ask, but answers are not forthcoming."[23] Unlike *First Blood,* Canby noted, the action in *Rambo* "is supported only by what appears to be the star's ego and a large budget for special effects."

Were it simply another action film, or even another of the *Missing in Action* series, *Rambo* might very well have faded quickly from screens. But a variety of circumstances converged to help create what would quickly become known as "Rambomania" in the summer of 1985.[24] To begin with, Sylvester Stallone was at the time one of the biggest box-office draws in the United States. Building on the success of *First Blood* and the *Rocky* franchise, the makers of *Rambo* put on a major publicity blitz to hype the film. Upon its release, *Rambo* opened in 2,165 theaters—a record number at the time.[25] Within three weeks the film had grossed over $75 million; *First Blood* had been considered successful when it grossed $15 million over the same period.[26]

Several scholars have noted how *Rambo* also shaped and was shaped by other cultural forces in society. As Susan Jeffords demonstrates in her book, *The Remasculinization of America,* the American war in Vietnam "provided the context in which American males could most clearly be identified as victims of a wide range of factors."[27] *Rambo* and other representations of the war helped white American men to recover and reassert the masculine identity that had been called into question after the war. The spectacle of shirtless young men adorned with plastic rifles and ammunition belts entering Stallone look-alike contests, with winners gaining a job delivering "Rambograms," testifies to the truth of Jeffords's analysis.[28] Critical theorist and cultural critic Douglas Kellner has also linked the success of *Rambo* to the film's role as propaganda for Ronald Reagan's domestic and foreign policy. For Kellner, Rambo is an articulation of important elements of Reaganism: unilateral military intervention, and the radical individualist as anti-government activist.[29]

Reagan himself testified to the parallels between his world view and that of the film in the early summer of 1985. Preparing to address the nation to announce the release of hostages being held in Beirut, Reagan announced, "Boy, I saw Rambo last night. Now I know what to do next time this happens."[30] Although the White House claimed that the president was simply joking during a microphone test, the remark was picked up and carried in every major newspaper the next day.[31] Stephen Randall, the executive vice president for marketing at Tri-Star Pictures, the film's distributor, told *Business Week* that Reagan's comments may have added as much as $50 million to the domestic revenues of the film.[32] In Congress, lawmakers also appropriated the image of *Rambo* more than a dozen times while debating a foreign aid bill that included aid to "insurgents in Afghanistan and Cambodia," the very forces with which Rambo was aligned in *Rambo III*, and, implicitly, in *Rambo*.[33]

Rambo was immensely popular overseas as well. All three films in the series were financed by sales of the international distribution rights. *First Blood*, made for only $14 million, grossed over $50 million domestically and over $70 million abroad. *Rambo*, which cost $44 million, made more than $180 million abroad, $30 million more than it grossed in the United States.[34] Although very popular in areas ranging from Bolivia to Japan, the film did especially well in the Middle East, breaking several marks in Israel and shattering every box office record in Lebanon. One of the foreign distributors of *Rambo* speculated that because of his "lone-wolf style" of violence, "maybe he's a hero in the U.S. and a terrorist in other parts of the world."[35] Even some aboriginal tribes in Australia were documented appropriating Rambo's insurgent identity to further their reclamation projects in that nation.[36]

Not everyone outside the United States appreciated the film, however. *Rambo* was banned in places as diverse as India and Norway, and drew particular ire from the Soviet Union. The Soviet government decried what it termed the American "cult of violence," represented by attacks on Soviets in films such as *Rambo* and *Red Dawn*. A film reviewer for *TASS*, the official government news agency, wrote in December of 1985, "To brainwash the public, primarily American youth, U.S. propaganda experts urgently need a new 'hero'—a guy with muscles of iron who can deal with his enemies alone. Those who trampled on Grenada's freedom, those who direct the actions of hitmen and killers in Lebanon, Nicaragua, and Afghanistan . . . eagerly await such a hero."[37]

It is worth noting that the Russians, who come off far better than the Vietnamese in the film, did not come to the defense of their allies here, nor did they note the American support of anti-Vietnamese forces in Southeast Asia. Clearly the United States was not the only nation to which the ongoing, stalemated, Third Indochina War was merely a sideshow.

The varied responses to and appropriations of the Rambo image and identity in the United States and around the world testify to the need to explore texts less in search of their "meaning" or their "code" than in terms of how the texts circulate in particular contexts, how they relate to other texts, and how different groups respond to and use texts in specific historical moments. Certainly, the character became a new reference point in American commercial culture. Along with Rambograms, the United States was offered Rambo action figures, a Rambo cartoon series, Rambo toy guns and video games, and even Rambo-themed adult films.[38] It also became synonymous throughout the world with individual acts of massive violence, particularly those connected to or committed by veterans of the war. On December 5, 1986, for instance, Campo Delgado, a Colombian veteran of the American war in Vietnam, went on a killing spree in Bogota, murdering twenty-nine people, including his mother, before turning the gun on himself. The *Times* of London quickly dubbed the killings a "Rambo-style bloodbath."[39]

Back in the United States, a large number of Americans, including many veterans of the war, found the film both offensive and ridiculous. One veteran interviewed at the Vietnam Veterans Memorial in Washington, D.C., told a reporter he thought the film was "fake. It didn't represent me a bit."[40] Some took issue with the film's revisionism, while others blamed Stallone for glamorizing combat. Scholar Harry Haines, in his essay "The Pride Is Back," described a protest in Salt Lake City at which veterans handed out leaflets describing the movie as a "lie" and containing "An Open Letter to Sylvester Stallone." The letter read:

> First, we want to know where you were in 1968 when we needed you. [Stallone, who was twenty-one in 1968, was teaching at a girls' secondary school in Switzerland at the time.] What right do you have to make this kind of movie and allow people of this country who have never been to war to believe that this is how wars are fought?
>
> Many of our brothers went to their graves because they believed that you fought wars the way John Wayne did in his movies. Are you prepared to accept responsibility for the deaths that may happen in future wars as a result of youths who believe?[41]

Haines notes that the protest was intended as a response not simply to the film, but to the rise of a "teenage 'Rambo' cult" in the city.[42] In early 1986, a similar scene took place in Cambridge, where Harvard's Hasty Pudding Society had named Stallone its "Man of the Year" for 1985. Outside the club during the award ceremony, a group of veterans protested with signs that read "Reality vs. Rambo" and featured a silhouetted Rambo figure in a circle with a line through it. According to film scholar Kevin Bowen, a small group of teenagers waiting to get the actor's autograph taunted the veterans, calling Stallone "a real veteran."[43] The teens further accosted and even picked fights with several of the veterans.[44]

Some of the greatest damage done by *Rambo,* however, centered on its shameless propagandizing of the POW/MIA myth. Although it was neither the first nor last film to do so, its popularity allowed the myth a stronger hold on American culture, bringing it once again to the forefront of national affairs. With the release of the film, the radical posturing of the POW/MIA lobby gained prominence. "We still have men over there who could be in prison camps working in fields," one veteran told the *Washington Post* in July of 1985. "I still think there's people in there and in the government trying to hide it," added another.[45]

In October of 1985, National Security Advisor Robert MacFarlane told a private audience that "there have to be live Americans over there," setting off a flurry of articles as well as statements from related constituencies. Jeremiah Denton, a Republican senator from Alabama and former POW, seconded MacFarlane, adding that "the greatest motivation for me to believe that there are Americans there is the Communists' insistence that they are not."[46] Throughout the year, articles in numerous media outlets offered updates on the MIA missions under way in Southeast Asia, many noting that pressure for results had increased since *Rambo*'s release.[47] The Vietnamese continued to locate, excavate, and repatriate the remains of unaccounted-for American soldiers as if it were a standard practice in international relations. Yet every new discovery seemed to legitimize the unsubstantiated claims that the Vietnamese were holding live American prisoners. This view was only reinforced by the Reagan administration, which continued to accuse Hanoi in regard to the missing soldiers, "insisting," as one article put it, "that Hanoi must clear up the MIA controversy."[48]

The most significant legacy of *Rambo,* however, consists not in the text itself, nor even in the film's role in the treatment of larger social, political, and cultural issues described by Jeffords, Franklin, or Kellner. One of the largely unnoticed long-term consequences of the Rambo phenomenon is that it redrew the terms of debate over the cultural memory of the war. As the standard-bearer of the second wave, "revisionist" school of American films about the war in Vietnam, *Rambo* constructed and established a new matrix of representations within and against which the next wave of films would be framed. However ridiculous *Rambo* may have appeared to some, it became the model against which new versions of the war's "reality" would be judged.

FROM REALISM TO REALITY: *PLATOON* AS THE ANTI-*RAMBO*

All but lost amid the rabid Rambomania was an understated cinematic antidote to the updated cold warrior tales filling the screens of the mid-1980s. *Salvador,* a dark view of U.S. involvement in Central America, centered on the real-life experiences of Richard Boyle, a photojournalist who went to El Salvador "to reclaim his glory days from Vietnam." Starring James Woods and Jim Belushi, both of whom took cuts in their normal pay to make the picture, *Salvador* was the first directorial success for an up-and-coming filmmaker named Oliver Stone. Describing the impetus for the film, Stone said that he was "sick of happy endings. The 1980s is the era of phony endings. It's time to cycle a change." When asked if American filmgoers were ready "for such a heavy dose of political reality," Stone replied, "This will be a test case, won't it?"[49]

If *Salvador* was indeed the test case, the answer must have been "no." Although it received some critical acclaim, the film performed poorly at the box office, taking in only $1.5 million after production and distribution costs of $4.5 million. Not to be deterred, Stone emerged from *Salvador* ready to deliver another dark film that would give new meaning to the word "reality." Stone, who dropped out of Yale twice to go to Vietnam, first as a teacher in 1965, then as an infantryman in 1967, had been since the mid-1970s shopping around a screenplay based on his experiences in the war. Finding no interest and without the capital to make the film himself, he continued to write screenplays, breaking through with 1978's *Midnight Express,* for which he received an Academy Award. Despite the increased attention that the Oscar brought him, Stone still found no takers for his Vietnam film. In 1984, Stone did strike a deal with director Michael Cimino of *Deer Hunter* fame and producer Dino De Laurentiis of the De Laurentiis Entertainment Group: if Stone would write the screenplay for *Year of the Dragon,* a Cimino/De Laurentiis project, Cimino would produce Stone's film. *Year of the Dragon,* in which a Vietnam veteran fights drug traffickers in New York's Chinatown, flopped, and the deal to make Stone's picture fell through because of a problem with the distribution rights.[50] Finally, while Stone was making *Salvador,* a producer named Arnold Kopelson read his screenplay and decided to back the film, with a projected budget of only $6 million. A few months later Stone brought his production crew to the Philippines, just as Coppola had done a decade before, and began shooting *Platoon.*

Stone's screenplay was based on his own experiences in combat, a point that he and the studio never tired of emphasizing. Stone himself also believed that his film was a crucial historical intervention, a corrective to revisionist texts such as *Rambo* and *Top Gun,* two of the biggest films of the period, which Stone saw as "sinister" attempts to romanticize and rewrite the realities of warfare. "It's like a video game," he said of *Top Gun,* the Tom Cruise vehicle about Navy pilots, one of only two films that would out-gross *Platoon* at the box office in 1986. "There is no reality to it."[51] Stone's concern was not just with Rambomania, however. Even such earlier Vietnam war films, admired by Stone, as *Apocalypse Now* and *The Deer Hunter* "didn't really fundamentally deal with the reality that I saw over there as an infantryman." These films, Stone felt, had left a gaping hole in historical and popular narratives of the war: "I mean if we didn't make that story [*Platoon*], I felt we wouldn't be telling the truth, we would be denying history. America would be a trasher of history, blind to the past."[52]

In an attempt to accurately recreate his experiences, Stone put his actors through a month-long military-style training run by former Marine Captain Dale Dye. Dye, who served during the early years of direct American involvement in Vietnam, had set up a consulting firm to provide technical advice about the military to filmmakers. The firm, Warriors, Inc., was created by Dye in 1985 for reasons that echoed Stone's for making the film: "out of distaste for what he considered the metaphorical rambling of such films as *Apocalypse Now* and *The Deer Hunter* and for the revenge fantasies of the *Rambo* genre." Even though the politics of Stone and Dye differed (they reportedly referred to each other as "John Wayne" and "the Bolshevik" on set), the two were both determined to "set the record straight."[53]

Certainly, Stone's personal experience and Dye's presence contributed to the discourse concerning realism and reality that came to surround the film, but long before filming started it was clear that not everyone shared *Platoon*'s view of reality. Considering a request for assistance from one of Stone's earlier production companies, the military responded, "the script presents an unfair and inaccurate view of the Army . . . The entire script is rife with unrealistic and highly unfavorable depictions of the American soldier." Such a response to Hollywood was not entirely uncommon; as Lawrence Suid points out in his detailed study of the subject, even John Wayne's confirmedly pro-war vehicle, *The Green Berets* (1968), was initially denied military assistance.[54] Yet at the time of the response to Stone, both *Top Gun* and *Rambo* were set to have advice provided by the military. Dye, appearing on ABC's *20/20* with Stone, acknowledged that some of the specific complaints of the Army, including images of American soldiers raping and murdering children, were far from universal, but remained adamant that the film was far more realistic than other films receiving cooperation: "It is not fair to say that every infantryman experienced those things and that every infantry platoon carried those things out. And we hastened to point that out. But it is certainly fair to say those things happened. They're on the record, and if you want to deny the record, then go do *Rambo*."[55] This "record," though, would be hotly contested after audiences flocked to see *Platoon* during the winter and spring of 1987.]

The plot of Stone's film centers on the autobiographical character of Chris (Charlie Sheen), a college student who dropped out to join the war. The audience arrives in Vietnam with Chris in the opening scene and remains with him until the film ends. In the early sequences we follow Chris on his first ambush mission. The heat, the bugs, and the jungle are all palpable to viewers, as Chris passes out on the hike from carrying too much. Drawing on his own similar experiences, as he does throughout the film, Stone's Chris is paralyzed by fear on the ambush and allows a Viet Cong patrol to sneak up on the platoon. In the ensuing firefight, one member of the unit is killed, and Chris receives a minor injury.

After his stint in the hospital, Chris returns to base camp, where Stone introduces the divided platoon, composed primarily of two groups: the "regulars" or "lifers," who drink, play poker, and generally follow Sergeant Barnes (Tom Berenger); and "the heads," who smoke pot, dance together to Motown tunes, and follow Elias (Willem Dafoe).[The bulk of the film focuses on the internal conflict of the platoon, symbolized by the rivals Barnes and Elias. Although Chris immediately identifies with Elias, a Christ-like figure who looks out for him, his ongoing conflict with the monstrous Barnes comes equally to define his character. As the film goes on, Chris rejects the most evil of Barnes's actions, but nevertheless becomes masculinized through combat, turning into a fighting and killing machine as reminiscent of Barnes as he is of Elias.]

In the defining moment of *Platoon,* the unit discovers the body of Manny, one of their own, who has been grotesquely killed by Vietnamese forces. The camera follows the troops in a tracking shot, showing close-ups of each face staring blankly ahead, ending with Barnes, who snarls, "The motherfuckers." As the troops march toward a nearby village reportedly in the hands of the National Liberation Front, Chris's voiceover tells us that "The village, which had stood for maybe a thousand years, didn't know we were coming that day. If they had, they would have ran. Barnes was the focus of our rage. Through him, our Captain Ahab, we would get things right again. That day, we loved him."

In following the lead of Barnes, his "Ahab," Chris at the same time attempts to justify the events which are about to take place and points out the futility of the platoon's efforts. Like Ahab's quest for the elusive white whale, the platoon's search for "the enemy" will ultimately be a journey of senseless self-destruction. Although the ensuing scene attempts to give a sense of the destruction wrought on similar villages during the war, it ultimately serves as a backdrop for the larger plot device of the internal battle between good and evil in the platoon.

As the platoon enters the village, pushing the residents with their guns, knocking over containers of rice, and killing a pig, Barnes locates several villagers hiding in a bunker. When one refuses to come out, Barnes throws in a grenade. In one of the homes, Chris and Bunny (Kevin Dillon), a self-described "killer," threaten an old woman and her son, who appears to have developmental disabilities. Chris screams at the young man as another member of his squad (Corey Glover) attempts to calm him. Chris is unrepentant: "Oh, they're scared? *They're* scared? What about me? I'm sick of this shit!" Chris fires his weapon at the feet of the man, but stops short of executing him, at which point Bunny calls him a "pussy" for not "doing the gook," whom he charges with killing Manny as well as Sal, an earlier casualty. As they are leaving the hut, Bunny turns around and repeatedly rams the butt of his rifle into the boy's face, beating him to death.

Outside, the villagers have been rounded up and Barnes interrogates them through a translator (Johnny Depp). The male elder of the village denies that they are "VC," but admits that the NVA forces them to keep its rice and weapons there. Throughout the scene, the man's wife angrily yells and repeatedly tries to run toward Barnes, but is held back by members of the squad. Her voice gets louder and her rage more intense, until Barnes walks up to her and fires a single rifle shot through her head. As the man holds his dead wife, Barnes instructs the translator, "You tell them he starts talking, or I'll waste more of them." Others in the platoon cry out in agreement, one of them shouting, "Let's do the whole fucking village." Barnes takes the man's young daughter and holds a gun to her head, still demanding information. Elias, who had remained behind at a bunker complex, shows up to stop Barnes, resulting in a brawl between the two. But the village is burned, "suspected VC" rounded up and bound, and the atrocities continue, as Chris breaks up a group of soldiers raping two young girls. The scene is undoubtedly the most horrific sequence of any American film about the war in Vietnam, and was a major focal point of the public debate over the "reality" of the film.

Afterward, Chris continues to negotiate the rift in the platoon, noting through a voiceover that he doesn't "know what is right or wrong anymore . . . I can't believe we're fighting each other when we should be fighting them." Caught in a heated firefight, Elias goes off on his own to outflank the enemy troops, but is left behind as the platoon retreats. When Barnes finds Elias in the jungle, he "frags" him, shooting him and leaving him for dead. Chris turns back to try and find Elias, but Barnes orders him to retreat from the area, telling him that Elias is dead. As the platoon is choppered out, they see Elias being chased by what appears to be a full regiment of Vietnamese troops. He is shot several more times and eventually succumbs to his pursuers. Chris immediately suspects that Barnes murdered Elias, and back at the base plots with some of the other "heads" to frag Barnes in revenge. Barnes can't be killed, however, Rhah tells Chris. "The only thing that can kill Barnes is Barnes." Their discussion is interrupted by a half-drunken Barnes, who suddenly appears at the bunker entrance , his face half-shadowed—a visual sign, perhaps, of the platoon's divisive struggle to come to grips with the good and the evil in their leader. "Y'all talking 'bout killin'?" he asks. "Whadda y'all know 'bout killin'?" As he stumbles around the bunker, he chastises the heads for their idealism, their belief in Elias, and their cowardice. "You smoke this shit to escape from reality?" he asks them. "Me, I don't need this shit. *I am reality.*"

In that one short phrase, Barnes encapsulates the larger message of *Platoon:* that this is the way the war in Vietnam "really was." Barnes might as well be speaking directly to the audience, or, perhaps, to Rambo himself. War is about killing. It's about death, and guts, and survival. At first glance, this seems a more suitable message than the glory-seeking fantasies offered by *Rambo* and the like. It is crucial, however, to see what is unspoken and invisible in Barnes's and *Platoon*'s version(s) of reality. The scene in the bunker revolves around the murder of Elias, whose last moments are shown in excruciatingly slow motion while his troops watch helplessly from above. Although the atrocities in the village caused further divisions within the platoon, Chris and the others only begin to contemplate taking action when Barnes murders one of their own. *Platoon*'s reality is clearly that of a dark, divisive, and devastating war, but devastating for whom? The village is quickly forgotten (although not as quickly, as we will see, by American moviegoers, particularly veterans), becoming mere backdrop to the main conflict of the film, entirely internal to the platoon: brother versus brother, American against American. The war, *Platoon* reveals—as much as does any other film discussed here—was ultimately about the United States, and its legacy was chiefly a matter of what "the war" did "to us." In this sense, it is the culmination of the cinematic cultural productions that began with *Coming Home* nearly a decade earlier.

In the final scene of the movie, a long battle sequence in which North Vietnamese troops overrun the American encampment, Chris demonstrates his full transformation into a one-man fighting force. In a Rambo-esque moment he kills over a dozen Vietnamese soldiers single-handed. The Vietnamese troops overrun the American perimeter and the local commander (Dale Dye) calls in an air strike on his own troops. Chris and Barnes find themselves face to face amidst the chaos of the battle, but just as Barnes is ready to kill Chris, the air strike bleeds the entire screen white. In the aftermath of the battle, the next morning, Chris awakes to find Barnes slithering around on the ground. Chris stares blankly as Barnes orders him to call for help. Realizing what is about to take place, Barnes tells Chris to "do it." Without hesitation, Chris raises his weapon and fires two rounds into Barnes's chest, killing him.

Relief arrives, and Chris is taken away on a stretcher while hundreds of dead Vietnamese are tossed and bulldozed into a mass grave. As the helicopter carries Chris toward the heavens, a final voiceover brings closure to the narrative:

> I think now, looking back, we did not fight the enemy. We fought ourselves. And the enemy was in us. The war is over for me now, but it always will be there for the rest of my days—as I'm sure Elias will be—fighting with Barnes for what Rhah called the possession of my soul. There are times since when I feel like a child born of those two fathers. But be that as it may, those of us who did make it home have an obligation to build again; to teach others what we know; and to try with what's left of our lives to find a goodness and meaning to this life.

If the United States was not fighting an enemy, whose were the nameless, faceless bodies in the village or in the final battle scene? Why were they being killed? Like nearly every other American film about the war, *Platoon* refuses to deal with the larger historical and political questions concerning American involvement in Vietnam. Yet *Platoon* takes this dehistoricizing of the war a step further, seeking to erase the Vietnamese from the narrative altogether. To argue, as *Platoon* does, that the enemy was "us" is not simply to ignore why the United States became involved in Southeast Asia; it is also to render invisible the incredible devastation wrought on Vietnam at the hands of the United States over several decades.

From the original screenplay, through the struggle to get it made, through the production, release, and ensuing cultural dialogue about the film, *Platoon* has been discursively constructed almost exclusively around a single word: reality. The constructions of reality that accompany *Platoon*, however, are based as much on previous representations of the war, particularly *Rambo*, as on the "reality" of the war itself. Those constructions also draw upon a very narrow view of the war that reinforces the myopia of earlier Hollywood representations of it and continues to render the Vietnamese invisible. Although it is not surprising that any American representations of the war silence the voices or points of view of the Vietnamese, the absence of those voices is nevertheless crucial to the constructions of the war offered by those representations, particularly of the victimization of American subjects at the hands of the Vietnamese. Only by marginalizing and silencing the voices of the Vietnamese are such representations able to focus their attention entirely on the effects of the war on the United States. But the discourse surrounding the film is even more telling than the text itself. By examining *Platoon*'s relationship to other texts and to other forms of expression, we can see how its version of reality achieved hegemony over the cultural memory of the war in the United States.

Released in December of 1986 in order to qualify for the Academy Awards, where it received the awards for Best Picture and Best Director, *Platoon*'s preview trailers declared it "the first real movie about the war in Vietnam." Stone, in interviews for both print and television, spoke about how his own experiences testified to the reality of the film. Immediately upon its New York release, it was hailed by most critics in language indistinguishable from the studio's marketing or Stone's own media campaign. David Ansen of *Newsweek* wrote that Stone's "elegy" was different from other films about the war. "For starters, he was there." Ansen was particularly impressed with the way Stone situated the audience "down in the muck with the grunts."[56] These sentiments were echoed by the *New York Times,* in which Vincent Canby lauded *Platoon* for taking as its subject "the life of the infantryman, endured at ground level, in heat and muck, with fatigue and ants and with fear as a constant, even during the druggy hours back in the comparative safety of the base."[57] Fred Burning, writing in *Maclean's,* claimed that *Platoon* left audiences feeling that "they had served a tour of duty too." "Now," he concluded, "we know exactly how bad it was" for the American troops.[58]

The ultimate compliment, however, came on January 26, 1987, when *Platoon* was featured on the cover of *Time,* a rare honor for a contemporary Hollywood film. Not even at the height of Rambomania, when the shirtless Stallone was a ubiquitous presence in American and even global culture, did his face grace the weekly's cover. Against a background of standard-issue Army camouflage, the *Time* cover showed a grim Elias, Barnes, and Chris, staring blankly ahead under the banner, "PLATOON: Viet Nam As It Really Was." Inside, a major feature by Richard Corliss, including sidebars on Stone and Dye, highlighted Stone's experiences in the war and opined that he had "created a time-capsule movie that explodes like a frag bomb in the consciousness of America, showing how it was back then, over there." Stone, Corliss concluded, "has devised a drama of palpable realism."[59] These and other reviews hailed the film's "realism," and praised Stone, clearly situated as an authority on the war, for telling it how it was. Interestingly, these reviews also revealed that in the aesthetic realism of the film, the "palpable" landscape representing Vietnam was as central to the construction of reality offered by *Platoon* as any fidelity to historical experience. The basic formula can be roughly summarized as follows: take Stone's experience, add a dose of "muck," and you have the reality of the American war in Vietnam. Gilbert Adair points to both these components in his discussion of *Platoon,* arguing that "we are bullied into craven submission" by the construction of "realness" in the film and the "certificate of authenticity" offered by Stone's experiential justifications.[60]

But there is a more subtle, and more important, factor at work in constructing *Platoon* as "the way it was," one overlooked by other studies of films about the American war in Vietnam. As film scholar Eben Muse later claimed, *Platoon* "established the conventions of reality for Vietnam."[61] This is certainly true, although it is significant that Muse chose to use "Vietnam" to stand in for Hollywood representations of the American war in Vietnam. But *Platoon* did not simply conjure up its reality from the muck of historical experience. Rather, Stone's film altered the matrix of "reality" for American films about the war by working against the conventions established by earlier representations. In nearly every review of *Platoon,* the author begins by setting the film up against earlier Hollywood productions, most commonly *The Deer Hunter, Apocalypse Now,* and, especially, *Rambo.* This is not surprising; it is common for films, particularly those dealing with a specific historical topic, to be compared to one another. But the frequency with which these three films are invoked in reviews of and debates about *Platoon* suggests that something more than comparison is at work. *Platoon* may look, sound, and feel more like the actual combat experience of American infantrymen in Vietnam, but it does so largely because Stone's Chris is not Cimino's Michael, Coppola's Willard, or Stallone's Rambo. And, with the success of *Platoon,* those earlier films came to be interpreted increasingly *less* as being about Vietnam the nation or even Vietnam the war, and more as being about "Vietnam: the American Experience."

We have already seen that both Stone and Dye brought to the project a desire to produce an explicit reversal of "the metaphorical rambling of such films as *Apocalypse Now* and *The Deer Hunter* and . . . the revenge fantasies of the *Rambo* genre," as Dye's motives were characterized. "There's no reality" to those pictures, Stone noted. The entire project of *Platoon* thus began with a particular view of reality framed as much by earlier filmic representations as by historical experience. In Ansen's *Newsweek* review, he begins by noting that while watching *Platoon,* "it dawns on you that most previous Hollywood movies about Vietnam weren't really about Vietnam." In the first film wave of the late 1970s, he writes, "Vietnam was not so much an issue as an opportunity to create epic cinema; for the makers of 'Rambo' and its comic-book ilk it was an opportunity to make money, while winning the war in a cinematic rematch."[62] Canby's review in the *Times* concurred, arguing that *Platoon* "is not like any other Vietnam film that's yet been made, certainly not like those revisionist comic strips 'Rambo' and 'Missing in Action.'" The film was also unlike Coppola's or Cimino's, he continued, which were "more about the mind of the America that fought the war than the Vietnam War itself."[63] Canby continued to press the point in a later piece, stating that, unlike *Platoon, Apocalypse Now* and *The Deer Hunter* "floated above the concerns of the American foot soldiers and saw the war in terms of mythology."[64]

In March of 1987, when *Platoon* once again grabbed headlines as the Oscars approached, no less a figure than David Halberstam, a legendary reporter during the war, weighed in on the film, further cementing the film's version of reality. In contrast to the films of the first wave, all of which Halberstam praises in some way, "*Platoon* is about Vietnam . . . It is painfully realistic." "What Mr. Stone has done," he continues, "in both a medium given to fantasy and in a political age given to longing (if not fantasy) is to strike an enormous blow for reality." But, he adds, "One cannot truly appreciate his achievement without comparing it to the work of Sylvester Stallone . . . Because of *Rambo,* I am that much more in Oliver Stone's debt." Halberstam could hardly fit enough superlatives in his piece: "genuinely authentic," "stunningly real," "the ultimate work of witness." What is most significant about Halberstam's piece, however, is his testimony as to the reality of the film from the "enemy" point of view. Not only does Stone accurately represent the American soldiers' experience, but in his film "the other side gets to shoot back"; they are shown as "professional and tough." "From the very early scene when the Americans set a night ambush, we see the N.V.A. regulars move into that ambush and we see how skillful and careful they are. In a World War II movie, all the N.V.A. soldiers would be blown away; in this one, although surprised, they fight with considerable skill." Halberstam again points to *Rambo* as crucial to the construction-by-contrast of the Vietnamese offered by *Platoon.* "Mr. Stallone," he writes, does an injustice to the American veterans of the war "because he diminishes their opponents." "In *Rambo* we are told that where an American battalion would have failed, one soldier-as-cowboy can do it all, wipe out hundreds of dinky little Vietnamese. With the barely covert racism of the movie, Mr. Stallone would undo what few lessons we have learned from Vietnam."[65]

Halberstam admits that the Vietnamese soldiers in the film are "more a shadow hovering constantly in the background than a fleshed out reality," but then, how are they different from the voices in the wilderness offered in *Apocalypse Now*? Contrasted with the caricatured Communist stooges in *Rambo,* would not *any* invisible enemy appear more realistic? In other words, without *Rambo,* how "realistic" would Stone's Vietnamese be? How "tough" and "professional" would they appear?

Halberstam points specifically to the early ambush scene, drawn from Stone's own experience. In that scene, briefly recounted above, the platoon sets up their position for the night. Chris is awakened to take his shift, which he does nervously but without incident, as a voiceover explains why he joined the war. Chris then awakens Junior, himself a fairly racist portrayal of a disgruntled, lazy black soldier, to take his shift.[66] Later, Chris wakes to find that Junior has fallen asleep and notices shadowy figures in the distance approaching the unit's perimeter. As they move closer, Chris remains paralyzed by fear, watching the enemy forces advance. They are almost on top of him when one trips the wire protecting the perimeter, sending up flares and awakening the platoon. Chris then fumbles the activation of the claymore mines, further hampering the American unit's defense. During and after the brief but intense fight, we see close-ups of the American wounded, one of whom dies, and of Chris, who receives a minor wound but a great deal of attention from the unit and the camera. The Vietnamese forces scamper off into the night, shadows retreating back into the jungle. Needless to say, the audience never receives that unit's casualty report. Certainly, a film need not give as much attention to the Vietnamese forces as it does to the American troops to be considered fair, but what in this scene justifies Halberstam's claim that the Vietnamese are shown to fight with "considerable skill"? The Vietnamese walk right up on the American platoon, only to set off a tripwire and announce their presence; they get in a shot or two, and then retreat just as quickly as they came. One could argue that this is an improvement over *Rambo,* but it affords little basis for Halberstam's claim that we have been given a representation of Vietnamese soldiers as heroic and skillful.

The ambush scene is the only one specifically mentioned by Halberstam, but there seems scant evidence elsewhere in the film to support his argument. In every encounter, the agency of the Vietnamese is essentially disparaged or dismissed, and their fates depicted as mere postscript. During the atrocity sequence, Chris notes that if the villagers had known he and his platoon were coming, "they would have run." Where, one is tempted to ask, would they have run? Could the villagers really have been surprised when the Americans showed up? By the final battle scene, Chris has matured into a killing machine, and makes up for the supposed cowardice of other members of the unit by staying to fight, taking out dozens of Vietnamese. Although different in scale from John Rambo's exploits, is Chris's rampage all that different, in terms of its representation of the enemy, from what Halberstam refers to as the exploits of "the soldier as cowboy" who "wipes out hundreds of dinky Vietnamese"? After the battle, the audience again sees agonizing close-ups of wounded Americans, while the faceless and nameless Vietnamese are simply bulldozed into a mass grave. Even in *Time,* which ran the only major piece on *Platoon* even to point out the arguably problematic representation, it was quickly explained away: "[T]he Vietnamese are either pathetic victims or the invisible, inhuman enemy. In the scheme of *Platoon* (and not just *Platoon*) they do not matter. The nearly one million Vietnamese casualties are deemed trivial compared with America's loss of innocence, of allies, of geopolitical face. And the tragedy of Viet Nam is seen as this: not that they died, but that we debased ourselves in killing them. Of course, *Platoon* need not be every possible Viet Nam film to be the best one so far. It is enough that Stone has devised a drama of palpable realism."[67]

Even here, where Stone's depiction of the Vietnamese is briefly set in a fuller context, once again any potential problems with the film, any contradictions in its construction of reality, are justified by immediately placing *Platoon* alongside *more* problematic, earlier representations of the war. What this review fails to acknowledge is that the "invisible enemy" is not a casual by-product of the film's focus on the experience of American soldiers. Rather, it is a crucial factor in allowing the American-centered narrative to be established as such.

In the end, the Vietnamese are clearly an afterthought to *Platoon,* which, as *Time* pointed out, does not distinguish it from other American films about the war. There may be good reasons for such self-limiting representations, having little to do with the presumably weaker commercial viability of a film more attentive or sympathetic to the Vietnamese people; as Stone argued when discussing *Salvador,* he could not "get inside the Salvadoran peasant's head. That would be presumptuous of me."[68] It could very well be that a representation that allows the Vietnamese subjects to remain invisible and silent, rather than attempting to speak for them, is an improvement over the racism of *Rambo*. In the final sequence, however, Stone proposes a further revisionist erasure of the Vietnamese. Recall that, as he rides away in the helicopter, Chris tells the audience, "we did not fight the enemy. We fought ourselves. And the enemy was in us." Those shadowy figures in the jungle, the girls being raped in the village, the mass grave full of Vietnamese bodies—in *its* final analysis, *Platoon* tells us that they no longer matter. What matters, as in *Coming Home, The Deer Hunter, Apocalypse Now,* and *Rambo,* is what the war did "to us."

The point here is not to discuss the film that Stone or others could have made; rather, I wish to show that *Platoon*'s "reality"—to which the filmmaker, studio, actors, critics, and reviewers insistently testified—is necessarily incomplete. For a filmic war to be constructed, through self-promotion and critical discourse, as "the way it really was," with only the slightest regard for what the war did to the nation and people of Vietnam, is as problematic as the absurdities offered by *Rambo* and its progeny. Perhaps even more so. The makers of *Rambo* or the *Missing in Action* films, while neverexpressing any remorse over their limited representations, also never tried to pawn off their movies as portraying the "reality" of the American War in Vietnam. Joe Zito, director of *Missing in Action* and *Missing in Action II,* was admirably forthright. "I tried to make video games out of them," he said, "and audiences had to know that we weren't playing realistically . . . It's not as if we set out to make a realistic war movie and failed."[69]

In the end, despite their quite differing intentions, *Platoon* and *Rambo* have been inextricably linked to one another from the start, in the battle over the cultural memory of the American war in Vietnam. We have already seen how certain critics and reviewers constructed the discourse concerning *Platoon*'s "reality" against the counter-instance of *Rambo*'s cartoonish fare. Others joined in on the *Platoon*-mania of early 1987 in much the same terms. On January 25, the *Los Angeles Times* devoted its "Calendar" section to *Platoon,* showing an overwhelming response to its proposed forum, "A Reason to Reflect on War."[70] Critics, veterans, and members of the movie industry weighed in—often discussing the film's relation to the *Rambo* films and frequently denying *Platoon*'s claims of a monopoly on the reality of the war. Chuck Norris, star of the *Missing in Action* franchise, called *Platoon* a "slap in the face" to American veterans, adding, "My God, it's making us look like the bad guys, and the VC like the good guys."[71] On the same page, though, Jane Fonda served as counterweight to Norris, calling all *Rambo*-esque fantasies "revisionist cinema" that "obscures the truth."[72]

More significant than the Hollywood stars, however, were the anonymous or at least less well-known figures quoted in the piece. Radio talk show hosts revealed that they were being forced to limit the amount of airtime devoted to listeners' comments on *Platoon* because the film was "all they wanted to talk about." "A woman called to say her husband, who was a former Marine, didn't find it realistic," noted a Chicago host. "The phones rang off the hook after that from people defending it."[73] Several veterans are cited in the same article as finding the film too difficult to sit through; they ended up in the lobby weeping. Yet, for every veteran who found the film all too realistic, there seems to have been one who found *Platoon* to be an affront to their own experience. "I was insulted by it," claimed Al Santoli, a combat veteran and author. "In my division, we didn't burn down any villages, we didn't slaughter villagers. It says no more about the war than *The Deer Hunter* or any of the others. It's just one person's view of it."[74]

The most intriguing part of the *LA Times* forum, for this study, is a brief side story devoted to responses to the film from Vietnamese refugees settled in the United States. The piece is titled, "Viet Refugees Give Platoon Good Reviews," but once again the reaction to the film is seen through the lens of *Rambo* and other films. To many Vietnamese refugees, the story begins by telling us, "the best that can be said for *Platoon*" is that it "isn't just another Rambo." "We have never taken the earlier films seriously," noted an Orange County resident, because they "are so unreal, the situations so preposterous." A student at UC–Irvine called *Platoon* "very real. It is not make believe. It is not a lot of Stallone or Chuck Norris." As among American veterans, however, the reality of the film was sharply contested by many Vietnamese-Americans. Yen Do, editor of a Vietnamese paper in California, accepted that an American film that did justice to a Vietnamese view of the war was unlikely, but wanted to make clear that *Platoon* "was no more about Vietnam and its people than was *Deer Hunter* or any of the others. This is to be expected. They were made by Americans for Americans." Yet in the end, Do conceded: "Yes, it is better than *Rambo*. We can be glad for that, can't we?"[75]

Do was not the only one grateful for the appearance of *Platoon*. Early in January of 1987, a father wrote to the *New York Times* praising *Platoon* as an antidote to *Rambo*. His son, the man wrote, had become "enthralled" with Rambo's escapades as a lone warrior. As he informed readers, movies such as *Rambo*—and Clint Eastwood's *Heartbreak Ridge*, which portrays the invasion of Grenada as an antidote to the Vietnam "syndrome"—"reinforced my son's plans to join [the Marines]." *Platoon*, by contrast, "worked a dramatic cure." Its images of "filth and blood," of a war in which "death wasn't clean," led his son to rethink his enlistment plans and his Rambo fantasies. "*Platoon* is rated R for good reasons," this father admitted, but "[f]or the sake of the Rambo generation, it ought to be PG-13."[76]

So, was *Platoon* an improvement over *Rambo*? Would the "Rambo generation" have been better off with the stark realism of Stone than with the cartoonish fare of Stallone? The questions themselves obscure the significant similarities of the two films. It may be that the answers to these questions lie not in a reading of these texts themselves, but in an examination of how they interact with other fields and other forms of cultural production.

THE 'NAM—COMIC-BOOK BATTLEGROUND

As *Platoon*'s version of reality was ensconced in American culture, its trickle-down effects were seen not simply in other films, but in other media and contexts as well. Inevitably, in a medium such as television, an already questionable and problematic representation of the war was further sanitized in accordance with the commercial and political precepts of cultural production. All the major networks were contemplating Vietnam War–related projects in the summer of 1987. NBC reportedly had in the works a Vietnam version of *M*A*S*H*, and ABC was developing a similar project that would eventually become the very successful *China Beach* series.[77] When CBS launched *Tour of Duty* in the fall of 1987, the same season as HBO's *Vietnam War Story*, it quickly became clear that network television would not be able to reproduce *Platoon* without significant concessions. Although HBO's series was allowed at least some latitude in its use of salty language and violence, CBS's was roundly criticized for its oversimplifications and overly sanitized portrayal of war. As one critic wrote, "Nary a single GI is shown puffing a joint. Breakdowns in military discipline—the atrocities committed against Vietnamese civilians and the 'fragging' of U.S. officers—are as absent as references to the war's political divisiveness or depictions of its gory cost." These problems, however, were explained away by the limitations of network programming: "Still, it's hard to imagine any filmmaker obliged to answer to affiliates, sponsors, and government overseers doing this subject much differently. And just the fact that CBS decided to take on Vietnam merits a commendation."[78]

In the final analysis the most dangerous aspect of *Platoon* was not that in and of itself it was more or less "unrealistic." By recasting the lines of the perceived reality of the war, *Platoon* set up a context in which representations to follow—including those working within the confines, histories, and modes of production of other media—could come up far short of *Platoon*'s degree of realism and still be accepted as falling within the new framework of "reality."

An important issue that arose as these representations reached a wider audience concerned how to teach a new generation of "post-Vietnam" Americans about the war. One article in *U.S News and World Report* even credited Stone's film with helping to instill in young people a new curiosity about the American war in Vietnam: "Until now, the views of the young have been shaped more often by Hollywood in films such as *The Deer Hunter* and *Rambo* than by history books," but new curricula and movies such as *Platoon* were "casting Vietnam in a more realistic light."[79] As the article pointed out, however, because of the way high school history classes are taught, the Vietnam War is often presented late in the year. It is not uncommon for classes to move through their curricula more slowly than was planned, and in the rush to make up for lost time students might not even have a chance to fully discuss the war—leaving many to learn about the war largely through films and other representations.[80]

If students and others, then, were learning about the war outside of the classroom, many observers no doubt continued to take refuge in their belief that *Platoon* had replaced the "comic book ilk" of *Rambo* as the primary popular historical treatment of the war in American culture. But in at least one medium, the seemingly opposed modes of *Platoon*'s realism and *Rambo*'s fantasies came together to constitute a new battleground on the cultural front of the American war on Vietnam.

In December of 1986, Marvel Comics released the first issue of its new Vietnam War comic, *The 'Nam*. Within a year, the book and its creators would be featured on the CBS *Evening News* with Dan Rather, receive an award from the Vietnam Veterans of America, and become one of the hottest-selling comics in the Marvel family. *The 'Nam* was not meant to be just another war comic; it was designed to play *Platoon* to G.I. Joe's *Rambo*. In the first issue, " 'Nam: First Patrol," after following PFC Ed Marks on a journey that replicates Chris Taylor's initial story in *Platoon*, the series editors described their goals for the book:

> The 'NAM is the real thing—or at least as close to the real thing as we can get—in a newsstand comic bearing the Comics Code seal. Every action, every firefight is based on fact . . . Furthermore, the events in the 'Nam happen in real time. When thirty days pass for the reader, thirty days also pass for the characters in the story . . . Now, I can't promise that we will show everything, every action that everyone's father or brother ever took part in during the Viet Nam war. But I will promise that we will show, in basic terms, what the War was really like for those who fought in it.[81]

That disclaimer is followed by a section called "'Nam Notes," a glossary of "grunt jargon" that appeared in very issue. "To give a true feel of the real Viet Nam, we will use this jargon whenever we can," explained the editors. For example, in the first issue the glossary included LZ (landing zone), M-16, R&R, and "Victor Charlie (or sometimes just CHARLIE): the Viet Cong, in short, the enemy."[82] The next issue offered a diagram of military hierarchies, a few additional phrases, and an updated definition for "Charlie": "The Viet Cong, Charlie Cong, the VC, the enemy, the bad guys."[83] *The 'Nam* made no secret of its allegiances. Not only are the "Viet Cong," who are never referred to by the more accurate "National Liberation Front," described as "the enemy," without any explanation of why they are contesting the American presence in Vietnam, they are also clearly labeled "the bad guys." No guesses are needed to determine who "the good guys" are.

In its limited, structured realism, working within the confines of the Comics Code, which regulates violence, sexuality, and language for comic books much in the same way as the ratings system does for films, *The 'Nam* quickly became hailed by readers, many of them first-time comic readers according to their letters, as a "realistic" comic—one committed, like *Platoon,* to showing "how it really was." More importantly, however, the comic became a site of struggle over the cultural memory of the war, a space for debates over the form and substance of memories of war and a means of transmitting knowledge to future generations. As readers responded to *The 'Nam,* they also claimed the text as a pedagogical site, and, as such, a crucial point of inquiry for the relationship between Vietnam and American popular culture.

Despite claims of realism from its creators, the comic offers many troubling representations of the war, the Vietnamese, and the antiwar movement. It also offers a very limited and sanitized portrayal of the American "grunt's" combat experience. Although much of this is to be expected given the history and mode of production of the medium and genre, the images and ideas need to be understood as part of the larger construction of the "reality" of the war taking place in American culture in the latter half of the 1980s. The point here is not to dismiss one set of texts as "false," but rather to note that, far from a singular historical reality, texts, especially popular texts, necessarily offer competing versions of the same events. By using the tropes of experience and "historical accuracy" to claim their version of reality as *the* reality, texts such as *Platoon* and *The 'Nam* particularly demonstrate the need to identify and dissect the contradictions and silences embedded in their stories.

For the most part, *The 'Nam* worked within the established matrix of representations defined by films about the American war in Vietnam, rendering Vietnamese subjects almost entirely invisible and focusing attention on what the war did to Americans. It was similar to *Platoon* in its focus on portraying the war from the "grunt's point of view." As with other progeny of *Platoon* in other media, *The 'Nam* reinforced a view of the war in which American soldiers play the role of the good guys to the marginalized Vietnamese enemy. Unlike *Platoon,* there is little mention of drugs in *The 'Nam* and there are no atrocity scenes or rapes of young girls. When it comes to representations of the enemy, however, the comic follows *Platoon* closely. With a few exceptions, the Vietnamese in *The 'Nam* do not speak. We do not see their faces and they do not shoot back, although they always instigate the fighting. The bombing and napalming of villages is always justified by showing that a village was controlled by the VC. Vietnamese die in groups, and we see nameless and faceless piles of bodies; individual American deaths, few and far between, are depicted in long, anguishing scenes. The creators of the comics did all of this not only based on the codes, formal and informal, of comic production, but because of their own views of the war and of other popular representations of the war.

In the fifth issue, "Humpin' the Boonies," readers are shown the first close view of the Vietnamese. After the unit stumbles upon a massive pile of bodies, villagers murdered by the NLF, one of the troops hears a squad of soldiers who turn out to be the executioners, drunkenly stumbling down the road. "They get careless when they think they're safe," one of the Americans says. "Must be a pretty big camp nearby. Let's find it!"[84] In the next pane, the American unit shows up, completely undetected, a few yards away from the base. "See the livestock. They must have 'liberated' it from the village. These are the boys that like to play with machetes." They call for reinforcements, the VC base is shelled, and we see fearful Vietnamese soldiers being blown apart by artillery; the entire base is wiped out without a fight. As in other representations discussed in this and previous chapters, when the Vietnamese forces are shown at all, they are often shown as incompetent or corrupt. Similar images appear with incredible regularity in the comic.

In the next issue, "Monsoon," the racist caricatures of Vietnamese villagers go well beyond comic book simplifications. In the crude artwork, the villagers in this issue grin menacingly throughout the following "realistic" dialogue:

VIETNAMESE VILLAGER: Hello Joe! Welcome to our old poor village.
AMERICAN SOLDIER: Thank you. We are just passing through, looking for numbah ten guerillas. Have you seen any?
VILLAGER (now surrounded by four other grinning locals): Guerillas! Here? This is just a peaceful village.
SOLDIER: I am glad it is so peaceful. We will not disturb you, but surely you won't mind if we walk through and avoid the mud of the fields?
VILLAGER: We would be proud to have our American friends visit. Just follow this dike for another two or three clicks. We will go ahead to prepare a welcome.

Unsurprisingly, the Americans see through the villagers' charade. The "welcome" consists of a few dozen members of the VC, heavily armed and idly waiting for the approaching Americans. It is the Americans who ambush the Vietnamese, all of whom are killed.

In two issues, however, the creators of *The 'Nam* stretch the limits by attempting to present the war from the "enemy's point of view." In number 7, "Good Old Days," the cover shows an old, run-down Vietnamese soldier against a backdrop of two rifles, a silhouetted map of Vietnam, and a pastiche of flags related to the occupation and liberation of the country. Ed Marks, the "star" of the first year's series, asks Duong, a former NLF soldier, "why he switched." The entire story offers a condensed history of Vietnam from 1940 to 1967, reinscribed within a narrative that "explains" the American war. In case readers questioned the accuracy of the story, Doug Murray, the story's author, attached a note to the second page: "The elements of this story *are completely true.* Duong's story is actually a composite of the stories of three different VC . . . By using these stories, I think we've given a clear picture of the roots of the war—the reason Charlie fought as long and hard as he did."[85] Duong narrates the story, which begins with French Vichy officials executing his wife, who resisted the Japanese-French occupation during World War Two. After attending college in France and being exposed to Vietnamese nationalist thought, Duong returned to join the Viet Minh in their fight against the occupying powers. As the Viet Minh unit liberated his village, Duong began to be suspicious of the revolutionaries, and returned to his life as "a simple farmer." In 1945, "it all came apart again . . . war had come again," and Duong again joined the Viet Minh to fight the French. "Finally, at Dienbienphu, the war was over," he continues, "but that wasn't the end of it. The diplomats talked and my country still wasn't free. It was split in two. And the South was still under the hand of the colonialists."[86] Describing the repression from both Diem's regime in the South and land reform in the North, Duong notes that "there seemed no justice anywhere."

Then, with large numbers of troops, "the Americans came":

> They began to build great bases, where they could feel secure. Then they went in to our cities, and tried to buy everything [including, the image tells us, Vietnamese women]. But they were never really secure. Not in their bases. Not in our cities. They were never safe. [Images of Americans having their throats slit and being gunned down by Vietnamese.] But the Americans got better, and more confident. Meanwhile

> I kept fighting. But it was not the same. You Americans wanted to help [American soldiers assisting Vietnamese children], while my people—I do not know what my people were trying to do! [A young Vietnamese boy attacks American soldiers with a grenade, killing them both.] As time passed, I became more and more unsure that I was on the right side. [Viet Minh gunning down unarmed students, women, and children.] Finally, I made my decision. I came to your people, where I have been accepted.[87]

This attempt at conveying the "enemy's" point of view, far from showing "why Charlie fought as long and hard as he did," echoes the assertions by the Kennedy and Johnson administrations that the United States was inherently different from, and better than, the imperial powers that previously sought to colonize Vietnam—and thus supports the popular 1980s view that the war was a noble cause. The story also completely masks the long and complex history of American involvement in Southeast Asia, which began long before 1965, and ignores altogether the history of American atrocities and war crimes in Vietnam while highlighting those of the Viet Minh and NLF. Although the story does attempt to show the nationalist roots of the Vietnamese revolutionary forces, it makes them out to be little more than murderers and tyrants, while the American servicemen are cast as the innocent victims of young urban terrorists on motorbikes. In the end, whether the revolutionary forces of Vietnam were primarily Communist or nationalist is irrelevant; they were simply terrorists who attacked the friendly Americans—in acts that this seasoned nationalist fighter is unable to comprehend.

Less troubling is issue number 22, "Thanks for Thanksgiving," which offers a surprisingly dignified representation of Vietnamese forces, if only for a few pages. Sheltering from American fire in an underground tunnel complex, Vietnamese subjects, far from being the racist caricatures seen in other issues, are observed treating their wounded and speaking in full sentences ("translated from the Vietnamese"). For the rest of the book, the action reverts back to the American unit, which cooks up a large Thanksgiving feast while in the field. When they return to the base, the Americans leave several cases of food behind, which the Vietnamese forces take into the bunkers to feed their wounded. "You see, Doctor. You see?" one of the wounded says. "It is as I said! The Americans have much! So much! And it just slips through their fingers. So it will be with our country! With all their might! It will slip though their fingers." "I hope you are right, my friend," the doctor replies. "I just hope you are right."[88] The issue is fairly remarkable, for a comic-book representation of the American war in Vietnam, but it needs to be placed in the context of the rest of the issues. This is the only issue among the first fifty that offers a representation of the Vietnamese as something other than invisible, silent enemies, racist, dehumanized caricatures, or helpless, fearful villagers. Overall, the comic follows these previous patterns of representing the "Other," working within the larger pattern of cultural inversion we have seen in other media and texts so far.

The 'Nam also regularly revised the history of the war though the distortion of particular incidents and images. In number 24, "The Beginning of the End," set during the 1968 Tet Offensive, the story follows the troops through their battle at the American Embassy in Saigon, after which they meet up with General Nguyen Ngoc Loan, the head of the brutal South Vietnamese police forces. The cover of the book offers a different take on one of the most widely recognized images to come out of the war, of General Loan executing a Viet Cong prisoner, Nguyen Van Lem, on a Saigon street on February 1, 1968. In Eddie Adams's original Pulitzer Prize-winning photograph, Lem faces the camera; on the comic-book cover we are looking from behind the prisoner, with the unidentified cameraman in the center of the frame. Inside, as a photographer and his Vietnamese guide survey the streets, the American unit discovers that Loan's family and one of his assistants have been killed by the VC. In the key frame that follows, the famous image is revisited, and now literally inverted: the panel is nearly filled by the photographer's camera lens, which reflects Loan firing a bullet into the head of the prisoner. The prisoner, however, is mostly obscured by the frame. The image thus focuses attention on the camera—that is, on the media's coverage of the event rather than the execution itself. In the panel that follows, the American soldiers looking on are concerned not by the barbarous act, but by the fact that photos of the incident will be on the "front page of every newspaper" back home in the United States.[89]

Bruce Franklin, in his *Vietnam and Other American Fantasies,* placed *The 'Nam*'s inversion of this image within the larger process of cultural inversion begun by *The Deer Hunter* a decade earlier:

> The prisoner appears merely as an arm, a shoulder, and a sliver of a body on the left. The only face shown belongs to the chief of the security police, who displays the righteous—even heroic—indignation that has led him to carry out this justifiable revenge against the treacherous "Viet Cong" pictured in the story. The climactic image is a full page in

which the execution scene appears as a reflection in the gigantic lens of the camera above the leering mouth of the photographer, from which comes a bubble with his greedy words, "Keep Shooting! Just keep shooting!" "Shooting" a picture here had become synonymous with murder and treason.[90]

Franklin goes on to discuss the comic's indictment of the media, noting that it preaches what has been understood by many to be a "lesson" of the American war in Vietnam. "The logic of this comic book militarism is inescapable," he writes. "[P]hotographers should be allowed to show the public only what the military deems suitable."[91]

The processes of historical revision and inversion do not end with the stories and images themselves, however. Readers of the comic are free to examine the representations, weigh them against their own knowledge and experience, and construct their own meanings. Unfortunately, if readers' responses are any measure, a large segment of *The Nam*'s audience seems to have accepted without question the "inverted" lesson offered by the comic. In later issues, several readers wrote in to praise "The Beginning of the End" for both its artistic and educational value. In the February 1989 number, three issues after the story appeared, one reader lauded the "magnificent" cover and the writer's attention to the "context" of the photo: "it is always easy so easy to forget that the photo doesn't exist by itself, in some sort of historical limbo . . . Thank you for taking the mystique away from the enemy"[92]

A more disturbing letter in the next isssue comes from a young reader: "Thanks for the truth about the Vietnam War. I'm 14, so this comic is the only way to see THE NAM without sneaking into movie theaters. My history classes ignore the war. Our education on Vietnam consists of being told there was a war and seeing a documentary about the invasion of the embassy. I learned more in issue #24 than I did in two weeks of edited documentaries that show the V.C. as heroes and the grunts as child killers."[93]

The readers of *The 'Nam* were not all young, "post-Vietnam" schoolchildren learning their first lessons about the war. Many were veterans and amateur historians who wrote in from time to time to discuss the "reality" presented in the comic. Yet almost invariably, their remarks focused on relatively incidental details such as military symbols and command structures. One correspondent, as an example, criticized the issue just discussed (number 24) over details concerning the timing of the attack on the embassy, a civilian in the embassy to whom an American soldier threw a pistol, and the NLF takeover of a local radio station tower. The author responded by invoking dramatic license. "The events are correct," he claimed. "The people are fictitious."[94] In other instances, the comic completely rewrites events themselves, in a revisionist approach to the war that goes far beyond the symbolic inversion offered in the Tet issue. In number 9, for instance, the story opens with Ed reading an issue of *Stars and Stripes,* the official military newspaper.[95] (Above Ed, a banner notes that, in keeping with the "real-time" narrative, the story takes place in October of 1966.) The image on the front of the paper is of a seated figure engulfed by flames. The ensuing dialogue confirms that this is indeed an allusion to one of the many acts of self-immolation undertaken by Buddhist monks in South Vietnam, the most famous of which was that of Thich Quang Duc, who took his own life on a crowded Saigon street in June of 1963 to protest the Diem regime's repression of religious freedom in South Vietnam. Assuming from the year in which we are told the story is set that the image we see in Ed's newspaper refers to another self-immolation, not Thich's, the explanation given for the photo in the Incoming section of the book, several issues later, is disturbingly inaccurate. In response to a letter from a young reader, author Doug Murray allows the correspondent's significant historical error to pass without correction:

> I am writing to you to ask about the picture on the cover of the STARS AND STRIPES in Ed Marks's hands on page 1 of issue # 9. Is this supposed to be a photo of the time when a Buddhist monk set himself on fire in the street *to protest communism*? . . . Maybe you should have let the readers understand more clearly exactly what it was in the photo. Maybe Ed could have read the headline out loud, or you could have made the headline visible to the reader.[96]
>
> Murray responded:
>
> Yes, that was a photo of a Buddhist monk immolating himself *in a protest.* Such things happened many times in the course of the Vietnam war and became so near-common that people didn't even mention it most of the time. We don't really feel it necessary to call attention to such things because they are part of the background . . . It's there for readers like you, who care enough to pay attention to the whole story, not just the combat sequences.[97]

The historical reality of the act, a protest against the repressive, anti-Buddhist actions of the American-supported regimes in South Vietnam, is clearly erased and its purpose and meaning inverted here. Doug allows the assertion in Joe's letter, that the monk sacrificed himself to protest *Communism,* to stand unchallenged. He does further injustice to the legacy of the monks by arguing that such acts were so commonplace as to become simply "part of the background." Overtly relegating such actions to the backdrop of the comic's "action" pointedly demonstrates the extent to which the effects of the war on Vietnam and the Vietnamese are marginalized by the text. Bringing Duc's story into the narrative in any truthful way would have forced an acknowledgment of the repressive nature of the American-backed regime in the South. Having clearly explained at the outset that "the VC" were "the bad guys" in the war, such complications are left outside the realm of normative discourse in the text.

Perhaps, in regard to the problematic representations of the Vietnamese and sanitized version of the war presented throughout the run of this comic book, there is little worthy of criticism in and of itself, given the medium and genre. However, in light of *The 'Nam*'s claims to historical accuracy, realism, and attention to detail—and of the fact that many readers were accepting this particular cultural production *as history,* very probably in the context of a relative absence of fact-based historical correctives alluded to above—such misrepresentations are both discouraging and dangerous. Were these images and versions of the past simply standing on their own, they might be dismissed as subtle, if ultimately untenable, distortions. But *The 'Nam* offers evidence, through its Incoming section, that its representations of the war were reaching and connecting with readers.

Indeed, the Incoming page is an interesting and important site for observing the battle over the cultural memory of the war. Over the course of the first fifty issues, from December of 1986 through November of 1990 (the comic ran until September of 1993), *The 'Nam* printed close to two hundred letters from readers, including American, Australian, and Canadian veterans of the war, children of American soldiers who fought in the war, students attempting to learn more about the war, and comic book fans who seemed to have little interest in the war at all. The Incoming pages form a space in which an inverted reality of the war is constructed for a specific audience, with readers themselves attesting to or accepting the comic's accuracy and educational value, and the creators further ensconcing their own version of the reality of the war, an updated "way it really was."

Out of the two hundred or so letters reviewed, roughly one-third praised the comic for its realism. For some, a clear distinction was drawn in reference to other comics, primarily *G.I. Joe,* or films such as *Rambo*. Many also commented on the similarities of *The 'Nam* to *Platoon*. (About 14 percent of the letters mentioned Stone's film by name; an almost identical number referenced *Rambo, Missing in Action,* or *G.I. Joe*.) The space was also used to debate issues not of the war but related to the war, such as the treatment of veterans, the anti-war movement, and the POW/MIA issue. In most instances, resting on his authority as the comic's creator and his status as a veteran, Doug Murray framed discussions to support his views on these and other issues, all the while holding up his depictions and interpretations as *the* reality of the war.

On the first Incoming page to include reader contributions, in February of 1987, five of the seven letters used the word "real" or some derivative thereof to describe the first two issues of *The 'Nam*. "I hope to see this magazine continue to tell the true story," wrote one veteran. "War is not a game, it is not 'RAMBO' or 'G.I. JOE.' " A younger reader concurred: "THE 'NAM isn't super heroes, it's not 'GI JOE,' it's not 'RAMBO' . . . It bears a closer relationship to some recent war films than it does to 'Sgt. Rock' [another war comic]." For this reader, the fact that the "enemy" was largely invisible was a bonus: "The enemy is never portrayed as evil or monstrous, in fact, they remain unseen throughout the whole story—a literary tactic, which when employed in propaganda is designed to dehumanize the enemy and make them easier to hate and kill, but here actually serve [sic] to make war more baffling." Others added praise for the "rugged realism" or "honest and insightful" message of the book.[98]

Letters such as these poured in throughout its run, contributing to the redefinition of reality. "I envisioned four-color adaptations of such travesties as RAMBO or MISSING IN ACTION," wrote a European reader. "I feel it is a pernicious tendency in the popular media today to trivialize what was a very traumatic experience, not only for the U.S. but also for the rest of the *Western* world."[99] "GI Joe and Rambo are okay for fantasy," wrote a longtime comics fan, "but this real life depiction of war is great." Another gushed, "THE NAM is probably the most realistic and fabulous comic I have ever read."[100] "I am glad to see a comic that deals with the reality of this war," added a reader who was "too young to remember much about the Vietnam era." He went on, "I hope that kids do read THE NAM. We have to be reminded that war is not GI JOE, that people die and lives are torn. We need to know just what happened in Vietnam. I intend to be with THE NAM throughout the entire war. I don't want to place blame for what happened in Vietnam—I only want to understand."[101]

Clearly, for these and other readers, *The 'Nam* fit the mold of the new reality for the American war in Vietnam. Just as *Platoon* was upheld as "the way it was" largely because *Rambo* had shown the way it wasn't, *The 'Nam*'s version of the war must have been the way it was because the comic was working within a different mode of representation than both *Rambo* and *G.I. Joe*. As one reader described the book, "The people who were there can say, 'Yeah, that's the way it really was,' the people who were never there can look at it and say, 'Yeah, that's the way it really must have been.'"[102]

By contrast, only a token few of the letters criticized the comic's lack of realism, and most of these, as with the Tet issue described above, focused on items such as the correct order of battle or the correct spelling for the name of an Air Force base.[103] Others were concerned with the dictates of the comics code and its relationship to the content of *The 'Nam,* but even in these letters, the influence of *Platoon* was made clear. In issue 11, for instance, one letter argued that "adhering to the code has done more than inhibit the language—it has totally ruled out a realistic portrayal of the war. I'm sure we won't see any of the rape, drug use, or fragging of superior officers that was so prevalent among the troops in Vietnam . . . PLATOON catches the reality, THE NAM is nothing more than a watered-down kiddie version."[104]

Murray's response to this letter is intriguing. He takes note of several other letters from readers who had also seen *Platoon,* but came to different conclusions, and writes, "Platoon is a very realistic looking movie; however, it is *not* a totally realistic portrayal of the Vietnam War! Fraggings, rape, destruction of villages, all of the stuff the TV and newspaper reporters of the late 60's and 70's made such a big thing out of were not, I repeat, not the everyday affairs of life in the Vietnam war. Atrocities did happen, officers and NCO's were fragged, but this was the exception, not the rule. Reality may not be exciting and titillating as entertainment—but it does exist."[105] In the space of a brief paragraph, Murray accomplishes a number of things, all of which demonstrate a great deal about the tone of his comic. First, as he did with the Tet issue, he blames the media for misrepresenting the "everyday affairs" of the American war, for "making such a big thing" out of the occasional rape or atrocity. Second, he demonstrates the extent to which the comic focuses on the American experience. Even if such events were not "everyday" occurrences, the destruction of villages and the deaths of civilians in particular must have seemed far from "the exception" to Vietnamese citizens. Most important for our purposes, however, he betrays how the matrix constructed by and around *Platoon* defined the terms of debate over the historical realities of the war. This is of course useful to Murray, because any attention paid to American war crimes in Vietnam would begin to focus attention on the effects of the war on the Vietnamese people, and that would greatly complicate *The 'Nam*'s sanitized version of the war.

More commonly found in Incoming than this debate, however, was one over whether or not young people should be the target of a war comic. Few letters expressed concern about exposing children to graphic images, but many correspondents called for more salty, violent, and gory stories for themselves. In number 5, a reader praised the artwork but took Murray to task for over-sanitizing and oversimplifying. "I was hoping we could have a *real* account of the Vietnam War," he wrote. "Why do we have to gear the book toward the twelve-year-old market?" But Murray defended his decision to produce a "Code" book, specifically focusing on the educational value he saw in it: "THE NAM is not just aimed at people like you and the vets, it's meant as a sort of primer on the Vietnam War to anyone that will read it."[106]

It was precisely this use of the comic as a supplement, answer, or antidote to one's historical knowledge of the war that drew a number of readers to *The 'Nam*. One reader acknowledged that he would rather see *The 'Nam* as a non-Code book, but did not want the creators to "forego a golden opportunity to do something genuinely worthwhile in the comic medium." He supported Murray's project, saying, "I think you should aim at not only entertaining your readers but also educating them about the true nature of war."[107] For many young readers, this was exactly what they believed they were getting. "Before this came out I never knew much about Vietnam," wrote a young fan. "I like this book because it tells me what adults won't. I hope that this lasts a long time and I hope all the other kids out there are learning as much as I am."[108] Another issue features a young reader who wanted to express his "feelings of joy" that "the world of comics is being lifted from its station as an entertainment form to become a tool of education and enlightenment." He noted that he had had his interest in the war piqued in school, but "saw the need to learn about [the war] and to spread that learning to other young people. Movies like *Platoon* and *Full Metal Jacket* are a start, but can only reach so many people."[109] For some, the comic was even a substitute for school. "THE NAM gives us superior insight into the war as opposed to the films and books (particularly history texts) on the subject," commented one reader.[110]

These testimonials should not be surprising. Cultural studies scholars have long made the point that popular culture can be both a site of contested hegemony and a space of pedagogical value. What is surprising and problematic about the Incoming section of *The 'Nam* are the testimonials offered to the reality of the war as presented by it: not that the comic offers a history of the war, alternative, revisionist, or otherwise, but that, like *Platoon,* it offers *the* history—"the way it really was." This view comes across even more clearly when examining the Incoming page's treatment of other controversial issues.

The POW/MIA issue first arose in number 13, when a twenty-eight-year-old reader wrote in to congratulate the creators on a "worthy project." After the obligatory contrasts with *G.I. Joe* and *Rambo,* this fan asked several serious questions about issues related to the war, including the frequency of American atrocities ("Yes, I am aware that the VC/NVA did things several times worse, but . . .") and the existence of American MIAs being held in Vietnam. Like many of the other historical questions recounted above, this reader had good questions to ask about the issue, and clearly felt Doug Murray to be a qualified person to query. The man admitted that he was skeptical about the myth, largely because he was "suspicious of any cause that's made so much money for Sylvester Stallone and Chuck Norris." But, he continued, "there is some very compelling, credible evidence. Just because photos can be faked, and witnesses can lie, doesn't mean they are and they do . . . I would hate to reject facts just because they are unpleasant." In response to these questions, Murray noted that the comic would show an American being taken captive in a future issue. He also offered his own opinion, which had been solicited by the reader: "I personally believe that there are still American MIA's in the 'Nam, possibly being held against the U.S. paying the reparations agreed to provisionally in Paris in '72. I doubt whether they'll ever be released, however."[111]

Murray continued to perpetuate this myth in future issues. In number 24, a teenage reader wrote in, appealing for a special issue related the POW/MIAs he believed to exist. "No Rambo rescue missions," he requested, "just cold, hard facts." "There are still (approximately) 2500 missing and unaccounted-for men in Vietnam," he added. "I wear an MIA/POW bracelet in hopes that SSG Elbert Bush will return home alive. Those that are still living need the U.S.'s support." Doug praised the young man in his response: "The M.I.A. issue is one of the most frustrating and shameful sides of the whole war. Anything that can be done to help is both vital and noteworthy."[112] In another issue, a reader asked Murray if he thought any of his friends from the war were still being held in Hanoi. His response began with an affirmation of his faith in the myth: "I personally believe that there are still Americans in Vietnam—whether you want to call them POW's or MIA's is unimportant. I also believe that they will never come back, simply because of the political outrage that would result. On the personal side . . . I really don't know if friends I left behind are still there."[113]

The perpetuation of the POW/MIA myth seems benign, however, when compared with the manner in which the antiwar movement was raked over the coals in *The 'Nam*. The furor over this issue began with number 15, "Notes from the World," when PFC Ed Marks returned to "the world" after his tour of duty. The cover featured Marks standing in line at the airport between two "hippies," one skinny and scowling, another rather obese and apparently yelling something at the returning soldier. In the story, Marks comes home to feel unappreciated, misunderstood, amazed at the antiwar movement, and angry about the media's coverage of the war. At first, this seems a reasonable representation, pointing to the lack of support offered many American veterans returning from service in Vietnam and the indifference or even hostility they encountered from certain quarters. *The 'Nam*, however, again offers a very limited view, both of the experience of returning vets and of the antiwar movement.

In a letter to his buddies still in Vietnam, Marks writes of seeing a major protest on television: "There were college students in Wisconsin . . . trying to do . . . I don't know what, something about a representative for Dow Chemicals [sic] and them trying to stop Dow from making napalm." In the next scene, a shocked Marks continues, "Napalm! How many times did a napalm drop save our butts?" Interestingly, it is his father who tries to explain the protestors' views to him, but Marks will have none of it. He soon reenlists and becomes a drill instructor for a short time, after which he returns to college, because "someone who understood what it's really like in the Nam had to tell its story."[114]

Immediately, the letters poured in—including ones from readers upset by *The 'Nam*'s representation of the antiwar movement. Two especially angry letters appeared in number 18. The first defended the antiwar movement, calling "Notes from the World" a "gross insult to those of us who gave so much to try to bring an end to this war," and defending the right of dissent in wartime. The second, written by someone from the comics industry, was less tempered and sensitive than the first. It took issue, mildly enough, with the defense of Dow Chemical, but also chided those who held the notion that "we're supposed to feel sorry for Ed Marks because he didn't get a ticker tape parade," and even argued that the portrayal of the war through the stories of sympathetic individual soldiers was "something like doing a book called AUSCHWITZ and presenting the Nazi guards as people too."[115]

Doug Murray's lengthy response to both letters began with a defense of soldiers "who had fought a dirty and unpleasant war because their government had asked us to." He then launched into a diatribe against "those who reviled returning troops simply because they felt those young men should not have fought" (it is worth noting here that neither the story nor the letters dealt with any specific ill treatment of returning veterans). Murray then took on the writer of the second letter, which he labeled "unreasoning elitist tripe":

> As for you, Mr. Karter, do you believe that each individual American must make his own choice on when and where to fight and what is and is not a "just" war? There is a word for that—the word is anarchy, and that way lies the death and obliteration of everything we (even you) hold dear.
>
> Your contention that napalm was bad because Dow Chemical made money on it is downright imbecilic. Do you try and make money with your "Dreamwell Comics?" If so, does that automatically make them bad? Making money is part of the American way. If, while making that money, you do some good (and I feel that saving American troops' lives is good), then it is all the better.[116]

Given that this is, at least in part, an argument over *napalm*, it is striking that once again the Vietnamese have been positioned completely outside the terms of the debate. In fact, neither of the "antiwar" letters even mentions the effects of the war on the Vietnamese (except by implication in the grossly overstated reference to Auschwitz). The entire discussion of Dow Chemical, from both sides, fails to address the reason so much anger was directed at that firm's profiting from the use of napalm: namely that, in "saving the butts" of American servicemen, Dow's weaponry savagely burned, maimed, and killed innocent Vietnamese and destroyed millions of acres of Vietnamese land.

Several fans wrote in to echo Murray's response to these letters. Others made their own points, most of which centered specifically on the treatment of veterans at the hands of the antiwar movement. One letter went so far as to proclaim that "the only real tragedy of the 'Nam war [was that] no one, absolutely no one ever went up to a Nam vet and said: 'You did a good job.'"[117] In a later issue, a veteran wrote in to state that he and his fellow veterans "have made our peace with our treatment." But this peace was conditional; this reader was only willing to grant forgiveness for the past sins of the antiwar movement in exchange for deference to those "who were there": "If THE 'NAM is not a realistic portrayal of the war, I wish someone would tell me what I was in. Yes, 'Platoon' and 'A Rumor of War' may be an example of one facet of the war, but they are not the be all and end all of Vietnam. If this is your memory of your time there, then please see a counselor to help you handle the problems you will face in the not too distant future. If, on the other hand, you were not there, then keep your bleepin mouth SHUT!"[118]

In one fell swoop, this veteran summarizes the cultural work accomplished by the late 1980s through the reconstruction of the reality of the American war in Vietnam: the placement of American soldiers and veterans at the center of the historical narrative; the claim of exclusive reality for a narrow version of history, presented and defended first by *Platoon* and then *The 'Nam;* the silencing of voices and stories that did not accord with this privileged narrative, including those from the antiwar movement, the Vietnamese, and anyone "who wasn't there."

By 1988, the Third Indochina War was nearing an end as Vietnam continued to remove its troops from Cambodia. Those events in Southeast Asia received little attention in the American press, however, certainly nothing approaching that given to the 1985–87 cultural phenomena of Rambomania and Platoon-mania.

As an indication of the dearth of understanding of either the situation in Southeast Asia or the state of U.S.-Vietnamese relations toward the end of the 1980s, consider the essay "No Hard Feelings?" in the December 1988 issue of the *Atlantic Monthly.* Penned by the accomplished James Fallows, who some years earlier had written one of the most eloquent pieces about the gross inequities in the American draft, "No Hard Feelings?" was based in part on Fallows's trip to Southeast Asia in 1987. The author bothers to mention the still ongoing war with Cambodia only once, in passing—yet at the same time expresses surprise that the Vietnamese are seemingly not as interested at the moment in the American war on their country as the United States still is. That sentiment, Fallows noted, was to be found in several other Southeast Asian nations he visited, which led him to state that "[t]he Vietnamese obviously care more about their war than their neighbors do, but what I saw reinforced the conclusion I had reached in the neighboring countries: *The Vietnam War will be important only for what it did internally to the United States.* What it did internally is immense, but the effects may be easier to deal with if we recognize that we are talking *about something Americans did to one another,* not an event that changed world history."[119]

Again, we can see the pervasive effects of the *Platoon* syndrome in American society. We can also see its function, for the transformation is now complete. In the space of little more than a decade, "Vietnam" had gone from something "we" did to the Vietnamese, to something Vietnam did to "us," and finally to something "we" did to ourselves. By the end of the 1980s, the Vietnamese, astonishingly, had ceased *even to be a required component* of the matrix of representations of the American war in Vietnam.

Fallows ended his article by suggesting that the United States should normalize relations with Vietnam. It should treat Vietnam as "just another bad country," much like Burma; after all, there was no real harm in having relationships with bad countries.[120] In fact, with the end of the war in Cambodia, and with the historical/cultural inversion of the American war in Vietnam being essentially complete by the end of the 1980s, there was seemingly little standing in the way of normalizing relations with this "bad country." As the United States and Vietnam entered the 1990s, the possibility of reconciliation between the two nations was, once again, at hand.

PEACE IS AT HAND ROADMAPS, ROADBLOCKS, AND ONE-WAY STREETS, 1990–1995

Throughout the Gulf War of 1990–1991, the administration of George H. W. Bush made clear that the United States was not simply at war with Iraq; it was at war with the memory of the war in Vietnam. While much of this rhetoric was to be expected—all U.S. military adventures since 1975 had been viewed though the lens of the Vietnam War—the Bush White House seemed almost singularly obsessed with "curing" what had become known as America's Vietnam "syndrome."[1] In his inaugural address three years earlier, Bush became only the second U.S. president ever to use the word "Vietnam" in that forum, declaring, "the final lesson of Vietnam is that no great nation can long afford to be sundered by a memory."[2] On November 30, with over 300,000 American troops already assembled in the Persian Gulf region, Bush assured the nation that this war would "not be another Vietnam." After the end of hostilities, the president famously declared, "By God, we've kicked the Vietnam syndrome once and for all."[3] In his testimony to a Senate panel the following month, Assistant Secretary of State Richard Solomon opened by telling the committee, "Let me begin by saying the war is over. As the President has said, our Vietnam syndrome is behind us."[4] It was unclear to which war the secretary was referring; for the White House, the war with Vietnam and the war with Iraq had become one and the same.

Mary McGrory pointed out in her *Washington Post* column shortly after the end of the Gulf War that if Bush wished to "formalize the defeat of the 'Vietnam syndrome,'" he could begin by normalizing relations with the nation of Vietnam, and certainly by lifting the trade embargo that was nearing its fifteenth anniversary. As McGrory noted, America was ready for such a step forward. The president was enjoying a 90 percent approval rating at the time, and polls showed that, although Americans were less inclined to support full recognition of Vietnam, 70 percent favored lifting the embargo.[5] With the cold war nearly over, the syndrome apparently cured, nearly all of the Vietnamese troops gone from Cambodia (an estimated five thousand "advisors" remained at the time), continued progress being made on the POW/MIA issue as a result of the Vessey Mission, and American business interests clamoring for access to the Vietnamese market, the time certainly appeared right to end the sanctions program.[6]

Although many policymakers during this period became fond of describing the transition of "Vietnam" in American culture from signifying a war to referring to a nation, this only masks the construction that was most important to the shift in policy: Vietnam as market. Ironically, this final shift in the way in which Americans talked, wrote, and debated about Vietnam returned U.S. policy toward Southeast Asia to where it had been fifty years earlier at the dawn of the cold war, when the American architects of the postwar world sought to develop the region as a market in raw materials, labor, and finished consumer goods, tied to Japan. By the end of the twentieth century Vietnam would come nearly full circle in the designs of the United States: from market to nation to war to cultural construct, and back, finally, to market.

THE "ROADMAP"

On the heels of its victory in the Gulf, the Bush administration was moving forward with normalization plans in the spring of 1991. At the United Nations on April 9, Solomon met with Vietnamese diplomat Trinh Xuan Lang, presenting him with the Bush administration's four-step "roadmap" to gradually normalized relations. The steps all hinged upon a final settlement in Cambodia and Vietnamese "cooperation" on the POW/MIA issue. Phase one consisted of a final peace agreement with Cambodia and accelerated progress on the POW/MIA issue, in exchange for the easing of U.S. travel restrictions on American citizens. Phase two included a lasting Cambodian ceasefire and more progress on POW/MIAs, in exchange for a partial lifting of the American trade embargo. In phase three, to be completed after a United Nations peacekeeping force had been in Cambodia for at least six months, there would be continued progress on the POW/MIA issue, a full end to the American embargo, the establishment of diplomatic offices in each country, and an easing of restrictions on international lending. Finally, phase four would entail UN-supervised elections in Cambodia, continued progress on POW/MIAs, U.S. support for international loans, and full normalization of political and economic relations.[7]

Despite a lukewarm reception by Hanoi, which was understandably frustrated by this ongoing linkage between the embargo and the POW/MIA issue, as well as by the fact that the Cambodian peace negotiations being supported and brokered by the United States continued to include representatives of the Khmer Rouge, the Vietnamese had little choice but to accept the American framework. That year, aid from the Soviet Union had been cut in half, from $2 billion to $1 billion. Before the end of the summer the Soviet Union would collapse completely, leaving Vietnam without its principal source of aid. Even with increased trade from the ASEAN nations, Japan, and Europe since its withdrawal from Cambodia, Vietnam required access to large amounts of capital to finance its most pressing need: renovating the nation's infrastructure, much of it still in tatters from the American war and grossly neglected during the 1980s.

There were several possible solutions to this infrastructure problem, all limited to some degree by the American sanctions program. Most international corporations were unwilling or unable to invest or engage in reconstruction programs by themselves, while many of the firms best suited to the size and scope of the work required were U.S. companies, still banned from the bidding process. The projects might also be funded by bilateral aid, but likely candidates such as France and Japan were still at least nominally supporting the U.S. embargo. Although both countries had formally resumed trade with Vietnam, they remained unwilling to provide the levels of direct aid necessary for large infrastructure projects. Finally, the most plausible if not the most ideal scenario for funding the projects was to secure loans from an international financial institution (IFI). Because of the American-led ban on loans to Vietnam, however, the IMF, World Bank, and Asian Development Bank were all prohibited from making such arrangements with Hanoi. While France and other nations had pushed for an end to the policy since the withdrawal of Vietnamese troops from Cambodia in 1989, the United States and Japan had lobbied to keep the ban in place. By the end of 1991, though, Japan joined France in leading the charge for a resumption of lending and restructuring of Vietnam's existing debt—still in the face of stiff opposition from the U.S.[8]

The intransigence of the Bush administration on the issue of IFI lending is, at first glance, the most glaring oddity of the roadmap. Why would the administration place the resumption of international lending to Vietnam—a relatively minor step, at least politically, compared with full normalization—in the final phase of the roadmap, only after the end of the American trade embargo? Why would it actively prevent Vietnam from financing its own projects, or other nations from helping to finance those projects, through IFIs? The lingering animus of many U.S. policymakers toward Vietnam provides a partial explanation, as does the ongoing desire by Washington to use the IMF and World Bank as tools to enforce American foreign policy. The complete explanation, however, would only become publicly apparent in later congressional hearings. As was then made clear, under the terms of the current U.S. sanctions regime American firms would still be barred from bidding on or participating in any IFI-sponsored projects if lending to Vietnam resumed. The Bush administration thus designed the roadmap's steps to prolong the politicization of the IFIs: so that American firms would not lose further business opportunities to their international counterparts, the United States would continue to obstruct IFI participation in the reconstruction of Vietnam until American companies were free to enter the market—with access, of course, to industry-favorable IFI financing terms. As a result of such policies, as well as the regularly encountered speed bumps provided by the POW/MIA community, Vietnam would have to wait several more years to reach the end of the road to normalization.

In the spring of 1991, though, many in the administration claimed normalization could happen sooner rather than later. On April 11, Solomon told Congress that if the Vietnamese cooperated fully with the plan, full normalization would occur "in short order." On April 20, after two days of negotiations between U.S. Envoy General John Vessey and Vietnamese Foreign Minister Thach, the administration announced that a U.S. office designed to facilitate progress on the POW/MIA issue would be established in Hanoi. Testifying again before the Senate Subcommittee on East Asian and Pacific Affairs on April 25, Secretary Solomon announced that, as a positive gesture acknowledging recent progress on the POW/MIA issue, the U.S. would make its first aid donation to Vietnam since 1975: one million dollars, to be distributed by private agencies and NGOs for the production of prosthetic devices to help Vietnamese amputees from the American war.[10] From the point of view of the White House, the roadmap initiative was already ahead of schedule and yielding results.

Claims of progress were met with skepticism on Capitol Hill, however. Members of Congress with wildly differing views on the situation in Cambodia and relations with Vietnam were quick to criticize the administration's policy from all sides. Senators and Vietnam veterans John Kerry and John McCain, for instance, pointed out that as long as the Chinese continued to back the Khmer Rouge forces, a lasting peace in Cambodia would remain a distant hope. Thus, they reasoned, it seemed unfair and illogical to hold the Vietnamese accountable for Khmer Rouge actions—which would be, after all, the effect of the roadmap's strict tying of the normalization process to specific steps toward peace and democratic elections in Cambodia—when Vietnam had for the past decade been the only nation to actively fight against the former genocidal regime. "If we were applying as much pressure to the Chinese as we are on the Vietnamese," McCain told the *Washington Post*, "I'd be more optimistic."[11] Kerry was more pointed in his criticisms. Sparring with Secretary Solomon at the April hearings, the junior senator from Massachusetts pointed to the inconsistencies in American policy: "You know what Vietnam did? They did what nobody else was willing to do. They went into Cambodia and kicked the Khmer Rouge out and nobody in the world said thank you. We responded with an embargo . . . Why is it that we are driven to treat Vietnam differently from Iraq, from China, from Chile and Pinochet, from countless other governments?"[12]

In fact, the Vietnamese continued to be the only force actively resisting the return to power of the Khmer Rouge. Earlier that week, some of the Vietnamese military personnel remaining in Cambodia had helped put down an uprising by members of the former regime.[13] The United States, meanwhile, continued to support the inclusion of the Khmer Rouge in the transitional Cambodian government.[14]

Another group of senators was attacking administration policy from a different angle, arguing that, far from accelerating progress on the POW/MIA issue, as Kerry and McCain maintained it would, "accommodating" Vietnam by gradually easing the embargo would mean abandoning the only leverage the United States continued to hold over Vietnam. Leading this charge were senators Jesse Helms of North Carolina and Bob Smith of New Hampshire. Ironically, although these rigidly anti-Communist senators held no brief for Vietnam, they continued to see the U.S. government as the primary obstacle to a full accounting of American personnel lost in the war. Smith in particular was an open supporter of various conspiracy theories purporting that the American government was actively suppressing information on American servicemen being held in Southeast Asia. Helms agreed with Smith, taking a page out of the *Rambo* script in his dissent from the roadmap policy: "I'm not criticizing Vietnam as much as I am our own government."[15] In May, less than a month after the formal proclamation of the roadmap, they took up the most controversial aspect of the policy—"satisfactory progress" toward a "full accounting" by Vietnam of all missing American servicemen—by producing a wildly inaccurate report on the history of the POW/MIA issue.[16]

Led by Smith and Helms, both of them members of the Senate Foreign Relations Committee as well as committed devotees of the POW mythology, POW/MIA activists built on this latest "report" and began to lobby for the creation of yet another Senate select committee to investigate the fate of the unaccounted-for soldiers. Many years had passed since the height of Rambomania, however. Even those in Congress and the White House who still assumed the worst about Vietnam were, by 1991, more likely to believe that rapprochement rather than isolation was the best course of action. The roadmap—and the growing power of the pro-Vietnam business lobby—were steering U.S.-Vietnamese relations toward a path where the promise of access would trump the supposed power of leverage.

THE 1991 EMBARGO HEARINGS

With Vietnam's troops gone from Cambodia, and ongoing Vietnamese cooperation in recovering the bodies of U.S. personnel placating all but the most radical elements of the POW/MIA lobby, there was little basis for arguing in favor of keeping the embargo in place. In fact, the first congressional hearings in fifteen years dedicated solely to the embargo on Vietnam, held in June of 1991, marked a significant turning point in public discourse about U.S.-Vietnamese relations. Indicative of the new direction of policy, the hearings were a joint meeting of Solarz's Subcommittee on Asian and Pacific Affairs and the Subcommittee on International Economic Policy and Trade, chaired by Sam Gejdenson of Connecticut. Gejdenson and others interested in lifting the embargo were not concerned with its effects on Vietnam, but focused instead on the embargo's ineffectiveness as a policy tool and its negative effects on American business interests. The diplomatic, internationalist approach long favored by Solarz was, particularly after the fall of the Berlin Wall, increasingly open to challenge from those advocating a more trade-oriented approach, who argued that "market forces" would ultimately work to minimize differences between nations and thus be more conducive to cooperation on matters such as human rights.

The opening statements of the two chairmen reflected these divergent approaches to Vietnam in the 1990s. Whereas Solarz pressed to keep the embargo in place in order to ensure "Vietnamese cooperation" on the political settlement in Cambodia, Gejdenson argued that the embargo "no longer makes sense." He continued, "We have only to look for examples of Eastern Europe, the Soviet Union, to know that exposures to Americans and American ideas of freedom and democracy and free enterprise is what will be most successful in pressuring the Vietnamese to change. Sixteen years of a U.S. economic embargo on Vietnam has only succeeded in denying Americans their rights and in sheltering the Vietnamese from Americans and American ideals that would threaten their totalitarian government."[17] A number of business lobbyists and other witnesses would testify in support of Gejdenson's position, arguing that the way to "end the war" and foster a lasting peace between the countries was to bring capitalism to Vietnam, just as it had been brought to the rest of Southeast Asia. With trade barriers removed, ideological barriers would easily break down—and along with unfettered access to Vietnam's markets, resources, and cheap, abundant labor force would come the answers sought by the families of unaccounted-for American personnel.

The question of access was brought into striking relief at the hearings by Frank Murkowski, senator from Alaska, who was called to testify on a piece of legislation he had recently introduced, the Vietnam Access Act of 1991. The bill called for lifting only the most stringent aspects of the embargo, effectively lifting Vietnam out of Category Z into a less-restricted classification of export control. This easing of the embargo, Murkowski argued, would "lead to greater access within Vietnam."[18] The senator noted that there was substantial support in his chamber for an easing of the sanctions. The Foreign Relations Committee on which he sat had recently passed, by a twelve-to-one margin, a resolution declaring that "the goals of U.S. foreign policy would be advanced by increased access to Vietnam and by a lifting of the trade embargo against Vietnam."[19] Questioning Murkowski about the bill, Solarz took pains to point out that a number of groups, including the National League of Families of American Prisoners and Missing in Southeast Asia (hereafter, "National League of Families," or NLOF), opposed any easing of the embargo. Murkowski countered that the isolationist approach supported by the NLOF had failed to produce satisfactory results, adding that the Vietnam Veterans of America, the largest group representing American veterans of the war, supported his position.[20]

Putting aside this sparring among legislators, the hearing was ultimately designed to provide the increasingly organized business community a chance to weigh in on the embargo. Led by Virginia Foote, director of the U.S.-Vietnam Trade Council, a parade of corporate executives testified and submitted written statements for the record arguing that the embargo was outdated, ineffective, and harmful to American interests. Dwight Jasmann, managing director of AT&T's Pacific operations, explained to the committee that the ban on providing direct phone service to Vietnam—one of only three countries, along with Cambodia and North Korea, on which such a ban existed—was not only ineffective in isolating Vietnam, but, ironically, worked directly *against* American policy goals. Because the ban was easily subverted by connecting through a conference call based in, say, Canada, not only could the Vietnamese government easily provide communications to the United States, but it received payment from the non-U.S. carriers in the type of hard-currency deals the ban was designed to prevent. Giving American communications companies control over the phone lines, he argued, was the only plausible way to enforce the ban.[21] Other witnesses, primarily from the petroleum and communications industries, testified that they were losing precious market share to their European counterparts. If the American embargo was designed to isolate Vietnam from international capital, they pointed out, the policy was failing miserably. Despite the administration's claims that the embargo was part of an international reaction to Vietnam's lingering presence in Cambodia, the hearings helped magnify the fact that other nations, including the closest U.S. allies in the region, had long since abandoned their own bilateral sanctions. While Japan had not yet restored its regular aid program to Vietnam, by the summer of 1991 it was trading with it to the tune of close to $1 billion, including $400 million worth of crude oil.[22]

Throughout the 1980s, the Reagan and Bush administrations, along with a cohort of supporters in Congress that included Solarz, had justified the embargo by claiming that it was simply adding muscle to the ASEAN policy of isolating Vietnam. By 1991, however, the United States was the only nation still pursuing a policy of total isolation. Even China had normalized relations with Vietnam the previous year, and the two countries had begun substantial trade. Nevertheless, Solarz pressed all the witnesses to explain how the United States could continue to exert leverage on Vietnam, particularly with regard to Cambodia, without the embargo in place. In particular, he proclaimed the need to show support for the Cambodian settlement plan proposed by the "P-5," the permanent members of the United Nations Security Council (China, Great Britain, France, the United States, and the Soviet Union). As Virginia Foote made clear in her testimony, however, all four other members of the P-5 maintained bilateral trade with Vietnam.[23] Thus, although the Vietnamese had long expressed their desire for American trade, to them it was far from the necessity—and consequent source of leverage—implied by Solarz and others. By the summer of 1991, any harm from the lack of trade with the United States was more than offset by increasing trade with and investment by other nations, including America's allies.

THE 1993 SENATE SELECT COMMITTEE

Whatever progress was being made on the roadmap framework by the early summer of 1991 was shattered in July, when three separate series of photos, supposedly depicting American POWs, took the U.S. media by storm. Newspapers, magazines, and nightly newscasts prominently featured the pictures, helping to advance the claims made by senators Smith and Helms and the POW/MIA lobby that the pictures were evidence of American servicemen still being held against their will in Southeast Asia.[24] In the furor over the images, including a call from the *Wall Street Journal* to "Bring on Rambo," the worst fears of policymakers and the most extreme claims of conspiracy theorists were seemingly realized.[25] As Bruce Franklin noted, on the same day the *Journal* piece appeared, a "stampeded" Senate voted unanimously to create the Senate Select Committee on POW/MIA Affairs. The pictures were eventually discredited as forgeries, but the Select Committee would spend much of the next year, and millions of dollars, following up on these and similar charges.

Not to be outdone by the more high-profile Senate committee, Stephen Solarz and the House Subcommittee on Asian and Pacific Affairs also seized the opportunity to hold hearings on this "new evidence" and its implications regarding the path to normalized relations. In late July, stealing a march on the Senate, Solarz's committee held the first hearings on the photographs. At the time of the hearings, a team from the Defense Department was already on the ground in Vietnam and Laos, working with the Vietnamese to investigate the photos, and the Sandia National Laboratories' New Mexico facility had already completed its analysis of the first photo. The team on the ground found nothing to corroborate the identity of the men in the picture, and the lab, along with the Defense Intelligence Agency, was of the opinion that the photo was almost certainly a hoax. The image in question had actually been doctored, according to the Sandia report, from a 1923 picture in a Soviet magazine.[26] Although the other pictures would also be exposed as fabrications, Congressional committees would still be debating the images two years later.

As the Senate Select Committee convened the first of what were to be many hearings in November of 1991, members of the House Subcommittee met once again, pursuing many of the same questions and expressing the same concerns as their Senate counterparts. Although each committee contained a representative sample from the ideological spectrum, it became clear over the course of the hearings that even previously more detached figures such as Solarz had moved closer in position on the POW/MIA issue to their conspiracy-minded colleagues, such as representatives Robert Dornan and Robert Lagomarsino of California, and Bob Smith, who was appointed John Kerry's co-chair on the Senate Select Committee. Solarz, who had passionately advocated a negotiated settlement in Cambodia, became increasingly convinced throughout the 1980s and early 1990s that Vietnam was deliberately withholding evidence about American military personnel, some of whom may have been held alive at some point.[27] Kerry, while he remained more moderate in his stance on the issue than either his co-chair Smith or Solarz, was instrumental in structuring the hearings so as to represent only the two narrowly defined "sides" of the debate that achieved hegemony during the 1980s: one providing assurance that the government was actively looking for POW/MIAs it believed might be alive, and the other claiming that the government was actively covering up the existence of the prisoners.[28] Bruce Franklin, the most well-known advocate of an alternate view—that the entire idea of POW/MIAs being held in Southeast Asia was a pernicious and pervasive myth—was denied the opportunity to testify.[29]

Despite this, John Kerry was more often than not a force of relative reason in the hearings. Kerry made, for instance, what would appear to be a fairly basic yet important point: that, during the 1980s, it was extremely rare to see "a Caucasian" in Vietnam, particularly outside of the major cities. He spoke of the "significant curiosity" aroused by his own visits, when he would walk into a village and immediately cause a major stir. "It is very hard to understand," Kerry argued, "how Americans [that is, American POWs] could be moved or moving without a community noticing it in a way that would create ripples of information at some point." Furthermore, although Americans working on body recovery continued to be somewhat restricted in their movement by the Vietnamese, diplomats and aid workers from other nations and NGOs enjoyed the unfettered access sought by the United States. If these various groups, including representatives of many close U.S. allies, had not seen or heard any evidence of American prisoners during their travels, it would certainly bolster the case against there being any prisoners.[30]

On another occasion, which is more indicative of his generally equivocating position on the issue, Kerry related the story of when he became the first U.S. citizen to meet with the Vietnamese Politburo's general secretary. The Vietnamese delegation could not understand why, in 1991, the issue of unaccounted-for U.S. personnel was being discussed, when it was hardly mentioned during the normalization talks of 1978. In retrospect, Kerry offered a fairly concise and interesting summary of how the issue gained such currency: "So I, frankly, went through this long explanation to him of what happened with the problems of Jimmy Carter's presidency and what happened in the desert in Iran and the sense of lack of power in the country and along came Ronald Reagan and he made this a big issue, to his credit, and raised the consciousness, and then movies appeared and books appeared, and Sly Stallone made a cult, and off we went, and it entered the American consciousness and body politic." As he went on to explain, the congressional delegation left with the Vietnamese a large collection of articles from the American media and other information demonstrating the prominence of the issue in the United States. The general secretary, according to Kerry, was somewhat taken aback to see that the issue was indeed seen as "real" and "serious." "He had no idea that this was anything but an American trick in the 1980s and nineties to sort of find a different way to prosecute the war against Vietnam."[31] Yet despite his skepticism, Kerry's insistence that Reagan should receive "credit" for exacerbating the POW/MIA issue reveals that, within the confines constructed by the Select Committee, even the more reasonable positions were staked out within the confines of the powerful POW/MIA mythology.

As a result, the committee spent endless hours discussing the gamut of POW/MIA hoaxes, from the already discredited photos to the "warehouse" myth. One of the most enduring tales from this phase of the POW/MIA drama, this particular myth held that there existed a warehouse deep in the jungles of Southeast Asia where the Vietnamese were secretly keeping the remains of hundreds of American service personnel. The basis for this myth came from a lone intelligence source, mysteriously nicknamed "the Mortician," who claimed that Vietnam, in the early 1980s, had at least four hundred sets of remains locked away in storage. This shadowy figure was an ethnic Chinese who fled Vietnam shortly after the Chinese invasion in 1979 and was debriefed by American intelligence after his defection. Supporters of the Mortician's statements were never able to produce any evidence to support his claims, nor could they even claim that the alleged remains were American, but those who believed his story, including high-level figures in the Bush administration's Defense Department, used it to add fuel to the fire.[32] Senator Bob Smith would help keep this myth alive with a new twist when, on several occasions during hearings of the Select Committee, he claimed that a holding cell of *live* prisoners was located under Ho Chi Minh's mausoleum in Hanoi.[33]

Driven by such outlandish stories, the POW/MIA hearings of 1991 and 1992 illuminate the standard working assumptions of the United States government with regard to Vietnam during the "roadmap" period. To begin with, the hearings reveal that, despite the claims to the contrary by conspiracy theorists in the POW/MIA community, the classification of the issue as a "matter of the highest national priority" was not simply lip service. The Department of Defense had spent over $20 million just for the POW/MIA work being done by the U.S. Pacific Command in 1990, and close to $100 million overall.[34] Before the Solarz committee on November 6, 1991, Deputy Defense Secretary Carl Ford testified that the Bush administration, under the direction of Defense Secretary Dick Cheney, had created the special position of deputy assistant secretary of defense for POW/MIA affairs, and had increased the Pentagon staff directly responsible solely for POW/MIA-related issues from three to fourteen. At that same hearing, and as the Senate Select Committee helped to make clear over the next year, the resolution of the "live prisoner" issue was indeed the primary focus of U.S. government policy with respect to Vietnam. As Ford told the Solarz committee:

> Our most urgent priority is investigating whether or not live Americans are held again their will in Southeast Asia. The *live prisoner* issue has been at the forefront of our investigations. While the governments of Indochina have consistently denied that they are still holding American prisoners, their denials have not deterred us from pursuing the *live prisoner* issue directly on each and every occasion, and at all levels, with them for several years. We intend to keep the pressure on. Although we have thus far been unable to prove that Americans are still detained against their will, information available precludes ruling out that possibility. Our assumption is that at least some Americans are still held captive.[35]

This emphasis—not just of a particular phrase, which is as thus in the original, but on the quest for live prisoners as potentially influencing the entire range and course of U.S. policies toward Vietnam—is important for several reasons. First, it makes plain that even in 1991 the fundamental assumption of the United States government—and thus the starting point for all official inquiries into the issue—was that the Vietnamese and/or Laotian governments were, in fact, holding live American prisoners, and had been for at least sixteen years. The government's official position therefore continued to place the onus on Hanoi of proving the *non*existence of these figures.

More immediately and concretely, however, the live prisoner issue was obscuring and delaying the arguably more important work of locating, repatriating, and identifying actually existing remains of U.S. servicemen. Particularly useful in illuminating this problem was the testimony of Ted Schweitzer. Appearing before the Select Committee on December 4, 1992, Schweitzer, who had been working closely with Vietnamese authorities in archives throughout the country, testified that the POW/MIA community's focus on live prisoners had been among the biggest obstacles to obtaining the "full accounting" that the United States continued to demand of Vietnam. Along with the hostile policies of the United States, the "unsound methods" being employed by American body recovery teams, and "the almost religious resistance among the official and unofficial POW/MIA community and the United States against any serious scholarly research on dead MIAs," Schweitzer told the committee, "the live prisoner issue has cost us years in the search for answers." As he informed them, "I personally spent tens of thousands of dollars, and nearly three years of my life, trying to get someone, anyone, to believe me that there was a mountain of information on dead Americans in Hanoi. I even showed pictures of dead MIAs to dozens of influential people, and still no one was interested, not even Ross Perot."[36]

Schweitzer's mention of Perot is especially significant, given the Texas billionaire's central role in financing and publicizing many of the more provocative elements in the POW/MIA campaigns, not to mention his significant role in the previous month's presidential election, in which President Bush's policies toward Vietnam were called into question. Schweitzer noted that he had personally implored Perot and others to focus on the "treasure-trove of American war artifacts in Hanoi." Yet, "Ross Perot and the others all replied that those men are dead, and I'm not interested in dead men."[37] Rather than commit to the work that would most likely result in the resolution of discrepancy cases, the government continued to press the live prisoner issue, offending and confounding the Vietnamese, lending credence to the conspiracy theorists, and prolonging the agony of American families.

The live prisoner issue was also complicating matters on the ground in the region, wasting the time and energy of everyone involved. One particular concern of the United States was the desire for "unfettered access" to the Vietnamese countryside so that teams could react immediately to any reported sightings of live prisoners. Because of the continued unease in relations between the United States and Vietnam, delegations were closely monitored and placed under stringent travel restrictions. Although bilateral cooperation on the issue had increased dramatically since the announcement of the roadmap, the Vietnamese understandably maintained some restrictions on the movement of American military personnel in their country. Those restrictions, however, continued to be a source of great acrimony among the military, members of congress, and the POW/MIA lobby. The specific concern of the U.S. teams, predicated on the belief that live prisoners were still being held, was ostensibly logistical. In order to investigate a live sighting report, American personnel had to apply for and receive official clearance to investigate in the area, which often took several days. If the Vietnamese, Cambodian, or Laotian government was holding American prisoners in secret camps, the argument went, they could easily relocate those camps with a few days notice. For instance, when a U.S. team was investigating the case of Donald Carr—believed to be the figure in the third photo to surface in the summer of 1991—they received word that Carr was being held in a prison camp near the Laotian Plain of Jars region. When the camp could not be located after several attempts, rather than conclude that they had received bad information, the team kept insisting that the camp had been repeatedly moved. At the Select Committee hearings, this case was used as evidence in support of the argument for increased access.[38]

Based on examples of this sort, the military personnel in charge of POW/MIA recovery in Southeast Asia reported to Congress that they required "full and unfettered access" to any location in the region, so that they could, on a moment's notice, investigate any live sighting reports. Testifying in November of 1991, Major General George Christmas, director of operations for the U.S. Pacific Command, argued that the best solution to the live sighting investigation problem was for the Vietnamese to allow the U.S. recovery teams to use American military helicopters to patrol the countryside.[39] At the time, the teams were being shuttled in Russian-made helicopters operated by Vietnamese pilots. Eventually, the governments agreed on a plan that would allow the U.S. to use rented helicopters, but the suggestion that the Vietnamese should allow the use of American military helicopters is remarkable, given the state of relations between the two countries in the fall of 1991. Only the day before the general's testimony, President Bush and Secretary of Defense Dick Cheney had pledged "decisive action" should any confirmation of live prisoners be made, continuing at the highest and most public level the implication that Hanoi had been holding American prisoners for two decades while at the same time threatening immediate military action against Vietnam.[40]

Even assuming that the Vietnamese might ever entertain the rather astonishing notion of allowing the United States to roam their countryside in U.S. military helicopters, since they were in fact not keeping prisoners, the belligerence of Washington was hardly the type of demonstration that would cause Hanoi to rethink their stance on the increased presence of American military. Furthermore, despite the slight easing of restrictions under the embargo, the United States continued officially to categorize Vietnam as an "enemy" nation under the Trading With the Enemy Act. In the fall of 1991, the only other countries classified as such were Cuba, Libya, and North Korea. It is difficult to imagine these nations allowing even the *presence* of American military personnel permitted by Vietnam at the time, let alone granting a request for unfettered access to search the countryside and classified military records. For the previous decade, the United States had funded the forces fighting Vietnam in Cambodia; only two years earlier it denied a license to a private group seeking to donate wheelchairs to Vietnamese amputees from the American war; and, at the time of the request, the U.S. continued to exercise its veto power in the international financial institutions to prohibit international loans to Vietnam.[41] In nearly every manner, the United States continued to treat Vietnam as an enemy nation, yet it displayed no sense of irony—let alone temperate diplomacy—as it sought to dictate to Hanoi an entrenched American military presence most U.S. *allies* would have had a difficult time accepting.

The helicopter request is indicative of the fundamental inability of anyone involved in these hearings even to begin to approach the issue from a Vietnamese perspective. At no point in any of the testimony did anyone raise the issue of how villages throughout the country would react to the reappearance of the same American helicopters that for years had terrorized Vietnamese civilians from the sky. Similarly, only Ted Schweitzer, in his testimony to the Select Committee, pointed out that if it wished greater enthusiasm and cooperation from Hanoi in accounting for the small number of "discrepancy cases," the U.S. might express a greater concern for the estimated 300,000 Vietnamese soldiers, not to mention countless civilians, still unaccounted for. As Schweitzer pointed out to the committee, this would not only be an appropriate gesture, but would actually assist in the recovery of American remains: "Many cases of American missing are closely intertwined in the archives with cases of Vietnamese missing. Had we shown real interest in helping Vietnam with its missing, we would certainly have come upon this correlation sooner, and been able to resolve many of our own MIA cases earlier."[42]

The U.S. disregard for Vietnamese MIAs was also apparent in the way in which it dealt with recovered remains. When American teams shipped a set of remains to its labs in Hawaii, more often than not a large percentage of them were not American.[43] Instead of taking the opportunity to use their findings to assist in the search for unaccounted-for Vietnamese soldiers and civilians, the lack of correlation to American servicemen's records was regularly turned back on the Vietnamese, with groups like the National League of Families accusing Vietnam of stalling or deceiving the American public by using phony remains. This tactic would continue through 1993, with the NLOF and others blaming the Vietnamese when their archives, which naturally consisted of Vietnamese military records, failed to produce documents that matched the needs of the POW/MIA lobby. As is the case with so many aspects of the ongoing war on Vietnam after 1975, the United States failed to take into account any Vietnamese views, aims, or needs, in a callous policy that worked directly against the interests of American citizens.

The inability of U.S. policymakers to empathize with the Vietnamese position went far beyond mere insensitivity. The failure to grasp Hanoi's approach to the American POW/MIA issue led to fundamental misconceptions about the Vietnamese government's level of cooperation. Whereas the United States, since early in the Reagan administration, had designated the issue as being of the "highest national priority," the Vietnamese, understandably, had very different priorities, from recovering their own missing, to wars with Cambodia and China, to a radical transformation of an economic system still recovering from the effects of the American war and the ongoing economic sanctions program. Yet when the Vietnamese failed to mobilize resources in the manner demanded by the POW/MIA lobby and policymakers in the U.S., they were portrayed as intransigent, or, worse, actively engaged in deceiving the American government and the families of the service personnel in question. In this respect, the hearings once again revealed the heavy burden being placed on the Vietnamese: to dig themselves out of the hole dug for them by the POW/MIA lobby.

In order to satisfy the conditions laid out in U.S. policy, the Vietnamese government had to provide either the "live prisoner," the remains of the person in question, or "convincing evidence" of why it could not provide the remains. Only then could U.S. personnel be considered "accounted for," and thus taken off the official POW/MIA list. Even in a case where the family of the person in question had publicly acknowledged that he was dead, and had obtained a photograph apparently showing his corpse, the person remained on the POW/MIA list, and, as such, unaccounted for. This classification scheme has its root in the decision of the Nixon administration to blur the distinction between the different military categories of POW, MIA, and KIA/BNR (Killed in Action, Body Not Recovered), but it remained a powerful force in U.S. policy into the 1990s.[44] Ann Mills Griffiths, executive director of the National League of Families and a regular witness at any hearing connected to Vietnam or the POW/MIA issue, offered an example of this intransigence in her testimony during one of the Select Committee hearings. Responding to questions about why a certain soldier was still listed as POW/MIA, Griffiths responded, "Because he isn't accounted for":

KERRY: What do you mean, he is not accounted for?
GRIFFITHS: Because there's no convincing—
KERRY: What do you mean he is not accounted for? He is dead.
GRIFFITHS: No. His death has been confirmed. He's not accounted for unless—
KERRY: But he is not—
GRIFFITHS: Excuse me, let me finish.
KERRY: He is not a POW.
GRIFFITHS: No, no.
KERRY: He is not a live person.
GRIFFITHS: He's dead.
KERRY: He is not an MIA.
GRIFFITHS: He is killed in action, body not recovered.
KERRY: Correct.
GRIFFITHS: But they have not provided convincing evidence as to why they cannot repatriate his remains.[45]

Griffiths later added, "what we're talking about here is the unilateral repatriation of remains that are already recovered or easily recoverable." Under further questioning, she admitted that she had no evidence to support the allegations that the Vietnamese had the remains in question or that they were "easily recoverable."[46]

Perhaps no issue in the entire history of the POW/MIA myth is so misunderstood as the belief, perpetuated at every opportunity by Griffiths and the POW/MIA lobby, that the Vietnamese had "easy" access to remains of U.S. personnel scattered throughout the country. In this regard, the testimony of Ted Schweitzer was perhaps the most significant in the lengthy proceedings of the Select Committee. Along with his important contribution to dispelling the "warehouse" myth and his damning indictment of the focus on live prisoners, Schweitzer was nearly alone among the many witnesses before the committee in describing the actual situation on the ground in Vietnam. In his descriptions, Schweitzer dispelled several pernicious myths about the Vietnamese. To begin with, he pointed out, the Vietnamese did indeed have a stockpile of information relevant to U.S. concerns. Yet contrary to the claims of the POW/MIA lobby, the "archive" in question was neither secretive nor centralized. Rather, it was a massive "collection" of memorabilia, documents, "souvenirs," and other residue from airplane and helicopter crashes, battles, and missions over the past half-century of warfare in Vietnam, involving not simply the United States, but the French, British, Japanese, Chinese, and various incarnations of Vietnamese resistance forces. Moreover, this "collection," described by Schweitzer as a "mountain of information," was literally scattered throughout Vietnam, and most of it was in possession of Vietnamese citizens at the village and province level.[47]

The people of Vietnam, Schweitzer noted, were thus the most important resource in the elusive quest for a full accounting. Given the circumstances, it would be up to the United States, not the Vietnamese government, to seek out the information. "The leadership of Vietnam," he argued, "cannot simply order 70 million Vietnamese citizens to bring this mountain of material to Hanoi." In perhaps the most significant testimony of the entire proceedings, Schweitzer continued:

> [assisting the U.S. search program] has to be something that the Vietnamese, the common Vietnamese citizen, feels in his heart he wants to do for America. If he has a souvenir, war memorabilia, something that he has picked up from a crash or a war site in the highlands in 1967 or from a crash up in the mountains someplace, say a piece of an airplane that he's been using as a side of his house or a little package of things

he picked up somehow, maybe the man who picked it up is dead and his children have it and have no idea what it is even. But they're not going to make—the common person of Vietnam just isn't going to come forward with all that mountain of information unless they really have the feeling in their heart that they want to do this for America. It can't be dictated on high that you will bring forward everything that you possess on America. It just won't happen that way.[48]

Later, Schweitzer reinforced the point: "Even with the fullest cooperation from the Vietnamese government, it will take an enormous amount of goodwill, time, and work to locate the materials, collect them, and catalog them."[49]

The need to engage with villagers throughout Vietnam was driven home by several examples offered by Schweitzer and others working in the country. In one case, from an area outside of Da Nang, in central Vietnam, a U.S. recovery team was presented with five sets of remains that local Vietnamese citizens had personally discovered several years earlier. When asked, "Why did you wait five years to turn these remains in to us?" they replied, "Because you never came to our village."[50] In another case, Schweitzer related the story of a Navy pilot who had been shot down over the Vietnamese coast. Local villagers took their boat out, dragged the plane to shore, and buried the remains of the pilot near the beach. The next day, an American bombing raid carpeted the area, destroying the grave. "Even though they had the remains and pictures," Schweitzer told the committee, "the remains are now completely unrecoverable."[51] This was not the only confirmed report of recoverable remains being destroyed by U.S. bombings. In yet another case uncovered through conversations with locals, a North Vietnamese Army team returning to Hanoi with reports of soldiers from both sides who had been captured or killed was struck by American bombs, killing all members of the team and destroying the report.[52]

More than any other witness, Schweitzer outlined the ironies and inconsistencies inherent in the POW/MIA issue. That is what makes it so significant that none of his testimony was included in the Final Report issued by the Select Committee on January 13, 1993. Schweitzer's work in Hanoi had been publicly hailed by President Bush as a "breakthrough" in October of 1992. While Bush's comments had as much to do with his own final push toward the November election, the press took note of Schweitzer's efforts in their reports, which contributed to Schweitzer's return for testimony before the Select committee in December.[53] When the

Final Report was assembled in late December and early January, however, all references to Schweitzer's testimony were left out. His name does not even appear on the official list of witnesses.

Sixteen years and one month to the day after the 1976 Select Committee on POW/MIAs released its report, the 1993 incarnation renounced the earlier findings. While "previous committees" had determined that no American personnel remained alive in Southeast Asia, the new report noted, "This committee has uncovered evidence that precludes it from taking the same view. We acknowledge that there is no proof that U.S. POWs survived, but neither is there proof that all of those who did not return had died. There is evidence, moreover, that indicates the possibility of survival, at least for a small number, after Operation Homecoming."[54] The "evidence" "uncovered" by the committee amounted to little more than specious claims gathered by way of questionable intelligence sources and practices:

> First, there are the Americans known or thought possibly to have been alive in captivity who did not come back; we cannot dismiss the chance that some of these known prisoners remained captive past Operation Homecoming.
>
> Second, leaders of the Pathet Lao claimed throughout the war that they were holding American prisoners in Laos. Those claims were believed—and, up to a point, validated—at the time; they cannot be dismissed summarily today.
>
> Third, U.S. defense and intelligence officials hoped that forty or forty-one prisoners captured in Laos would be released at Operation Homecoming, instead of the twelve who were actually repatriated. These reports were taken seriously enough at the time to prompt recommendations by some officials for military action aimed at gaining the release of the additional prisoners thought to be held.
>
> Fourth, information collected by U.S. intelligence agencies during the last years, in the form of live-sighting, hearsay, and other intelligence reports, raises questions about the possibility that a small number of unidentified U.S. POWs who did not return may have survived in captivity.
>
> Finally, even after Operation Homecoming and returnee debriefs, more than 70 Americans were officially listed as POWs based on information gathered prior to the signing of the peace agreement; while the remains of many of these Americans have been repatriated, the fates of some continue unknown to this day.[55]

Reading these findings raises the question of what, if anything, the hearings accomplished other than the transmogrification of the faint hopes of families and the spurious assumptions of the POW/MIA lobby into "fact." All of this supposed evidence rests on the fundamental assumption that Americans *must have been* held after 1973. Ironically, much of the confusion over the unresolved cases is traceable to the most significant finding of the 1976 report so disparaged by the 1993 committee: that the U.S. military was deficient in its record-keeping regarding soldiers classified as MIA, KIA/BNR, or POW. Unlike the 1976 report, which attempted to clear the way for normalization, the 1993 report overtly declared that the issue was far from resolved. "We want to make clear," the introduction noted, "that this report is not intended to close the door on this issue. It is meant to open it."[56]

The one issue on which the committee did attempt to provide a sense of finality was the belief that the U.S. government was actively covering up the existence of live POWs. While implying that Americans were still being held by the Vietnamese or Laotians, the committee took pains to argue that, as to the question of whether "American POWs were knowingly abandoned in Southeast Asia," the answer was "clearly no."[57] Thus, if it suggests anything, the Final Report seems to indicate that the primary outcome of the committee's work was not to resolve the POW/MIA issue, nor to exonerate the Vietnamese, but rather to refocus attention on Vietnam by disproving the conspiracy theories directed at the United States. This is reflected not only by the unsubstantiated "evidence" of live prisoners but by the failure to include in the Final Report the testimony by Schweitzer and others who demonstrated that the Vietnamese were *already* cooperating, as well as the general lack of care put into the sections of the report dedicated to discussions of relations with Vietnam. The Final Report also contains several references to "North Vietnam" as still existing at the time of its writing, such as, "The U.S. has long suspected that the North Vietnamese *have been* holding a considerable amount of information bearing on the fate of missing Americans."[58] The occasional slip of referring to "North" or "South" Vietnam during a congressional hearing or a statement to the press was far from uncommon after 1975, but by 1993 "South Vietnam" had been gone almost as long as it was ever in existence. For such phrasing to be included in an official Senate report of such magnitude twenty years after the American military withdrawal from Vietnam only testifies to the decidedly anti-Vietnamese tone of the Senate Select Committee.

In the face of ongoing accusations by the more radical elements taking part in the hearings, Vietnamese officials were quick to point out that they were providing the U.S. with highly classified military records, even when American officials refused to provide their own relevant classified materials.[59] In addition to this very public accession by Vietnam to U.S. demands, another condition set forth in the roadmap had been met over the summer when the Cambodian ceasefire agreement entered its second phase: preparing for UN-supervised elections, albeit without the support of the Khmer Rouge. At the same time he had praised the "breakthrough" made by Schweitzer, Bush told reporters on the campaign trail that he thought he was ready "to begin writing the last chapter of the Vietnam War."[60] As the Select Committee was wrapping up its hearings and readying its report, American businesses were gearing up for what they assumed would be a relatively swift end to the sanctions in early 1993. Pharmaceutical representatives, investors, and members of the airline industry began to flock to Vietnam, following the lead of their counterparts in the oil and telecommunications industry, who had been actively working to develop bases of operations in the country since late 1991. The Australian-based *Vietnam Investment Review* playfully noted that there had been a dramatic upsurge in "live sightings" of Americans toward the end of the 1992, including representatives of Procter and Gamble, Coca-Cola, Boeing, and Eastman Kodak.[61] It is likely that the Bush administration was waiting for the Final Report of the Select Committee to be released in 1993 to announce further easing of the sanctions, if not an outright end to the embargo.

THE CLINTON YEARS

By the time the Select Committee had wrapped up its hearings in December, however, the political landscape of Washington had been altered. After twelve years of Ronald Reagan and George Bush, Bill Clinton and Al Gore swept into the White House in the fall of 1992. The specter of the war in Vietnam had once again been raised in the campaign, with Bush supporters charging Clinton with being a "draft dodger." Clinton had been marginally active in antiwar activities, particularly during his days as a Rhodes scholar at Oxford, but reports during the campaign revealed that he had used connections to avoid military service.[62] Regardless, the fact that the first president to come of age during the war in Vietnam was generally allied with the antiwar movement was significant. None other than Robert McNamara wrote the president-elect a letter which enthused, "For me—and I believe for the nation as well—the Vietnam War finally ended the day you were elected President."[63]

Despite McNamara's sentiments, however, the war was far from over. For Clinton to follow the roadmap to normalization with Vietnam, he would have to navigate rough political waters, fending off charges of "selling out" the families of unaccounted-for servicemen from some veteran groups and the National League of Families. It certainly helped that the Bush administration continued along its slow path to normalization by further easing the embargo in December, allowing American companies to sign tentative contracts to do business in Vietnam. The contracts were not allowed to be finalized until the sanctions were lifted, but American companies could at least enter the Vietnamese market and compete with European and Asian firms.[64] The most restrictive measures of the sanctions program remained in place, however, including the ban on access to IFI funds. Despite the snail's pace of progress, it did finally appear that the pieces were in place for normalization to occur. As Frederick Brown put it in a paper for the Overseas Development Council, the United States was finally in a position to "win" in Vietnam. It would be up to the new administration to finish the job of allowing Vietnam to fully integrate with the regional and global economies.[65] Even the *Wall Street Journal,* which only a year earlier had continued to oppose any normalization of relations as long as Vietnam retained any remnants of a centrally planned economy, was ready to lift the embargo by the spring of 1993.[66] "President Clinton," the *Journal* pleaded on March 8, "Normalize Ties with Vietnam."[67]

Although it remains unclear if Clinton was ready for full normalization by the spring, an April 28 IMF meeting in Washington loomed on the near horizon and forced the administration to declare its intentions. The White House was prepared to offer a slight detour from the roadmap at the meeting by ending its opposition to loans to Vietnam and to the Franco-Japanese plan to restructure Vietnam's existing debt. At the very least, this suggested that the full embargo would be lifted by September, when the Trading With the Enemy Act provisions would have to be renewed for the sanctions to continue. On April 12, *The Wall Street Journal* again weighed in, in favor of the move, but warned of "an orchestrated campaign" to prevent progress on normalization. "As if on cue," Bruce Franklin wrote the following month, another cruel and fraudulent campaign by anti-Vietnam forces began on the same day the *Journal*'s warning appeared, leading to a major roadblock.[68]

Working in the Moscow archives of the former Communist Party of the Soviet Union, Australian scholar Stephen Morris, then a fellow at Harvard University, unearthed a document purporting to show that the Vietnamese held back hundreds of American prisoners after the Paris accords. The *New York Times,* which first reported Morris's claim, was quickest to jump to conclusions, adding fuel to the fire by seeking out Carter administration National Security Advisor Zbigniew Brzezinski to assess the claim. Brzezinski told the *Times,* in a statement picked up by newspapers and television stations across the country, "the great likelihood" was not that the Vietnamese continued to hold those prisoners, but rather "that the Vietnamese took hundreds of American officers out and shot them in cold blood."[69] In the initial news cycle following Brzezinski's comments, the focus was therefore not on the accuracy of the document or its claims, but on whether or not the prisoners were more likely to have been executed in the late 1970s or to still be held captive in Southeast Asia. As Bruce Franklin recounts the fallout:

> In a replay of the phony photo gambits of 1991, the "smoking gun" now exploded as the lead story on every TV network, including PBS, whose balanced coverage showcased a *MacNeil/Lehrer Newshour* panel on April 13, consisting of three disinterested "experts"—Brzezinski, Kissinger, and Morris himself. Brzezinski's massacre scenario was repeated in editorials across the country. Headlines blared "North Vietnam Kept 700 POWs After War: 'Smoking Gun File Exposes 20 Years of Duplicity' "; "POWs: The Awful Truth?"; and "We Can't Set Up Ties with Killers of Our POWs."[70]

Although neither the document, Morris's claims, nor Brzezinski's allegation held up under investigation, the damage had been done in the first round of coverage, as the press did not nearly go to the same lengths to disprove the claims as it had to spread them.

Franklin, Nayan Chanda, the U.S. Defense Department, and others familiar with the issues quickly found the document to be inaccurate on a number of points. Writing in *The Nation* and *Far Eastern Economic Review,* respectively, Franklin and Chanda pointed out several flaws with the document, ranging from terminology never used by the Vietnamese to the wrong names of significant Vietnamese leaders, to the segregation of POWs by rank (which was not the normal practice) and wildly inaccurate numbers given for known prisoners being held at the time.[71] Chanda's article quoted military officials investigating the claim who further confirmed the report was likely a "fabrication." "The more textual analysis you make," one of the investigators told Chanda, "the more ridiculous it is . . . It is illiterate."[72] Chanda's scathing piece drew an angry response from Morris, who was unable to refute any of the direct claims made by Chanda, Franklin, or other investigators, arguing at best that the obvious inaccuracies in the report were the result of a faulty translation from Vietnamese to Russian. More commonly, however, Morris's response was to assume the de facto position of the POW/MIA lobby and the likes of Kissinger and Brzezinski: that any discrepancies related to American prisoners were the result of the lying and deceitful leaders in Hanoi. The Vietnamese were never to be trusted on their word, even when it conformed precisely to the historical records in question.[73]

When Morris remained adamant about the accuracy of the document, some in the press began to question his personal motives. Morris, the *Washington Post* pointed out, had long been a public critic of Vietnamese leaders and a staunch supporter of Henry Kissinger. Moreover, as Morris freely admitted in the *Post* piece, "If I find out the Soviets had poor intelligence, all my research has been in vain . . . I'm basing the whole credibility of what I'm doing on the validity of their intelligence."[74] Morris shrugged off those who disagreed with him, including General Vessey, who flew to Vietnam to investigate the document first-hand. Those sympathetic to Morris tried to deflect criticism of him by pointing out that while the document may have been "authentic," and while the Soviets may have believed the document at the time, it did not necessarily follow that the information was accurate. Morris rejected this distinction, once again asserting that "it cannot be true" that the basis for his entire research project was so flawed.[75] Although the document was clearly inaccurate, the damage to Vietnamese-American relations was already done. With the POW/MIA myth once again at the center of national attention, the Clinton administration was forced to postpone the lifting of its IMF veto.

By summer the initial furor over the Morris incident had been quelled and progress toward normalization slowly resumed. The Cambodia-related aspects of phase three of the roadmap had been fulfilled when UN-supervised elections were held in May, with a massive turnout. The newly elected national assembly named Prince Sihanouk head of state and approved a coalition government, without the Khmer Rouge, which had announced earlier in the year that it would not participate in the elections. Despite sporadic violence from the Khmer Rouge forces, a constitution and government would be in place by the fall.[76] The official interagency report on the Morris document was also released, concluding that it was unreliable. Finally, on the night of July 2, after the daily news cycle had already ended, the administration quietly announced it was lifting the ban on IFI lending to Vietnam.[77] The administration's decision was supported by a bipartisan letter from several members of Congress stating that further Vietnamese cooperation would be "in jeopardy if our nation does not make a gesture to acknowledge the contributions of the Vietnamese."[78] The move was promptly criticized by the POW/MIA community for abandoning "leverage" with the Vietnamese. It was also disparaged for not going far enough, by business interests which, under the remaining aspects of the embargo, were not permitted to bid on projects that would presumably result from the resumption of lending to Vietnam.

The tension between the POW/MIA lobby and the forces of the American business community continued to define the course of U.S. policy toward Vietnam, as a series of congressional hearings resulting from the decision to lift the restrictions demonstrated. The first of these, "POW's/MIA's: Missing Pieces of the Puzzle," was convened on July 14, 1993, with another session on July 22. The first session featured four "experts" who would speak on the Morris document: Morris himself, Al Santoli, Jim Sanders, and George Carver, Jr. All four men were on the record as believing that Vietnam had kept American prisoners after the Paris agreements of 1973.[79] None of the witnesses were able to refute the claims of inaccuracy made by others who had investigated the document; rather, they criticized the government for not adequately exploring the report and speculated about why neither the U.S. government nor the Vietnamese were to be believed. Morris's statements to the Committee were full of the misrepresentation and hyperbole about Hanoi for which he had gained a reputation. Morris insisted that the document must be accurate because "we have abundant evidence of other massive violations of the Paris Peace Agreement, and in fact of every other peace agreement the Vietnamese communist leaders have ever signed—most notably the Geneva agreement of 1954 ending hostilities in Indochina and the Geneva agreement of 1962 on Laos."[80] Morris further argued that many within the State and Defense Departments, including General Vessey, had "pursued their assignment [of determining the accuracy of the information in the document] with inappropriate prejudice."[81] The official government representatives at the hearings refused to give prominence to the Morris document, which had been termed the "1205 Report" after the number of prisoners it alleged the Vietnamese had held. Acting Assistant Secretary of Defense for POW/MIA Affairs Ed Ross noted briefly in his opening statement only that, "While portions of the document are plausible, evidence in support of its accuracy is far outweighed by errors, omissions, and propaganda that detract from its credibility."[82]

The Senate hearing that summer was a more balanced and productive affair, exploring many of the ironies and inconsistencies of American policy toward Vietnam. The hearing would be the last significant appraisal of the policy before the embargo was lifted early in 1994. In a prepared statement to the committee, Senator John Kerry acknowledged the ongoing war against Vietnam, if not the ramifications: "Since 1975, the U.S.-Vietnamese relationship had remained essentially frozen, like a still photograph from that traumatic day when the last Americans left Saigon by helicopter from the U.S. embassy roof. Diplomatic relations have remained severed; Vietnamese assets have been frozen; trade has been embargoed. The war has gone on in another form, less bloody, but still damaging to our national psyche."[83] Although Kerry's portrayal of this phase of the war focused on the damage done to Americans, the acknowledgement of an ongoing warlike state of relations between the two nations was a rarity in congressional debates on the topic. Other familiar faces from the Senate appeared to testify at the hearings, including Senator Bob Kerrey of Nebraska, who spoke passionately about incorporating human rights considerations in discussions of relations with Vietnam, an issue that was absent from the roadmap plan but had been vigorously debated in recent sessions of Congress with regard to China's trade status.[84]

The hearings also featured John Terzano, president of Vietnam Veterans of America, the leading organization for American veterans of the war and a strong supporter of normalizing relations with Vietnam. Terzano provided an eloquent argument offering many reasons to move forward on normalization with Vietnam, but his testimony was particularly significant in another respect: for the first time since 1975, a congressional hearing featured a witness decrying the American embargo on Vietnam because of its effects on the people of Vietnam.[85] If the U.S. government planned to consider the human rights records of other nations in formulating its foreign policy, he argued, it should begin with a reconsideration of its own impact on rights around the world:

> I believe this policy [the embargo] was always wrong and immoral, but it now violates increasingly accepted principles of human rights. This June, the World Conference on Human Rights upheld "the right to development" as a basic human right. And, for the first time, the U.S.

> recognized it by signing on to the declaration. How do we continue to justify our attempt to cause suffering to the Vietnamese people, former allies and enemies alike, over policies over which they have no control? Twenty years after the last American soldier left Vietnam, why are we still punishing these people?[86]

That last remark, about "the last American" leaving Vietnam, offered a subtle jab at the POW/MIA lobby and Ann Mills Griffiths of the NLOF, who was to testify shortly after Terzano. Griffiths and the rest of the POW lobby must have begun to realize by this time that their efforts to prevent normalization were failing. Over the course of the past several years, most hearings related to Vietnam had featured at least one new document or report about a particular unresolved case in Defense Department files. Yet as each new live sighting report or "declassified" document turned up, only to be dismissed and discredited, and as actual remains of American soldiers continued to be returned home from the jungles of Southeast Asia through the help of the Vietnamese people, there was no legitimate argument left to make for upholding the embargo. The best Griffiths could do at these hearings in support of her position was to submit remarks by former Reagan National Security Advisor Robert McFarlane, who had criticized the Clinton administration's approach at the recently concluded 24th Annual Meeting of the NLOF.[87]

Business interests were clearly overtaking the POW/MIA lobby as the prime source of testimony at these hearings. In addition to the U.S.-Vietnam Trade Council, other pro-business lobbying groups were beginning to coalesce around the effort to end the embargo. At the July Senate hearings, Al Baker, CEO of Halliburton, testified on behalf of the National Foreign Trade Council, a coalition of over five hundred large U.S. firms engaged in trade and investment around the world. The U.S. Chamber of Commerce was also lined up in favor of lifting the embargo, submitting a detailed prepared statement describing the "lost opportunities" for American businesses in Vietnam. Baker pointed to the combination of Vietnam's growing economy and the large potential market share for various industries—particularly petroleum exploration and development, one of Halliburton's specialties—arguing that the embargo was only harming United States interests. While Baker and the NFTC supported the administration's decision to lift the IMF restrictions, they criticized the president for not going far enough. Under the embargo, U.S. firms were still banned from bidding on or participating in the many infrastructure projects likely to result from the new IMF loans. Thus, Baker pointed out, American businesses found themselves "in the unusual position of having its own government use U.S. tax dollars directly or indirectly to fund economic activity from which they are legally barred."[88]

Perhaps no issue sums up the central tension of American policy—access versus leverage—better than the question of U.S. opposition to loans from the IMF. During the normalization debates of the late 1970s one of the major concerns among policymakers was the "politicization" of IFIs. The Carter administration and such IFI representatives as Robert McNamara, president of the World Bank, opposed using the institutions to enforce U.S. policy in developing countries. A decade later, their concerns had been forgotten in the debate over lifting the embargo. The institutions were by 1991 clearly under the thumb of the United States—which continued to exercise its veto to ensure that there would be no loans to Vietnam from the IMF, World Bank, or Asian Development Bank. Absent any discussion of whether or not it was legitimate for the United States to use the institutions to punish the Vietnamese, the only issue by then was how long to continue the ban. Meanwhile, the standard assumption of various anti-Vietnamese constituencies, particularly the POW/MIA lobby, was that the Vietnamese not only wanted but needed the loans. The reality was far more complex.

Although it was barred from direct lending to Vietnam, the IMF was active in Hanoi. Representatives of the fund were not barred by U.S. policy from advising Vietnam, and they continued to do so throughout the 1980s, peddling such neoliberal "reform" measures as privatizing state-controlled resources and programs (including health care and education), liberalization of investment codes (particularly, foreign ownership regulations), and ending subsidies for agriculture and industry. By the end of 1987, as part of its market-based *doi moi* economic program, Hanoi had, in the words of historian Gabriel Kolko, agreed to "the entire IMF package, one that many countries are reluctant to accept, much less implement." As Kolko persuasively demonstrates in his close study of the transformation of Vietnam's political economy after 1975, the IMF was a key contributor in the development of the Vietnamese "reforms" of the 1980s: "Whatever the Communist Party's rhetoric or its pretensions, Vietnam's economic and social direction since 1986 is comprehensible only in the context of the IMF's central influence. The party's ideologues still evoke Marx, Lenin, and Ho Chi Minh devoutly, but the IMF's inspiration has been far more decisive, and it has determined the nation's crucial priorities."[89] Had Vietnam not followed the IMF's advice in its economic program for the late 1980s, the question among U.S. law- and policymakers regarding the resumption of lending in the early 1990s would have been moot. Even so, it would be a while before the United States would finally cease to block both requests for new funding and any proposals to restructure Vietnamese arrears for current debt. But the Vietnamese did, as Kolko outlines, follow the IMF program—ironically, helping the country become both ripe for and vulnerable in the face of foreign investment.

Although Vietnam maintained a liberal foreign investment code, many firms were reluctant to do business there because of corruption and other bureaucratic and legal problems. In that sense, for the IMF to resume supporting projects in Vietnam would have been an important sign of security for investors. As the fund's representatives in Hanoi put it, "It would help reassure investors that the country [is] on the right economic path."[90] That the resumption of lending would be good for investors in the U.S. and elsewhere was, however, only one consideration. More pressing was the question of what impact further IMF dictates would have on the Vietnamese economy and the Vietnamese people going forward, particularly as the U.S. and other sanctions of the 1980s had now all but disappeared, and bilateral trade with nations in the region and around the globe was steadily increasing.

The Vietnamese Politburo remained in 1993, as it had been through most of the 1980s, divided as to whether the significant injection of capital that multilateral aid would provide was sufficiently necessary, given the potential costs. Those who favored a major influx of foreign capital pointed to the country's still-neglected infrastructure and the drastic drops in aid since the collapse of the Soviet Union in 1991. Others argued that finally gaining economic independence from the Soviets had forced Vietnam to become more self-sufficient—even if by borrowing. They had a hard row to hoe, in many respects. As a member of the Party told Nayan Chanda in 1995, "We started to develop only in 1991, when the Soviet aid stopped and the U.S. still had its embargo. We were like babies who stopped drinking milk and were starting to eat on their own."[91] While the record of progress for most nations that have put themselves under IMF—dictated reforms is checkered at best, there is evidence to recommend the position taken at the time by Chanda's source. Even with massive Soviet aid in the late 1980s, the Vietnamese economy was largely stagnant. Yet, in 1992, when the Soviet well had completely dried up, the Vietnamese economy grew by 8.3%, almost doubling in size from 1991. Inflation, historically one of

Vietnam's biggest problems, was held to 18%. Perhaps most significantly, Vietnam's trade deficit had been all but erased by 1992, despite the ongoing U.S. trade embargo and the disappearance of bilateral aid and trade either from or to the Soviet Union.[92]

Citing this progress, many in Vietnam questioned whether a massive influx of aid would be ultimately beneficial to the Vietnamese people. While there were any number of projects that called for significant financing—roads, bridges, and electrical infrastructure, notably—some wondered if the Party had the knowledge or the sense of priority to lead and control the rebuilding effort. "We're desperately short of capital," a Vietnamese representative of the Institute for Scientific and Technological Forecasting acknowledged, "but in my opinion our biggest difficulty is the lack of economic know-how." The bulk of training over the past several decades, he pointed out, had been dedicated to military, not economic planning, let alone market economics.[93] Even an American working for the World Bank was so impressed by the effective liberalizations that were already taking hold in the Vietnamese economy as to wonder whether the resumption of loans might even be in the country's interest: "[T]he World Bank is always looking for new clients and trying to push money on them. But Vietnam can push domestic reform further without multilateral aid. It might even be good for Vietnam not to have access to aid."[94]

Economists and historians remain sharply divided over whether the IMF-based reform measures have benefited the Vietnamese people as a whole.[95] Only after more time has passed and a generation has come of age under Vietnamese "market socialism" will we really have enough information to form useful conclusions. The crucial point here, as we leave 1993, is the manner in which the terms of debate in the United States, between those advocating either "leverage" or "access" as the focal point of American policy toward Vietnam, continued to render the Vietnamese people invisible. The apologists for leverage had never done anything but—while those advocating access were unquestionably correct in assuming that increased contact with the Vietnamese people would lead not only to greater opportunity and profit for American firms but to new progress in the search for the remains of American servicemen. In neither camp was much thought given to the effects of either course on the people of Vietnam.

Where once there had been talk of "lost opportunities" for peace—still so common in historical treatments of the war in Vietnam—there was now talk of lost opportunities for market share, and competitive bids. "Vietnam as market" was gradually replacing "Vietnam as war" (let alone "Vietnam as nation") as the construct's most common representation in American culture. Unfortunately, the U.S. government as a whole still chose to ignore events on the ground: this latest construction did nothing to make the Vietnamese people more visible in policy discussions. As the September deadline for renewing the Trading With the Enemy Act approached, the administration signaled that it was not prepared to unilaterally lift the sanctions, although it did indicate that it planned to allow American businesses to bid on IMF projects "pending the lifting of the embargo." (Which was lifted formally in December.) The United States' attempted global economic warfare on Vietnam was winding down, and the battle for access was over. On September 14, 1993, the American embargo of Vietnam entered the last of its eighteen years.

TRADING WITH THE ENEMY, 1994–1995

When the 103rd Congress of the United States returned to Washington for its second session, nearly all of the pieces were finally in place for the White House to lift the embargo. As *Time* put it in early 1994, "the issue of normalizing relations with Vietnam no longer hinges on the unanswered—or unanswerable—questions of what happened to America's missing soldiers; instead it has become a debate about whether the war is finally, conclusively over."[96] The only consideration left for Clinton was purely political: could the White House survive the inevitable onslaught of criticism from the POW/MIA lobby? The "leverage" argument of the National League of Families and its allies in Congress—that the embargo was the last bargaining chip left on the table in dealing with Vietnam—was no longer sustainable. While the basis for moving forward was obviously an economic one, the decision to end the sanctions would still have to be couched politically, and specifically in terms of an ongoing commitment to the POW/MIA-recovery cause. A *New York Times*/CBS News poll conducted in mid-January 1994 revealed that, although a small plurality of those questioned favored lifting the embargo (46 percent in favor versus 40 against), a significantly greater number, 56 percent, believed that Americans were still being held prisoner in Southeast Asia. In the face of such numbers, and of public perceptions of his record during and on the war, Clinton needed what the news media at the time termed "political cover."[97]

On January 27, 1994, the Senate held a lengthy, contentious debate over whether to give the president that cover. The floor fight, on a resolution recommending that the president end the embargo once and for all, introduced by Democrat John Kerry and Republican John McCain, brought out the animosity to be expected from anti-Vietnamese forces from both inside and outside the Senate chambers. Against the claims of Kerry and McCain that it was "time to put the war behind us," Senator Smith concurred with the VFW and NLOF, calling the idea of putting an end to the sanctions "immoral and incomprehensible."[98] But opponents of normalization were far outweighed by pro-business forces as well as by others who saw the embargo as an impediment to progress on the POW/MIA issue.

In the early hours of the 28th, a nonbinding resolution calling on the president to lift the embargo passed by a vote of 62–38. Although the administration tried to downplay its role in pushing for the resolution, it had, by all accounts, closely orchestrated its passage with Kerry and other supporters. While Kerry towed the administration's line as he placed himself at the center of the story, McCain was able to be more forthcoming in his statements to the press, telling the *Washington Post* that "The White House staff felt it was very important to pass this [resolution], given the problems that the President's lack of military background gives him on this sort of issue." Three days later, when it received word that the Justice Department was prepared to clear Commerce Secretary Ron Brown of charges that he had accepted a large payoff from Vietnamese-American businessmen in exchange for help in lifting the sanctions, the administration cleared the final political roadblock to changing the course of U.S.-Vietnamese relations.[99]

On February 3rd the *Washington Post* ran a story describing the "last bitter days of the personal Vietnam war" still being fought by "a handful of distressed and angry Americans." There had been almost no such characterization of the POW/MIA lobby in the mainstream press before. Murmurs from the White House indicating that the end of the embargo was imminent had led representatives of the NLOF and VFW to huddle in the Capitol for a last-minute "strategy session" with Bob Smith and Ross Perot. Smith and Perot "pleaded" for any suggestions on how to "head off" the White House plans, but were unable to come up with any serious proposals, and the entire group declared defeat. One member told the *Post* that all in attendance had come to recognize "that the handwriting was on the wall."[100] The POW/MIA lobby, at long last, had no more tricks up its sleeve.

Later that day, ringed by several veterans and members of Congress, Bill Clinton lifted the American embargo on Vietnam. He told the assembled guests and media that he was "absolutely convinced that [this] offers the best way to resolve the fate of those who remain missing and about whom we are not sure."[101] The president made it clear, though, that while the embargo had been lifted, full normalization of political and economic relations could still take some time. After detailing some of the progress that had been made in resolving outstanding cases, he made his case to the various groups opposing the move: "I want to be clear: These actions do not constitute a normalization of our relationships. Before that happens, we must have more progress, more cooperation, and more answers."[102]

The embargo, however, was at an end, and that moved a new set of questions to the forefront. Clinton's fervent rhetoric about the ongoing commitment to the POW/MIA issue only served to mask the new, economic focus of U.S.-Vietnamese relations. After his remarks, the first barrage of questions from the press was telling: "Mr. President, aren't you giving up some leverage, though? Could we ask about that? And what do you anticipate in terms of American trade? What's the size of the market? What do you think the opportunities are?" As he had for the past year, Clinton assured the public that economics played no role in his decision, insisting that he had not even received briefings on the benefits that lifting the embargo would provide for American business. "I thought it was very important," he responded, "that that not be a part of this decision."[103] American corporations, in any case, had no need for prognostications from Clinton. They had long been aware of the opportunities available to them in the Vietnamese market and were ready to seize their chance the moment the embargo was officially lifted.

The announcement from the White House set off a frenzy of contract signing, announcements of new services, and distributions of free samples from New York to Hanoi. Within an hour of Clinton's remarks, representatives of Pepsi set up an inflatable soda can and began handing out forty thousand free bottles of the soft drink in Ho Chi Minh City. A few hours later, about the same time that American Express signed a contract to be the first credit card accepted in Vietnam, United Airlines announced it was ready to begin service from Los Angeles to Ho Chi Minh City, pending final approval from Hanoi. Not to be outdone by its rival, Coca-Cola later that day unveiled a billboard in Ho Chi Minh City with the phrase, "Nice to see you again." Coke, which spent $250,000 on marketing and advertising in the first ten days after the embargo was lifted, proclaimed that it would spend $45 million on production in Vietnam over the next five years.[104] Pepsi responded a few days later, unleashing a new advertising campaign featuring the current Miss Vietnam.[105]

The headlines in the United States were unanimous in their predictions:

the war was finally over and a long, bitter, chilly relationship would soon be warmed by the prospect of trade. *Time* magazine featured a cartoon of Ho Chi Minh holding up an order of French fries sporting the likeness of Colonel Sanders, the fictional spokesperson of Kentucky Fried Chicken. "Vietnam," the *Washington Post*'s William Branigin declared, "can finally become for America a country instead of a war, a place of real people with a history and a future instead of U.S. national nightmare."[106] Yet the American media seemed unable to describe the new nation without resorting to the tropes of warfare. The marketplace of Saigon, papers declared, was the site of "the new Vietnam war," the latest "campaign for the hearts and minds of Vietnam's 71 million people." "Vietnam Braces for a New Invasion," declared *Newsweek*.[107] In particular, the American "cola wars" were seen as opening a new front in Vietnam. The *New York Times* proclaimed Coke-versus-Pepsi to be "the new Vietnam Combat"; in its pages and elsewhere the "battle" between the two soft drink giants was being followed closely, with Pepsi winning "the opening skirmish" but Coke "fighting back" strongly. The *Times* admitted to the irony of the situation, noting that fighting the cola wars on the streets of Hanoi was likely "the realization of the worst nightmare of a generation of dedicated Vietnamese Communists."[108]

While providing an accurate representation of the seemingly unbridled enthusiasm of American business interests breaking into the new market, the clever headlines and playful anecdotes were not indicative of the more cautious note struck in Vietnam itself. Were it not for the spectacle-laden antics of Pepsi and Coke, many Vietnamese might not have even been aware that the embargo had been lifted. The state television station ran the embargo story seventh on its morning broadcast. "The Vietnam issue has created many emotions in the United States," Deputy Foreign Minister Le Mai offered. "We Vietnamese have less emotions."[109] Official statements from Hanoi expressed cautious optimism regarding the long-awaited end to the sanctions, hailing "a new page in U.S.-Vietnam relations."[110] Accompanying such reactions, however, were calls for full diplomatic normalization and the establishment of most favored nation (MFN) status for Vietnam. Vietnamese leaders were acutely aware that they remained at a major disadvantage in the global economy without a full trade agreement with the United States. Ending the Trading With the Enemy Act "only allows American companies to sell in Vietnam," Le Van Bang, Vietnamese ambassador to the United Nations, told the *Far Eastern Economic Review* the night before Clinton's announcement. "It is not both ways because without MFN, we cannot compete and sell in the U.S."[111] Although the end of the sanctions was praised as a step in the right direction and, in the short term, a stimulus for American investment, without MFN status Vietnam would be unable to develop a balanced trade program.

The effects of this lack of reciprocity were apparent in the case of Vietnam's negotiations with Boeing. The American aerospace giant had agreed in principle with the Vietnamese government to a sale of four 737 aircraft only a few months earlier. Because the White House had not yet lifted the embargo, however, Boeing lost its chance at the $160 million contract, passed over for the European firm Airbus. Ironically, Airbus could only lease its aircraft to Vietnam because they had a sufficient number of U.S.-manufactured components to be prohibited by the embargo. Both Boeing and Hanoi were thus happy to revive their deal in 1994. After the lifting of the embargo, Boeing announced that it expected Vietnam to buy at least sixty aircraft over the next decade, to the tune of around $4 billion. The Vietnamese were not as optimistic. While they needed the planes, the Vietnamese economist Le Dan Doanh argued, Hanoi would be unable to purchase such a fleet without a reduction in American tariffs on Vietnamese goods sold to the United States: "Now Vietnam can buy Boeings, but it can't sell textiles in the U.S. A one-way street can't be maintained for a long time. Vietnam needs to pay for its imports."[112]

Thus, despite the warnings of the POW/MIA lobby, the Vietnamese had been far from emboldened by the lifting of the sanctions. If anything, the reaction from Hanoi should have reinforced the view that the United States was clearly still in a position of power relative to Vietnam. In Washington, however, the various anti-Vietnamese constituencies were not prepared to go quietly. A week after Clinton announced the end of the embargo, the House Subcommittee on Asia and the Pacific held a hearing appropriately named "POW/MIA: Where Do We Go from Here?" The last hearing of its type to be held before the United States and Vietnam normalized diplomatic relations, the testimony demonstrates the tatters in which the POW/MIA lobby found itself, and the extent to which it continued to misread the power dynamics of American relations with Vietnam.

Gary Ackerman, the representative from New York who had taken over as chair of the subcommittee after the departure of Solarz, opened by stating that, in light of the lifting the embargo, the United States "must immediately move to ensure that Hanoi does not interpret this action to mean that it is off the hook on providing a full accounting of our missing Vietnam war heroes."[113] Other members of the committee made similarly worded opening remarks, calling for diligence on the POW/MIA issue while assuring the many members of the POW/MIA lobby in attendance that the end of the embargo did not constitute normalized relations or a commitment of U.S. aid. Representative Dana Rohrabacher claimed that the administration had "just given up the tremendous leverage that we had on South Vietnam [*sic*] by lifting the embargo."[114] Luis Gutierrez of Illinois argued that the final chapter of the war had not yet been written, contrary to all accounts in the news media. That would be accomplished only when the United States could "find out all of the information of those who went to Vietnam, but did not return."[115]

A member of the "POW/MIA grassroots organization" dug up the issue of the 1973 Nixon reparations letter, arguing that it continued to serve as Hanoi's basis for withholding live American prisoners. "Can we not for once, just once," she pleaded, "put aside all other considerations except for to secure the release of any Americans being held against their will?"[116] Former POW Michael Benege provided perhaps the most outrageous comments of the hearings, stating matter-of-factly, "Hanoi knows where the bodies are buried. Why would Hanoi hold POWs? The Vietnamese Communists are not born-again Christians. They are not Mr. Nice Guy." Benege went on to accuse Hanoi of continuing to hold prisoners from the First Indochina War as well. "This is documented, that they hold French POWs." "By lifting the trade embargo," Benege concluded, "President Clinton lost a unique opportunity to heal the wounds of the Vietnam War."[117]

If the purpose of the hearings was, in part, to determine the future direction of the POW/MIA lobby, prospects for the movement were not bright. In fact, statements from members of the committee as well as witnesses only serve to confirm how out of step they were with the new direction of relations with Vietnam. The rigidly anti-Vietnamese sentiments expressed by Benege and others clearly represented the attitudes of a minority both of the American public and among American policy makers after the lifting of the embargo. Images of an America held hostage by devilish Asian Communists had long disappeared, replaced by a triumphant cold war victory and the demise of the Soviet Union. Once the centerpiece and driving force behind American policy toward Vietnam, the POW/MIA lobby by 1994 was largely reduced to an afterthought. Policymakers continued to pledge their ongoing commitment to the mission of obtaining a "full accounting" from the Vietnamese, but the direction of U.S.-Vietnamese relations was now being dictated largely by the forces of the global economy and the Vietnamese market.

In line with this new economic focus, the issue of settling outstanding corporate claims against Vietnam was raised at the hearings. Robert Torricelli, designated spokesman in Congress for the corporate claimants, made a brief appearance at the outset of the session, asserting that the corporate victims of the war should not be abandoned in the push for normalization. Like the POW/MIA activists, Torricelli wanted "to continue pressure on the Vietnamese"—but it was to be a different kind of pressure, the opportunity for which was now provided by the evolving economic dynamics of U.S.-Vietnamese relations. In the year ahead, it would be Torricelli's corporate claims, not the claims of the POW/MIA lobby, that would be the basis of the bilateral negotiations between Washington and Hanoi.

THE FINAL STEP: REVERSE REPARATIONS AND NORMALIZATION

As 1995 began, the pieces for constructing a new era of relations between Vietnam and the United States were seemingly in hand. With the embargo lifted and international lending fully restored, American trade with and investment in Vietnam increased significantly, as did U.S. participation in bilateral and multilateral aid. In 1993, the Vietnamese government reported $500 million in foreign assistance, up from an average of less than $100 million during the late 1980s and early 1990s. At the fall 1993 IMF and World Bank meetings, with no more U.S. opposition, Hanoi received aid pledges of nearly $2 billion. Under the limited waiver opportunities permitted under the embargo during 1993, American companies exported about $7 million worth of products to Vietnam. In 1994, the exports jumped to $160 million.[118] The prospects for aid and trade only increased in the final five years of the century, but several obstacles to increased U.S. business activity in Vietnam and to full economic normalization for the Vietnamese remained.

Although the end of the embargo brought a long-awaited groundswell of foreign investment, many of the legal safeguards to which American firms working overseas had grown accustomed could not be put in place without further measures. The Overseas Private Investment Corporation (OPIC), and the Export-Import Bank of the United States (Ex-Im Bank), both of which provided support for American businesses operating internationally, continued to be prohibited from working with Vietnam because of "a complex set of statutory constraints," most of which stemmed from Vietnam's status as a nonmarket economy.[119] Many of these restraints were odd relics of the cold war that seemed particularly ill-suited to dealing with the most central aspects of U.S. foreign economic policy in 1995. Section 620(f) of the Foreign Assistance Act, for instance, required the president to issue a waiver in order for OPIC or the United States Trade and Development Agency to assist American firms doing business with any Communist country. The presidential determination was required to substantiate that "(a) the assistance is vital to U.S. security, (b) the country is not controlled by the international Communist conspiracy and (c) the assistance will promote independence from International communism."[120] Less severe was the Jackson-Vanik waiver, required by the Trade Act of 1974, an annual presidential waiver asserting either that the governments of the named nonmarket-economy countries allowed their citizens to emigrate freely, or that the waiver would help promote reform and progress on emigration issues.[121]

The Foreign Assistance Act also prohibited the U.S. government from promoting trade with or providing aid to countries that had illegally expropriated American property—private or government—or had defaulted on previous loans from the United States.[122] Vietnam fit both these categories: the property seized in 1975 was taken in violation of international law, and the collapse of the Saigon regime in April of that year left the United States with around $150 million in unpaid loans from the defunct Republic of South Vietnam. Given the enormous economic—let alone human—costs that the United States inflicted on Vietnam both during and after the military phase of the war, it might have been reasonable for the United States to make exceptions in order to "heal the wounds of war," as the normalization process was avowedly designed to do. Vietnam, however, remained at a distinct disadvantage throughout the normalization process, with no real leverage to speak of. From the point of view of the United States government, the settlement of these outstanding claims was the final obstacle to normalization—and the Vietnamese would once again acquiesce to American demands.

For several years, the claims issue arose sporadically at government hearings on policies toward Vietnam or Cambodia, with the most significant point of contention being whether or not to include the claims of private American companies and individuals simultaneously with those of the U.S. government. The issue was first openly debated in 1979, when the claims against Vietnam were formally referred to the Foreign Claims Settlement Commission (FCSC) and the International Claims Settlement Act of 1949 was amended to include reference to Vietnam.[123] After a six-year investigation, the commission ruled in 1986 that 192 of the 534 claims met the requirements for compensation. Over half (58%) of the 192 confirmed claims had been brought by a handful of petroleum companies. The total amount of the claims awarded was just under $100 million dollars.[124] Ironically, by 1980, when the commission was charged with investigating the outstanding claims against Vietnam, the Vietnamese assets that had been frozen by the U.S. in 1975 were worth almost exactly this amount.[125]

The assets continued to appreciate considerably. Originally valued at $70 million when they were frozen in 1975, they were estimated to be worth $150 million in 1983; by 1989, $245 million; and by 1994 they were commonly valued at $290 million (although by some estimates at well over $300 million).[126] As Robert Torricelli told a House committee at the time the embargo was lifted, this amount was "far more than necessary to pay the claims."[127] The claims, however, were also subject to appreciation. According to the terms provided by the settlement legislation, all approved claims were to be adjusted by simple interest calculations at a rate of 6 percent per year, retroactive to 1975. Thus the claims were worth $99 million in 1986, $200 million in 1989, and nearly $220 million by 1995.[128] These amounts reflected only private claims, though, and did not include the $150 million in outstanding loans claimed by the U.S. government. Combining the government and private claims, the total reached approximately $370 million in 1995, well over the estimated $300 million-plus value of the frozen Vietnamese assets. In effect, the U.S. was negotiating political and economic normalization with the Vietnamese from the stance that it was *owed* tens, if not hundreds, of millions of dollars.

Some in Congress had for years been trying to pay out claims from the frozen assets without reaching a full agreement with the Vietnamese government. Since the bulk of the assets held in the United States were formerly property of the Republic of Vietnam, which had ceased to exist in 1975, some in Congress responded positively to legislation, authored by lawyers representing the corporate claimants, asserting that the current government of Vietnam had no legal right to the frozen funds. The case was bolstered by the fact that the United States had not yet legally recognized the government of the Socialist Republic of Vietnam.[129] The SRV had formally accepted the international responsibilities of the former North and South Vietnam in 1975 and 1976, and it was a commonplace of international law that a new government was entitled and obligated to assume both the rights and liabilities of the previous one—which would clear the way to direct claims against the Vietnamese government, but would also dictate that the United States release the frozen assets to the Vietnamese. In the eyes of the United States, however, as one litigator argued in 1989: "Vietnam is not, however, the normal case, and the normal rule does not automatically apply."[130]

After a twenty-year impasse, on January 28, 1995, the United States and Vietnam signed a historic Agreement Concerning the Settlement of Certain Property Claims. The agreement arranged for Vietnam to pay private claims of United States nationals ("both natural and juridical persons") in the amount of $208,510,481.[131] The claims of the United States government for the RVN loans were not covered by this arrangement. Only in 1997 did the two governments reach an agreement on this issue, when Treasury Secretary Robert Rubin and Finance Minister Nguyen Sinh Hung agreed that the SRV would repay $145 million in loans from the former Saigon regime. The agreement also called for a "down payment" of $8.5 million to cover the interest on the loans. The down payment was due within 30 days; the full loan was to be paid off through "regular payments" until 2019.[132]

"BINDING OUR WOUNDS"

With the corporate claims issue settled, there was no longer anything standing in the way of normalization. Although the White House would still have to fend off criticism from the POW/MIA lobby, the American media were beginning to dismiss the increasingly desperate antics of some of the groups and individuals still carrying on the fight. In June, as speculation grew that normalization was imminent, former North Carolina Congressman Billy Hendon, a longtime advocate of various POW conspiracy theories, repeatedly chained himself to the headquarters of the U.S. POW/MIA office in Hanoi. Hendon, who appeared several times at various congressional hearings and was responsible for some of the most outrageous assertions about live prisoners, claimed that he knew where American prisoners were being held. Refusing to divulge the location, he informed authorities that he would lead them to the men. Eventually, a U.S. government team investigated Hendon's purported underground prison, fifty miles outside of Hanoi. The spot turned out to be a depot for military vehicles. No evidence related to American prisoners was found.[133]

Around the same time as Hendon's grandstanding, another American team received permission to undertake a massive excavation at a series of Vietnamese military cemeteries. It unearthed hundreds of Vietnamese corpses in the vague hope of finding a few isolated remains of American servicemen. None were found. “Imagine,” Jonathan Alter wondered in *Newsweek,* “if the Government of Vietnam believed that one of its estimated 300,000 MIAs had been mistakenly buried in Arlington national cemetery. Would the United States allow the Vietnamese to go into Arlington in the middle of the night and dig up old bones?” Yet the Vietnamese continued to cooperate and to assist the American teams with their efforts. The younger Vietnamese, in particular, Alter pointed out, were “sympathetic to all this but a bit perplexed by the American obsession with the war.”[134] Back home, Bob Smith, joined now by Senator Bob Dole, made a last-ditch effort to derail diplomatic recognition of Vietnam by preempting the approval of funds for an American embassy, should relations be normalized.

On July 11, 1995, however, in a solemn, brief, and understated ceremony in the East Room of the White House, President Bill Clinton announced that the United States was establishing diplomatic relations with Vietnam. Couching the announcement, as ever, in the language of continued progress on a full accounting of those listed as POW/MIA, Clinton noted that only fifty-five “discrepancy cases” remained open. Normalization would help the United States “move forward on an issue that has separated Americans from one another for too long now,” Clinton predicted. “This moment offers us the opportunity to bind up our own wounds. They have resisted time for too long. We can now move on to common ground. Whatever divided us before, let us consign to the past. Let this moment, in the words of Scripture, ‘Be a time to heal, and a time to build.’ ”[135] Try as he might, though, Clinton could not consign these specifically American wounds to the past.

Angered by the administration’s action, the Republican-controlled Congress seized it as an opportunity, reviving the Smith-Dole bill that would have denied funding for an American embassy in Vietnam. The debate was carried on in full rhetorical mode. “A slap in the face” to the “friends and families of American MIAs,” one member of the House International Affairs Committee labeled normalization. “A blot, a stain on our government,” cried another.[136] But there was little enthusiasm among the public for the punitive proposal. In a *New York Times* survey conducted immediately after the normalization announcement, nearly all the respondents supported rapprochement with Vietnam. Even some who believed that Americans were still being held in Vietnamese prison camps recognized that the time had come. “The question should be, can Vietnam forgive us,” said one respondent. “If we had won,” argued another, “this wouldn’t be an issue." Not everyone was convinced, of course. "It's the same Vietnam that took our sons and brothers," said a woman who lost family in the war. "I could never forgive them for that."[137]

That August, in a grand public ceremony held in Hanoi, Secretary of State Warren Christopher and Foreign Minister Nguyen Canh Cam signed the official papers opening the American embassy. The ceremony was upbeat, including a champagne toast. Cam told the assembled guests that a new era in U.S.-Vietnamese relations had, at long last, arrived: "We want Americans to view Vietnam as a country, and not as a war." As the American flag was raised over the embassy, it seemed that the United States was finally prepared to do just that. Yet, for twenty years, the American war in Vietnam had proved itself singularly resistant to all attempts at closure—at least in the United States, where there was still no definitive ending to the multiple narratives the war had produced. The period after 1995 would continue that trend, bringing new battles in the ongoing American war with the nation, the market—and the memory—of Vietnam.

INVISIBLE ENEMIES
SEARCHING FOR VIETNAM AT THE WALL(S)

I didn't want a monument,
not even one as sober as that
vast black wall of broken lives.
I didn't want a road beside the Delaware
River with a sign proclaiming:
"Vietnam Veterans Memorial Highway."
What I wanted was a simple recognition
of the limits of our power as a nation
to inflict our will on others.
What I wanted was an understanding
that the world is neither black-and-white
nor ours.
What I wanted was an end to monuments.
W. D. Erhardt, "The Invasion of Grenada,"
from *To Those Who Have Gone Home Tired: New and Selected Poems* (1984)

Nothing more aptly sums up the story, for the United States and its people, of the American war on Vietnam after 1975 as the establishment of the Vietnam Veterans Memorial in Washington, D.C. From the first proposal in 1979 to build such a memorial, to the initial construction in the early 1980s toward Maya Lin's design, through the passage of legislation in late 2003 to add an "Education Center" to the site, the history of "The Wall," as the memorial is commonly called in the United States, spanned nearly the entire post-military phase of the war. Over that time, the Wall has been a key battleground in the contest over cultural memories of the war: a powerful symbol for various veterans' constituencies and the POW/MIA lobby; a common setting, even a motif, in works of fiction and nonfiction about the war; a symbol used by legislators to advance and publicize an array of policy positions. 

But the Wall also speaks for itself. Unfortunately, just as is found elsewhere along the cultural front in the ongoing war in Vietnam, the Wall consistently renders the nation and people of Vietnam invisible—

demonstrating, if anything does, how unavoidably central that absence is to the reconstruction of American nationalism and American imperialism after 1975.

It is not surprising that a national monument to veterans of a war, even one as divisive as the American war in Vietnam, would focus on the deaths of Americans rather than those of allied soldiers, civilians, or enemy forces. Indeed, the invisibility of the Vietnamese at the Wall (and its progeny) is predictable, and more easily explained than their nearly utter absence elsewhere on the cultural front. What makes the absence of any mention of the Vietnamese at the Wall particularly glaring, however, is the fact that ever since its inception the memorial has consistently been challenged to become more "inclusive" as a site of public history and memory.

Over the past two decades, various groups and individuals, feeling that the site could not contain or represent their stories and memories, have sought to point out and address the limitations of the memorial. Throughout the often bitter political and cultural battles over the changes that have been made to the original design, the absence of any mention of Vietnam or the Vietnamese has become more and more conspicuous. By exploring these battles, and the narrative structure of the memorial(s)—the ways in which material, spatial, and contextual elements structure visitors' bodies and experience in particular ways—we can identify some of the means by which, upon the still active cultural front of the American war on Vietnam, the war has been re-inscribed in American cultural memory.[1]

THE WALL GOES UP

The Vietnam Veterans Memorial began with Jan Scruggs, an American veteran of the war. After seeing *The Deer Hunter* in the spring of 1979, Scruggs awoke from a night of traumatic flashbacks to tell his wife, "I'm going to build a memorial to all the guys who served in Vietnam. It'll have the name of everyone killed."[2] It went without saying that, by "everyone," he meant Americans. Scruggs and his fellow veterans embarked on a remarkable campaign, raising awareness of veterans issues as they raised millions of dollars from individuals, private organizations, and American corporations to fund the memorial. After they had battled members of Congress and endured the first of many battles with the National Park Service, legislation designating a two-acre spot on the National Mall for the memorial was signed into law by President Carter in June of 1980.

When the Vietnam Veterans Memorial Fund (VVMF), the organization set up by Scruggs to finance construction, announced the design competition for the memorial, it began the process of defining the narrative boundaries of the site. Only two explicit rules were laid out for the contest: entries were to incorporate the names of American soldiers who died in Vietnam, and they were not to be "political" in nature. The mission statement for the design competition set forth a theme of reconciliation that the VVMF saw as apolitical in nature: "The Memorial will make no political statement about the war or its conduct. It will transcend those issues. The hope is that the creation of the Memorial will begin a healing process."[3] As Scruggs and his partners were soon to find out, both of the requirements would prove to be points of contention. The question of whose name would be allowed to be included on the Wall would provide the driving force for several additions to the site in the ensuing years. More to the point, it was impossible for anything related to the American war in Vietnam to be apolitical.

At the end of the contest, the largest of its kind in American history at the time, the unlikely winner emerged: Maya Ying Lin, a twenty-one-year-old undergraduate architecture student at Yale. Lin, born in Ohio, was a particular surprise to many because of her Asian American heritage. She would later write that at the time of the contest she had been "naïve" about her "racial identity." When her design was announced as the winner, a reporter asked her, "Isn't it ironic that the war in Vietnam was fought in Asia and you are of Asian descent?" Lin dismissed the question as "completely racist—and completely irrelevant." When she saw the story in the *Washington Post* the following day, however, she realized that "we were going to have problems." The article, which focused on elements of Taoism and Zen present in the design, labeled Lin "an Asian artist for an Asian war." As Lin recalled, "Eventually, though, it occurred to me to ask the veterans if my race mattered. They seemed embarrassed—and it was then that I realized that people were having problems with the fact that a 'gook' had designed the memorial. It left me chilled."[4]

The unease of some over Lin's identity would subside somewhat, at least publicly, over the course of the site's development. It was her design that would prove to be the real focus of controversy. Although the design would endure through the various alterations that were to be imposed on the site, Lin herself would be overtly marginalized in the process. Over the course of negotiations, Lin, who represented the "Other" to so many involved in the memorial, was nearly rendered as invisible as the ghostly Vietnamese presence at the Wall.

Lin's design had been praised by the selection jury for its simplicity and minimalism: two long, black granite walls descending into the earth, with the names of the dead listed in chronological order of their death. As Lin described her memorial years later:

> At the intersection of these walls, on the right side, at the wall's top, is carved the date of the first death. It is followed by the names of those who have died in the war in chronological order. These names continue on this wall, appearing to recede into the earth at the wall's end. The names resume on the left wall as the wall emerges from the earth back to the origin where the date is carved at the bottom of this wall. Thus, the war's beginning and end meet. The war is complete, coming full circle yet broken by the earth that bounds the angle's open side and contained within the earth itself. As we turn to leave, we see these walls stretching into the distances, directing us to the Washington Monument to the left, and the Lincoln Memorial to the right, thus bringing the Vietnam memorial into historical context. We the living are brought to a concrete realization of these deaths. Brought to a sharp awareness of such a loss, it is up to each individual to resolve or come to terms with this loss.[5]

This uniquely nonlinear chronological listing of the names was a point of contention for some of the veterans groups associated with the construction of the memorial, but they eventually agreed that the "narrative framework," as Marita Sturken puts it, "provides a spatial reference for their experience of the war, a kind of memory map." "The refusal of linearity" in Lin's design, Sturken adds, "is appropriate to a conflict that has no narrative closure."[6] Rejecting the traditional role of the war memorial, Lin's memorial refuses to allow the war in Vietnam to be contained "within the particular master narratives" of history. Rather, the Wall "refuses to sanction the closure of the conflict."[7]

Indeed, the lack of "closure" provided by the design is the single most important factor in its narrative structure. The Wall is inherently open-ended—and thus participatory. The list of names in and of itself, as Kristin Haas suggests, requires "a certain amount of participation" by visitors.[8] Even more generally, however, the memorial was designed to leave the task of interpretation to the individual visitors. As one of the jury members said, "People can bring to it whatever they want."[9] Although the "historical context" described by Lin was a key component in the design and does situate the memorial, and thus the war in Vietnam, in relation to the larger narrative space of the mall, that relationship is, at best, ambiguous. In the end, the historical referents were less important to Lin than the cathartic potential of the site. "Death is in the end a personal and private matter," she wrote of her design, "and the area contained within this memorial is a quiet place, meant for personal reflection and private reckoning."[10] The original discursive structure of the Wall, then, was centered around personal narratives and private acts of memory, leaving the larger questions "about the war or its conduct" appropriately unresolved.

Not everyone shared the jury's reading of the design, however. For many, the ambiguity of the proposal and the open-ended narrative structure, although seemingly in line with the competition's guidelines, were threatening. Many disparaged Lin's design for not being sufficiently upbeat and patriotic. A group of Republicans in Congress sent a letter to President Reagan, labeling the design "a political statement of shame and dishonor."[11] Author Tom Wolfe called it "a tribute to Jane Fonda."[12] Tom Cahart, a veteran and member of the VVMF who had offered his own design in the competition, labeled the Wall "a black gash of shame." Cahart, whose own proposal featured an officer offering a dead GI up to heaven while standing in a large purple heart, went on to lead the public relations battle against accepting Lin's design.[13] The conservative magazine *National Review* provided yet another scathing critique of the proposal, labeling it "an Orwellian Glop." It even went after Lin for following the most basic criterion of the competition, listing the names of all the Americans who died in the war: "The mode of listing the names makes them individual deaths, not deaths in a cause: they might as well have been traffic accidents."[14] Lin later claimed, making the same point as did many of the design's supporters at the time, that the names, "seemingly infinite in number, convey the overwhelming numbers while unifying the individuals as a whole. For this memorial is meant not as a monument to the individual, but rather as a memorial to the men and women who died in the war as a whole."[15] Such arguments were no use, however. In the face of the small but vocal outcry, the White House directed Interior Secretary James Watt to delay the planned groundbreaking of the memorial, scheduled for that spring, until a "compromise" could be reached.

Despite a raft of defenders on the jury and among the veterans groups sponsoring the memorial, Lin was abandoned by many key players, including Scruggs, who feared losing the site altogether and favored a quick resolution to the dispute. The VVMF chose to work out a deal with opposing forces so that the construction of the memorial could proceed on schedule. The original compromise called for a flagpole to be placed on top of the intersection of the two component walls and a statue, described in advance as "a strong commanding figure symbolizing all who served in Vietnam," to be placed directly in front of the Wall. Reports also circulated that inscriptions would be added, including one that would read, "For those who fought for it, freedom has a flavor," and another quoting former American POW Jeremiah Denton: "We are honored to have had the opportunity to serve our country under difficult circumstances. God Bless America!"[16] Lin was understandably upset at the proposed changes to her design, though she attempted throughout the ordeal to accommodate the disparate demands of various groups. While the flag and statue would later be situated away from their proposed locations and the inscriptions would be dropped altogether, for Lin the damage was already done. When the groundbreaking ceremony was held on March 27, 1982, she was noticeably absent, as she was that November when the Wall was officially opened.

Although it was not in place for either the groundbreaking or the dedication, the statue continued to be a source of controversy. In July 1982, Lin broke her silence and offered public criticism of the addition. With the agreement incorporating the statue finalized, Lin accused the sculptor, Frederick Hart, of "drawing mustaches on other people's portraits."[17] The statue, which would be cast and installed in 1984, portrays three stoic American soldiers of diverse ethnic backgrounds staring across to the Wall. Haas describes the figures as "strong, masculine, and heroic," the prescribed antidote, for many, to Lin's more ambiguous Wall.[18] When it was finally unveiled, Lin said of the statue, "Three men standing there before the world—it's trite. It's a generalization, a simplification. Hart gives you an image—he's illustrating a book." Others weighed in as well. The art critic for the *Boston Globe* called Hart's piece a "Starsky and Hutch pose."[19] Scruggs defended the statue, claiming that, far from detracting from Lin's vision, Hart's piece "makes it 100 percent better, much more beautiful." Members of the selection committee, including architect Harry Weese, sympathized with Lin: "It's as if Michelangelo had the Secretary of the Interior climb onto the scaffold and muck around with his work."[20] Perhaps the *Economist* put it most aptly, however, when it opined, "This 'improvement' would make the V-shaped memorial more like other memorials, but it cannot make Vietnam more like other wars."[21]

When the statue was officially added to the site on Veterans Day in 1984, two years after the initial dedication of the Wall, Lin was again absent; her name was not even mentioned during the proceedings that day. Unlike the 1982 dedication, when President Reagan stayed away due to "security concerns," in 1984 he lent authority to the addition of the statue by showing up to accept, on behalf of the federal government, the memorial as a gift from the VVMF.[22] With the statue now keeping watch over the Wall from across the knoll, many at the ceremony felt the memorial was finally ready to fulfill its avowed purpose of promoting healing and reconciliation among Americans. The *New York Times*, writing of the dedication ceremony, claimed that the statue finally "completed" the memorial.[23]

The battle to include the statue and flagpole was only the first of many over the narrative structure of the memorial. The imposition of the more overtly political, patriotic, and heroic statue was intended to situate visitors in a less ambiguous discursive framework. Despite the manner in which the additions were handled and the way in which Lin was treated during the ordeal, Hart's addition proved to be a fairly benign addition to the site. Lin's more open-ended structure was designed to allow visitors to come to their own conclusions and interpretations, and Hart's sculpture did not impose closure on the memorial. Rather, it provides an arguably useful and appropriate tension to the site, representing a different vision of the war in Vietnam and its legacy for the American soldiers who fought and died there. Even Lin would later admit, "In a funny sense, the compromise brings the memorial closer to the truth. What is also memorialized is that people still cannot resolve that war, nor can they separate the issues, the politics, from it."[24]

As would be the case with future battles, various groups and figures attempted to put and end to such campaigns by declaring, as the *Times* did in 1984, that the memorial was "finished," or "completed." But the Wall, like the larger signifier of "Vietnam" in American culture, steadily and stubbornly resisted attempts to pronounce it finished. Yet, although her design had been altered thanks to political considerations, Lin's vision of the Wall persevered. Visitors began to flock to the memorial, immediately making it the most visited monument in Washington. Regardless of the changes made at the site, the powerful tension created—between the Wall as "a quiet place, meant for personal reflection and private reckoning," and the profoundly national space formed by its insertion in the National Mall—would continue to exert a powerful force on the established narrative boundaries of both the site and its setting.

As Sturken points out, the Wall "functions in opposition to the codes of remembrance evidenced on the Washington Mall."[25] In contrast to the traditional elevated white structures, the Wall, with its reflective black surfaces set below ground level of the mall's broad expanse, is designed both to be partially hidden from the larger narrative of the mall—chiefly structured by the Washington Monument and the Lincoln Memorial—and to stand out: to be different, to mark an interruption in the grand narrative sweep of American history. That tension extends to the personal interactions and private experiences that occur in this place, still, of living memory. Uncertain as most are, as to how exactly the war in Vietnam fits into United States history, most visitors to the Wall are similarly dealing with how the war has affected them personally, be it in regard to the image they have of their nation, or in light of what the war did to them and their families. Visitors to—participants in—the site are thus, as a result of the narrative structure of the memorial, placed in a situation where cultural memory, national history, and private loss (for almost all, at some level) come together, and in which visitors are forced to confront conflicting frameworks and interpretations of the past. As David Thelen describes it, "Maya Lin designed a memorial that brilliantly allowed those with large political agendas and those with intimate private memories to come together."[26]

More than anything else, the Wall was designed to be interactive. Although no one imagined the eventual scope or degree of that interaction between visitor and memorial, the literally reflective face of the memorial in itself forced a degree of interaction not present with other structures on the mall. Visitors see themselves in the shiny granite face of the Wall, and, from many angles, they also see reflected the Washington and Lincoln memorials and the additional statues at the Wall site itself. And this play of reflections, of course—visual, mental—is set in motion against a background of or as background to (alternately) the engraved names of the dead.

Furthermore, visitors must *allow their bodies to be taken in:* in this structure which, uniquely among the mall's great memorials, must be approached to within touching distance if one is to gain any true impression of it, visitors go down to the depth of the Wall, guided by and into the structure of the site, bounded, by ropes on one side of their path and the Wall itself on the other. They are at the same time structured into, made part of, the memorial's narrative—fleetingly but literally, in the black granite's reflective face—and invited, encouraged, allowed to act as their own narrators and guides. Each visitor, reflected there for himself, herself, or anyone else to see, redraws and remakes the always unfinished memorial. This will go on as a function of the Wall's structure long past living memory; for as long as the construct "Vietnam" means anything in American consciousness, it promises to transcend the personal. This is precisely the type of terrain that Sturken would describe as a place of cultural memory, a continually fluctuating, contested battleground in struggles over the meaning of the past.

The most readable, publicly revealed form of interaction with the Wall, however, arises from the tradition of visitors leaving artifacts at the memorial. This practice, which began almost immediately back in 1982 and continues to this day, is the focus of Kristin Haas's book, *Carried to the Wall.* Leaving these items, visitors to the site both experience and perform acts of memory, bringing their own narratives of or regarding the war to the Wall, and negotiating both memory and interpretation within the narrative structure provided by the Wall. The visitor knows that these added marks of memory will not remain—though each day, they are added to the National Park Service's archive—yet they continue to appear, left at the base of the Wall in a participatory and supremely privatized memorialization.

But what, exactly, do these objects represent? Haas examines these artifacts for the insight they may offer, and finds, most notably, a marking of the narrative limits of the monument itself—perhaps not entirely unlike that effected by insertion of the flag, the statues, and the "In Memory" plaque. "The restive memory of the war changed American public commemoration," Haas writes, "because the memory could not be expressed or contained by Lin's powerful and suggestive design alone. The deep need to remember the war and the challenges that it presented to the idea of the nation, the soldier, and the citizen met in Lin's design and inspired hundreds of thousands of Americans to bring their own memorials to the Wall. These intensely individuated public memorials forge a richly textured memory of the war and its legacies."[27] That the objects left by visitors go beyond and thus mark a limitation in the narrative structure of the memorial is sufficiently clear; the more interesting question has to do with the extent to which Haas's "intensely individuated" memorials are at the same time "public."

While Haas offers a fascinating description of items left at the Wall, and rightly notes that a complex of memories are both brought to and born at the site, her assertion that this constitutes a "public debate" over the meaning of the war is ultimately unconvincing. The memory or memories negotiated and contested, privately and publicly, at the Real Wall (as opposed to the Virtual Walls discussed below, which terms I use without prejudice to those in either category) may have arisen from a divisive and devastating war, but the acts of memory performed at the Wall offer little if any evidence of public debate about the public meaning of the war. They are acts concerned primarily with the memories of American individuals, families, and friends. Although these memories are, in fact, often negotiated by way of conflict with the shared narrative shaped by the memorial itself, this particular monument powerfully serves as a space for individual emotion, and that is how it appears by almost all to be used. The proliferation of individual forms of remembrance does little to challenge the dominance of the national narrative at the wall. Occasionally, as we have already seen, the war over cultural memory at the Wall becomes more inclusive and more "public." Such struggles have sometimes resulted in actual physical changes to the memorial. In almost all cases, the driving force is the tension implicit in resolving individual, yet inexorably grouped, narratives with the national narrative of the site.

This was particularly evident in the 1993 addition of Glenda Goodacre's Vietnam Women's Memorial. Sturken points out that the decision to include this statue, which features three nurses caring for a fallen soldier, was based on a more or less acknowledged concern among all parties for "inclusion and recognition." Certainly, American women who served in the war are not represented by the Wall; there are few female names on the memorial. This absence may be seen, as Haas suggests, as part of a long practice in American society of rendering "women's war work" invisible.[28] For one thing, there is a long tradition in the United States of not fully recognizing all its branches of service. In many ways, however, the addition of Goodacre's statue has to be read alongside the addition of Hart's Three Servicemen even more so than the Wall itself. While the Wall exclusively memorializes the dead, Hart's piece seemed to offer a particularly masculinized form of remembrance. The addition of the Vietnam Women's Memorial, however, was seen by many as an unnecessary intervention at the site. It was widely criticized, including by Maya Lin, for setting a disturbing precedent of adding "special interest memorials." "One monument too many," exclaimed the *Washington Post*."[29] The entire episode represents another rupture in the evolving narrative structure of the site, another tension between personal and national narratives that could not be privately negotiated. It would not be the last battle for resolution of such tension.

Indeed, among the more widely noted intersections of the personal and the national at the memorial, most have focused on the issue of just whose names can and cannot be placed on or near the Wall—that is, as members of an identifiable but not yet included class, as in the case of Goodacre's memorial. Most recently, battle has been joined over the addition of the "In Memory" plaque commemorating American veterans who have died since their return from the war. It reads, "In Memory of the men and women who served in the Vietnam War and later died as a result of their service. We honor and remember their sacrifice." The bill to add the plaque was sponsored by over a hundred House representatives and eventually passed both houses unanimously. President Clinton signed it into law on June 15, 2000. The plaque was finally put in place on April 15, 2002.

The Vietnam Veterans Memorial Fund has received numerous suggestions for additions over the years. Why was this one accepted?

Unlike other proposals, such as for branch-specific markers for the Army or the Marine dead, the "In Memory" plaque clearly steps outside the intended narrative structure of the memorial's original design, and execution, in straightforward temporal terms. Unable to reconcile their personal loss with the fact that those they lost are not included within the chronological limits set by the Wall, those who have nonetheless lost loved ones have, since the first days following the Wall's dedication, challenged Department of Defense rules regarding whose names could be added to the Wall. "Each day we receive inquiries from family members asking how can they get the name of their father, brother, or sister included on the Wall," as Jim Doyle of Vietnam Veterans of America attested before the Subcommittee on National Parks, Historic Preservation, and Recreation. "We must tell them that there is no memorial to the sacrifice of their father, mother, husband, or mother." [30]

Robert Doubek, an advisor to the VVMF in the original design contest, gave, in his testimony before the same subcommittee, some indication of the sentiment involved in the decision to add the plaque. Although he opposed the addition of the "Three Fightingmen" statue and the Women's Memorial, Doubek was of the opinion that "With the hindsight of two decades, it is now clear that the casualties of Vietnam were not only those named on The Wall. The casualties include thousands who returned home to family and friends but who have died prematurely as an indirect result of their Vietnam service. These include those exposed to Agent Orange, and those subject to severe post traumatic stress syndrome. The 'In Memory' plaque will honor them. It will provide a special tribute to their unique sacrifice. It will comfort their loved ones by providing a societal acknowledgment of their loss." [31]

Strikingly, Doubek went on to state his support for the 'In Memory' plaque because, rather than setting precedent for further additions, the addition "closes the book and completes the memorial." [32] But, just as when the memorial was declared "finished" with the addition of Hart's statue, this assertion of closure was premature. The narrative structure of the memorial itself refuses linearity and closure, allowing spaces for a variety of individual memories to interact with the national context of the memorial and its location on the mall. The Wall's openness to so many stories and contradictions continues to undermine the efforts of those wishing to have done with the ongoing reinterpretation of the memorial.

There are still stories that are not bounded by the Wall's narrative structure, or even represented in it. Although the narrative structure has now been altered so that the stories of perhaps most Americans *can* be represented, there remains the question of those who died in their efforts to *stop* the American war in Vietnam. Are they not part of the narrative of that war, and of the national space in which the memorial stands? And, of course, most glaringly, there are those who many would consider to be the greatest victims of the war, the millions of Vietnamese and other Southeast Asians who died in the conflict, not to mention those Vietnamese who, even more so than American veterans, continue to suffer from the effects of Agent Orange and other forms of chemical and economic warfare.

Although it seems likely that the book will never be closed on the memorial as firmly as Doubek would have liked, it does seem unlikely that these stories will ever be represented at the Wall. They pose a far greater threat to the national narrative represented by the site and the mall than the existing additions, which are all fairly easily subsumed under the larger nationalist project of the mall. As the VVMF insisted, the memorial itself still does not endorse any particular view of the war. Yet, just as there can never be an apolitical statement about the American war in Vietnam, there can be no apolitical structure on the National Mall. Every addition has further constricted the limits of remembrance at the Wall, endorsing an increasingly orthodox, nationalist interpretation of the war in Vietnam. Sturken has been especially eloquent on this point. First, she notes, as with any memorial or representation of memory, certain things must be forgotten so that others might be remembered. In the case of a national monument, this is often a political decision. "Framed within the context of the Washington Mall," she writes, "the Vietnam Veterans Memorial must necessarily 'forget' the Vietnamese and cast the Vietnam veterans as the primary victims of the war."[33] Later, in describing Chris Burden's alternative memorial-sculpture, "The Other Vietnam Memorial," which contains three million Vietnamese names, Sturken asks the fundamental question, "Why must a national memorial reenact conflict by showing only one side of the conflict?"[34]

The question is a useful reminder that, while it appears perfectly normal that the Wall would focus attention on American combat soldiers, the ability of the site to absorb and delimit insurgent acts of memory actually reflects a large degree of cultural and ideological work. The persistence of a nationalist narrative of the war's role in American history becomes even more pronounced when examining the digitization of the Vietnam Veterans Memorial.

THE VIRTUAL WALLS

Searching for "Vietnam" on the Internet immediately alerts one to the heavy use of the medium made by American veterans of the war. A Web search will provide well over 200 million hits, with the top positions regularly going, first, to Vietnam's official tourism site and, second, to the Vietnam Veterans of America site, www.vietvet.org. The Real Wall has its own official Website, maintained by the National Park Service, which offered its own description of the Wall: "The Vietnam Veterans Memorial serves as a testament to the sacrifice of American military personnel during one of this nation's least popular wars. The memorial consists of three distinct sections. 'The Wall,' the Three Servicemen statue and flagpole and the women in service to the Vietnam war statue. The purpose of this memorial is to separate the issue of the sacrifices of the veterans from the U.S. policy in the war, thereby creating a venue for reconciliation."[35]

While hundreds of course syllabi devoted to the American war in Vietnam also appear in Internet searches, as do chronologies of the war and links to various American television shows and exhibits about the war, the prominence of U.S. veterans' groups on the Web is unsurprising. American veterans of the war were among the first organized groups to make wide use of the Web, launching vietvet.org on Veterans Day in 1994. Since then, the number of sites devoted to veterans' issues has expanded exponentially.

The most common form of site devoted to American veterans of the war is the "cybermemorial"—which I will define here as an interactive site devoted to memorializing those who died in or as a result of their service in the war. Among these, www.thewall-usa.com, launched in 1996, claims to be the "the first Internet site dedicated to honoring those who died in the Vietnam War." Also known as "The Vietnam Veterans Memorial Web Page," the site was started and maintained by members of the Fourth Battalion of the Ninth Infantry Regiment and has collected over twenty-thousand "remembrances" since it went online. The title of "first"

Virtual Wall, however, more accurately rests with www.vietvet.org, which contains sections devoted to remembrance that date back to the site's 1994 inception. It also includes "The Wall on the Web," a page dedicated to the Real Wall, which lists all the names from the Wall, as well as a links page pointing to, among other resources, www.noquarter.org, a "Vietnam Casualty Search Engine" that provides standard background information about those listed on the Wall.[36] Vietvet.org also has its own "Remembrance" section, subtitled "Reflections, Memories, and Images of Vietnam Past," that contains stories, poems, and memoirs written by veterans as well as personal memorials to Americans who died in the war.[37]

Most notably, however, the site features the "Taps Gallery," which developed the basic format used by many later cybermemorials.[38] The "Taps Gallery" includes images, text, and links dedicated to those who served and died in Vietnam. For example:

> PFC Frank Fettuccia
> US Army medic
> D. Co., 2nd. BN, 35th. INF RGT, 4th. INF Div.
> KIA 1 March, 1968
>
> He was there for less than 1 year.
>
> I would like to get in contact with his former teamates [*sic;* see endnote] from that div.; anyone who knew him well. I'd like to hear the stories and fotos; I have 2 old ones to exchange.
>
> Every year, on his date of death in March, I try to have a Mass said for his soul.
>
> I miss him so much. He was a good and true friend.
>
> please contact: Maureen Cawley Monteiro[39]

Those who construct these memorials are performing acts of memory not possible within the confines of the Wall. Using the medium available to them, they have expanded upon the narrative possibilities of the original site to create memorials that are, at once, both public and private—individuated acts of memory, yet lasting additions to the larger public space first opened up by the memorial.

For vietvet.org and the visitors who have constructed its remembrance sections, the "Taps Gallery" is not only a place to move beyond the *structural* narrative constraints of the Real Wall, it is also a space to share stories whose *content* was limited by that site. For instance, the American veterans who died after their return as a result of their service were for many years not explicitly acknowledged at the Real Wall—even now, a source of tension in regard to the memorial. The "Taps Gallery" provided both a forum and a format for many of these stories to be told:

James Frank Supulver
24 December 1948–12 June 2001
United States Army
Vietnam Veteran

My father did three tours to Vietnam earning the Bronze Star twice and he thought what he was doing was right; for his family, his parents and his country. He was a huey technician inspector.

He committed suicide last month and I believe in the way that he did it he truly never left Vietnam. My father did not have a high tolerance for pain and so I think that his guilt hurt him so deep inside because he loved his baby girl with every ounce of his being, but he couldn't tolerate the pain anymore. The only hell story I ever heard was when they went down to pick up people and everyone was shot and he had to fly the helicopter out himself. But he left behind his heart along with many wounded.

The only thing anyone ever got from Vietnam was pain and sorrow. Vietnam took my dad. His Grandchildren are beautiful gifts he will never treasure.

And I hope to see him someday to smell his Old Spice aftershave and tell him that I love him.

His Baby Girl
Erin[40]

Others told of the deadly legacies of American chemical warfare:

Johnny Ingram Streater
United States Army
Vietnam Veteran 1969–1970

Johnny was my husband who passed away on November 16, 2003 of liver disease. He was 100% service connected for PTSD and lived with the haunting memories of Vietnam and several medical conditions related to his service for 33 years. Of course the VA would never admit he was even exposed to agent orange even though he told me that he would radio the planes where to drop and then wade through the chemical afterward.

There were times when I wondered if he might take his own life but thank God his family meant so much to him that he never did.

Immediately after he passed three people whose lives he saved since Vietnam contacted me to tell me their stories. He was a true hero in every sense of the word. I'm sure the angels in heaven are singing "Welcome Home" to their brother.

Until we meet again dear Husband.

Your wife,

Shirlean[41]

And many used the space to link to memorial pages they had created on other Web sites:

Bobby Joe Williams
VNVMC Alabama
Died May 2002

BJ was the most wonderful brother. BJ suffered terribly from PTSD and he died of cancer caused by Agent Orange after a long and hard struggle.

God only knows how he is missed by all of us each and everyday. You can view his memorial site at this link.[42]

For these users, the "Taps Gallery" was a separate site, distinctly and intentionally separated from the "Wall on the Web" section, and carrying few explicit references to the Real Wall. However, vietvet.org, along with thewall-usa.com, demonstrates the possibilities offered by the Internet to move beyond the structural and content limits placed on memorial practices at the Wall. Two subsequent sites, each titled "The Virtual Wall," would build on these frameworks to reconstruct, powerfully and convincingly, both the national context of the Wall and the more flexible, personal narrative structure provided by Web-based technologies of memory.[43]

The first Virtual Wall (or, as I will occasionally refer to it, VW1) was put online in March of 1997.[44] Run by a small group of American veterans of the war, VW1 is a nonprofit endeavor that even rejects donations, aside from the free Web space provided by a local Internet service provider. *The Virtual Wall Vietnam Veterans Memorial* describes itself as

> an interactive World Wide Web site that attempts to take portions of the experience and emotions of a visit to the Vietnam Veterans Memorial (The Wall) into homes and schools of internet visitors. The Virtual Wall endeavors to duplicate and convey the dignity and solemnity of the Vietnam Veterans Memorial and to maintain the tradition of care and compassion of National Park Service volunteers at The Wall. The Virtual

> Wall reflects an environment like The Wall itself: a memorial created and maintained by volunteers, with no commercials, no noisy or flashy distractions, and no hands held out for donations.[45]

The Virtual Wall appears as a list of names of those who died or were listed as MIA in the war, the same groups eligible to be placed on the Real Wall. The names are listed alphabetically, not chronologically as on the Real Wall, although visitors can choose to view the names chronologically, by state and city, by military unit, or by the number of the panel on which the name appears on the Real Wall. Each name links to information about that person, including such things as name, rank, and dates of birth and death—but the pages can also include images and words left by those who have visitors. Sometimes these messages are from members of the deceased's unit, sometimes from family and friends, and occasionally from anonymous visitors. VW1 began with the names of twenty-seven of the Webmaster's friends: some from high school, some from flight school, and some from his unit in Vietnam. Due to staff and time restraints, VW1 does not have a page for each name on the Real Wall, only those requested by visitors.

The second Virtual Wall (VW2) went online in November of 1998 as a joint venture between Winstar Communications and the Vietnam Veterans Memorial Fund, the same group that funded the Real Wall. Since its separate launch, VW2 has been folded into the VVMF site, which also includes, among other things, "Teach Vietnam," a section devoted to educational materials and programs related to the war and the Wall.[46] Regarding the Virtual Wall itself, this site seems intent on delivering a "personal" experience. As its home page once read—although the language has since been removed—"The Virtual Wall creates a unique experience for each visitor . . . Create your own personal journey." Obviously maintained by a professional, full-time staff, VW2 doesn't just seek to duplicate the purpose of the Real Wall: it attempts a "virtual replica" of the Real Wall itself.

Unlike its counterpart, VW2 lists and has a linked page for *every* name found on the Real Wall (although most pages do not have messages or images posted by visitors); as with VW1, visitors can search for individual names. But by clicking on "Experience the Wall," users start a Flash application that offers a user experience entirely different from that of searching for specific people or browsing pages of visitors' personal memorials. After the words "Sacrifice" and "Honor" display against a backdrop image of the Wall, one reads, "58,220 gave their lives in Vietnam—Millions

Remember." The screen then dissolves into a simple digital-graphic representation of the Wall: a *v*-shaped, "granite"-textured, black and gray wall seen across a lawn of digitized green grass.

Using a mouse and an onscreen navigation tool, users can open up a row-by-row transcription of the names on a particular panel—or move from panel to panel, simulating, to some degree, a walk past the Real Wall. We can "enter" the memorial, encountering at the top and to the right of the Virtual Wall's line of intersection, as we would at the Real Wall, the name of the first American "officially" killed in Vietnam. Unlike at the Real Wall, however, we click on the name to learn that

> MAURICE FLOURNOY was born on July 7, 1929. He became a member of the Air Force while in El Camdo, Texas and attained the rank of SSGT (E5). On February 21, 1960, at the age of 30, MAURICE FLOURNOY gave his life in the service of our country in South Vietnam, Quang Tri Province. You can find MAURICE FLOURNOY honored on the Vietnam Memorial Wall on Panel 1E, Row 1.[47]

VW2 once contained a "Community" area where users could discuss the war and its legacy, recent events, and American foreign policy. Mostly, however, visitors used the space to try to connect with former buddies or family members—much as they still do, as we will see, on the pages of other Virtual Walls. The discussion area was taken down due to lack of interest, although the site still features occasional live chats with public figures and veterans.

The VW1 and VW2 memorial pages differ in appearance, but the stories told on them are remarkably similar. In them, we glimpse the everyday negotiation of personal and national narratives. While most VW2 pages do not contain images or messages left by visitors, those that do generally fall into three categories, similar to those found on VW1. The first are messages left *to* the person being remembered, very much like letters left at the Real Wall, except that these are enduringly public messages, left to be read by anyone. The brother of Edward Eugene Cannon offers the simple remembrance: "My Brother, you'll always be in our hearts forever, God be with you and all our brothers who gave there 'All' we miss you dearly. Your Twin Brother–Robert."[48]

Far more common at all the Virtual Walls, however, are messages written *about* those who died in Vietnam. Many of these stories relate their experiences to the POW/MIA issue. A private cybermemorial dedicated to

Richard M. Cole, Jr., though not at a Virtual Wall, captures the mood of many. It tells the story not only of Cole, but of frustration with a government that "has been LYING to us for 30 years about our loved ones, and CONTINUES to LIE."[49] In relation to the POW/MIA myth as a whole, such pages offer a forceful example of personal memories seeking inclusion in the larger national narrative of loss, healing, and recuperative nationalism. Less dramatic, perhaps, but equally moving, are the stories which simply give the visitor a little more information about the name on the Wall. Patrick J. O'Shaughnessy's page on VW1 offers the following from a high school friend: "Pat O'Shaughnessy was a fine young man and a very good athlete. We attended high school together . . . I felt his loss and think our community was robbed of someone who would mark his mark in life. I never watch a baseball game without thinking of Pat."[50]

Finally, some of the most intriguing of the Virtual Wall entries seek connections with the family and friends of those lost. On the VW1 page for Harold Warren Cummings, Jr., we see the following message: "I would like to contact the widow or other family of Harold Cummings Jr. I was with Harry when he was taken in ambush and must fulfill his last request," followed by the contact information.[51] Similarly, the widow of Edward Arnold Birmingham makes this request on his page: "I am Edward's widow. He left three children: 2 sons and 1 daughter. I am sure they would love to learn more about the Father they never got to know. Please send us email . . . Sallie Birmingham."[52]

While we do not know the outcomes of such attempts at communication, it is clear that people use these sites in ways for which the Real Wall was not designed. The stories told on these pages are more communal in nature, designed for the public eye with the goal of telling stories, sharing information, and initiating contact. As opposed to what occurs at the Real Wall, the vast majority of the online messages are *about* the dead and those they left behind, not letters written *to* or objects left *for* those lost in the war. Users of the Virtual Walls take advantage of the sites, which are more conducive to communication, to create and follow up on the types of stories that they cannot share at the Real Wall.

These messages are quite evidently part of an ongoing conversation about the legacy of the war. Yet, at the same time, the "public" nature of these acts of memory must be questioned. The acts of memory manifested on the pages of the Virtual Walls, as we have seen, are different in style and nature from those performed at the Real Wall. They are designed for public viewing, and are often explicit attempts at communication with others. But it is important to note that the communication enabled by the Virtual Walls remains largely private. Edward Birmingham's widow does not post the responses she receives from her message, nor does Harold Cummings's buddy offer visitors any update on whether or not he has fulfilled Harry's last request. In fact, we do not know if any connections have been made at all. Perhaps we are not supposed to. While the structure of the Virtual Walls offers the potential for a more publicly oriented discourse, what we see are visitors using the space for personal communication. Connections are sought out, but they remain focused on individual, localized stories. As such, they reflect the larger political and cultural environment of the Real Wall, which does not offer a public space for public debate about the war and its legacies, but rather a liminal space for private acts of memory.

That the Virtual Walls offer a space more conducive to the resolution of the personal and the national than the Real Wall is in part a function, of course, of the fact that they are removed from the overwhelmingly public physical context of the National Mall. They are also more accessible: users can visit as often as they like, not constrained by the need to travel. The VVMF has attempted to deal with this problem by way of "The Wall That Heals," a scaled-down replica of the Real Wall that tours the United States, yet this comment by a veteran who served in Vietnam in 1968–69 makes it clear that the narrative space of the Virtual Walls provides for an experience that cannot be had either at the Real Wall or its simulacrum: "I spend time adding things on [the Virtual Wall] for members of our unit lost in VietNam. I have been to the moving wall three times in three states, but never got to Washington DC yet. Matter of money to go—not choice—or feelings about wall or war. The Virtual Wall gives each of us a chance to say special things about people, not names in rock."[53]

The first Virtual Wall was in fact created in response to the inconvenience presented by the Real Wall's real location. Jim Schueckler, one of its founders, had worked for years as a National Park Service volunteer at the Real Wall, but the nine-hour drive from upstate New York meant that he could only get there a few times a year.[54] So Jim, his cofounders, and volunteers constructed and maintain a space that can be more easily accessed—and one that is, in significant ways, a space designed for private experience.

Yet the public/private dynamics of such sites are rather complex. On the one hand, their separation from the imposing national context of the mall removes a key public element inherent in the Real Wall's narrative structure. At the same time, however, while the decentered nature of the

Virtual Walls makes them more conducive to personalized acts of memory than the Real Wall, the influence of the national narrative is far from removed—particularly at VW2, where the red, white, and blue VVMF logo and other images as well as text serve to recontextualize it. And here, as at all the Virtual Walls, users collaborate in actively reconstructing the national narrative, most obviously when they invoke such themes as "duty," "sacrifice," "heroism," and "patriotism."

One veteran, posting a message on VW2 about a fallen friend, invoked both the American flag and the POW/MIA flag to speak of the values of honor and duty his friend's story represented to him: "In front of my house is a flag pole on which fly two flags, the Stars and Stripes, of course, and a POW/MIA flag. The first honors this country and all who have or will defend it, the second flies for William Tamm Arnold and all who never returned. It flies 24/7 and will remain there as long as there is life in these tired old bones. God Bless You."[55] A less personal but similar message was left elsewhere on the same site by a fellow veteran:

> I want to thank you Earl Lee Wilson, for your courageous and valiant service, your years of faithfully contributing, and your most holy sacrifice given to this great country of ours!
>
> Your Spirit is alive—and strong, therefore Marine, you shall never be forgotten, nor has your death been in vain!
>
> It's Heroes like you, that made it possible for others like myself to return home and lead free and full lives!
>
> Again, although we never met personally, thank you SSGT Earl Lee Wilson, for a job well done!
>
> REST IN ETERNAL PEACE MY MARINE FRIEND[56]

As we see demonstrated here, perhaps most telling of the latent impulse to reconstruct the national narrative at the Virtual Walls are the messages posted by users who have no connection at all to the person memorialized on the page. In this vein, several teachers have assigned their students to post remembrances on VW2, contributing to the great number of this type of personal, yet impersonal, remembrance, often with an eloquence that expresses what those more immediately affected have felt:

> In my history class at my high school, we are currently carrying out the Gridley High School posting project to ensure that no soldier who died in Vietnam is forgotten. You have paid a price. That price was death, but by paying that terrible cost, you gave to those still living

> freedom, and an example. Your example of sacrifice and patriotism will live on, inspiring others to act courageously and bravely to serve and better their country. For that service, that sacrifice, I thank you. You will not be forgotten.[57]

One entire sixth grade class posted the following message to several pages with the subject line "Remembering a serviceman from our county": "We would like to say thank you for serving your country and sacrificing your life. We appreciate you very much!"[59]

Students participating in projects are not the only ones expressing such sentiments. It is also common to find more spontaneous and anonymous postings on the pages, for instance, of VW2, including this one from a Navy veteran:

> Although we never met personally, I want to thank you Bobby Lynn Weathers, for your courageous and valiant service, faithful contribution, and your most holy sacrifice given to this great country of ours![60]

As with the objects and letters left at the Real Wall, we do not know the intentions of such messages. Nevertheless, it is striking that these postings, taken from a wide array of dates and pages, are so similar to one another. The language of duty, honor, patriotism, and sacrifice, so central to the re-inscription of the War in Vietnam into the national narrative, has clearly been absorbed, accepted, and reproduced by a variety of users. Regardless of their intentions, by posting these messages on the pages of (to them) anonymous veterans, they have invoked and reimposed the national context from which the Virtual Walls were originally removed.

Thus, while users have taken advantage of the discursive possibilities provided by the Virtual Walls to expand the narrative structure of the memorials, the acts of memory performed on the pages of these sites only serve to reinforce the triumph of the recuperative national narrative described by Sturken. The end result, therefore, of both the Virtual and Real Walls is to focus attention on what the war did to individual Americans, their friends, and their families. The unstated assumption, then, is that the memory of the American war in Vietnam concerns Americans—not U.S. policy, and not the millions of non-American lives destroyed in Southeast Asia.

Marita Sturken writes of the ghostly presence of the Vietnamese dead at the Real Wall: "It is rarely mentioned that the discussion surrounding the memorial never mentions the Vietnamese people. This is not a memorial to their loss; they cannot even be mentioned in the context of the mall. Nor does the memorial itself allow for their mention; though it allows for an outpouring of grief, it does not speak to the intricate reasons why the lives represented by the inscribed names were lost in vain."[61] Note Sturken's phrase: *"they cannot even be mentioned."* It is literally impossible to do so within the current narrative structure of the site—and any scenario in which that structure would change to allow for a plaque commemorating even the lives lost among the United States' South Vietnamese *allies* seems improbable at best. Of course, such a commemoration could be accomplished rather easily on the Virtual Walls, by their Webmasters or even by visitors. I have yet to run across such a page. The messages on the Virtual Walls speak of the duty, sacrifice, and honor of American soldiers alone.

The point is neither to diminish the importance of the American lives lost in Vietnam nor to marginalize the very real sacrifices made by American veterans of the war. The point is that these decentered technologies of memory have succeeded in maintaining the power dynamics of the narrative structure of the Real Wall. Just as with the Real Wall, this is accomplished at the Virtual Walls not through what is said or represented, but through what is *not* said or represented; not through who or what is remembered, but through who or what is forgotten. Acts of sacrifice in the name of the nation are reinscribed while acts of imperialism are erased, rendered outside the narrative structure of the cultural memory being constructed at the memorials.

In the face of such a powerful cultural force, it becomes all the more important to return to Sturken's question: "Why must a national memorial reenact conflict by showing only one side of the conflict?"

THE WIDOWS OF WAR MEMORIAL AS TRANSNATIONAL CYBERMEMORIAL

Since the inception of the Virtual Walls in the late 1990s, a veritable cybermemorials industry has developed in the United States. The University of California–Berkeley now hosts a page where visitors can "view and create memorials online for faculty, staff, students, retirees, emeriti, and volunteers who have died."[62] Virtual-Memorials.com offers personalized service to those who wish to create "memorials that celebrate the lives and personalities of those we have lost."[63] In addition to those already discussed, other Vietnam-related memorials have also arisen. At one time, vietworld.com offered a virtual memorial to those who died while in Vietnam's "Re-education Camps" after the fall of the Republic of

Vietnam. Although the site has since been taken down, it commemorated hundreds who died in what the site referred to as the "Vietnamese Holocaust."[64]

One of the great strengths of the World Wide Web is its ability to facilitate transnational cultural and political flows. One project that took advantage of this possibility—and in doing so moved beyond the narrative limitations of the Virtual Walls—was the "Widows of War Living Memorial" (warwidows.org). The site was developed by Barbara Sonneborn after the release of her documentary film, *Regret to Inform,* in which she travels to Vietnam twenty years after her husband died there, and in which the voices of both American *and* Vietnamese war widows are heard. Following the lead of the film, warwidows.org was launched in 2000 as "a place where widows of all wars can record and share their stories with people throughout the world." Although the site was taken down in 2004, the way in which it was used during its brief existence suggests the possibility of an alternative form of cybermemorial.[65]

This site in many ways reproduced the same types of stories seen on the pages of the Virtual Walls, of individual families coping with personal loss—but by expanding the discussion to include widows of soldiers from places other than the United States and from wars other than Vietnam, the dynamics and implications of such stories change considerably. The postings on the site were, initially, mostly by American women who had lost their husbands in Vietnam, but the site quickly grew to include stories from women who had lost loved ones in battles in Armenia, Guatemala, Tibet, and Rwanda, to name a few. The site also included the writings of widows from World War Two, the Third Indochina War, and the American war in Iraq—and numerous contributions from Vietnamese widows.

Xuan Ngoc Nguyen's page began, "I was only 14 years old when my South Vietnamese village was burned to the ground. It was 1968, and my five year-old cousin was killed by a soldier in front of me. You can't comprehend the loss, you just try to go on."[66] She then recounted the story of her husband's death.

Nancy Le's account took her from the years of the American war into the postwar era, when other South Vietnamese like she and her family fled their homeland. "So in February 1981, I took my husband and my two oldest sons to the South China Sea. I watched them climb into a boat with 72 people and go into the water. I planned to join them later that year, but that day I cried all the way back to Saigon." Seven months later, she and her two younger sons made their own journey. "After nine days, we landed on a beach in Malaysia. My sons and I looked for my husband and my other sons. We didn't hear about them ever again. After two years, we got permission to go to the United States."[67]

The "victims" in the War in Vietnam, according to the narrative boundaries of this site, were not just Americans, but Southeast Asian men, women, and children as well. Furthermore, by including the stories of widows from numerous conflicts and wars, the widows' memorial transcended the confining narrative grasp of the American war in Vietnam. After the events of September 11, 2001, the ensuing United States invasion of Afghanistan, and the increased violence in Israel and Palestine, widows from those events and areas began to contribute to the site. One widow from Israel claimed the space as a memorial not to war, but in the name of peace: "And yet, without peace, I see no future in this region. The price of war is so high we must do everything to prevent it. The new weapons make war all the more devastating. All efforts must be made to create peace. Never mind the risks—we must take the risks of peace."[68] The site's owners offered a "statement" after September 11 that accurately summed up the larger cultural work of the project: "Our thoughts and prayers are with all those who have suffered or lost loved ones in this tragedy. Terrorism has been called a new kind of war. Our goal at the WarWidows International Peace Alliance is to end violence and war in all its incarnations."[69]

The Widows of War Living Memorial offered an opportunity for forms of remembrance that the Real and Virtual Walls cannot, at least in their present configurations. Freed from nationalistic narratives and from narrow definitions of who is a victim, the site moved beyond the narrative structure of the Walls, transcending the gendered and national space of those memorials to create a space in which war itself could be memorialized. As such, it offered a powerful example of the type of memorial the Virtual Walls might have been—and still could be—and further demonstrated the sway the national narrative continues to hold over those sites.

AN END TO MONUMENTS? TEACHING THE "LESSONS" OF VIETNAM AT THE REAL WALL

We have seen that visitors to the Virtual Walls have used the tools provided them by the medium to challenge and expand the narrative boundaries of the memorials by telling stories whose form and content is circumscribed by the narrative boundaries of the Real Wall. We have also seen, however, how those sites are dominated by the nationalist narrative that seeks to marginalize the significance of the American war in Vietnam, by reinscribing that conflict into the sweep of United States history as a story of the duty, honor, and sacrifice of American soldiers only. Although the basic narrative structure of the Real Wall has become more flexible and inclusive over time, it remains subject to forces seeking to further limit it by imposing a more monolithic vision of the war. A quarter-century after the end of the military phase of the American war in Vietnam, Maya Lin's design was still sufficiently liminal and ambiguous to provoke a new proposal for a major addition to the memorial.

In September 2000, Senator Chuck Hagel of Nebraska, a veteran of the war in Vietnam, introduced legislation calling for an "Education Center" to be constructed at the Wall. The proposal originated earlier that year in discussions related to the addition of the "In Memory" plaque. The "primary reason" for the center, according to the VVMF, which spearheaded the drive, "would be to educate young Americans about the Vietnam War and The Wall."[70] The proposed center would include historical information, rotating exhibits, and a photo gallery featuring pictures of all those listed on the Wall. In this sense, the center would in part mirror the Virtual Walls by allowing for more individualized and personalized forms of remembrance. But the focal point of the proposal was the need to pass the "lessons of Vietnam" on to future generations. Throughout the next three years, as the battle over the center continued, several constituencies expressed their concern that these "young Americans" had little knowledge of the war and thus would not learn the lessons offered by the war. While few disagreed with this assessment, the question of what exactly these lessons were—and which would be represented at the center—remained a sticking point. Among others, politicians, environmental groups, and the National Park Service joined battle over the proposed addition.[71]

In May 2003, the congressional subcommittee charged with marking up the legislation held hearings at the Wall to determine the impact of the center on the site and the mall. While arguments over the environmental and aesthetic impact of the center had remained fairly consistent over the years, the debate regarding its tone, content, and pedagogical style had taken on new meaning with the launching of the American war in Iraq in April. Pointing to the lack of historical context provided by the Wall itself, a diverse groups of witnesses, including actor Robert Duvall and author Stanley Karnow, weighed in on just which "lessons of Vietnam" should be conveyed at the center.

Duvall quoted a line from his role in *Apocalypse Now*—"You know, someday this war's going to end"—to frame his testimony that the "societal impact of the war is not over." Calling on Congress to allow the center to go forward, Duvall claimed that the educational mission of the center was a logical outgrowth of the Wall and the Wall That Heals: "America's youth must have the opportunity to learn patriotism and sacrifice at the Vietnam Veteran's Memorial."[72]

Alone among the witnesses, and nearly alone among those who have engaged in public discourse about the Wall, Stanley Karnow took a moment to remind those in attendance of the damage done to Vietnam and the Vietnamese during the war. "If I could just inject one more point, when we talk about the number of Americans who died in Vietnam—I know it is not within the purview of this—I want to remind people that something like 2 to 3 million Vietnamese also died in the war, and I am talking about Vietnamese on both sides."[73] It is interesting that, even as he made this comment in passing, Karnow deemed it necessary to acknowledge that the issue was essentially irrelevant: the Vietnamese were "not within the purview" of the discussion. His remark is especially telling when compared with his formal testimony inserted for the record, which contains no mention of the Vietnamese. Yet Karnow, a member of the center's advisory council, had in mind a different educational mission than Duvall and others at the hearings. Rather than extolling "patriotism" and "sacrifice," Karnow envisioned a center that would move beyond commemorating the dead to "become an instrument of goodwill and that elusive dream—peace on earth."[74]

John Peterson, a Republican committee member from Pennsylvania, offered a strikingly different vision. Peterson claimed that the center would be a valuable addition to the site because it would help "personalize" the war for Americans. He was less concerned about the lessons of the war; according to him, the wars in Iraq and Afghanistan were demonstrating that those "lessons had been learned." Nevertheless, he saw the center as a way to make sure those lessons were passed on, asserting that it was "vital to this country to understand the intricacies of the Vietnam War, the mistakes that were made there so that we don't repeat them." As to what specific lessons the Center might provide, Peterson offered, "I think as we watch [the Bush] administration as it came into some involvements, they didn't make some of the mistakes that were made in Vietnam. Because when we decide to have a conflict, we win, we get it over with. We don't do it in stages. We don't do it in degrees. We don't decide whether we should turn it over. When we make a decision, we win. And if we don't remember history, we have the likeliness to repeat it."[75]

Others went on to testify about the importance of the center as a pedagogical site that could help instill the values of "service," "sacrifice," and "patriotism," but perhaps the most telling testimony came from Duncan Hunter, chairman of the House Armed Services Committee. Hunter described with disdain the negative image of the American war in Vietnam in American culture, especially in films about the war (except *We Were Soldiers* and *The Green Berets,* which he approved of). He also railed against the Enola Gay exhibit at the Air and Space Museum of the Smithsonian Institution, which had caused an uproar nine years earlier by raising questions concerning the United States' use of nuclear weapons and offering what some viewed as too sympathetic a view of the Japanese victims of the bombs.[76] Like Peterson, Hunter saw the recent Iraq war as a step in the right direction, claiming that the media coverage of the invasion sent the "message" to the American people that "GIs are pretty good people. They had never seen that before." Along these lines, he continued, "visitors centers are darn good if they carry the right message." As for the specific center being proposed for the Wall, Hunter concluded that he was "all for this exhibit if it shows the honor and goodness of American GIs, and, I think, Mr. Chairman—and I speak for myself—the honor of the cause. The only time when Vietnam had any freedom, any modicum of freedom—and if anybody thinks that they have got a modicum of freedom over there today, please go on over and take a look—was when the Americans were there."[77] In the end, the center, in the words of Hunter, would tell the stories of "honor and determination" that were at the heart of the American war in Vietnam—a useful corrective to the "distorted view" of the war, and of the soldiers who fought it, in American culture.

A bill incorporating provisions for construction of a center was signed into law by President Bush in November 2003. The final version of the bill focused almost exclusively on limits to future building on the mall, and devoted only a few pages to the addition of the Vietnam Veterans Memorial Visitor Center. The law did not lay out specific guidelines for the center's programs and exhibits, stating only that it was to provide "appropriate educational and interpretive functions."[78] The design of the center is even now far from complete, and its exhibits and programs far from determined, but in its press release hailing the signing of the Vietnam Veterans Memorial Visitor Center Act the VVMF was already claiming that the center would "not only honor the memory of Vietnam veterans, but most importantly will educate visitors of the sacrifices our veterans have made in the name of freedom." Jan Scruggs, who had begun his quest for a Vietnam Veterans

Memorial nearly twenty-five years earlier, added his thanks to Bush for approving the center, thus "guaranteeing," as Scruggs put it, "that future generations will better understand the principles of service, sacrifice, and patriotism."[79]

These, then, are the true "lessons of Vietnam" that the Wall will pass on. As with the Virtual Walls, the discourse of duty, honor, and sacrifice provides the tropes for the reinscription of the national narrative, further rendering outside the realm of discussion any sense of what the war did to the nation and people of Vietnam. The center thus stands as possibly the final step in the reimposition of a grand national narrative at the Wall, reintegrating Vietnam—now viewed through the lenses of Iraq, Afghanistan, and a particular brand of patriotism—into the history of American foreign relations.

The Vietnam Veterans Memorial stood for over two decades as a complex, liminal space. Situated in the most national of contexts, the Wall also offered a remarkably personal space for those touched by the war to perform individual acts of memory, reconciling their personal narratives with the national narrative constructed at the memorial. I have argued here that, since its inception, the ambiguity so centrally built into the Wall has given rise to constant attack from those seeking a more cohesive and more inclusive (to a point) narrative. The additions of two statues, a flagpole, a commemorative plaque, and soon an educational Visitor Center have been both responses to and shaped by that ambiguity—and they have all shaped and will continue to shape the narrative structure of the site.

There will always be those who speak back in the face of such displays of power, but it does seem safe to assume that if the center's narrative of the war is constructed around the ideas and values described by Scruggs, critical questions about American foreign policy in Southeast Asia and elsewhere will be all but erased as a point of entry into the debate. While critical narratives of the war may continue to be constructed against such triumphant revisionism, one must ask where such stories will be told. It is very unlikely that they will be told at the Wall.

In his testimony in May of 2003, Robert Duvall claimed that "education is never dangerous."[80] Certainly, it is far too early in the process to see what the Vietnam Veterans Memorial Visitor Center will have to say about the American war in Vietnam, and it would be wrong to imply, without knowing those details, that an almost exclusive focus on "service, sacrifice, and patriotism" is in itself "dangerous." The real danger is not that the center will offer any particular narrative of the American war in Vietnam. It is that it will make the narrative structure of the overall site so rigid as to further exclude a greater range of stories, that it will further impose uniformity and de facto consensus on a necessarily fractured and indeed divisive heterogeneity of stories. Perhaps the greatest danger, though, is that the more we restrict the range of stories that are permitted expression in our memorials, the less likely it is that we will ever see, in W. D. Erhardt's memorable phrase, "an end to monuments."

EPILOGUE

THE UNEASY PEACE AND THE FLAGS THAT STILL FLY

Although I have situated the 1995 normalization and diplomatic recognition of Vietnam as the "end" of the American war on Vietnam, the period since normalization has been marked by a series of ongoing battles between the two nations, on trade, human rights issues, and the meaning of "Vietnam" in American society. Nevertheless, 1995 did mark, as Secretary of State Christopher put it at the time, "an end to a decade of war and two decades of estrangement."[1] Normalization also offered the opportunity for some in the United States to rethink the long war against Vietnam, and to see what lessons might be drawn from it. At the time, the message was clear. Thomas Friedman of the *New York Times* declared victory in Vietnam, "if winning is measured by a Vietnam that is economically, politically, and strategically pro-Western." "It's time that we declare victory," he added, "and go back to Vietnam and reap it."[2] The lesson of Vietnam, argued the *Washington Post*, "is that it makes a lot more sense to make markets than to make war."[3] Vietnam the market was attracting a lot of attention from American corporations; what effect the new relationship would have on Vietnam the nation remained to be seen.

After diplomatic normalization was completed, the economic windfall predicted by many was slow to develop, particularly for the Vietnamese. American corporations were finally free to set up operations in Vietnam, taking advantage of a skilled, hard-working, and cheap labor force. Within a year, however, stories of abusive labor practices and unsafe working conditions began to surface. Nike, Disney, and McDonalds were among the well-known companies implicated in various stories of sweatshops in Vietnam. In one example, labor monitoring groups found factories producing toys for McDonald's "Happy Meals" where many young Vietnamese women were being paid only six cents per hour.

As one news report of the situation noted, however, "low wages are not the workers' worst problem." In February of 1996, more than two hundred workers in the plant were forced to stop working as a result of acetone poisoning.[4] Later that year, in response to cases such as these, Vietnam Labor Watch was founded to monitor labor practices in the country.

As Vietnamese leaders made clear after the lifting of the embargo, the new era of relations would mean little economically without a trade agreement extending normal trade relations to Vietnam. Negotiations over the agreement proceeded at a snail's pace however, which meant that Vietnamese exports to the United States were still subject to high tariff rates. By the end of the twentieth century, the United States remained the only industrialized nation not to grant most favored nation status to Vietnam, and Vietnam remained one of only six countries not to receive that status from the United States.[5]

From 1997 to 2000, the Clinton administration granted Jackson-Vanik waivers to Vietnam, lessening the effects of the tariffs by granting temporary most favored nation status in regard to some Vietnamese goods. On each occasion, Congress was required to approve the waiver, and many members took the opportunity to criticize Vietnam for human rights violations, for lack of transparency in economic matters, and, of course, for not producing the remains of American service personnel. Although these hearings tended to focus more on issues of international trade than did those held prior to normalization, the same cast of characters could often be found at the witness table. In hearings on relations with Vietnam in the late 1990s, those who clung to the need for "leverage" with Vietnam, whether for political or economic reasons, maintained that the promise of normal trade relations status and, later, accession to the WTO continued to provide that leverage.[6] And, without fail, every major hearing would include Ann Mills Griffiths and other members of the POW/MIA lobby, who continued to lambaste the Vietnamese for not doing enough to assist in the recovery of American remains.[7] Despite such criticisms, and despite the determined efforts of many representatives in the House, the Jackson-Vanik waivers were upheld every year.

Not until the summer of 2000, however, did the two nations agree to the terms of the bilateral trade agreement. That document, too, was subject to the approval of legislatures in both countries, and the United States Congress would not receive the measure for over a year, after George W. Bush had assumed the Presidency. In September of 2001, the Senate passed the measure by a vote of 88–12, while the House required only a voice vote.

President Bush signed the bilateral trade agreement into law on October 16. In Vietnam, the National Assembly approved the agreement 278–85, and President Tran Duc Luong signed the bilateral trade agreement into law. After an exchange of letters acknowledging the accord, the bilateral trade agreement between Vietnam and the United States went into effect on December 10. Under the agreement, Vietnam received most favored nation—or normal trade relations—status, although that status is not permanent.[8] It remains subject to annual reviews by the White House and Congress, both of which must sign off on Vietnam's adherence to American conditions on immigration, human rights, and a number of other issues as laid out in the bilateral trade agreement.

While the bilateral trade agreement opened many doors into the American market for Vietnamese goods—imports to the U.S. reached $1.05 billion in 2001—it has, like the IMF/World Bank structural adjustment programs and the influx of foreign investment, produced mixed results for Vietnam. Consider the case of catfish. After the terms of the bilateral trade agreement were agreed upon in 2000, Vietnamese exports of catfish to the U.S. jumped from five million to thirty-four million pounds. Under the terms of the agreement, American catfish farmers filed suit with the Commerce Department in 2002 charging the Vietnamese with a number of complaints: that Vietnamese catfish were not really catfish; that the Vietnamese were "dumping" their "catfish" in the U.S. market; and, most ironically, that the Vietnamese fish might be unsafe for American consumers because they might be contaminated with dioxin from Agent Orange.[9] In July 2003, the U.S. International Trade Commission ruled unanimously in favor of the American catfish industry, clearing the way for the government to impose import duties of 37 to 64 percent on Vietnamese catfish fillets. While the catfish case was pending, the American shrimp industry filed a similar suit, which played out over the next several months with similar results.[10] In another protest, U.S. rice growers and numerous members of Congress from across the political spectrum expressed their displeasure when a contract for 70,000 metric tons of rice to be shipped to American-occupied Iraq was denied to American farmers. Instead, the contract, along with a UN contract for 152,000 additional metric tons, was awarded to Vietnam.[11]

Hopes were high among many in the United States and Southeast Asia that Vietnam might join the World Trade Organization as early as 2005, in which case further U.S. sanctions would be subject to WTO adjudication.[12] In the summer of 2005, however, the Vietnamese application was still in process, leaving the United States and Vietnam locked in their trade war. To be sure, skirmishes over shrimp and catfish are preferable to the literal wars of the preceding thirty years, yet these conflicts indicate the remaining hostility toward Vietnam on the part of some Americans, as well as Vietnamese distrust of the United States. They also indicate the extent to which major political and economic developments in Vietnam remain subject to the domestic politics of the United States.

"VIETNAM" IN TWENTY-FIRST-CENTURY AMERICAN CULTURE

It has been over a decade since the American embargo on Vietnam was lifted, and since the normalization of diplomatic relations between the two nations. The thirtieth anniversary of the end of the military phase of the American war in Vietnam has come and gone. At this point, it is worth reflecting on how much has changed in relations between United States and Vietnam—and how much has stayed the same.

Since 1975, a generation has come of age. In Vietnam, more than half of the current population was born after the end of the American war. While they know of and can see the effects of the horrors of war experienced by previous generations, they have also experienced the greatest period of economic expansion in modern Vietnamese history. This latest generation is marked more by the items they consume and the market ideology they expound than by their adherence to socialist policies.

When President Clinton made his historic visit to Vietnam in November 2000, he received an extraordinarily warm welcome. Although his flight landed after 11 p.m. in Hanoi, thousands of Vietnamese lined the streets and congregated in front of the hotel where the Clintons were staying. Many Vietnamese, according to various press accounts, thought well of Clinton not only because he had lifted the sanctions and normalized relations, but because they knew he had opposed the war in the 1960s and 1970s.[13] In an unprecedented move, Vietnamese officials allowed Clinton's address from Hanoi's National University to be carried live on national television. In the speech, Clinton referred to the ongoing efforts of the Vietnamese to recover the remains of American servicemen: "Your cooperation in that mission over these last eight years has made it possible for America to support international lending to Vietnam, to resume trade between our countries, to establish formal diplomatic relations and, this year, to sign a pivotal trade agreement. Finally, America is coming to see Vietnam as your people have asked for years—as a country, not a war."[14]

It is not clear, however, that this has been the case.

In the United States, Vietnam has become an important trading partner, the leading supplier of coffee and a major source of textiles. "Vietnam," however, remains a free-floating signifier in American society, standing in the rhetoric of both left and right for an entire complex of notions regarding American military misadventure. The 2003 invasion and resulting occupation of Iraq, in particular, has led to a sharp resurgence of "Vietnam" as a term of debate—which makes it all the more ironic when significant stories about Vietnam the nation, or even Vietnam the war, receive little if any attention in the American press.

For example, in October 2003 the *Toledo Blade* ran a major investigative piece revealing the previously unreported story of Tiger Force, an elite American unit that waged a campaign of terror in the Vietnamese central highlands in 1967. The story, which appeared in installments over several days, detailed how members of Tiger Force murdered—and dismembered, decapitated, and otherwise mutilated—hundreds of unarmed villagers, including women and children, over a period of several months. Most of the killings took place within fifty miles of My Lai, the site of the massacre previously thought by most Americans to be the worst of American war crimes in Vietnam. As Michael Sallah and Mitch Weiss reported, the Army learned of the Tiger Force crimes during its investigation of the My Lai murders, and promptly covered them up. Although the Pentagon's investigation found that several members of the Tiger Force platoon were guilty of war crimes, none were prosecuted.[15] As the *Blade* editorialized at the end of the story's run, "Tiger Force's Assaults Should Horrify the Nation."[16] Instead, the story was largely ignored. In the spring of 2004, Sallah and Weiss won a Pulitzer Prize, but the failure of the U.S. media to pick up their story remains telling.

A few weeks after the story appeared, Seymour Hersh, who first uncovered the My Lai massacre, noted that "the *Blade*'s extraordinary investigation of Tiger Force . . . remains all but invisible." None of the major news networks had picked up the story, and hardly any other newspapers had even mentioned the account.[17] Hersh's criticism led ABC News to run a feature on the Tiger Force story, but no other major outlets followed suit. Writing about the media's coverage (or lack thereof) of the story in the *Nation* in March of 2004, Scott Sherman noted that the "list of major news organizations that has yet to acknowledge the *Blade* series includes NBC, CBS, CNN, *Time, Newsweek, U.S. News and World Report,* and the *Wall Street Journal.*"[18] The *New York Times,* burying its belated acknowledgment of the story in a summary on page A-24 eight weeks later, admitted that, if its own staff had discovered the story, "it would have been on the front page."[19] Both Sherman and Hersh speculated, however, that the almost universal reluctance to reprint, follow up on, or further investigate the story was more than a case of journalistic rivalry, but arose from an unwillingness among the media to bring up such issues while the United States was at war in Iraq. In an interview on National Public Radio, *Blade* reporter Sallah stated, "there is a sense that we should not be too openly critical and evoke these painful memories of Vietnam when we're already in a conflict."[20]

Yet, while the Tiger Force story was being ignored, "Vietnam" was seemingly everywhere. Countless stories compared the war in Iraq to the war in Vietnam, speeches in Congress labeled Iraq "Bush's Vietnam," and the press pored over the wartime records of the two major candidates for president in 2004, Bush and Senator John Kerry. The cover of *Newsweek* gave prominence to several stories related to the American war. The first (February 23) featured wartime-era pictures of the two candidates, Bush in Alabama while a member of the National Guard, and Kerry on a gunboat in the Mekong Delta. A few weeks later (April 18), the cover showed a picture of a young American soldier next to the headline, "Crisis in Iraq: The Vietnam Factor." In that week's issue, several stories and columns compared the wars in Iraq and Vietnam.

The previous month (March 8), the magazine cover had highlighted a story on "The New Science of Strokes"—interestingly enough, the article's actual title was "The War on Strokes"—underneath a banner reading, "John Kerry & Agent Orange." The five-page story raised concerns over Kerry's health, since he had been exposed to the carcinogenic chemical agent while serving in Vietnam. It conveyed Kerry's own concern regarding the health of members of his unit and other American servicemen. It managed to give only glancing attention, however, to the obvious point that millions of Vietnamese had been exposed as well: "Agent Orange was one of the many tragedies of Vietnam. It may have killed or sickened, via long-incubating cancers and nerve disorders, thousands of American soldiers and sailors (not to mention many more Vietnamese)."[21]

In the space of eighteen hundred words which were, after all, referring to chemical warfare waged on Vietnam by the United States, the primary victims of the attacks merit a single, parenthetical aside. Among the then-current developments regarding the "many more" Vietnamese that might have been mentioned, Vietnamese victims had recently initiated legal action against the manufacturers of Agent Orange (following a path similar to that which led to the 1984 case in which American veterans of the war won a $180 million settlement from manufacturers including Monsanto and Dow Chemical), and studies had found both that dioxin from Agent Orange was still contaminating Vietnam's food and water supplies at extremely high levels, and that previous figures on dioxin levels per liter of Agent Orange were underestimated.[22] Instead, Vietnam once again received its traditional treatment in American public discourse: readily available to highlight the meaning of the war for the United States, and conspicuously invisible whenever a story raised the specter of American empire or dared address the legacy of the war for the Vietnamese. Vietnam continues to operate as a ghostly presence haunting American society, everywhere and nowhere at the same time. As ever, the Vietnamese remain invisible enemies—and invisible victims—of the United States.

THE FLAGS THAT STILL FLY

By way of conclusion, I want to point to three flags that symbolize the still ambiguous and contested place of Vietnam in American society, American cultural memory, and the rest of the world. To begin with, there is the POW/MIA flag, which can be found seemingly everywhere in American society. In 1997, Congress passed a law requiring post offices and other federal buildings to fly the flag several times a year.[23] This "second national flag," as Bruce Franklin has labeled it, serves as a powerful reminder of the hold the war has on American cultural memory, a reminder that the American war on Vietnam may never end, and that it will be remembered—and forgotten—in particular ways.[24]

Another sign of the continuing American desire to contest, revise, and erase particular memories of the war arose in January of 2003. State delegate Robert Hull—representing the northern Virginia suburb of Fairfax, home to one of the largest Vietnamese-American communities in the United States—introduced a bill in the state legislature requiring that the flag of the former Republic of Vietnam, rather than that of the actually existing Socialist Republic of Vietnam, be displayed at all public functions and state institutions, including public schools.[25] The RVN flag had long been a popular symbol for many of Virginia's Vietnamese-American citizens (numbering nearly forty thousand, according to the 2000 census), and was called "an eternal symbol of hope and love of freedom" by Governor Mark Warner when he declared June 19, 2002, to be "Vietnamese American Freedom Fighter Day."[26] Predictably enough, Vietnam took great offense at the proposal, calling it "insolent" and lodging a formal complaint with the U.S. Department of State. The State Department successfully lobbied for the bill to be killed, but Vietnamese-Americans in Virginia remained firm in their desire to raise the issue at a later date. One Arlington resident told the *Washington Post* that hanging the Vietnamese flag was "just like displaying the swastika in a community with a lot of people of Jewish background."[27] While the bitter feelings of some refugees are understandable, the attempt to ban the flag of an existing nation in favor of one representing a former American client state—which was in existence for less than twenty years—surely stands as one of the most remarkable displays of the desire to erase and rewrite the American war in Vietnam.[28]

The final flag, one that symbolizes much about the ever-changing relationship between the United States and today's Vietnam, can be found in the city of Hai Duong, which lays about halfway between Hanoi and Hai Phong. In this area that still bears a number of scars from the American war, there now stands a large American majority-owned automobile factory. Outside the factory stand three flagpoles, flying three different flags at the exact same height. The first is the flag of the Socialist Republic of Vietnam; the second is the flag of the United States of America; the third is the flag of the Ford Motor Company.

From Richmond to Hai Duong, each of these flags serves as a symbol of the ongoing contest for cultural memory in American society. And each of the flags, in its own way, hearkens back to the final line of the admittedly tongue-in-cheek Calvin Trillin poem that served as an epigraph for this book:

"Remind me, please: Why *did* we fight that war?"

NOTES

In tracking down hundreds of government documents over the course of this project, I have found it much easier, and more fruitful, to search by the title of the hearing or committee print document than by the name of the committee or subcommittee. That is particularly true in the years under consideration here, when committees such as the House Subcommittee on East Asian and Pacific Affairs changed names. Given the large number of congressional hearings used as sources for this study, I have chosen to list them, contrary to standard practice, by title first, then the appropriate committee or subcommittee. Readers wishing to examine the documents cited here should find it easier to distinguish and locate them, and to follow the notes themselves, in this format.

INTRODUCTION

1. Quoted in Stanley Karnow, *Vietnam: A History* (New York: Penguin, 1983), 683–84.

2. I have used a variety of news sources to reconstruct this history, but I rely heavily on accounts from five in particular: The *New York Times (NYT)*, the *Washington Post (WP)*, *Far Eastern Economic Review (FEER)*, *Newsweek*, and *Time*. There are several reasons for this. To begin with, during much of the period under consideration there were few American news organizations with bureaus in Southeast Asia. The *Times* and the *Post* were among the few, and it is clear that most other papers relied on these two sources in addition to the wire services. Limiting the focus on news articles to the *Times* and the *Post*—and, similarly, to *Time* and *Newsweek* as representing U.S. weekly news magazines—while reducing a huge range of possible sources, has not compromised the overall integrity of my findings or argument.

More important, with the exception of *FEER*, these are among the most widely read news sources in the United States; they are particularly popular among policymakers in Washington, D.C. As noted above and demonstrated throughout this project, articles from these sources are widely cited in congressional hearings and often included in appendices in congressional reports and hearings prints. As such, they are particularly useful in exploring how public discussions of American policy toward Vietnam were constructed, and how cultural memory of the American War in/on Vietnam was actively contested in this era.

3. Amy Kaplan, "Left Alone with America: The Absence of Empire in the Study of American Culture," in *Cultures of United States Imperialism*, ed. Amy Kaplan and Donald Pease, 1–17 (Durham, N.C.: Duke University Press, 1993), 11.

4. Amy Kaplan, "Violent Belongings and the Question of Empire Today: Presidential Address to the American Studies Association, Hartford, Connecticut, October 17, 2003," *American Quarterly* 56, no. 1 (March 2004): 1–18.

5. Janice A. Radway, "What's in a Name? Presidential Address to the American Studies Association, 20 November 1998," *American Quarterly* 51, no. 1 (March 1999): 1–32.

6. Michael H. Hunt, "Internationalizing U.S. Diplomatic History: A Practical Agenda," *Diplomatic History* 15 (Winter 1991): 1–11.

7. Emily Rosenberg, "Presidential Address—Revisiting Dollar Diplomacy: Narratives of Money and Manliness," *Diplomatic History* 22, no. 2 (Spring 1998): 155–76.

8. Robert J. McMahon, "Contested Memory: The Vietnam War and American Society, 1975–2001," *Diplomatic History* 26, no. 2 (Spring 2002): 159–84; the quote is from 184.

9. Kaplan and Pease, eds., *Cultures of United States Imperialism;* Amy Kaplan, *The Anarchy of Empire in the Making of U.S. Culture* (Cambridge: Harvard University Press, 2002); Mark Bradley, *Imagining Vietnam and America: The Making of Postcolonial Vietnam, 1919–1950* (Chapel Hill: University of North Carolina Press, 2000); Kristin Hoganson, *Fighting for American Manhood: How Gender Politics Provoked the Spanish-American and Philippine-American Wars* (New Haven: Yale University Press, 1998); Melani McAllister, *Epic Encounters: Culture, Media, and U.S. Interests in the Middle East, 1945–2000* (Berkeley: University of California Press, 2001); Mary Renda, *Taking Haiti: Military Occupation and the Culture of U.S. Imperialism* (Chapel Hill: University of North Carolina Press, 2001).

10. See Michel Foucault, "The Subject and Power," afterword in Hubert L. Dreyfus and Paul Rabinow, *Michel Foucault: Beyond Structuralism and Hermeneutics*, 208–26 (Chicago: University of Chicago Press, 1983), esp. 220–21.

11. Ibid., 221.

12. Jill Lepore, *The Name of War* (New York: Vintage, 1999), x.

13. Ibid., xxi.

CHAPTER ONE

1. Henry Kissinger, *Years of Renewal* (New York: Simon and Schuster, 1999), 541, 545.

2. "How Should Americans Feel?" *Time*, April 14, 1975.

3. *Newsweek*, March 31, 1975.

4. "How Should Americans Feel?"

5. *Adjudication of Claims Against Vietnam*, Hearing and Markup before the Subcommittees on Asian and Pacific Affairs and International Economic Policy and Trade, 96th Congress, 1st Session, July 27, 1979, 3.

6. Kissinger, *Years of Renewal*, 566.

7. Ibid., 575. In addition to Kissinger's memoirs, this reconstruction of events comes from Seymour Hersh, *The Price of Power* (New York: Summit Books, 1983), 639; and Ralph Wetterhahn, *The Last Battle: The Mayaguez Incident and the End of the Vietnam War* (New York: Carroll & Graf, 2001).

8. For the larger history and context of these and other pieces of legislation related to economic sanctions, trade embargoes, and asset controls, see Michael

Malloy, *United States Economic Sanctions: Theory and Practice* (The Hague: Kluwer Law International, 2001); Barry Carter, *International Economic Sanctions: Improving the Haphazard U.S. Legal Regime* (New York: Cambridge University Press, 1988); and Gary Clyde Hufbauer, Jeffrey J. Schott, and Kimberly Ann Elliott, eds., *Economic Sanctions Reconsidered: History and Current Policy* (Washington, D.C.: Institute for International Economics, 1985).

9. *United States Embargo of Trade with South Vietnam and Cambodia,* Hearing before the Subcommittee on International Trade and Commerce, House of Representatives, 94th Congress, 1st Session, June 4, 1975, 3.

10. Ibid., 1.

11. Ibid., 4, 5.

12. *Adjudication of Claims Against Vietnam,* 3.

13. *United States Embargo of Trade with South Vietnam and Cambodia,* 6.

14. Ibid., 11.

15. Ibid., 19.

16. Ibid., 9.

17. Ibid., 7.

18. Ibid., 9.

19. Ibid.

20. Ibid., 3.

21. *NYT,* June 4, 1975, cited in Stephen Hurst, *The Carter Administration and Vietnam* (New York: St. Martin's, 1996), 18.

22. Quoted in James Laurie, "Indochina: A Decision Based on Ideology," *FEER,* July 4, 1975, 13. See also Hurst, *The Carter Administration and Vietnam,* 10.

23. *U.S. MIA's in Southeast Asia,* Hearing before Committee on Foreign Relations, United States Senate, 95th Congress, 1st Session, April 1, 1977, 14.

24. Nayan Chanda, *Brother Enemy: The War after the War* (New York: Harcourt Brace Jovanovich, 1986), 145.

25. See, for instance, "U.S. Ready to Talk with Indochinese," *NYT,* November 15, 1975; "Trading with Indochina: Many U.S. Executives in Asia Urge Ban on Dealing with Vietnam and Cambodia," *WSJ,* November 1, 1975.

26. Marjorie Hyer, "Quakers Get Approval for Vietnam Aid," *WP,* November 15, 1975.

27. "A Silly War," *Los Angeles Times,* November 13, 1975.

28. *U.S. Embargo of Vietnam: Church Views,* Hearing before the Subcommittee on International Trade and Commerce, House of Representatives, 94th Congress, 1st Session, November 17, 1975, 1.

29. Ibid., 3–4.

30. Ibid., 10.

31. H. Bruce Franklin, *M.I.A., or Mythmaking in America* (New York: Lawrence Hill Books, 1992), 17.

32. Ibid., 40.

33. *Final Report of the Select Committee on Missing Persons in Southeast Asia,* 94th Congress, 2nd Session, December 13, 1976, 73–74. This will be cited hereafter

as *Final Report of the Select Committee on Missing Persons in Southeast Asia* (1976), to distinguish it from the final report of the 1993 Senate Select Committee on POW/MIA Affairs, discussed in chapter 5.

34. Ibid., 21; Franklin, *M.I.A.*, 12.

35. Franklin, *M.I.A.*, 68.

36. *Final Report of the Select Committee on Missing Persons in Southeast Asia* (1976), 208–9.

37. Franklin, *M.I.A.*, 90, 91.

38. Ibid., 122.

39. Ibid., 83. Also see Hurst, *The Carter Administration and Vietnam*, 41–44.

40. I will return to the POW/MIA issue at the beginning of the next chapter, which traces the significance of the issue in the context of the opening of the "cultural front" of the American War on Vietnam after 1975.

41. "Count Your Vietnams," *Economist*, August 9, 1975, 14; Louis Halasz, "Stalemate in the Halls of Diplomacy," *FEER*, August 22, 1975, 20.

42. "Count Your Vietnams."

43. Daniel Patrick Moynihan, *A Dangerous Place* (Boston: Little, Brown, 1978), 143.

44. Ibid., 145.

45. Ibid., 110, 146–48.

46. Ibid., 142.

47. T. Christopher Jespersen, "The Bitter End and the Lost Chance in Vietnam: Congress, the Ford Administration and the Battle Over Vietnam, 1975–76," *Diplomatic History* 24, no. 2 (Spring 2000): 279.

48. For a catalogue of such votes since 1978, see William Blum, "The United States Versus the World at the United Nations," in *Rogue State: A Guide to the World's Only Superpower*, 184–99 (Monroe, Maine: Common Courage Press, 2000).

49. Louis Halsalz, "Washington Put on the Spot," *FEER*, September 24, 1976, 20.

50. Joseph Zasloff and MacAlister Brown, *Communist Indochina and U.S. Foreign Policy: Postwar Realities* (Boulder, Colo.: Westview, 1978), 9.

51. Hasalz, "Washington Put on the Spot."

52. Jespersen, "The Bitter End," 289.

53. "Extending a Hand to Hanoi," *Time*, February 28, 1977, 30.

54. Ibid.

55. *NYT*, February 26, 1977, 1.

56. Ibid. Quoted in Hurst, *The Carter Administration and Vietnam*, 31.

57. Hurst, *The Carter Administration and Vietnam*, 32. Hurst is citing from Frederick Brown, *Second Chance: The United States and Indochina in the 1990s* (Washington, D.C.: Council on Foreign Relations Press, 1989), 23–24.

58. The Nixon letter is reprinted in Marvin E. Gettleman et al., eds., *Vietnam and America: A Documented History* (New York: Grove Press, 1995), 487–88.

59. Hurst, *The Carter Administration and Vietnam*, 32.

60. "A Bridgehead Is Won in Hanoi," *Time*, March 28, 1977, 17.

61. Ibid.

62. "Vietnam: Mission Accomplished," *Economist*, April 4, 1977, 47.

63. "Report of the Presidential Commission on U.S. Missing and Unaccounted For in Southeast Asia," included in *U.S. MIA's in Southeast Asia*.

64. Ibid., 13.

65. Nayan Chanda, "Vietnam: Breakthrough in Aid," *FEER*, April 1, 1977, 42.

66. Revision of Trading With the Enemy Act," Markup before the Committee on International Relations, U.S. House of Representatives, 95th Congress, 1st Session, June 16, 17, 20, 1977 (Washington D.C.: U.S. Government Printing Office, 1977), 2.

67. Ibid.

68. Elizabeth Becker, *When the War Was Over: The Voices of Cambodia's Revolution and Its People* (New York: Simon and Schuster, 1986), 390.

69. Ibid.; Hurst, *The Carter Administration and Vietnam*, 35.

70. Becker, *When the War Was Over*, 391.

71. Ibid.; Hurst, *The Carter Administration and Vietnam*, 41; *World News Digest*, May 7, 1977, A1.

72. "Claiming Assets in Vietnam," *FEER*, April 29, 1977, 43.

73. *Final Report of the Select Committee on Missing Persons in Southeast Asia* (1976), 235.

74. Chanda, *Brother Enemy*, 154.

75. *U.S. Aid to Vietnam*, Hearing before the Subcommittee on Asian and Pacific Affairs, 95th Congress, 1st Session, July 19, 1977 (Washington, D.C.: GPO, 1979).

76. Zasloff and Brown, *Communist Indochina and U.S. Foreign Policy*, 25.

77. Susumu Awanohara, "Aid: Change of Mood in Washington," *FEER*, November 4, 1977, 46.

78. "Bid to Cut Out Indochina," *FEER*, June 17, 1977, 106.

79. "Carter Gets the Amber Light," *FEER*, September 9, 1977, 18; *NYT*, July 29, 1977, 1; Hurst, *The Carter Administration and Vietnam*, 40.

80. Awanohara, "Aid: Change of Mood in Washington"; see also "Protectionism: Hamstringing the Aid Effort," *FEER*, August 5, 1977, 32.

81. For an excellent overview of the workings of the IMF and World Bank, see Joseph Stiglitz, *Globalization and its Discontents* (New York: W.W. Norton, 2002).

82. Zasloff and Brown, *Communist Indochina and U.S. Foreign Policy*, 24–25.

83. Hurst, *The Carter Administration and Vietnam*, 43.

84. Chanda, *Brother Enemy*, 156.

85. Hurst, *The Carter Administration and Vietnam*, 44–45.

86. "More Francs for Vietnam," *FEER*, May 20, 1977.

87. Zasloff and Brown, *Communist Indochina and U.S. Foreign Policy*, 20. Also see Heinrich Dahm, *French and Japanese Economic Relations with Vietnam since 1975* (Surrey, U.K.: Curzon Press, 1999).

CHAPTER TWO

1. Environmental Conference on Cambodia, Laos and Vietnam, *Long-Term Consequences of the Vietnam War,* 43–44, http://www.nnn.se/vietnam/ethics.pdf (accessed July 1, 2005). These numbers reflect bombing data not only for Vietnam, but for Laos and Cambodia as well.

2. Ibid.

3. Ibid.; "Vietnam War's New Victims," *BBC News Online,* November 15, 2000, http://news.bbc.co.uk/1/hi/world/asia-pacific/1024627.stm (accessed February 18, 2004).

4. *Long-Term Consequences of the Vietnam War,* 43; Arnold Schecter et al., "Food as a Source of Dioxin Exposure in the Residents of Bien Hoa City, Vietnam," *Journal of Occupational and Environmental Medicine* 45, no. 8 (August 2003): 781–88; "Decades Later, Vietnam War Toxin Still Torments," *WP,* February 16, 2004; "New Study into Agent Orange," *BBC News Online,* March 10, 2002, http://news.bbc.co.uk/2/hi/world/asia-pacific/1865730.stm (accessed February 18, 2004). For more on Agent Orange, see Robert Dreyfuss, "Agent Orange: The Next Generation," *Mother Jones* (January–February 2000); and Phillip Jones Griffiths, *Agent Orange: Collateral Damage in Vietnam* (London: Trolley Press, 2003).

5. "Report of the United Nations Mission to North and South Viet-Nam," reprinted in *Aftermath of War: Humanitarian Problems of Southeast Asia,* staff report prepared for the Committee on the Judiciary, Subcommittee to Investigate Problems Connected with Refugees and Escapees, 94th Congress, 2nd Session, May 17, 1976 (emphasis in original).

6. "Preface," in *Aftermath of War,* v.

7. T. Christopher Jespersen, "The Bitter End and the Lost Chance in Vietnam: Congress, the Ford Administration and the Battle Over Vietnam, 1975–76," *Diplomatic History* 24, no. 2 (Spring 2000): 267.

8. H. Bruce Franklin, *M.I.A., or Mythmaking in America* (New York: Lawrence Hill Books, 1992), 4.

9. Ibid., 39.

10. *Final Report of the House Select Committee on Missing Persons in Southeast Asia* (1976), 107.

11. Testimony before House Committee on International Relations, 92nd Congress, 2nd Session, February 3, 1972, 14; excerpted in *Final Report of the House Select Committee on Missing Persons in Southeast Asia,* 107–8.

12. Franklin, *M.I.A.,* 49–50n196. The *NYT* editorial appeared on May 29, 1969.

13. Franklin, *M.I.A.,* 54.

14. "Remarks at Press Briefing, March 24, 1977," *Public Papers of the Presidents of the United States: Jimmy Carter, 1977* (Washington, D.C.: GPO, 1979), 1:499–500.

15. "Remarks at Press Briefing," 501 (emphasis added).

16. Julian Smith, *Looking Away: Hollywood and Vietnam* (New York: Scribners, 1975).

17. Rick Berg, "Losing Vietnam: Covering the War in an Age of Technology," in Rick Berg and John Carlos Rowe, eds., *The Vietnam War and American Culture* (New York: Columbia University Press, 1991), 127.

18. Melani McAllister, *Epic Encounters: Culture, Media, and U.S. Interests in the Middle East, 1945–2000* (Berkeley: University of California Press, 2001), 8.

19. Peter Marin, "Coming to Terms with Vietnam," *Harper's,* December 1980, 44 (emphasis in original).

20. "Hollywood Tackles Vietnam War," *NYT,* August 2, 1977, C23.

21. Ibid.

22. "Coming Home with the War," *WP,* November 4, 1977.

23. On this matter, see "Screen: 'Company C,'" *NYT,* February 2, 1978, C15; "At the Movies," *NYT,* February 3, 1978, C6; "Hollywood Focuses on Vietnam at Last," *NYT,* February 19, 1978, D1; and Weekend Films, *WP,* February 3, 1978.

24. "Hollywood Focuses on Vietnam."

25. "The Five-Year Struggle to Make 'Coming Home,'" *NYT,* February 19, 1978.

26. Eben J. Muse, *The Land of Nam: The Vietnam War in American Film* (Lanham, Md.: Scarecrow Press, 1995), 99.

27. "The Five-Year Struggle to Make 'Coming Home.'"

28. Gilbert Adair, *Hollywood's Vietnam: From the Green Berets to Full Metal Jacket* (London: Heinemann, 1989), 72 (emphasis in original).

29. Morris Dickstein, "Bringing It All Back Home," *Partisan Review* 45, no. 4 (Winter 1978): 630.

30. "The Five-Year Struggle to Make 'Coming Home.'"

31. Marin, "Coming to Terms with Vietnam," 46; Frank Rich, "The Dark at the End of the Tunnel," *Time,* February 20, 1978, 84.

32. Dickstein, "Bringing It All Back Home," 632.

33. Ibid.

34. Muse, *The Land of Nam,* 99.

35. For instance, see Jack Kroll's review of *The Deer Hunter* in *Newsweek,* which contrasts the politics of the two films. Kroll, "Life-or-Death Gambles," *Newsweek,* December 11, 1978, 113–14.

36.Hans Koning, "Films and Plays about Vietnam Treat Everything but the War," *NYT,* May 27, 1979, D1.

37. "Ready for Vietnam? A Talk with Michael Cimino," *NYT,* December 10, 1978, D15.

38. "Stalking Us All: 'The Deer Hunter,' Loaded for Bear," *WP,* February 19, 1978.

39. Kroll, "Life-or-Death Gambles."

40. H. Bruce Franklin, *Vietnam and Other American Fantasies* (Amherst: University of Massachusetts Press, 2000), 15.

41. Hellmann, *American Myth and the Legacy of Vietnam* (New York: Columbia University Press, 1986), 172.

42. Marin, "Coming to Terms," 45.

43. Arnett, "Vietnam's Last Atrocity," *Los Angeles Times,* April 4, 1979, quoted in Berg, "Losing Vietnam," 139n42.

44. "Vietnam Comes Home," *Time,* April 23, 1979, 22–28.

45. Adair, *Hollywood's Vietnam,* 88.

46. Berg, "Losing Vietnam," 139–40.

47. Leonard Quart, "*The Deer Hunter:* Superman in Vietnam," in Linda Dittmar and Gene Michaud, eds., *From Hanoi to Hollywood: The Vietnam War in American Film,* 159–68 (New Brunswick, N.J.: Rutgers University Press, 1990), 167.

48. Frank Rich, "Vietnam without a Map," *Time,* December 18, 1978.

49. Kroll, "Life or Death Gambles," *Newsweek,* December 11, 1978.

50. Quart, "Superman in Vietnam," 166–67.

51. "Ready for Vietnam? A Talk with Michael Cimino."

52. "A Vietnam Movie That Does Not Knock America," *NYT,* August 7, 1977, D11.

53. "Vietnam Comes Home," *Time,* April 23, 1979.

54. "Films and Plays about Vietnam Treat Everything but the War," *NYT,* May 27, 1979, D1.

55. " 'Apocalypse Now' Will Open, At Last," *NYT,* January 25, 1979, C15.

56. Maureen Orth, "Watching the Apocalypse," *Newsweek,* June 13, 1978, 57–64.

57. Marin, "Coming to Terms with Vietnam," 47.

58. Richard Thompson, "Stoked: An Interview with John Milius," *Film Comment* 12, no. 4 (July–August 1976), quoted in Frank Tomasulo, "The Politics of Ambivalence: *Apocalypse Now* as Prowar and Antiwar Film," in Linda Dittmar and Gene Michaud, eds., *From Hanoi to Hollywood: The Vietnam War in American Film,* 145–58 (New Brunswick, N.J.: Rutgers University Press, 1990), 156.

59. "Coppola's Film is a Battle Royal," *NYT,* May 15, 1977.

60. Richard Thompson, "Stoked," quoted in Muse, *The Land of Nam,* 114.

61. In the redux version of the film, released in 2001, many additional scenes were inserted, including, interestingly, footage in the surfing scene where Kilgore goes out of his way to order the evacuation of a Vietnamese woman and her wounded baby, further complicating the representation of American violence in the scene.

62. Orth, "Watching the Apocalypse."

63. Muse, *The Land of Nam,* 114, 118.

64. "Finally, 'Apocalypse Now,' " *Newsweek,* May 28, 1979, 100.

65. For an example of this, see "Finally, 'Apocalypse Now.' "

66. "Coppola's War Epic," *Newsweek,* August 20, 1979, 57.

67. "Briefs on the Arts," *NYT,* August 23, 1979, C15.

68. "The Screen: Apocalypse Now," *NYT,* August 15, 1979, C15.

69. Marin, "Coming to Terms with Vietnam," 47.

70. "The Screening of Vietnam," *WP,* August 19, 1979.

71. "Mangled Revelations: 'Apocalypse' At Last," *WP,* October 3, 1979.

72. "Apocalypse Now: A Long Trip for a Short Struggle," *WP*, October 5, 1979.

73. Frank Tomasulo, "The Politics of Ambivalence."

74. Ibid., 157 (emphasis in original).

75. Statistics from http://www.worldwideboxoffice.com (accessed December 1, 2005).

76. "Powerful and Convincing 'Spartans': Capturing the Elusive Spirit of the Vietnam War," *WP*, July 28, 1978.

77. "Vietnamese Refugees Find Work—In a War Movie," *NYT*, October 4, 1977.

78. "Powerful and Convincing 'Spartans;'" Martin, "The Indigestibility Of a Whole War," *WP*, August 4, 1978.

79. "The Dirty Little War," *Newsweek*, October 2, 1978, 85.

80. Marin, "Coming to Terms with Vietnam," 43.

CHAPTER THREE

1. *Nhan Dan* (Hanoi), February 2, 1976, quoted in David Marr and Christine White, Introduction to Marr and White, eds., *Postwar Vietnam: Dilemmas in Socialist Development* (Ithaca: Cornell University Press, 1988), 1.

2. For further discussion of these "three revolutions," see William Duiker, *Vietnam Since the Fall of Saigon* (Athens, Ohio: Center for International Studies, 1985), esp. 3–29.

3. Charles Harvie and Tran Van Hoa, *Vietnam's Reforms and Economic Growth* (New York: St. Martin's, 1997), 46.

4. Ho Chi Minh, *Testament*, quoted in Duiker, *Vietnam Since the Fall of Saigon*, 3: "Once the American invaders have been defeated, we will rebuild our land ten times more beautiful."

5. Harvie and Hoa, *Vietnam's Reforms and Economic Growth.*

6. ASEAN is the Association of Southeast Asian Nations, founded in 1967 in part to replace the Southeast Asia Treaty Organization (SEATO), a collective security arrangement that had included the United States and Australia as well as several Southeast Asian nations. ASEAN was initially made up of "the five": Indonesia, Malaysia, the Philippines, Singapore, and Thailand. Brunei was added after gaining independence in 1982.

7. For more background on the Cambodian revolution and the rise to power of the Khmer Rouge, see Elizabeth Becker, *When the War Was Over: The Voices of Cambodia's Revolution and Its People* (New York: Simon and Schuster, 1986); Shawcross, *Sideshow* (New York, Simon & Schuster, 1979) and *The Quality of Mercy* (New York, Simon & Schuster, 1984); Ben Kiernan, *The Pol Pot Regime* (New Haven: Yale University, 1996); several works by David Chandler, including *Brother Number One* (Boulder: Westview, 1999) and *A History of Cambodia* (Boulder: Westview, 1996); and Kenton Clymer's *The United States and Cambodia*, vol. 1, *From Curiosity to Transformation, 1870–1969*, and vol. 2, *A Troubled Relationship, 1969–2000* (New York: RoutledgeCurzon, 2004).

8. Shawcross, *The Quality of Mercy*, 63.

9. *Human Rights in Cambodia,* Hearing before the House Subcommittee on International Organizations, 95th Congress, 1st Session, May 3, 1977 (Washington, D.C.: GPO, 1977), 14.

10. Ibid., 32.

11. Ibid., 17.

12. Ibid., 40.

13. Ibid.

14. Ibid., 33.

15. See ibid., 53.

16. *Human Rights in Cambodia [Second of Two Hearings],* Hearing before the House Subcommittee on International Organizations, 95th Congress, 1st Session, July 26, 1977, 3.

17. Ibid., 8.

18. Ibid., 22.

19. For more on the place of Cambodia and the Khmer Rouge in the POW/MIA situation, see H. Bruce Franklin, *M.I.A., or Mythmaking in America* (New York: Lawrence Hill Books, 1992), 105–8.

20. Ibid., 107.

21. For the complexities of the aid situation in Cambodia, particularly during the Vietnamese occupation, see Shawcross, *The Quality of Mercy,* esp. 95–111.

22. Richard Holbrooke, "U.S. Policy in Asia: Changing Perspectives," *Department of State Bulletin: Current Policy* 24 (June 1978), 7.

23. Quoted in Stephen Hurst, *The Carter Administration and Vietnam* (New York: St. Martin's, 1996), 70; *NYT,* July 11, 1978, A6.

24. *St. Louis Post Dispatch,* August 20, 1978, quoted in Hurst, *The Carter Administration and Vietnam,* 71.

25. *Indochina,* Hearing before the Senate Subcommittee on East Asian and Pacific Affairs, 95th Congress, 2nd session (Washington, D.C.: GPO, 1978), 30.

26. Hurst, *The Carter Administration and Vietnam,* 71–90.

27. The study is discussed in Gareth Porter, "The Decline of US Diplomacy in Southeast Asia," *SAIS Review,* no. 1 (Winter 1981): 149–60, cited in Hurst, *The Carter Administration and Vietnam,* 94.

28. Derek Davies, "Carter's Neglect, Moscow's Victory," *FEER,* February 2, 1979, 16.

29. Hurst, *The Carter Administration and Vietnam,* 96.

30. "Hanoi: We Want to Be Your Good Friends," *Newsweek,* September 4, 1978, 35.

31. Davies, "Carter's Neglect, Moscow's Victory."

32. Gareth Porter, "Vietnam's Soviet Alliance: A Challenge to U.S. Policy," *Indochina Issues* (Indochina Project, Washington, D.C.,), no. 6 (May 1980), quoted in Nayan Chanda, *Brother Enemy: The War after the War* (New York: Harcourt Brace Jovanovich, 1986), 322.

33. "State Department Answers to Additional Questions Submitted by Senator Glenn," in *Indochina,* 42.

34. Michael Haas, *Cambodia, Pol Pot, and the United States: The Faustian Pact* (Westport, Conn.: Praeger, 1991).

35. On the Vietnamese decision to invade Cambodia, see Duiker, *Vietnam Since the Fall of Saigon*, 115–20; and Chanda, *Brother Enemy*, 333–41.

36. *Indochina*, 1.

37. Ibid., 23.

38. Ibid.

39. Ibid., 24.

40. Ibid., 32.

41. Ibid., 33–34.

42. Douglas Pike, *Vietnam-Cambodia Conflict*, Report Prepared by the Congressional Research Service for the House Subcommittee on Asian and Pacific Affairs, October 4, 1978 (Washington, D.C.: GPO, 1978), 17–18.

43. Chanda, *Brother Enemy*, 266.

44. Hurst, *The Carter Administration and Vietnam*, 96–97.

45. Douglas Pike, *Vietnam's Future Foreign Policy*, Report Prepared by the Congressional Research Service for the House Subcommittee on Asian and Pacific Affairs, October 24, 1978, reprinted in *Indochina*, 221.

46. *Indochina*, 222–23.

47. Ibid., 226–27.

48. Douglas Pike, *Viet Cong: The Organization and Techniques of the National Liberation Front of South Vietnam* (Cambridge, Mass.: MIT Press, 1966), xi, x.

49. Pike, *Vietnam's Future Foreign Policy*, 160.

50. Chanda, *Brother Enemy*, 290.

51. Ibid., 321–22.

52. See ibid., 325–35, for further discussion of Chinese-American normalization.

53. Ibid., 342.

54. Ibid., 349.

55. Historians have differed on the extent to which the United States was complicit in China's "punitive" invasion of Vietnam. Nayan Chanda and Elizabeth Becker have been stern in their criticisms of the Carter administration. Stephen Hurst has defended Carter's stance, arguing that Chanda, in particular, misreads many of the administration's statements. Hurst argues that, far from appeasing the Chinese, the United States sternly denounced China's actions, much to the surprise of Beijing. In Becker's account, however, which Hurst largely ignores in order to focus on Chanda, even Brzezinski himself, in an interview with the author, described American policy as a "semipublic wink" at the Chinese plans. This "wink," Becker explains, helped to set the stage for future U.S. proxy support of the Chinese and their Khmer Rouge clients. "We could never support" Pol Pot, Brzezinski told Becker, "but China could." For the specific discussions of these topics, see Chanda, *Brother Enemy*, 352–62; Becker, *When the War Was Over*, 439–41; Hurst, *The Carter Administration and Vietnam*, 118–24. Also see "Carter, The Unwilling Ally," *FEER*, March 9, 1979, 16.

56. Hurst, *The Carter Administration and Vietnam,* 118–19; Chanda, *Brother Enemy,* 359.

57. Carter stated that "in the last few weeks, we have seen a Vietnamese invasion of Cambodia and, as a result, a Chinese border penetration in Vietnam." Chanda situates this statement as part of the rationalization of U.S. support for China's actions, while Hurst argues that a "more logical conclusion" is that "it is simply a statement of fact" (Hurst, *The Carter Administration and Vietnam,* 118). But Hurst's own account misquotes Chanda's quotation from Carter. In Hurst's citation, Carter uses the term "Chinese border invasion," rather than the (correct) language from Chanda: "Chinese border penetration." Hurst's claim of neutrality and balance on behalf of the administration is thus suspect. Clearly, in Carter's distinction of terms, an all-out Vietnamese "invasion" is constructed as more dire than, and as a precursor to and cause of, a less offensive "penetration" by the Chinese. Hurst also takes Chanda to task for misreading other statements by the White House, a result, he claims, of Chanda "misunderstanding the dynamics" of the administration (119). While Hurst focuses on the public statements of the administration, a function of his methodology, he fails to pay sufficient attention to the actions, or lack thereof, of the United States during the escalating war in Southeast Asia. In the long run, Chanda's version of events appears to be upheld, particularly when one moves beyond the limited scope of Hurst's focus.

58. *Southeast Asia Refugee Crisis,* Hearing before the Senate Subcommittee on East Asia and Pacific Affairs, 96th Congress, 1st Session, September 27, 1979, 29; Murray Heibert, "Waiting in Ruins for the Next Installment," *FEER,* June 15, 1979, 12.

59. Chanda, *Brother Enemy,* 361.

60. Heibert, "Waiting in Ruins for the Next Installment."

61. Quoted in Shawcross, *The Quality of Mercy,* 116.

62. Ibid., 95–96.

63. *Cambodian Famine and U.S. Contingency Relief Plans,* Hearing before the Senate Subcommittee on Arms Control, Oceans, International Operations and Environment, 96th Congress, 1st Session, November 8, 1979, 3.

64. For a thorough discussion of the interrelation of food and diplomacy, see Shawcross, *The Quality of Mercy,* esp. 95–111.

65. *Cambodian Famine and U.S. Contingency Relief Plans,* 5.

66. Ibid., 14–15; Becker, *When the War Was Over,* 444.

67. Along with Becker, *When the War Was Over,* and Shawcross, *The Quality of Mercy,* see Anthony Lewis, "Cambodia: Time to Act," *NYT,* September 27, 1979.

68. Becker, *When the War Was Over,* 444.

69. Douglas Pike, *Vietnam's Foreign Relations, 1975–78,* Report Prepared by the Congressional Research Service for the Subcommittee on Asian and Pacific Affairs (Washington, D.C.: GPO, 1979), 1.

70. Davies, "Carter's Neglect, Moscow's Victory."

71. Shawcross, *The Quality of Mercy,* 74.

72. Ibid., 330.

73. "Vietnam and the UN," *Economist,* March 3, 1979, 54.

74. "Remarks by the President," April 21, 1978, *Public Papers of the Presidents of the United States: Jimmy Carter, 1978* (Washington, D.C.: GPO, 1980), 1:717–18. For a fascinating discussion of the crafting of this statement, see Kenton Clymer, "Jimmy Carter, Human Rights and Cambodia," *Diplomatic History* 27, no. 2 (April, 2003), 245–278.

75. Chanda, *Brother Enemy,* 377.

76. As Chanda recounts the story, the United States representative to the Credentials Committee arose after casting the U.S. vote in favor of the CGDK to find someone grabbing his hand in congratulations. "I looked up and saw it was [Pol Pot's lieutenant] Ieng Sary," he told a reporter. "I wanted to wash my hand." Chanda, *Brother Enemy,* 454n23. Chanda is quoting from Gareth Porter, "Kampuchea's UN Seat: Cutting the Pol Pot Connection," *Indochina Issues* (Indochina Project, Washington, D.C.), no. 8 (July 1980), 1.

77. *Southeast Asian Refugee Crisis,* 28.

78. Ibid.

79. Ibid.

80. *Southeast Asia,* Hearing before the Senate Subcommittee on East Asian and Pacific Affairs, 96th Congress, 2nd Session, March 24 and 25, 1980 (Washington, D.C.: GPO, 1980), 1.

81. Ibid., 26.

82. Chanda, *Brother Enemy,* 389. For a full description of the conference, see 387–90.

83. Ibid, 388–89.

84. Shawcross, *The Quality of Mercy,* 356.

85. *Kampuchea and American Foreign Policy Interests,* Hearing before the House Subcommittee on Asian and Pacific Affairs, 97th Congress, 1st Session, July 23, 1981, 2–3.

86. *U.S. Policy toward Indochina since Vietnam's Occupation of Kampuchea,* Hearings before the Subcommittee on Asian and Pacific Affairs, 97th Congress, 1st Session, October 15, 21, and 22, 1981, 5.

87. Ibid., 50–51.

88. Ibid., 53.

89. Ibid., 255.

90. Ibid., 264.

91. Ibid., 166.

92. Ibid., 257; Christopher Brady, *United States Foreign Policy toward Cambodia, 1977–92: A Question of Realities* (New York: St. Martin's, 1999), 74–75.

93. Michael Haas, *Genocide by Proxy: Cambodian Pawn on a Superpower Chessboard* (New York: Praeger, 1991), 48.

94. *The Democratic Kampuchea Seat at the United Nations and American Interests,* Hearing before the Subcommittees on Asian and Pacific Affairs and on Human Rights and International Organizations, 97th Congress, 1st Session, September 15, 1982, 28.

95. Ibid., 29.

96. Ibid., 32–33.

97. "CIA Covertly Aiding Pro-West Cambodians," *WP*, July 8, 1985, A1.

98. "Statement to Press, July 8, 1985," Private Papers of Stephen Solarz, Brandeis University Library, Folder "Camb: 1985 NCR Aid."

99. "CIA Covertly Aiding Pro-West Cambodians."

100. *Foreign Assistance and Related Programs Appropriations for 1986,* Hearings before the House Subcommittee on Appropriations, March 27, 1985, 242. Cited in Brady, *United States Foreign Policy toward Cambodia,* 112n74.

101. Stephen Solarz, "Why the U.S. Is Helping Cambodia," *NYT*, July 30, 1985, 22A.

102. Mark P. Lagon, *The Reagan Doctrine: Sources of American Conduct in the Cold War's Last Chapter* (Westport, Conn.: Praeger, 1994), 1.

103. "Waging War by Proxy," *Newsweek,* December 23, 1985, 32–34.

104. On the dubious distinction between humanitarian and development aid in particular, see Shawcross, *The Quality of Mercy,* 380.

105. Solarz's efforts on Cambodia were also bolstered by the 1984 release of *The Killing Fields,* a film about the reign of the Khmer Rouge based on the real-life story of Dith Pran, a survivor of the Cambodian holocaust who had worked for the *New York Times* during the American Wars in Vietnam and Cambodia in the 1970s. Pran and Dr. Haing Ngor, the virulently anti-Communist actor who played Pran in the film, became increasingly public figures in the United States, writing books, giving lectures, and even testifying at congressional hearings on the war in Cambodia.

106. Letter from William Ball to Dante Fascell, April 24, 1985, Private Papers of Stephen Solarz, Brandeis University Library, Folder "Camb: 1985 NCR Aid."

107. "House Approves Foreign Aid Bill Opposing Marxists around the World," *NYT*, July 12, 1985, A1.

108. H.J. Resolution 602, included in *Hope for Cambodia: Preventing the Return of the Khmer Rouge and Aiding the Refugees,* Hearing and Markup before the House Subcommittee on Asian and Pacific Affairs, 100th Congress, 2nd Session, June 30 and July 28, 1988, 81.

109. *Hope for Cambodia,* 38.

110. Ibid., 39 (emphasis added).

111. Ibid., 57.

112. Brady, *United States Foreign Policy toward Cambodia,* 121.

113. "Sihanouk Hints at Military Aid," *NYT*, October 14, 1988, A3.

114. "How Scandal Almost Sunk Our Secret Cambodia War," *WP,* October 30, 1988, C1.

115. "Tainted Cambodian Aid: New Details," *NYT*, November 1, 1988, A3.

116. "Amid Congressional Unease, U.S. Weighs Cambodia Arms Aid," *WP,* June 16, 1989, A12; "House Panel Assails U.S. Policy on Khmer Rouge," *NYT*, September 15, 1989, A9.

117. "From the Killing Fields," *ABC News Special Report,* April 26, 1990.

118. "Beyond Vietnam," *ABC News Special Report,* April 26, 1990.

CHAPTER FOUR

1. Jonathan Alter, "Live from Ho Chi Minh City," *Newsweek,* April 22, 1985, 72.

2. Ibid. Also see Tom Shales, "TV's Return to Vietnam," *WP,* May 2, 1985.

3. Maureen Dowd, "Kissinger and Le Duc Tho Meet Again, and Bitterness Shows," *NYT,* May 1, 1985.

4. Shales, "TV's Return to Vietnam."

5. Ibid.

6. "The Legacy of Vietnam," *Newsweek,* April 15, 1985; "The War That Went Wrong, the Lessons It Taught," *Time,* April 15, 1985.

7. "The War That Won't Go Away," *Newsweek,* April 15, 1985, 32.

8. "We're Still Prisoners of War," *Newsweek,* April 15, 1985, 34–35.

9. "A Wounded Land," *Newsweek,* April 15, 1985, 59.

10. Ibid., 58.

11. Noam Chomsky, "The United States and Indochina: Far from an Aberration," in Douglas Allen and Ngo Vinh Long, eds., *Coming to Terms: Indochina, The United States, and the War* (Boulder, Colo.: Westview, 1991), 172, 186n20.

12. "A Bloody Rite of Passage," *Time,* April 15, 1985, 22–23.

13. Ibid., 31. After obsessing on what "Vietnam did" to American politics, gender and race relations, and nationalism, the *Time* section went on to include a brief essay on life in Vietnam, the primary fascination of which was, apparently, that many Southern Vietnamese had failed to embrace socialism and continued to have access to cognac and Coca-Cola. After this one-page essay, six pages explored the implications of the war in regard to the use of American military power, under the title "Lessons from a Lost War."

14. The films mentioned form part of what several authors have referred to as a "neo-fascist aesthetic" in American film during the late cold war, evidenced also in such others as *Red Dawn* (1982), *Conan the Barbarian* (1984), and *Invasion U.S.A.* (1985). For discussion of the "fascist aesthetic" debate, see Harry Haines, "The Pride Is Back: *Rambo, Magnum P.I.,* and the Return Trip to Vietnam," in Richard Morris and Peter Ehrenhaus, eds., *Cultural Legacies of Vietnam: Uses of the Past in the Present,* 99–123 (Norwood, N.J.: Ablex, 1990), 108. Also see H. Bruce Franklin, *M.I.A., or Mythmaking in America* (New York: Lawrence Hill Books, 1992), 140–41; and Susan Jeffords, *The Remasculinization of America: Gender and the Vietnam War* (Bloomington: Indiana University Press, 1989).

15. See Franklin, *M.I.A.,* 137–38.

16. Ibid., 149.

17. On the relationship of Stallone and his hyper-masculine body to the politics of the 1980s, see Jeffords, *The Remasculinization of America,* and Susan Jeffords, *Hard Bodies: Hollywood Masculinity in the Reagan Era* (New Brunswick, N.J.: Rutgers University Press, 1994).

18. Like *The Deer Hunter* and several other films, *Rambo* uses mostly Chinese actors to fill the roles of the Vietnamese. This interchangeability of third world subjects has been a hallmark of the Rambo films. In the final installment of the trilogy, *Rambo III,* in which Rambo fights alongside the Mujahideen in Afghanistan, this logic is taken a step further. The film, shot in Israel, uses Israeli actors to play the roles of the Islamic fundamentalists leading the resistance against the Russian occupation.

19. Richard Schickel, "Danger: Live Moral Issues," *Time,* May 26, 1985, 91.

20. Jack Kroll, "A One-Man Army," *Newsweek,* May 27, 1985.

21. Schickel, "Danger: Live Moral Issues."

22. Richard Cohen, "Next: Rambo Goes to Nicaragua?" *WP,* June 4, 1985.

23. Vincent Canby, "*Rambo* Delivers a Revenge Fantasy," *NYT,* May 26, 1985.

24. For an excellent summary and discussion of Rambomania, see Douglas Kellner, *Media Culture: Cultural Studies, Identity, and Politics between the Modern and the Postmodern* (New York: Routledge, 1995), chap. 2, "Media Culture, Politics, and Ideology: From Reagan to Rambo," 55–92.

25. "Blood, Sweat, and Cheers," *Newsweek,* June 3, 1985, 62.

26. Fred Bruning, "A Nation Succumbs to Rambomania," *Maclean's,* July 29, 1985, 7.

27. Jeffords, *The Remasculinization of America,* 121.

28. "Rocky and Rambo: Return of the American Hero," *Newsweek,* December 23, 1985, 61.

29. Kellner, *Media Culture,* 66.

30. Franklin, *M.I.A.,* 151.

31. For instance, see "Reagan Gets Idea from 'Rambo' for Next Time," *Los Angeles Times,* July 1, 1985, cited in Franklin, *M.I.A.,* 212n43.

32. "The U.S. Has Surrendered—Now Rambo Is Taking the World by Storm," *Business Week,* August 26, 1985, 109.

33. Steven Roberts, " 'Machismo' on Capitol Hill," *WP,* July 15, 1985. Also cited in Franklin, *M.I.A.,* 151.

34. *Rambonomics,* documentary by Laura Nix (Tri-Star Productions, 2001). Included in the *Rambo Trilogy* DVD set (Tri-Star, 2001).

35. "The U.S. Has Surrendered."

36. John Fiske, *Understanding Popular Culture* (New York: Routledge, 1989), 166–67.

37. Quoted in "Reds Launch Major Assault on *Rambo," Toronto Star,* December 20, 1985, D26.

38. "Rocky and Rambo: Return of the American Hero." See also Franklin, *M.I.A.,* 151. Franklin even mentions a few of the adult titles, including *Ramb-ohh!* (1986) and *Bimbo: Hot Blood Part I* (1985).

39. "Vietnam Veteran Kills 29 in Bogata," *Times* (London), December 6, 1986.

40. "How Real is *Rambo*?" *WP,* July 8, 1985, C1.

41. Haines, "The Pride Is Back," 112.

42. Ibid., 113.

43. Kevin Bowen, "'Strange Hells': Hollywood in Search of America's Lost War," in Linda Dittmar and Gene Michaud, eds., *From Hanoi to Hollywood: The Vietnam War in American Film,* 226–35 (New Brunswick, N.J.: Rutgers University Press, 1990), 229.

44. Harry Haines quotes from his interview of members of the group—and cites "Stallone Comes Through at Harvard," *Boston Globe,* February 19, 1986, 21—in "The Pride Is Back," 113.

45. "How Real Is Rambo?"

46. "POW's in Vietnam: Fact or Fiction," *U.S. News and World Report,* October 28, 1985, 12. MacFarlane's quote also appears in Franklin, *M.I.A.,* 157.

47. "POW's in Vietnam: Fact or Fiction." Also see, for example, "MIA's: A Surprise from Hanoi," *Newsweek,* July 22, 1985, 34, and "The Lost Americans," *Newsweek,* January 20, 1986, 26.

48. "The Lost Americans."

49. "Oh What an Ugly War," *Newsweek,* September 9, 1985, 89.

50. Oliver Stone, "My Brilliant Career," *Time,* January 26, 1986, 60.

51. *20/20,* March 26, 1987; cited in Lawrence H. Suid, *Guts and Glory: The Making of the American Military Image in Film* (Lexington: University of Kentucky Press, 2002), 504. The other film to make more money than *Platoon* from the domestic box office was *Crocodile Dundee.*

52. *Nightline,* December 19, 1986; cited in Suid, *Guts and Glory,* 505.

53. "How the War Was Won," *Time,* January 26, 1986, 58.

54. Suid, *Guts and Glory,* 503–4.

55. Ibid., 507.

56. David Ansen, "A Ferocious Vietnam Elegy," *Newsweek,* January 5, 1987, 57.

57. Vincent Canby, "The Vietnam War in Stone's *Platoon,*" *NYT,* December 19, 1986.

58. Fred Burning, "A Celluloid War of Credibility," *Maclean's,* March 16, 1987.

59. "Vietnam, The Way It Really Was," *Time,* January 26, 1987, 57.

60. Gilbert Adair, *Hollywood's Vietnam: From* The Green Berets *to* Full Metal Jacket (London: Heinemann, 1989), 150.

61. Eben J. Muse, "The Way It Really Was," in *The Land of Nam: The Vietnam War in American Film* (Lanham, Md.: Scarecrow Press, 1995), 169.

62. Ansen, "A Ferocious Vietnam Elegy."

63. Canby, "The Vietnam War in Stone's *Platoon.*"

64. Canby, "*Platoon* Finds New Life in Old War Movie," *NYT,* January 11, 1987.

65. David Halberstam, "Two Who Were There View *Platoon,*" *NYT,* March 8, 1987.

66. Stone drew a fair amount of criticism for his portrayal of black soldiers in *Platoon.* In its initial denial of military assistance in making the film, the Army took Stone to task for "stereotyping black soldiers" (Suid, *Guts and Glory,* 503). *Time* noted that black soldiers are occasionally patronized and sentimentalized

("Vietnam: The Way It Really Was," 58). For a fuller treatment of the issue, see Clyde Taylor, "The Colonialist Subtext in *Platoon,*" in Dittmar and Michaud, *From Hanoi to Hollywood,* 171–74.

67. "Vietnam: The Way It Really Was," 58.

68. "Oh What an Ugly War."

69. Quoted in *"Platoon*—Hollywood Steps on a Gold Mine," *LA Times,* January 25, 1987, Calendar Section, 39.

70. "A Reason to Reflect on War," *LA Times,* January 25, 1987, Calendar Section, 1.

71. "Drawing Flak from Norris," *LA Times,* January 25, 1987, Calendar Section, 3.

72. "After Seeing *Platoon,* Fonda Wept," *LA Times,* January 25, 1987, Calendar Section, 3.

73. "Platoon—Hollywood Steps on a Goldmine," 5.

74. Ibid., 6.

75. "Viet Refugees Give *Platoon* Good Reviews," *LA Times,* January 25, 1987, Calendar Section, 5.

76. *"Platoon* Meets *Rambo," NYT,* January 22, 1987, A26.

77. "Prime Time for Vietnam," *Newsweek,* August 31, 1987, 68.

78. Ibid., 69.

79. "Vietnam Comes of Age," *U.S. News and World Report,* February 2, 1987, 58.

80. For a fuller discussion of the topic, see Edwin A. Martini, "Quagmire in the Classroom: Teaching the Vietnam War to Post-Vietnam Generations," B.A. thesis, Pitzer College, 1998, available from the author.

81. "Incoming," *The 'Nam,* no. 1 (New York: Marvel Comics), December 1986.

82. " 'Nam Notes," *The 'Nam,* no. 1, December 1986.

83. " 'Nam Notes," *The 'Nam,* no. 2, January 1987.

84. "Humpin' the Boonies," *The 'Nam,* no. 5, April 1987.

85. "Good Old Days," *The 'Nam,* no. 7, June 1987 (emphasis added).

86. Ibid., 13.

87. Ibid., 16–22.

88. "Thanks for Thanksgiving," *The 'Nam,* no. 22, September 1988.

89. "The Beginning of the End," *The 'Nam,* no. 24, November 1988.

90. H. Bruce Franklin, *Vietnam and Other American Fantasies* (Amherst: University of Massachusetts Press, 2000), 18.

91. Ibid.

92. "Incoming," *The 'Nam,* no. 27, February 1989.

93. "Incoming," *The 'Nam,* no. 28, March 1989.

94. "Incoming," *The 'Nam,* no. 29, April 1989.

95. "Pride Goeth . . . ," *The 'Nam,* no. 9, August 1987.

96. "Incoming," *The 'Nam,* no. 14, January 1988 (emphasis added; ellipsis in original).

97. Ibid. (emphasis added).

98. "Incoming," *The 'Nam*, no. 3, February 1987.

99. "Incoming," *The 'Nam*, no. 6, May 1987 (emphasis added).

100. "Incoming," *The 'Nam*, no. 8, July 1987.

101. Ibid.

102. "Incoming," *The 'Nam*, no. 3, February 1987.

103. See, for instance, "Incoming," *The 'Nam*, no. 9, August 1987, and no. 20, July 1988.

104. "Incoming," *The 'Nam*, no. 11, October 1987.

105. Ibid. (emphasis in original).

106. "Incoming," *The 'Nam*, no. 5, April 1987.

107. "Incoming," *The 'Nam*, no. 6, May 1987.

108. "Incoming," *The 'Nam*, no. 7, June 1987.

109. "Incoming," *The 'Nam*, no. 14, January 1988.

110. "Incoming," *The 'Nam*, no. 15, February 1988.

111. "Incoming," *The 'Nam*, no. 13, December 1987.

112. "Incoming," *The 'Nam*, no. 24, November 1988.

113. "Incoming," *The 'Nam*, no. 25, December 1988.

114. "Notes from the World," *The 'Nam*, no. 15, February 1988.

115. "Incoming," *The 'Nam*, no. 18, May 1988.

116. Ibid.

117. "Incoming," *The 'Nam*, no. 27, February 1989.

118. "Incoming," *The 'Nam*, no. 33, August 1989.

119. James Fallows, "No Hard Feelings?" *Atlantic Monthly*, December 1988, 76.

120. Ibid., 78.

CHAPTER FIVE

1. For an interesting discussion of the Vietnam Syndrome and its relation to the American War in Vietnam and American foreign policy after 1975, see Geoff Simons, *Vietnam Syndrome: Impact on US Foreign Policy* (New York: St. Martin's, 1998). On the various ways in which Vietnam shaped American receptions of the Gulf War, see Susan Jeffords and Lauren Rabinovitz, eds., *Seeing Through the Media: The Persian Gulf War* (New Brunswick, N.J.: Rutgers University Press, 1992).

2. "Inaugural Address, January 20, 1989," *Public Papers of the Presidents of the United States: George Bush, 1989* (Washington, D.C.: GPO, 1990), 1:3.

3. "Kicking the Vietnam Syndrome," *WP*, March 4, 1991.

4. *Vietnam: The Road Ahead*, Testimony before the Senate Subcommittee on East Asian and Pacific Affairs, April 25, 1991, reprinted in *U.S. Department of State Dispatch* 2, no. 18 (May 6, 1991).

5. "The Real 'Vietnam Syndrome,'" *WP*, March 7, 1991.

6. *The Vessey Mission to Hanoi*, Hearing before the House Subcommittee on Asian and Pacific Affairs, 100th Congress, 2nd Session, September 30, 1987. Led by retired General John Vessey, the Vessey Mission was sent to Vietnam by President Reagan to gauge the level of progress on the POW/MIA issue in Vietnam.

7. Don Oberdorfer, "U.S Details Plan for Normalizing Vietnam Relations," *WP*, April 10, 1991; "US Lays Conditions for an Opening to Vietnam: Deal on My Terms," *FEER*, April 18, 1991, 13.

8. "US to Hurdle Vietnam's IMF/World Bank Ties," *FEER*, October 17, 1991; see also "The Next Great Leap," *FEER*, April 22, 1993, 68; "Aid: Ghosts at the Feast," *FEER*, April 22, 1993, 72.

9. *Effects of the Continued Diplomatic Stalemate in Cambodia*, Hearing before the Senate Subcommittee on East Asian and Pacific Affairs, 102nd Congress, 1st Session, April 11, 1991, 22.

10. *Vietnam: The Road Ahead*; "U.S. to Give Vietnam $1 Million," *NYT*, April 26, 1991.

11. Oberdorfer, "U.S. Details Plan for Normalizing Vietnam Relations."

12. *Effects of the Continued Diplomatic Stalemate in Cambodia*, 28.

13. Oberdorfer, "U.S. Details Plan for Normalizing Vietnam Relations."

14. *Effects of the Continued Diplomatic Stalemate in Cambodia*, 29.

15. "U.S. to Give Vietnam $1 Million."

16. *An Examination of U.S. Policy toward POW/MIAs*, Report Prepared by the Republican Staff of U.S. Senate Committee on Foreign Relations, May 1991, cited in H. Bruce Franklin, *Vietnam and Other American Fantasies* (Amherst: University of Massachusetts Press, 2000), 196.

17. *U.S. Economic Embargo on Vietnam*, Joint Hearing before the House Subcommittees on Asian and Pacific Affairs and International Economic Policy and Trade, 102nd Congress, 1st Session, June 25, 1991, 1–2.

18. Ibid., 4.

19. Ibid., 5.

20. Ibid., 10–12.

21. Ibid., 18–19.

22. Ibid., 76–77; Henrich Dahm, *French and Japanese Relations with Vietnam since 1975* (Surrey: Curzon Press, 2000), 113.

23. *U.S. Economic Embargo on Vietnam*, 75–79.

24. See, for example, "Hoping Against Hope," *Newsweek*, July 29, 1991; "Are They or Aren't They?" *Time*, July 29, 1991, 41.

25. "Bring On Rambo," *WSJ*, August 2, 1991, A1, cited in Franklin, *Vietnam and Other American Fantasies*, 197.

26. *Resolving the POW/MIA Issue: A Status Report*, Hearing before the House Subcommittee on Asian and Pacific Affairs, 102nd Congress, 1st Session, July 17, 1991, "Appendix Two: Analysis of the Purported Robertson, Lundy, and Steven POW/MIA Image," reprinted in *American POW's in Southeast Asia: The Questions Remain*, Hearings before the House Subcommittee on Asian and Pacific Affairs, July 31 and August 2, 1991, 175. Also see Franklin, *Vietnam and Other American Fantasies*, 197. Franklin notes that the following summer, the Defense Department confirmed that the picture was "a 1923 photograph reproduced in a 1989 Soviet magazine."

27. For the full evolution of Solarz's position on Vietnam and the POW ques-

tion, see Stephen Solarz and Richard Childress, "Vietnam: Detours on the Path to Normalization," in C. Richard Nelson and Kenneth Weisbrode, eds., *Reversing Relations with Former Adversaries: U.S. Foreign Policy after the Cold War,* 88–125 (Gainesville: University Press of Florida, 1998).

28. H. Bruce Franklin, *M.I.A., or Mythmaking in America* (New York: Lawrence Hill Books, 1992), 157–58.

29. Franklin recounts the story as a footnote in his *Vietnam and Other American Fantasies,* 233n78: "My own efforts to testify, in which I persisted from February to December 1992, were officially rebuffed not only by the committee and in letters from Senator Kerry but also by Senator Kerry and Senator [Chuck] Grassley [of Iowa, another member of the Select Committee], when I appeared with them on national television."

30. *U.S. Government's Post-War POW/MIA Efforts,* Hearings before the Senate Select Committee on POW/MIA Affairs, 102nd Congress, 2nd Session, August 11–12, 1992 (Washington, D.C.: GPO, 1993), 282–83.

31. *Oversight Hearings: Department of Defense, POW/MIA Family Issues, and Private Sector Issues,* Hearings before the Senate Select Committee on POW/MIA Affairs, 102nd Congress, 2nd Session, December 1–4, 1992, 1295.

32. For testimony on the "Mortician" and the warehouse, see *American POW/MIA's in Southeast Asia: An Update on U.S. Policy and Current Investigations,* Hearings before the House Subcommittee on Asian and Pacific Affairs, 102nd Congress, 1st Session, November 6, 1991, 74–76; and *Oversight Hearings,* 1190.

33. *U.S. Government's Post-War POW/MIA Efforts; Oversight Hearings,* 14–16.

34. *POWs/MIAs: Missing Pieces in the Puzzle,* Hearings before the House Subcommittee on Asian and Pacific Affairs, July 14, 1993, 66. The $100 million figure comes from the *Final Report of the Senate Select Committee on POW/MIA Affairs,* Senate Report 103–1, January 13, 1993 (Washington, D.C.: GPO, 1993), 8 (hereafter, *Final Report of the Senate Select Committee on POW/MIA Affairs* (1993).

35. *American POW/MIA's in Southeast Asia,* 29 (emphasis in original).

36. *Oversight Hearings,* 1188–89.

37. Ibid., 1188.

38. Ibid.

39. *American POW/MIA's in Southeast Asia,* 81–82.

40. Cited in ibid., 82.

41. *The Vessey Mission to Hanoi,* 50; *Issues Affecting the Question of United States Relations with Vietnam,* Hearing before the House Subcommittees on Asian and Pacific Affairs and on International Economic Policy and Trade of the Committee on Foreign Affairs, 101st Congress, 1st Session, November 17, 1989., 55.

42. *Oversight Hearings,* 1189.

43. *American POW/MIA's in Southeast Asia,* 9.

44. On the classification decision, see Franklin, *M.I.A.,* 16–17.

45. *Oversight Hearings,* 1293.

46. Ibid., 1294.

47. Ibid.

48. *Oversight Hearings*, 1185.

49. Ibid., 1187.

50. Ibid., 1195.

51. Ibid., 1186.

52. Ibid.

53. "U.S. Ex-Operative in Hanoi Obtained MIA Photos," *WP*, October 22, 1992; "Bush Hails 'Breakthrough' in Vietnam War MIA Cases," *WP*, October 24, 1992. The tone of the reports made it appear that Hanoi had been withholding information. As discussed above, this was far from the case; the Vietnamese were quick to allow access to documents and photographs, many of which they were previously unaware they possessed.

54. *Final Report of the Senate Select Committee on POW/MIA Affairs* (1993), 7.

55. Ibid.

56. Ibid., 4.

57. The report went on to add, "But there remains the troubling question of whether the Americans who were expected to return but did not were, as a group, shunted aside and discounted by government and population alike. The answer to that question is essentially yes." *Final Report of the Senate Select Committee on POW/MIA Affairs* (1993), 7.

58. Ibid., 28. A later section detailing the cooperation of the ASEAN nations after 1984 also refers to "North Vietnam" (285).

59. "Vietnam Underlines Cooperation on MIAs," *WP*, October 31, 1992.

60. "Bush Sees Gain in U.S.-Vietnam Ties," *Los Angeles Times*, October 24, 1992, cited in Franklin, *Vietnam and Other American Fantasies*, 199.

61. "Vietnam: The Big Buildup Begins," *WP*, December 6, 1992.

62. On Clinton's own account of his activities during the war, see his memoir, *My Life* (New York: Knopf, 2004), esp. 157–60.

63. Ibid., 469.

64. "Statement by Press Secretary Fitzwater on Relations with Vietnam, December 4, 1992," *Public Papers of the Presidents of the United States: George Bush, 1992–1993* (Washington, D.C.: GPO, 1993), 1:2187; "Embargo is Eased after Hanoi's Help on MIAs," *WP*, December 15, 1993.

65. Brown's paper is cited in "Vietnam: The Big Buildup Begins."

66. "President Clinton: Normalize Ties with Vietnam," *WSJ*, March 8, 1993, A12. On October 23, 1991, the *Journal*'s lead editorial encouraged the US to wait until communism collapsed in Southeast Asia before "fling[ing] wide the doors of the developed world." "Vietnam Glitch," *WSJ*, October 23, 1991, A1.

67. "President Clinton: Normalize Ties with Vietnam," *WSJ*, March 8, 1993.

68. H. Bruce Franklin, "MIASMA," *Nation*, May 10, 1993, 616; also see Franklin, "Missing in Action in the Twenty-first Century," chap. 8 in *Vietnam and Other American Fantasies*, 173–201.

69. "U.S. to Press Hanoi to Explain '72 POW Report," *NYT*, April 13, 1993; "POW Document Renews Bitter Arguments," *WP*, April 14, 1993.

70. Franklin, *Vietnam and Other American Fantasies*, 200. Franklin's headlines

and editorials (233n87) are taken from the *Washington Times,* April 12, 1993; *USA Today,* April 12, 1993; *WP,* April 15, 1993; and *Jersey Journal,* April 18, 1993.

71. Franklin, "*MIASMA*"; Nayan Chanda, "Research and Destroy," *FEER,* May 6, 1993, 20.

72. Chanda, "Research and Destroy" (ellipsis in original).

73. Morris, "Documenting the Truth," *FEER,* July 15, 1993, 4.

74. "A Researcher's Dream Find on U.S. POWs Turns Into a Nightmare," *WP,* April 25, 1993.

75. Ibid. The actual "1205 Report" is included as an appendix in *POW/MIA: Where Do We Go from Here?,* Hearing before the House Subcommittee on Asia and the Pacific, 103rd Congress, 2nd Session, February 10, 1994, 315–30.

76. For a detailed discussion of the Cambodian elections, see MacAlister Brown and Joseph J. Zasloff, *Cambodia Confounds the Peacemakers, 1979–1998* (Ithaca, N.Y.: Cornell University Press, 1998), esp. chap. 3, "Implementing the Paris Agreements, 1991–1993," and chap. 4, "Conducting the Election, 1992–1993."

77. "The Wages of Peace," *FEER,* July 15, 1993, 10.

78. "U.S. Drops Opposition to Loans for Vietnam," *WP,* July 3, 1993.

79. *POW's/MIA's: Missing Pieces of the Puzzle,* Hearings before the House Subcommittee on Asia and the Pacific, July 14 and 22, 1993. All of these witnesses demonstrate their beliefs in the Vietnamese holding prisoners after 1973 during the hearings.

80. Ibid., 113.

81. Ibid.

82. Ibid., 191.

83. *United States Policy toward Vietnam,* Hearing before the Senate Subcommittee on East Asian and Pacific Affairs, 103rd Congress, 1st Session, July 21, 1993, 13.

84. Ibid., 18, 45.

85. The previous examples of testimony focusing on the plight of the Vietnamese under the embargo came in the November 1975 hearings, *U.S. Trade Embargo of Vietnam: Church Views,* discussed in chapter 1.

86. *United States Policy toward Vietnam,* 63.

87. Robert McFarlane, "The Last Battle," remarks at the National League of Families 24th Annual Meeting Dinner, July 16, 1993, reprinted in *United States Policy toward Vietnam,* 79–81.

88. *United States Policy toward Vietnam,* 69.

89. Gabriel Kolko, *Vietnam: Anatomy of a Peace* (New York: Routledge, 1997), 33.

90. "The Next Great Leap," *FEER,* April 22, 1993, 68.

91. "Vietnam: War and Peace," *FEER,* May 4, 1995, 20.

92. "The Next Great Leap"; John Dodsworth et al., *Vietnam: Transition to a Market Economy,* Occasional Paper 35, International Monetary Fund (Washington, D.C., 1996).

93. "Vietnam: War and Peace."

94. "The Wages of Peace."

95. For a negative view of the IMF and World Bank role in Vietnam, see Kolko, *Vietnam: Anatomy of a Peace.* For more positive reviews, see Dodsworth et al., *Vietnam: Transition to a Market Economy;* and Peter Wolff, *Vietnam: The Incomplete Transformation* (London: Frank Cass, 1999), 118–21.

96. "Does Clinton Need This?" *Time,* February 7, 1994, 47.

97. Ibid.; "Senate Urges End to U.S. Embargo against Vietnam," *WP,* January 28, 1994; "The Wages of Peace," *FEER,* July 15, 1993, 10.

98. "Senate Urges End to U.S. Embargo against Vietnam."

99. "Justice Department Set to Clear Ron Brown," *WP,* February 2, 1994.

100. "MIA Activists Fight on for Vietnam Embargo," *WP,* February 3, 1994.

101. "Remarks on Lifting the Trade Embargo on Vietnam and an Exchange with Reporters, February 3, 1994," *Public Papers of the Presidents of the United States: William J. Clinton, 1994* (Washington, D.C.: GPO, 1995), 1:178.

102. Ibid., 179; "Clinton Lifts Vietnam Trade Embargo," *WP,* February 4, 1994.

103. "Remarks on Lifting the Trade Embargo on Vietnam," 180.

104. "Watch This Space: Advertisers Covet Vietnam's Growing Consumer Market," *FEER,* March 31, 1994, 66.

105. "Vietnam Welcomes U.S. Decision on Embargo," *NYT,* February 5, 1994; "Peace Finally at Hand," *Time,* February 14, 1994; "New Vietnam Combat: Coke Versus Pepsi," *NYT,* February 7, 1994; "The War—To Cash In," *Newsweek,* February 14, 1994, 33.

106. "As Trade Opens, War Closes," *WP,* February 6, 1994.

107. "The War—To Cash In"; "New Vietnam Combat."

108. "New Vietnam Combat"; "As Trade Opens, War Closes."

109. "A Lukewarm Welcome," *FEER,* February 17, 1994.

110. "Vietnam Welcomes U.S. Decision on Embargo."

111. "A Lukewarm Welcome."

112. "Making Up for Lost Time," *FEER,* February 17, 1994, 17.

113. *POW/MIA: Where Do We Go from Here?,* 4.

114. Ibid., 8.

115. Ibid., 9.

116. Ibid., 19.

117. Ibid., 21–22, 24.

118. *U.S.-Vietnam Relations: Issues and Implications,* Report to Congressional Committees by the General Accounting Office (Washington, D.C.: GPO, 1995), 6, 9.

119. Ibid., 13.

120. Ibid., 15.

121. For an example of the process involved in the Jackson-Vanik waiver determination, see "Waiver under the Trade Act of 1974 with Respect to Vietnam: Communication from the President of the United States to the House Committee on Ways and Means," April 21, 1998 (Washington, D.C.: GPO, 1998); and *Approving*

the Extension of Nondiscriminatory Treatment (Normal Trade Relations) to the Products of the Socialist Republic of Vietnam, Report of the Senate Finance Committee to Accompany S.J. Res. 16, 107th Congress, 1st Session, July 27, 2001 (Washington, D.C.: GPO, 2001).

122. *U.S.-Vietnam Relations: Issues and Implications,* 15–16.

123. *Adjudication of Claims against Vietnam.* Also see chap. 1.

124. *Issues Affecting the Question of United States Relations with Vietnam,* 14.

125. *Adjudication of Claims against Vietnam,* 3.

126. *POW/MIA: Where Do We Go from Here?,* 2. The 1995 GAO report claimed that the assets were worth "more than $350 million."

127. *POW/MIA: Where Do We Go from Here?,* 3; *Issues Affecting the Question of United States Relations with Vietnam,* 100.

128. *Issues Affecting the Question of United States Relations with Vietnam,* 3.

129. Ibid., 67.

130. Ibid., 68.

131. "Claims: Agreement between the United States of America and Vietnam," U.S. Department of State document, January 28, 1995 (Washington, D.C.: GPO, 1995).

132. "United States and Vietnam Sign Debt Agreement," U.S. Department of the Treasury press release, April 7, 1997.

133. "MIA Hunter Chains Himself to Gate," *NYT,* June 5, 1995; "U.S. Finds No POWs at Vietnam Military Site," *NYT,* June 19, 1995.

134. "Binding Up Old Wounds," *Newsweek,* June 26, 1995, 34.

135. "Opening to Vietnam," *NYT,* July 12, 1995.

136. "Republicans Attack Clinton on Vietnam," *NYT,* July 13, 1995.

137. "Reflecting on Vietnam Ties, Many Agree That It's Time," *NYT,* July 15, 1995.

CHAPTER SIX

1. In this context, it is worth pointing to certain ideas about narrative structure in social constructs, beginning as perhaps one must with those of Michel Foucault. Historian Hayden V. White has also written enlighteningly on the subject in *The Content and the Form: Narrative Discourse and Historical Representation* (Baltimore, Md.: Johns Hopkins, 1987). Scholars of what has come to be called narratology have further developed the concept. See in particular the work of Mieke Bal in her *Narratology: Introduction to the Theory of the Narrative* (Toronto: University of Toronto, 1985, rev. 1997). Bal has been at the forefront of interdisciplinary work that seeks to apply analysis of narrative structure to other fields, including to material and political culture.

As for my own discussion here, I do not intend to put forth a determinist model, in which the structures of, for instance, war memorials would overdetermine the stories that were told at the different sites, but rather a dynamic situation in which these structures shape and in turn are shaped by the experiences of visitors. The narrative structure does not determine experience, then, but rather serves as a boundary or limit of normative and accepted practices for users who bring a seemingly boundless number of stories with them when they visit these sites. As I argue throughout this work, these normative boundaries are important not because they actively silence some narratives at the expense of others, but because of how the structural limitations of dominant discourses render some forms of stories outside, in Foucault's words, the "possible field of action," Michel Foucault, "The Subject and Power," afterword in Hubert L. Dreyfus and Paul Rabinow, *Michel Foucault: Beyond Structuralism and Hermeneutics,* 208–26 (Chicago: The University of Chicago Press, 1983), 221.

2. Jan C. Scruggs and Joel L. Swerdlow, *To Heal a Nation: The Vietnam Veterans Memorial* (New York: Harper and Row, 1985), 7.

3. Ibid., 53.

4. Maya Lin, *Boundaries* (New York: Simon and Schuster, 2000), excerpted in "'As American as Anyone Else'—But Asian Too," *WP,* November 12, 2000.

5. Christina M. Gillis, ed., *Grounds for Remembering: Monuments, Memorials, Texts,* Doreen B. Townsend Center Occasional Papers 3 (Berkeley: Doreen B. Townsend Center for the Humanities, 1995), 12.

6. Marita Sturken, *Tangled Memories* (Berkeley: University of California Press, 1997), 61.

7. Ibid., 51.

8. Kristin Ann Haas, *Carried to the Wall* (Berkeley: University of California Press, 1998), 15.

9. "Epitaph for Vietnam," *WP,* May 7, 1981.

10. Gillis, ed., *Grounds for Remembering;* also quoted in "The Statue and The Wall," *WP,* November 10, 1984.

11. "Memorial Delayed: Vietnam Memorial to be Reviewed," *WP,* February 27, 1982.

12. Tom Wolfe, "Art Disputes War," *WP,* October 13, 1992.

13. Scruggs and Swerdlow, *To Heal A Nation,* 80.

14. "Stop That Monument," *National Review,* September 18, 1981, 1064; quoted in Scruggs and Swerdlow, *To Heal a Nation,* 81, and Sturken, *Tangled Memories,* 52.

15. Gillis, ed., *Grounds for Remembering,* 11.

16. "Ground Broken in Capital for Memorial on Vietnam," *NYT,* March 27, 1982.

17. "'Art War' Erupts Over Vietnam Veterans Memorial," *WP,* July 8, 1982.

18. Haas, *Carried to the Wall,* 18.

19. Scruggs and Swerdlow, *To Heal a Nation,* 129.

20. "'Art War' Erupts Over Vietnam Veterans Memorial."

21. Quoted in Scruggs and Swerdlow, *To Heal a Nation,* 130.

22. "President Accepts Vietnam Memorial," *NYT,* November 12, 1984.

23. "Statue Completes Vietnam Memorial," *NYT,* November 10, 1984.

24. Quoted in Scruggs and Swerdlow, *To Heal a Nation,* 133.

25. Sturken, *Tangled Memories,* 46.

26. David Thelen, "Memory and American History," *Journal of American History* 75 (Spring 1989): 1128.

27. Haas, *Carried to the Wall*, 2.

28. Ibid., 19.

29. Ibid; Sturken, *Tangled Memories*, 69.

30. http://energy.senate.gov/hearings/national_parks/4_27Cats&Dogs/Doyle.htm (accessed March 14, 2004).

31. http://energy.senate.gov/hearings/national_parks/4_27Cats&Dogs/Doubek.htm (accessed March 14, 2004).

32. Ibid.

33. Sturken, *Tangled Memories*, 63.

34. Ibid., 83.

35. http://www.nps.gov/vive/ (accessed November 2, 2000).

36. http://www.vietvet.org/thewall/thewallm.html (accessed November 2, 2000).

37. http://www.vietvet.org/thepast.htm (accessedNovember 2, 2000).

38. http://www.vietvet.org/tapsgal.htm (accessed November 2, 2000).

39. Ibid. Quotations from Web pages have not been corrected for spelling or grammar, although words run together in the original have been separated for clarity.

It is always perilous to write about emerging technologies such as virtual memorials. At the time this chapter was originally crafted, the sites discussed here all had a consistent presence on the Web. Since that time, many of the sites have changed their URL, and others, such as the Widows of War memorial discussed below, have been completely removed. I have provided access dates in citations and have tried to steer readers to the present location of sites wherever possible.

40. http://www.vietvet.org/tapsgal.htm (accessed November 2, 2000).

41. Ibid.

42. Ibid.

43. The phrase "technologies of memory" is taken from Sturken, *Tangled Memories*, 9.

44. http://www.virtualwall.org (accessed November 5, 2002).

45. http://www.virtualwall.org/announce.html (accessed November 5, 2002). The welcome page was later changed to http://virtualwall.org/about.htm (accessed November 21, 2006).

46. http://www.vvmf.org (the entire VVMF site is still accessible via the URL http://www.thevirtualwall.org).

47. http://www.vvmf.org//index.cfm?SectionID=110&Wall_Id_No=16508.0 (accessed November 30, 2006). The Virtual Wall regularly changes its searching methods to keep pace with advances in web technologies. Although some of the URLs featured here have changed as a result of these developments, the URLs and information contained on the pages were accurate at time they were accessed. Current profiles for the pages from the Virtual Wall cited here can be found through a search at the site using the full names of the soldiers.

48. http://www.vvmf.org//index.cfm?SectionID=110&anClip=16668 (accessed November 20, 2006).

49. http://www.angelfire.com/fl5/voicesmemory/(accessed November 21, 2006).

50. http://www.virtualwall.org/do/OShaughnessyPJ01a.htm (accessed November 7, 2002).

51. http://www.virtualwall.org/dc/CummingsHW01a.htm (accessed November 7, 2002).

52. http://www.virtualwall.org/db/BirminghamEA01a.htm (accessed November 6, 2002).

53. Email to author, February 4, 2000.

54. Email to author, November 8, 1999.

55. http://www.vvmf.org/index.cfm?SectionID=110&anClip=27044 (accessed November 21, 2006).

56. http://www.vvmf.org/index.cfm?SectionID=110&anClip=121310 (accessed November 21, 2006).

57. http://www.vvmf.org/index.cfm?SectionID=110&anClip=121285 (accessed November 21, 2006).

59. http://www.vvmf.org/index.cfm?SectionID=110&anClip=121312 (accessed November 30, 2006).

60. http://www.vvmf.org//index.cfm?SectionID=110&anClip=121302 (accssed November 21, 2006).

61. Sturken, *Tangled Memories*, 82.

62. http://death-response.chance.berkeley.edu/memorial (accessed November 5, 2002).

63. http://www.virtual-memorials.com (accessed November 5, 2002).

64. http://www.vietworld.com/Holocaust/index.html (accessed November 5, 2002).

65. Sites like the Widows of War memorial that have been removed from the web can normally still be accessed by using the Internet Archive (http://www.archive.org/index.php) and its Wayback Machine (http://www.archive.org/web/web.php). As of December 1, 2006, the pages cited below were all accessible via the Internet Archive.

66. http://www.warwidows.org/xuan_ngoc_nguyen.html (accessed December 5, 2001).

67. http://www.warwidows.org/nancy_le.html (accessed December 5, 2001).

68. http://www.warwidows.org/Memorial/eva_alaluf.html (accessed December 5, 2001).

69. http://www.warwidows.org/Memorial/response901.html (accessed December 5, 2001).

70. "Background: An Education Center at the Vietnam Veterans Memorial," http://thevirtualwall.org/index.cfm?SectionID=315 (accessed March 17, 2003).

71. The Education Center proposal hit its first snag almost immediately. The National Park Service had for several years resisted a number of proposed addi-

tions to the mall, including a Franklin Roosevelt Memorial, Korean War Memorial, and World War Two Memorial. It worried that the center would take away from the experience of the Wall, further clutter the mall as a whole, and set a precedent for similar centers at other monuments. The Park Service was supported by several environmental groups, including the National Coalition to Save Our Mall, which offered a counterproposal that pamphlets be handed to visitors instead. For several legislative sessions, the proposed center was attached to legislation, otherwise supported by these groups, that would have placed strict limitations on any further additions to the mall. A more surprising source of opposition came from Phil Gramm. The Republican senator from Texas had by 2001 twice taken the Education Center off of the Senate's unanimous consent calendar, dooming the measure to die in committee. Gramm's reason for opposing the center had nothing to do with environmental concerns or with the war and its legacies; he was opposed to either building or banning any more memorials until a monument to Ronald Reagan was approved. Through his stalwart opposition, Gramm almost single-handedly blocked not only the center but the ban on future additions to the mall. Ironically, Reagan himself had signed the original legislation which the ban would have amended: the 1986 Commemorative Works Act, which specified that no monument to an individual could be built on the mall until twenty-five years after the person's death. The irony was not lost on the Bush administration, which supported the ban and reminded Gramm not only that Reagan, in his early nineties at the time of the proposal, had signed the legislation, but that the famously anti-government president already had the Washington, D.C., airport and another federal building named after him. When Gramm retired in 2002, the proposal was cleared to move forward, although not without continued opposition from the National Park Service. For the details of these conflicts, see "Background: An Education Center at the Vietnam Veterans Memorial," and *Legislative Field Hearing to Authorize the Design and Construction of a Visitor's Center for the Vietnam Veterans Memorial,* Hearing before the House Subcommittee on National Parks, Recreation, and Public Lands, 108th Congress, 1st Session, May 21, 2003.

72. *Legislative Field Hearing,* 10.

73. Ibid., 17.

74. Ibid., 19.

75. Ibid., 22.

76. Ibid., 24. On the Enola Gay controversy and some interesting connections to Vietnam, see Edward Linenthal and Tom Engelhardt, eds., *History Wars: The Enola Gay and Other Battles for the American Past* (New York: Metropolitan Books, 1996).

77. *Legislative Field Hearing,* 24.

78. Text of H.R. 1442, available at http://www.vvmf.org/index.cfm?SectionID=4 (accessed March 10, 2004). The site has since taken down the link to the text of H.R. 1442, but the press release discussing it can be found at http://www.vvmf.org/index.cfm?SectionID=298 (accessed November 30, 2006).

79. "President Bush Signs Visitor Center Bill," www.thevirtualwall.org/index.cfm?SectionID=298 (accessed March 10, 2004).

80. *Legislative Field Hearing*, 9.

EPILOGUE

1. Quoted in "U.S.-Vietnamese Ties," *NYT*, August 6, 1995.

2. "Good Morning, Vietnam," *NYT*, January 18, 1995.

3. "Make Money, Not War," *WP*, February 15, 1995.

4. "McDonald's 'Happy Meals' Sad For Workers," Interpress Service, May 9, 1996, www.oneworld.org/ips2/may/Vietnam.html (accessed February 25, 2004). For similar stories, see Irene Norlund, "Nike and Labour in Vietnam," *Nordic Newsletter of Asian Studies* 3 (October 1998): 15–18; and Eyal Press, "Vietnam: A Nike Sneak," *Nation* 268, no. 13 (April 5, 1999): 6.

5. Mark E. Manyin, *The Vietnam-U.S. Bilateral Trade Agreement*, Congressional Research Service report to Congress, June 20, 2001 (Washington: GPO, 2001); *United States-Vietnam Bilateral Trade Agreement*, Hearing before the Senate Committee on Finance, 107th Congress, 1st Session, June 26, 2001.

6. See, for example, the statement of Ambassador Douglas "Pete" Peterson in *United States-Vietnam Trade Relations*, Hearing before the House Subcommittee on Trade, 106th Congress, 1st Session, June 17, 1999 (Washington: GPO, 2000), 33.

7. Ibid., 99; *U.S.-Vietnam Relations*, Hearing before the House Subcommittee on Asia and the Pacific, 105th Congress, 1st Session, June 18, 1997, 59.

8. Manyin, *Vietnam-U.S. Bilateral Trade Agreement*, 1–2. In 1998, the U.S. government's official terminology shifted from "most favored nation" to "normal trade relations."

9. "Free Trade's Muddy Waters," *WP*, July 13, 2003; "Vietnam Shuns U.S. Sanctions on Catfish," *WP*, June 18, 2003.

10. "Trade Ruling Favors U.S. Catfish Farmers over Vietnamese," *WP*, July 24, 2003; "Vietnam Worried About Shrimp Sanctions," *WP*, July 24, 2003.

11. "U.S. Rice Growers Want to Sell to Iraq," *WP*, March 14, 2004.

12. On Vietnam and the WTO, see Kym Anderson, *Vietnam's Transforming Economy and WTO Accession* (Singapore: Institute of Southeast Asian Studies, 1999).

13. "Clinton Gets Late-Night Welcome in Vietnam," Reuters, November 16, 2000.

14. "Remarks by the President to Vietnam's National University," November 17, 2000, available at http://www.dtic.mil/dpmo/news/2000/001117_white_house_national_univ_remarks.htm.

15. Among the many stories run by the *Blade* in October and November 2003, see, in particular, "Untold Story of Savage Force," October 19, 2003; and "Vietnam Inquiry Yields No Justice," October 20, 2003.

16. "Buried Secrets," *Toledo Blade*, October 24, 2004, A-26. Sallah and Weiss

later turned the articles into a fascinating and horrifying book, *Tiger Force: A True Story of Men and War* (New York: Little, Brown, 2006).

17. "Uncovered" ("Talk of the Town" item), *New Yorker,* November 10, 2003, 41.

18. Scott Sherman, "The Other My Lai," *Nation,* March 1, 2004, 9.

19. Ibid. The statement came from *Times* editor Bill Keller and was quoted by public editor Daniel Okrent.

20. Ibid. Tiger Force was at the time on active duty in Iraq.

21. "Kerry and Agent Orange," *Newsweek,* March 8, 2004.

22. "Legal Action by Vietnamese Agent Orange Victims Was Inevitable," Agence France-Presse, February 9, 2004. See also Environmental Conference on Cambodia, Laos and Vietnam, *Long-Term Consequences of the Vietnam War,* 43, http://www.nnn.se/vietnam/ethics.pdf; Arnold Schecter et al., "Food as a Source of Dioxin Exposure in the Residents of Bien Hoa City, Vietnam," *Journal of Occupational and Environmental Medicine* 45, no. 8 (August 2003): 781–88; "Decades Later, Vietnam War Toxin Still Torments," *WP,* February 16, 2004; "New Study into Agent Orange," *BBC News Online,* March 10, 2002, http://news.bbc.co.uk/2/hi/world/asia-pacific/1865730.stm. For more on Agent Orange, see Robert Dreyfuss, "Apocalypse Still," *Mother Jones* 25, no. 1 (January–February 2000): 42–51; and Philip Jones Griffiths, *Agent Orange: Collateral Damage in Vietnam* (London: Trolley, 2003).

23. H. Bruce Franklin, *Vietnam and Other American Fantasies* (Amherst: University of Massachusetts Press, 2000), 173.

24. Ibid., 174.

25. "Bid to Honor South Vietnamese Elicits Anger," *WP,* January 29, 2003.

26. Ibid.

27. "Va. Bill Promoting South Vietnamese Flag Dies," *WP,* February 17, 2003.

28. A similar bill was proposed, and eventually defeated, in 2005 in California, home of nearly 500,000 Vietnamese Americans.

INDEX